Mozambique

Who Calls
the Shots?

Mozambique

Who Calls the Shots?

Joseph Hanlon

James Currey
LONDON

Indiana University Press
BLOOMINGTON AND INDIANAPOLIS

James Currey Ltd
54b Thornhill Square, London N1 1BE

Indiana University Press
Bloomington, Indiana 47405

British Library Cataloguing in Publication Data
Hanlon, Joseph *1941–*
      Mozambique : who calls the shots?
       1. Mozambique. Foreign assistance
       I. Title
  338.9117220679

  ISBN 0-85255-347-1
  ISBN 0-85255-346-3 pbk

Library of Congress Cataloging-in-Publication Data

Hanlon, Joseph.
      Mozambique : who calls the shots? / by Joseph Hanlon
      p. cm.
      Includes bibliographical references.
      ISBN 0-253-32696-6.
      1. Economic assistance--Mozambique. 2. Mozambique--Economic
conditions--1975- 3. Mozambique--Economic policy. I. Title.
HC890-H36   1991
338.9679--dc20   91-17006
1 2 3 4 5 95 94 93 92 91

Manufactured in Great Britain

Typeset in 10/10½ pt Bembo by Opus 43
Printed and bound in Great Britain
by Villiers Publications, London N6

To my friend
Teresa

Contents

Appendices

List of text tables

List of maps,
photographs & illustrations

Abbreviations

Água Rural	Rural water programme
Agricom	Parastatal agricultural marketing board
AID	see USAID
ANC	African National Congress
Apparatchik	State or party functionary; orig. functionary in the communist party of the USSR
ASDI	*see* SIDA
Beira corridor	Zone in central Mozambique containing the road, railway, oil pipe-line, and power line which link the port of Beira to Zimbabwe
bn	billion = 1,000,000,000
CDM	Camionagem de Maputo, parastatal trucking company
CEA	Centro de Estudos Africanos, Centre of African Studies of Universidade Eduardo Mondlane
CENE	Comissão Executiva Nacional de Emergência, National Executive Commission for the Emergency
CIA	US Central Intelligence Agency
CIDA	Canadian International Development Agency
CMEA	Former socialist bloc Council for Mutual Economic Assistance, also Comecon
COE	Comité Operacional de Emergência, Emergency Operations Committee of CENE
Colonato	Colonial settlement zone for Portuguese peasants
Comecon	*see* CMEA
Cooperante	Foreign technician sent by a solidarity organization and working for the Mozambique government
CREE	Comissão de Relações Económicas Externas, Foreign Economic Relations Commission
DIA	US Defense Intelligence Agency, US military intelligence
DPCCN	Departamento de Prevenção e Combate às Calamidades Naturais, Department for the Prevention and Combat of Natural Disasters
EC	European Community (sometimes erroneously called "EEC")
ECA	UN Economic Commission for Africa
EDM	Electricidade de Moçambique, parastatal electricity company
ERP	*see* PRE

FAO	UN Food and Agriculture Organization
Forex	Foreign exchange, hard currency such as UK£ or US$
Frelimo	Ruling party, originally Frente de Libertação de Moçambique, Front for the Liberation of Mozambique
FY	US fiscal year
GATT	General Agreement on Tariffs and Trade
GD	Groupo Dinamizador, dynamising group (neighbourhood or factory committee)
GDP	Gross domestic product = total output of goods and services
Glasnost	Openness; orig. USSR
GNP	Gross national product = value added claimed by residents = GDP plus income from abroad less certain payments made abroad
GPRM	US abbreviation for "government of the People's Republic of Mozambique"
Hortofrutícola	Parastatal fruit and vegetable wholesaler
ICRC	International Committee for the Red Cross
IFAD	International Fund for Agricultural Development
ILO	International Labour Organization
IMF	International Monetary Fund
Intervention	A form of bankruptcy, under which the Mozambican state operates an abandoned company
Kcal	Kilocalories
kt	1000 tonnes
LAM	Linhas Aéreas de Moçambique, Mozambique air line
Like-minded	Group of countries: the Nordic states plus Netherlands and Canada
Loja Franca	Foreign currency shop
Lomé	Convention or agreement between the EC and many African, Caribbean, and Pacific developing countries
London Club	Cartel of banks and other private creditors
LSU	Logistic Support Unit of DPCCN
Maputo	Capital of Mozambique
Medimoc	Parastatal pharmaceuticals import company
MI	South Africa Military Intelligence
MIO	Mozambique Information Office in London
mn	million = 1,000,000
MNR	Movimento Nacional de Resistência de Moçambique, Mozambique National Resistance Movement; also NRM; later Renamo
MoH	Ministry of Health
MSF	Médecins sans Frontières
MSF-F	MSF-France
NATO	North Atlantic Treaty Organization
Navique	Parastatal coastal shipping company
NGO	Non-government organization
Nkomati	Accord between Mozambique and South Africa, signed 16 March 1984, under which South Africa agreed to stop supporting Renamo
Nomenclatura	State and party elite; lit. list of names; orig. USSR
Nordic	Group of countries: Denmark, Finland, Norway, Sweden, and, sometimes, Iceland
NRM	see MNR
NSC	US National Security Council
OAU	Organization for African Unity
OECD	Organization for Economic Cooperation and Development

OEOA	UN Office for Emergency Operations in Africa
OFDA	US Office of Foreign Disaster Assistance
OMM	Organização da Mulher Moçambicana, Mozambican Women's Organization
OPEC	Organization of Petroleum Exporting Countries
Paris Club	Cartel of government creditors
PDP	Programa dos Distritos Prioritários, Priority District Programme
Perestroika	Economic restructuring; orig. USSR
PHC	Primary health care
PRE	Programa de Reabilitação Económica, Economic Rehabilitation Programme
PRES	Programa de Reabilitação Económica e Social, Economic and Social Rehabilitation Programme (renamed PRE from 1990)
PTA	Preferential Trade Area for Eastern and Southern Africa
PVO	Private voluntary organization, NGO
Régulo	"Traditional" clan chief or headman, normally appointed by the Portuguese in the colonial era
Renamo	Resistência Nacional Moçambicana, Mozambique National Resistance; formerly MNR or NRM
SADCC	Southern African Development Coordination Conference; Angola, Botswana, Lesotho, Malawi, Mozambique, Swaziland, Tanzania, Zambia, Zimbabwe, and (from 1990) Namibia
SCF	Save the Children Fund
SDA	Social Dimensions of Adjustment, part of World Bank programmes
SIDA	Swedish International Development Agency (ASDI in Mozambique)
SNAAD	Sistema Não-Administrativo de Alocação de Divisas, system for non-administrative allocation of foreign exchange
t	tonne, 1000 kg, 2205 lb
TNC	Trans-national corporation
UCPI	Unidade de Coordinação de Programas de Importação, Agency to Coordinate Import Programmes
UDI	Rhodesia's 1965 unilateral declaration of independence
UK	United Kingdom of Great Britain and Northern Ireland
UN	United Nations
Unctad	UN Conference on Trade and Development
UNDP	UN Development Programme
Undro	UN Disaster Relief Organization
UNHCR	Office of the UN High Commissioner for Refugees
Unicef	UN Children's Fund
Unido	UN Industrial Development Organization
UNSCERO	UN Special Coordinator for Emergency Relief Operations in Mozambique
US	United States of America
USAID	US Agency for International Development
USSR	Union of Soviet Socialist Republics
WFP	UN World Food Programme (part of FAO)
WHO	UN World Health Organization
World Bank	International Bank for Reconstruction and Development
WV	World Vision International
WVRO	World Vision Relief Organization, later WVRD
WVRD	World Vision Relief & Development
WV-USA	World Vision USA

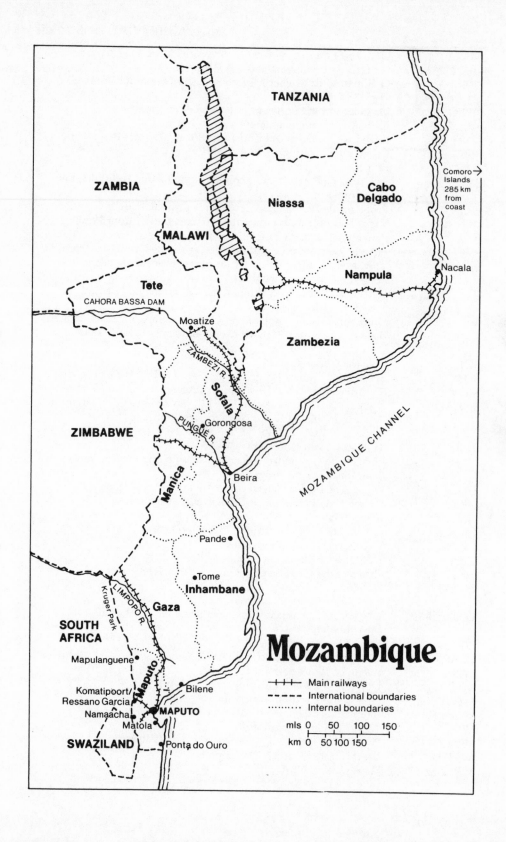

TANZANIA

ZAMBIA

Comoro
Islands
285 km
from
coast

Niassa

Cabo
Delgado

MALAWI

Nampula

Nacala

Tete

CAHORA BASSA DAM

Moatize

ZAMBEZI R.

Zambezia

Sofala

ZIMBABWE

PUNGUE R.

Gorongosa

MOZAMBIQUE CHANNEL

Manica

Beira

Pande

SOUTH
AFRICA

Tome

Inhambane

LIMPOPO R.

Gaza

Kruger Park

Mapulanguene

Maputo

Bilene

Komatipoort/
Ressano Garcia

MAPUTO

Namaacha

Matola

SWAZILAND

Ponta do Ouro

Mozambique

┼┼┼ Main railways
╌╌╌ International boundaries
...... Internal boundaries

mls 0   50   100   150

km 0   50 100 150

INTRODUCTION

Aid and recolonization

British and South African companies establish huge plantations covering hundreds of square miles and patrolled by private armies; the chartered companies of 50 years ago would approve. European doctors fly out to minister to rural peasants, in a modern version of the colonial mission hospitals. In Maputo, foreign white men issue orders in many ministries. They come from the World Bank and donor agencies, but they are little different from colonial administrators. And the Portuguese are coming back. They or their children are reclaiming businesses and houses that they abandoned 15 years ago. Portuguese and English companies are again being given exclusive rights over peasant cotton production.

This is not *neo*colonialism; it is the *re*colonization of Mozambique, with Britain and South Africa dominating the economy and the Portuguese taking on their traditional role of "shopkeeper colonists" who run small businesses. If history does not repeat itself exactly, the similarities with the colonial era are nevertheless striking. The pressure is on to roll back the independence of Mozambique and overturn the victory of the liberation war. Mozambique's very sovereignty is being challenged.

Forced to accept aid

Mozambique is the world's poorest, hungriest, most indebted, most aid-dependent country, according to the World Bank's *World Development Report 1990* (WB 1990e: Tables 1, 20, 23, 28). The purpose of this book is to show how that happened, and how the groundwork was laid for the recolonization. I look particularly at the role of outside agencies – multilateral bodies such as the IMF, bilateral donors, and non-government organizations (NGOs). The argument is that destabilization ended the socialist experiment and weakened the Mozambican state to such an extent that donors were able to move in and reconstruct Mozambique in a more acceptable way.

With independence in 1975, Mozambique set out to follow a different path from many other developing countries. It wanted a non-aligned foreign policy and a socialist domestic policy; development was to benefit the mass of the people and not just a privileged handful. Mozambique recognized many of the well-documented problems of "foreign aid"; for the first nine years of its independence, it kept many aid agencies out and negotiated clear relationships with those it allowed in. Most NGOs were barred. Mozambique was not a member of the IMF, the World Bank, or the Lomé convention; it set its own goals and made its own mistakes.

Effective social policies made the government popular and the economy grew, albeit slowly. Thus Mozambique became a threat to the major Western powers and to their hegemony in the Third World. Destabilization was the result, at horrific cost: more than a million dead and a material cost of more than $18 billion (£11 billion) (see Chapter 3). Frelimo was forced to beg for the aid it had earlier refused. Mozambique joined the IMF and from 1984 the donors piled in with unseemly haste.

In a previous book, *Mozambique: The Revolution Under Fire* (Hanlon 1984a) I looked at the first decade of Mozambique's independence and at Frelimo's attempt at a more broadly based development that involved a degree of equity rare among developing countries. In two other books, *Beggar Your Neighbours* and *Apartheid's Second Front* (Hanlon 1986a and 1986b), I looked at the first years of destabilization. These books documented South Africa's central role in building and supporting Renamo, as well as Pretoria's brazen decision to ignore the 1984 Nkomati Accord in which it promised Mozambique that it would end that support. I will not cover that ground again here.

In this book, picking up the story in 1984, I show how the Western powers and donor agencies attempted to impose their will on a weakened Mozambique. Part I (Chapters 1-4) looks at the horrific impact of destabilization in creating widespread famine and misery, and at the special role of the United States. Part II (Chapters 5-8) looks at the international response to the crisis in Mozambique, and at the battles which ensued as donors tried to use "emergency aid" to displace and marginalize the government. A central demand of the Western powers was that Mozambique sign an agreement with the IMF and accept structural adjustment. Part III (Chapters 8-15) looks at this battle over the economy, at the impact of structural adjustment, and at the cogency of World Bank "second thoughts". It also considers specific battles over the role of the state in the economy and social services. Part IV looks in more detail at the Mozambican and foreign actors. Finally, Part V reassesses the phenomenon of recolonization, and asks if a tiny, embattled, poorly educated, bankrupt country can control its own destiny. Or does power really rest with the big countries and the wealthy aid agencies? Who calls the shots in Mozambique?

This last question remains unresolved. As I complete this book in late 1990, Mozambique seems set to enter a new phase. At last there seem to be genuine prospects of peace, both because the end of apartheid would weaken the main destabilizing force and because the Western powers are now impatient to harvest the fruits of victory. It is not possible to make detailed predictions of what will happen in the 1990s, but it does seem possible to set out general outlines. Clearly, the Western powers have achieved their initial goal: to prevent a socialist transformation. The next goal would appear to be to reintegrate Mozambique into the world economy, where it will again be a market for manufactured goods, a source of minerals and tropical agricultural products, and a port for inland countries.

Mozambique has been important to the West in a negative rather than a positive way. It required priority attention as a dangerous threat promoting an alternative development model, but despite its titanium and cashew nuts, it will never have a key role in the international economy. Nor will it attract major foreign investments. Thus the Western powers do not seem interested in direct control; they are happy to see Mozambique return to its colonial position of being doubly peripheral – being subordinate to Portugal and South Africa, themselves peripheral economies. With the prospect of majority rule in South Africa, it would suit the West to see a capitalist South Africa dominate the entire southern African region as it did in the 1960s.

For this reason, the strategy of recolonization emerged in the late 1980s. The process has only just begun, and peace will bring radical changes. Foreign agencies such as the World Bank and "aid donors" will continue to play a pivotal role. Mozambicans themselves are much more divided than they were a decade ago, and there will be continued struggles over the recolonization process.

Fear of success

It is important to put Mozambique into context. With the defeat of the US in Vietnam, the victories of liberation movements in the former Portuguese colonies and of the Sandinistas in Nicaragua, and the emergence of left governments in Grenada and Zimbabwe, it seemed as if socialism was gaining a limited foothold in the Third World.

In the period around 1980, notably in Mozambique and Nicaragua, there was optimism that an alternative development path could be followed; and in the US, there was fear that these countries might succeed. It is not my purpose here to argue that Mozambique would have succeeded, or that Frelimo's mistakes doomed the attempt to failure. The point is that in 1980 both Mozambicans and right-wing leaders in the West thought that Frelimo might create a prosperous, non-aligned, non-racial, socialist state. The election of Margaret Thatcher in the UK and Ronald Reagan in the US marked a sharp rightward shift in the West and a move toward East-West confrontation.

If in the 1970s the Western grip on the Third World weakened, in the 1980s the West reasserted its control. The invasions of Grenada, the Falklands, and Panama showed that the big stick was still there to be used, but the real mark of the decade was the use of low-intensity warfare and surrogate armies, notably in Nicaragua, Angola, and Mozambique. In each of the three an underlying pattern was varied to reflect local conditions. Thus, in southern Africa it was sufficient to encourage the newly elected P W Botha to destabilize his neighbours by taking on existing anti-government forces, while in Nicaragua the US had to create the Contras from scratch.

At first, the goal was simply to ensure that Nicaragua, Angola, and Mozambique failed in their attempts to create a non-aligned alternative. In John Saul's phrase, the goal was to destroy the dream of socialism; to prove to the people of the Third World that socialism could not work. Initially, then, destabilization was an end in itself.

As the decade progressed, this goal was refined and modified. In Nicaragua and Angola, the goal became putting the opposition into power. In Mozambique, however, the failure to turn Renamo into a credible alternative, combined with the weakness and poverty of Mozambique itself, led to a different strategy of coopting the Frelimo government (although, as I note in Chapter 4, this alternative was not totally accepted in the US). The scale of destruction meant that Mozambique could be rebuilt in a different way. The IMF, the World Bank, and the donors then became the agents of its restructuring. As the decade progressed, it became apparent that Mozambique could be recolonized. This book is about that process.

Conspiracy of interests

It is important not to see international action in terms of a cartoon conspiracy in which a group of fat, cigar-smoking men sit around a table deciding how to carve up Mozambique. Rather, it is what might be called a "conspiracy of interests" or "collective self-interest" in which a wide range of participants develop a common interest and then exert pressure in different ways, while encouraging and facilitating the actions of other participants. Thus, US officials did not order the South African military to destabilize Mozambique, but did provide encouragement and support. Similarly, a condition of ending destabilization became the acceptance of an IMF structural adjustment package. Susan George (1988: 40) describes a similar phenomenon as a "consortium". Consortium members, she writes, "share (mostly) common interests and therefore pursue similar goals. They don't conspire, but they do consult."

Central to this process was the international wave of privatization of the 1980s, affecting not just the economy and social services, but also the conduct of foreign policy. At a covert level, there was a shift to supporting low-intensity warfare through right-wing private groups and front companies set up with the encouragement and aid of the CIA, South African military intelligence, etc. The Iran-Contra affair showed the international role of covert non-government agencies. Not only did these companies take substantial commissions on their arms deals, but they also engaged in ivory, drug, and other illicit trading.

At the more public level, there was an increasing tendency to direct foreign aid through NGOs and, in some cases, UN agencies such as Unicef. Sometimes there was an overlap in the two forms of privatization; right-wing church NGOs dispensed aid, while also supporting the opponents of progressive governments. Even liberal NGOs became major government contractors, and by the late 1980s were among the dominant dispensers of charity in Mozambique.

Most organizations want to grow, and thus both the NGOs and the private backers of destabilization were anxious to promote a takeover of Mozambique that allowed them to profit and expand. They were also strongly motivated by ideological goals – the right-wing groups were anxious to overthrow a socialist government, while NGOs wanted to replace government structures with alternative non-governmental bodies. In a loose way, this could be orchestrated by the World Bank and by government contracts with NGOs and private firms. Although the process of privatization and fractionalization sometimes led to conflicts, it generally served to increase conservative US hegemony because of the conspiracy of interests.

Three caveats

This brief summary highlights three caveats, to keep in mind when reading what follows. First, an implication of privatization is that agencies acting in their own interests may also serve a set of broader policy goals without actually supporting those goals. Thus, NGOs which claim to be progressive sometimes also work to undermine the Mozambican government, both by becoming channels for funding which might otherwise go to the government, and because in their insistence that they work directly with "the people" they supplant the government in providing health care and agricultural extension services. So it is important to distinguish professed goals from the impact on the ground.

Second, it is important not to impute conspiracies. For example, the Heritage Foundation is cited at length in Chapter 4. Clearly, Heritage articulated and spelled out the conservative agenda, campaigned for and promoted it and played a direct role through support of Renamo. Nevertheless, this does not necessarily mean that Heritage was organizing a grand conspiracy; rather, it was one of many actors in the "conspiracy of interests".

Third, it must be remembered that policy and strategy evolved over time. There has never been a grand plan or blueprint for Mozambique. The handful of disgruntled people who dreamed of rolling back the events of 1975 and recolonizing Mozambique were ignored by those who formulated policy in 1981. Indeed, it could be argued that Western policy toward Mozambique has had a particularly short time horizon and has been created and modified on the hoof. Thus the shift in policy from destabilization to cooption to recolonization has been neither smooth nor fully endorsed by all participants.

Primary responsibility

Recently a number of writers have argued that the massive suffering in Mozambique is the "fault" of Frelimo. There are two distinct strands to this new approach. One sees Mozambique as the failure of socialism. The South African daily *Business Day* (14 March 1990) says the power cuts in Maputo are "the combined result of Renamo sabotage and central planning", though the power cuts are entirely due to blown-up pylons. This report was part of a warning to the ANC to "learn from Maputo's mistakes" that "should we follow the socialist route, we [South Africa] would then be reduced, as Mozambique now is, to a pauper of a nation".

The other strand, coming from both left and right, is more complex. It is that the failures of Frelimo to democratize, to involve traditional leaders, and to take adequate account of peasants' economic demands led directly to the success of Renamo. Although more subtle than the first, this strand, also blames Frelimo or socialism for the chaos and suffering.

The question is not whether Frelimo made mistakes. I raised questions about the lack of democracy and about economic failings in an earlier book (Hanlon 1984a: Chapters 12, 15, 23). Rather, the question is about the primary cause of the crisis – was it South African intervention and destabilization, or was it Frelimo errors and socialism?

In a recent interview Frelimo Politburo member Marcelino dos Santos said that "We admit that we made mistakes. But look at the quality of those errors. Were they fundamental mistakes or did we fall short on secondary aspects?" He argues that the fundamental problem was foreign intervention, but that Frelimo's "errors provided the holes though which the enemy entered" (*Domingo* 10 June 1990).

This is hardly a new idea. Nearly a decade ago, the South African theorist of destabilization, Deon Geldenhuys (1982), wrote that "the destabiliser will be guided by the target state's political, economic, and military vulnerability". And in an earlier book on destabilization I wrote a chapter entitled "Building on weakness", showing how South Africa had done just that (Hanlon 1986b: Chapter 11).

Nearly all countries have ethnic, regional, or language minorities with legitimate grievances about their cultures being marginalized or their regions being economically disadvantaged. Journalist Neal Ascherson wrote an article citing 46 sources of "tensions and potential trouble" in Europe, where ethnic and other disputes could lead to conflict – or, as in Cyprus and Northern Ireland, already have (*Independent on Sunday*, 18 February 1990). Similar flashpoints exist in the US and Canada. Consider what would happen if a powerful and wealthy neighbour were to train Welsh, Basque, Puerto Rican or Quebec nationalists, and then drop arms and other supplies, send submarines along the coast to land instructors, send commandos to blow up railway bridges, and set up an international propaganda campaign to boost the credibility of the new movement. The British government was rightly worried and outspoken about reports of foreign support for the IRA on a scale that was minuscule compared to South African support for Renamo.

It is necessary and important to understand the weaknesses South Africa and the US played on, but it is equally important to realize how vulnerable our own countries would be. That our own flashpoints and grumbling minorities have not generated large-scale wars is due more to the lack of foreign support than to any wisdom or skill by European or North American governments in resolving these problems.

The primary cause of suffering in Mozambique is destabilization and foreign intervention. Without that, the crisis would have been much less severe. No conceivable set of Frelimo errors could have resulted in a million dead and $18 billion in economic losses. To put the primary responsibility on Frelimo or socialism makes nonsense of history; it is blaming the victim.

The victors write the histories, and the rewriting of Mozambican history goes on apace. Not only are Frelimo and socialism increasingly blamed for the havoc wrought by destabilization, but the attempt is made to erase from memory Frelimo's successes. The World Bank fudges the economic data to conceal growth that took place before structural adjustment started, while donors choose to forget a health system that in the late 1970s won praise from the World Health Organization and progressive health experts the world over.

Frelimo inherited a bankrupt and backward country. Adult literacy was less than 15% and the Portuguese version of apartheid meant that few Mozambicans were trained for even semi-skilled jobs. South Africa cut off the subsidy it had given to fascist Portugal, and earnings were further cut when Mozambique imposed the mandatory UN sanctions against Rhodesia.

Faced with this extremely unpromising start, Frelimo halted the economic decline in only two years. Abandoned farms and factories began producing again. The ports and railways functioned. The years 1977–81 were actually a period of economic growth. Of course there were mistakes and massive inefficiencies. But overstretched and undertrained Mozambican officials turned around a broken and distorted colonial economy and were moving to correct some of their worst errors. And, most importantly, Frelimo remained immensely popular, winning credit for independence, the end of fascism, advances in health and education, for giving new rights and a voice to women, and for creating a limited democracy. Undoubtedly Frelimo did too little to promote democracy and women's emancipation; it made major economic errors; and it pushed too hard for rapid modernization, paying too little attention to traditional values. These were to provide the "holes through which the enemy entered".

At the beginning of the 1980s, however, these failings had not checked Frelimo's popularity. Independent Mozambique had made major and unexpected strides. Many Mozambicans believed that Frelimo could succeed. In Pretoria, Washington, and Lisbon key people were afraid that Frelimo might succeed. Destabilization was the result.

Explanations and thanks

In part, this is a book about "aid" to Mozambique and about the unequal relationship between recipient and donor. Mozambique is a special case, however, because it was forced to accept foreign aid. The need for aid came about because of destabilization, and not primarily because of natural disasters, economic factors, or a demand for large-scale foreign development assistance.

Mozambique is also a special case because it is one of the most aid-dependent countries in the world: in 1988 foreign aid was equivalent to an incredible 70% of gross domestic product (GDP) and it was receiving nearly $60 per capita in aid. (Others receiving as high a percentage of GDP, such as Guinea-Bissau, or more per capita, such as Israel, are all much smaller countries than Mozambique.) Thus Mozambique cannot be seen as typical; because of their money, donors have so much power that they may act in more extreme ways than elsewhere.

This book is not intended to be a catalogue of aid horror stories (although there are some here). Nor is it asking if aid is "good" or "bad". Indeed, in my travels in Mozambique I have seen aid workers doing imaginative, creative, helpful work. And I have seen aid workers doing serious harm. Rather, I have accepted that "aid" exists and is now essential in Mozambique; my interest is in the implication of Mozambique's being forced to accept aid, and to challenge some of the received wisdom about aid and donor agencies as it relates to Mozambique.

I hope I have been able to produce a more searching analysis than one finds in the accounts of journalists and aid tourists who usually only have a few days or weeks in Mozambique. Having been a journalist in Mozambique for five years (1979–84), I knew many people who were prepared to discuss these issues honestly with me. Because the aid invasion is very recent and was very rapid, people have fresh memories of the changes and the struggles, and thus it has been easier to chronicle.

To protect the guilty

I received extensive cooperation from Mozambicans, both officially and unofficially. In exchange, I agreed that I would not identify individual donor agencies. Except where the identification would be very difficult to disguise, I have adhered to this. Mozambicans are afraid that if agencies were publicly criticized, they would take their money elsewhere.

As I worked on this book, I soon came upon another reason not to identify agencies. I found aid workers coming to me to see if I was going to criticize them, and concluded that some agencies would have argued that, if I did not mention them, then they were doing well. Similarly, when I gave talks about my conclusions, I found donor officials demanding that I give them evidence of individual transgressions. This is to miss the point totally. There are more than 200 agencies spending hundreds of millions of dollars a year in Mozambique; there was never any possibility that I could look at all of them, or at all projects. That means both good and bad will inevitably be left out – and I do not want the presence or absence of comments on agencies to be given any weight in one way or the other. In any case, I did not find any agency which was totally "good" and "progressive", or totally "bad" and "reactionary".

The purpose of this book is not to highlight "good" or "bad" donors – it is to make points which I feel are general and widely applicable about the aid relationship in Mozambique. With respect to NGOs, for example, I am primarily concerned to make the case that NGOs are fulfilling the role of the "new missionaries"; I leave to the NGOs the problem of deciding how to be "good" missionaries.

Money and names

The Mozambican currency, the metical (MT), has been devalued rapidly from 40 MT to 1000 MT against the US$ (see Table A.1). During the period when this book was researched (1987–90), the official rate against the dollar ranged from 400 to 950 MT, or approximately 660 to 1600 MT against the pound sterling. The black market rate was normally just over double the official rate – about 900 to 2100 MT against the dollar. Wherever possible I have tried to give $ and £ equivalents, at the official rate at the time or at the year average. But for purposes of rough calculation, readers will not be far off it they take 1000 MT (known to Mozambicans as a "conto") to be roughly $1 or £1.

Foreign trade, commodity prices, aid, the cost of destabilization, and all other values of foreign exchange are normally reported by international agencies in dollars, and this form has been followed here. The value of the pound sterling has varied in the past 15 years between $1.30 and $2.40, which makes direct conversions difficult. I have used the average rates of £1 = $2 up to 1981 and £1 = $1.65 since 1982, rounded to the same degree of accuracy as the original US$ figure.

The word billion (bn) always means 1000 million (mn).

A brief note on the names MNR, NRM, and Renamo, which all denote the same organization. The main agent of destabilization in Mozambique is a group formed by Rhodesia and later backed by South Africa and right-wing forces in the US. Initially it was called Movimento Nacional de Resistência de Moçambique, meaning Mozambique National Resistance Movement, and the acronym MNR (or sometimes NRM) was used in both English and Portuguese. In an effort to sound more like Frelimo, the name was modified to Resistência Nacional Moçambicana with the acronym Renamo. I used MNR in my earlier books but Renamo has become more common and is largely used here. Nevertheless, MNR still appears in quotations, and I sometimes use it when describing the pre-1984 period. Some Mozambican place names have been changed at various times since independence, mainly to replace colonial names and spellings. In the text I have followed the orthography used in a recent survey by the Mozambican cartographer Fernando Pililão (1989). The maps use some older spellings.

Thanks and credits

The research for this book was partly funded by the Swedish International Development Agency (SIDA; ASDI in Mozambique). Special praise should go to SIDA because they agreed that the result would be a published book and that they make no comments on the manuscript. Indeed, even when I started to ask difficult questions about their projects, SIDA staff remained helpful and put no pressure on me.

This book cannot be taken to represent either SIDA or Mozambican government policy. Indeed, I suspect some people in both organizations will disagree quite forcefully with what is being said. In some cases, however, I am saying things that Mozambican officials want said, and have encouraged me to say, but which they cannot say publicly for fear of offending donors (and which they would deny if asked). Clearly I cannot say which is which, so the reader is advised to take the views expressed in this book entirely as my own.

Hundreds of people talked to me while I was preparing this book. Ordinary Mozambicans, as well as government officials and ministers, shared their hopes and experiences. Officials of foreign governments and aid agency workers discussed their roles with me. I cadged beds, hundreds of pages of photocopying, lifts, and plane seats. Without this help, and the trust of so many people, the book would have been impossible.

Many people spoke officially, on the record, and some of them are quoted in these pages. I was given many official reports and documents. In some cases I talked to people officially but off the record, sat in on meetings on the agreement that I did not report directly, and was given documents on the understanding that I did not quote directly from them. Finally, many people spoke with me unofficially and passed on confidential documents, on the clear understanding that I should not name or otherwise identify them. References in the text usually cite only published books and articles or official documents, and not anything which might compromise a source; this means readers will need to take some material on trust.

Because it would be invidious, and because I might inadvertently mention people who would prefer not to be identified, I have not included the normal list of thanks to individuals. My apologies to those who would like to have been mentioned, and my thanks to all of you. I hope you feel it was worth your effort, and judge the book a constructive contribution to the debate.

1 Destroying the Dream

1 Dreams fulfilled: 1975-80

Once a model of Third World development, Mozambique now endures a degree of suffering and aid dependence which makes it a warning to others. The transformation has been so rapid that it is important to recall why Mozambique was once seen as so successful, and to understand the complex factors that brought about its downfall.

Frelimo (originally the Front for the Liberation of Mozambique) launched its war in 1962 and won independence from Portugal in 1975. A traditional anti-colonial liberation struggle was simultaneously a struggle against the Portuguese dictatorship; independence came because the colonial wars eventually brought down the fascist government in Lisbon. In particular, this meant Frelimo was a non-racial and not a black nationalist movement. Frelimo also had the advantage of being the only liberation movement; it did not face the political problems that plagued Zimbabwe or Angola after independence.

But Frelimo inherited a bankrupt and crippled economy. Portugal had been the poorest and weakest of the colonial powers; it had done little to develop Mozambique and its earnings depended almost entirely on the exploitation of peasant labour. Widespread use of forced labour continued into the 1960s. The colony's main earnings came from port traffic and migrant labour for neighbouring states, particularly South Africa, and the export of agricultural crops such as sugar and tea which depended on seasonal labour. British, South African, and other non-Portuguese capital dominated. In an effort to avoid land reform at home, the fascist state had dumped tens of thousands of landless Portuguese peasants in Mozambique. The colony's balance of payments deficit was partly made up by a subsidy from South Africa, which was anxious to maintain white rule.

At independence, adult literacy was less than 15% – most Mozambicans were illiterate and many Portuguese peasants could not read and write. Health services were poor, limited to urban areas and a few mission hospitals. Within a few years, Frelimo transformed this dramatically, nationalizing all social services – health, education, legal, and funeral – and then rapidly expanding them at the most basic level. By 1980 the number of qualified school leavers had increased four-fold in both primary and secondary education (DNE 1985). In education, emphasis was placed on adult literacy and primary schooling.

Special stress was put on "primary health care" a year before the World Health Organization (WHO) began to promote the idea. Similarly, Mozambique adopted a restricted drugs list before WHO did, and it was one of the first countries to ban imports of inessential drugs not on the list. A vaccination campaign in 1976–78 reached 95% of the population and provided a highly accurate forecast for the 1980 census. By 1982 there

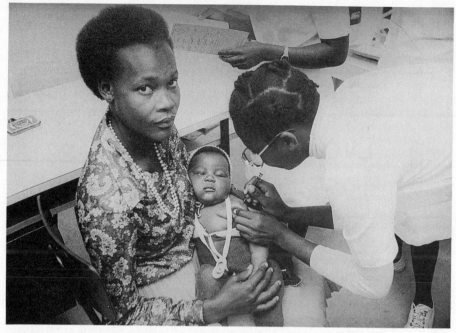

Child being vaccinated at the Mavalane health centre in Maputo. Vaccination was a high priority
(AIM: Alfredo Mueche)

were more than twice as many rural health posts and centres as there had been at independence (DNE 1985). The number of births in health units tripled. A WHO survey in 1982 showed that 81% of rural children had been seen at least once by a health worker – an incredible percentage for Africa – and two-thirds of rural health posts surveyed had a sufficient stock of essential drugs (Hanlon 1984a: Chapter 8). Mozambique became one of the success stories cited by WHO and other international health experts.

Halting economic collapse: 1975–76

Most Portuguese fled at the time of independence, ignoring Frelimo attempts to reassure them that they still had a place in Mozambique. Instead, they believed colonial propaganda about Frelimo terrorists, and they often smashed equipment and killed livestock before they left. This departure was a serious setback because Portuguese settlers, many recently arrived, had occupied nearly all middle-level positions; they were the taxi drivers, ticket collectors on trains, low-level civil servants, and so on. Nearly all farms with tractors and irrigation had been occupied by white settlers.

Under pressure of the liberation war, the Portuguese had made major social and economic changes in the late 1960s and early 1970s. Nevertheless, the economy and social services remained highly distorted, largely serving an urban elite. Recognizing this, Frelimo nationalized the social sectors along with land and rented property. But it nationalized only a few businesses: the oil refinery, the coal mine, insurance, and all but one of the banks. The flight of Portuguese owners and managers meant that thousands of shops, restaurants, and small factories were simply abandoned. Responding to the need to protect jobs and keep these units in production, the state began running them in a process known as "intervention"; it was similar to bankruptcy, where the state appoints an administrator but does not actually own the business. Nevertheless, private farms, factories, shops, and transport continued to operate.

Mass mobilization was the order of the day. Everywhere, communities set up small collective gardens. In 1974, during the transitional period before formal independence, villages, neighbourhoods, and workplaces elected Groupos Dinamizadores (GDs; dynamizing groups) in a new form of participatory democracy. The GDs filled the administrative gap caused by the collapse of the colonial government and the flight of the Portuguese, as well as providing a forum for articulating demands and introducing new policies. They combined the roles of courts, councils, debating groups, and mobilizers for latrine building and adult literacy classes. Mass meetings were common. And so, despite the skills gaps, Mozambique muddled through on a wave of mass mobilization and enthusiasm.

Not surprisingly, the already bankrupt economy declined further. But by 1977 it began to pick up, and there was steady growth until 1981 when, with exports rising, GDP was double the 1977 level and well above pre-independence levels (DNE 1985). (Appendix 2 sets out a periodization of post-independence Mozambique.)

This economic growth was all the more surprising because the country was already coming under attack from its neighbours. In 1976 Mozambique imposed the mandatory UN sanctions and closed the border with Rhodesia, then ruled by the Ian Smith regime following a "unilateral declaration of independence" (UDI) in 1965. This meant that Mozambique lost vital revenue earned by port and railway traffic from Rhodesia and Zambia. Increasingly fierce Rhodesian raids into Mozambique disrupted the central provinces; road, rail, port, hydroelectric, and oil facilities were damaged. The Rhodesian security services also created the MNR as a guerrilla force which attacked targets in Manica and Sofala provinces. According to UN estimates, imposing sanctions cost Mozambique nearly $600 million (£300 mn; USCD 1980). Although various promises were made at the time, little international assistance was forthcoming to compensate.

Meanwhile, South Africa, which had subsidized Portuguese rule in Mozambique, reversed its position. It imposed sanctions against Mozambique, cutting its use of the port of Maputo from 6 mn tonnes before independence to 3 mn tonnes in 1981 (and down to less than 1 mn tonnes later), while it cut the number of migrant Mozambican miners from 118,000 to 41,000 in just two years. Together, these measures cost Mozambique at least $800 mn (£400 mn) in lost earnings by 1983 (CNP 1984a).

Modernization and socialism: 1977–80

Just keeping the economy going in the face of Portuguese flight, and beginning the expansion of health and education, was a triumph. But Frelimo faced a much more serious problem: the economy was based on a degree of exploitation and coercion that simply could not be maintained. Social services and industry were designed to serve only a tiny urban elite, or to support export industries. Nothing less than a total transformation of the economy was required. Faced with this daunting task, Frelimo looked to the rapid industrialization and social transformation of eastern Europe. It followed a path trod in many other countries and tried to make a great modernizing leap, putting all its money and energies into the modern sector.

In industry, the stress was on the production of basic consumer goods for the masses rather than luxury goods, but in large factories and ultramodern textile mills rather than through the lower, decentralized technology tried in Tanzania, India, and China.

In agriculture, Frelimo clearly could not continue the colonial policy which was very inefficient and would not generate the necessary economic surplus. In any case, peasants were not prepared to grow cotton nor work long contracts on plantations except under duress. Instead, rural development was to be based on "socialization of the countryside", with people living in new "communal villages" where it would be easier to provide health services, education, water, and agricultural extension. To increase productivity, stress was put on mechanized state farms and cooperatives. About 2000 small farms had been abandoned by Portuguese peasants going home (WB 1989d: 48). In some cases they were returned to the peasants whose land had been taken some years before. More often, however, they were grouped into state farms or cooperatives, on the grounds that they were integrated colonial development projects with central services like irrigation which needed central management. Originally a defensive way of maintaining production, the state farms were then expanded as the quickest way to increase food supplies for the cities.

Finally, Frelimo decided to modernize the military. Faced with the threat of a conventional South African invasion as had occurred in Angola in 1975, it converted its guerrilla fighters into a modern, mechanized army, and started an air force.

Frelimo's policy had substantial popular support. Real wages increased. Urban jobs were protected. State farms provided more favourable rural employment than had been available during colonial times. Successful communal villages offered a better life. Factories and power lines were being built. State farms were producing significant amounts of urban food; in 1979 there were post-independence record exports of sugar, tea, and citrus – all from the state sector. The modernization of the army proved a success in late 1979 when accurate Mozambican artillery repelled the biggest Rhodesian invasion, ending Ian Smith's military aspirations and speeding the end of the Lancaster House talks. Thus, in 1979, President Samora Machel felt confident in declaring the 1980s "the decade of victory over underdevelopment".

In general, Mozambique's donors and foreign friends encouraged the modernization line. East European and Nordic donors and the UN Food and Agriculture Organization (FAO) all supported the state farm approach. The late 1970s were a period when international banks were still encouraging Third World borrowing, and Mozambique was offered generous loans and export credits to pay for the big new factories. The UN Industrial Development Organization (Unido) also backed Mozambique's attempt at rapid industrialization; foreign consultants encouraged Mozambique to think big. There were a few qualms expressed – for example, the East Europeans warned Mozambique to take a cautious line on cooperativization and start with peasant associations (Hanlon 1984a: 109) – but when these were waved aside the donors did not press the point too hard.

Social change

As part of its modernizing and socialist ideology, Frelimo set out to transform social and economic relations. The Portuguese had already abandoned their form of apartheid in the cities and ended forced labour and forced cultivation of cotton and rice; Frelimo was rightly given credit for these fundamental changes in most people's lives because they had only come about because of the pressure of the liberation war. After independence, Frelimo introduced a number of additional measures, including minimum employment protection, and rapidly expanded health and education.

More controversially, Frelimo took a strong stand against traditionalism, obscurantism, and cults; society was secularized. There were single national systems of law, of health, and of education. There were no traditional or tribal courts, as in some African states; mission hospitals and schools were nationalized; traditional healers were labelled witch doctors. Régulos ("traditional" clan chiefs or headmen appointed by the Portuguese) lost all official status.

In their place, there was a rapidly expanding state health and education system. Frelimo appointed village secretaries and eventually there were elected councils and local magistrates' courts. In some places a brother or cousin of the old régulo would be made Frelimo party secretary, so that he carried some traditional authority as well; more often traditional leaders were simply displaced. Roman Catholic priests and officials, who were much hated for their alliance with the Portuguese, were marginalized; Protestants (who had supported the independence struggle) and Muslims, who had both been restricted in colonial times, actually gained freedom after independence.

The traditional oppression of women was a particular target. Polygamy was discouraged and all elected bodies such as village councils and courts had to have at least one woman. In meetings, women spoke out for the first time and the local women's group often became a powerful force.

Although there were a few overt attacks on churches and other targets, the main attack on traditionalism was pursued through the party. Regular churchgoers, people who ran businesses or hired labour, and men who took extra wives after independence or who maltreated their wives were not allowed to join Frelimo; this meant they could not be elected to any body, which limited their local power and opportunities for advancement, and imposed a certain social pressure.

Democracy and responsiveness

Frelimo gave Mozambicans a voice. In colonial times they had little say; in the first years of independence there were meetings everywhere in which people spoke their minds. In the absence of any other authority, the GDs took on real power in villages, neighbourhoods, and workplaces.

The Third Congress in 1977 created a more formalized structure. Frelimo was converted from a mass organization into a Marxist-Leninist vanguard party; Mozambique was confirmed as a one-party state, the president of Frelimo being the president of Mozambique. (For that reason, in this book I sometimes use "Frelimo" and "the Mozambican government" interchangeably, particularly with respect to policy matters, until the late 1980s. The Fifth Congress in 1989 reversed the decision to set up a vanguard party, and in 1990 Frelimo decided to end the one-party state, thus ending this identity between party and state.)

People's assemblies were established as local and provincial councils and a national parliament. The election of people to the party and to assemblies was very open. Potential party members were nominated or put themselves forward, and their neighbours and co-workers had to discuss them at public meetings and say that they were "exemplary" citizens. Frelimo must have been one of very few Marxist parties where good character was the main condition for admission and the general public had the dominant voice.

For assembly elections, slates of candidates were put forward by the party and the candidates had to stand up before public meetings; I attended several such meetings and saw unacceptable people rejected. Clearly the system was undemocratic in that people not approved by Frelimo could not stand, which meant there was no debate on issues; nevertheless, my impression was that those elected did enjoy public confidence and that local councillors and MPs were at least as representative of, and acceptable to, their constituents as in Europe or the US. For a country with no democratic traditions, the new system was initially quite democratic and open.

Independence gave people the freedom to speak out, and public meetings were an initial form of democracy. This woman is speaking at a meeting in 1989 in Gilé, Zambézia province, of people displaced by Renamo raids. (AIM: Alfredo Mueche)

Local government and decentralization

But democracy is not just about elections; it is about the exercise of power, and it is intimately related to lower levels of government. The sharp contrast between the federal systems of the US and West Germany, on one hand, and the centralized systems of Britain and France, on the other, show there is no agreed system. The bitter controversy caused by the abolition of the Greater London Council by the government of Prime Minister Margaret Thatcher shows, too, that allegedly democratic governments may not be prepared to tolerate too much local democracy.

Unfortunately, Frelimo adopted a government structure little different from that of the Portuguese. The president was at the top and he appointed governors and ministers. Below that were appointed national and provincial directors and district administrators. The structure of the national government was replicated at provincial and district levels, with directors of health, education, etc. But governors, district administrators, and provincial and district directors had little previous administrative experience and rarely received any special training.

Furthermore, Frelimo never defined the role of provincial and local government, or of elected provincial and local assemblies. And national government was reluctant to devolve power. There was no system of local taxes, budgets, and decision-making power over local issues. Central planning and central budgeting covered areas like construction of schools, health posts, and small bridges which could have been decided on and carried out at local level. This destroyed local initiative and replaced it with a hierarchical and deferential structure which was totally incapable of carrying out the grand plans.

Every official saw himself (it was virtually never herself) as the representative of the president. Orders came from the top and those below were reluctant to question them. In some cases, an official in Maputo, a provincial director, or a farm administrator who lacked adequate knowledge gave totally inappropriate instructions which were carried out because it would have been disrespectful to disagree. On the other hand, local and provincial officials were often afraid to take even quite small local actions without approval from Maputo.

Furthermore, after the initial post-Congress spurt of enthusiasm, there was little attempt to regenerate and invigorate the party. Its structure resembled that of the state administration, with the president as head and a Politburo elected by the Central Committee; governors and administrators also served as provincial and district party secretaries. Thus party and government were effectively merged. Frelimo proclaimed "democratic centralism" which functioned to the extent that the party remained in touch with the base and could respond to popular demands. Mass meetings were of two very different kinds, depending on the orientation from the party.

If the party ruled that they were to be for information gathering, as in the run-up to party congresses or national conferences of the youth and women's organizations, they were open and outspoken. Most of the time, however, meetings simply consisted of officials chanting slogans and lecturing a group of peasants, passing on instructions from above that they sometimes did not understand themselves and which were totally meaningless to the audience. Information flowed from above; leaders preoccupied with keeping the country running began to lose touch with the base. The total failure to respond to peasant needs and demands in the 1979–82 period, and the total failure to appreciate the extent of the rural crisis, signalled how wide the gap had become: in a more democratic system representatives of rural areas would have made these problems widely known. A Frelimo member ruefully admitted to me that "the state became its own worst enemy. We ran too fast without looking where we were going."

In such a highly centralized system, what was the role of local party cells, mass organizations of women and youth, and elected assemblies? They became bodies to carry out instructions from above, rather than representative voices. It was this lack of power, rather than the method of election, that eventually made them undemocratic.

In retrospect, Frelimo's error lay in not building on the early era of mass mobilization; the GDs, in particular, could have provided a basis for formally elected bodies with power over local issues. Perhaps it was because the Frelimo leadership had no experience of local government and local democracy that it failed to understand the importance of it.

"Aspirants to the bourgeoisie"

The flight of the Portuguese meant the disappearance of most of the colonial bourgeoisie and petty bourgeoisie, and its replacement by a new group. The Central Committee report to the Fourth Congress in 1983 said that "our country has a social stratum that enjoys levels of consumption unavailable to the overwhelming majority of the people. From a social point of view, it consists chiefly of citizens originating from social strata that were already privileged in the colonial period." President Samora Machel said that "they are still 'aspirants to the bourgeoisie' because they do not yet have economic power." This remained a reasonable assessment into the late 1980s, although change was taking place (see Chapter 18). In an earlier book I argued that there were two different kinds of aspirants, a *state group* and a *commercial group*. The former is composed of directors and apparatchiks whose own power comes from control of state resources. The latter is based on trade and other small businesses (Hanlon 1984a: 185ff).

The state group evolved over time. In the early years of independence, the middle- and high-level leadership was dedicated, hardworking, and exceptionally honest. The ban on private rented housing meant that many officials who had a base inside the country abandoned homes they owned to move into houses rented from the state, rather than illicitly renting out the other house. The ban on employing labour meant that none set up private businesses. There were few privileges and when there were shortages, ministers went short as well. All energies were concentrated on building a new Mozambique. Frelimo officials often had three jobs – in the party, in the state, and helping to keep intervened businesses running – and worked punishing schedules. Just as the armed struggle required single-minded devotion, so did building the new socialist state. In particular, officials did not worry about providing for their children or their own old age because they were going to create a socialist state which provided for everyone's children and for all the aged.

The Frelimo leadership was committed to rapid transformation, and to socialism from the top. Thus they supported modernization, with large state farms and industry, rather than a decentralized, peasant-based development strategy which, they felt, would have been slower and more difficult to implement. Central planning and policy making by a strong hierarchical government was the way to do this. The decision at the 1977 Third Congress to convert Frelimo from a mass to a vanguard party was a logical action by a committed leadership in a hurry.

At the same time, members of this state group gained power and respect from the highly centralized government and party. They encouraged appointed rather than elected officials, and pushed the Third Congress to opt for a vanguard party because it would increase their power and reduce the democratic and popular checks provided by the GDs. Their influence showed in a series of speeches by President Samora Machel in late 1979 and early 1980 when he said "power is exercised by the manager; it is the manager who decides." In the newly modernized army, an officer corps was created.

The state group promoted a form of state capitalism, in which it did not own the means of production, but did control them. Bigger projects meant control of large amounts of resources. What the leadership initially saw as being in the best interests of the mass of the people eventually proved to be in its own interest as well. This state group is a combination of educated technocrats and leaders from the armed struggle who gained positions after independence. Generally, members of this group had been able to obtain a better education in colonial times which meant, by definition, that they had been privileged compared to most Mozambicans. They pushed for salary structures based strictly on educational qualifications, which ensured that they earned more than skilled workers. Although this group did not accumulate wealth, it increasingly did, as the Central Committee report commented, build a higher level of consumption by granting itself perks such as cars, special shops, and foreign travel.

The commercial group, too, had been better off before independence, although in an inferior position compared to the colonial bourgeoisie. This group included traders, often but not always of Asian origin, who had been in rural areas during the colonial period and moved into the cities to take over shops and other small businesses abandoned by the fleeing Portuguese. Others in this group were Portuguese small farmers and shopkeepers who had stayed on, and a handful of Mozambicans who had been encouraged to become kulak farmers by the Portuguese in a change of policy in the late 1960s.

Kenneth Hermele (1990: 3) argues that parts of this group had been kept from accumulating by the Portuguese and thus were part of the initial anti-colonial alliance. But this group was marginalized by Frelimo's policy of not replacing the old exploiters by new ones, so it worked against the new socialist and modernizing line after independence. Hermele (1988: 29) even argues that this group sabotaged state farms; middle peasants who had failed to gain settler land at independence became tractor drivers and lower-level administrators on the new state farms; they were hardly anxious to make those farms work.

The easing of Frelimo's antagonism to private business and the recovery of the economy that began in 1977 gave this commercial group confidence and allowed it to expand, rebuilding some of the rural trading network that had been abandoned at independence. By 1980 private traders were willing to take back intervened shops and other small firms which had been abandoned at independence and run by the state since then.

Although there was initially some hostility between these two groups, they increasingly cooperated as they saw that their interests did not conflict: the state group had little interest in small industry and petty trade. The growing alliance was shown in the 1980 sell-off of state and intervened shops and restaurants, when there was no attempt to encourage co-ops, protect workers, or keep well-run small businesses within the state sector.

1980: a year of promise

The first five years of independence produced dramatic gains for most Mozambicans. Freedom and a measure of democracy changed people's lives; women, especially, gained rights for the first time. Health and education became much more widely available. Mozambique did not suffer the racial and other ethnic tensions seen elsewhere. The economic decline had been reversed and the economy was growing. Victory over underdevelopment seemed possible.

1980 seemed to confirm all of Mozambique's hopes and dreams. Zimbabwe became independent and there was peace throughout the country. In Maputo, the soldiers guarding government office buildings were withdrawn; the street in front of the presidential palace which had been closed to traffic for fear of sabotage raids was opened and left unguarded. In June 1980 the government introduced a new currency, the metical; in just three days everyone happily exchanged their old colonial banknotes and coins for new ones with the pictures of revolutionary leaders Samora Machel and Eduardo Mondlane. In August the first post-independence census reached the farthest corners of this vast and sparsely populated country.

With the war over, economic development was at the top of the agenda. A new ten-year plan was produced, and work on development projects was started or accelerated. In November, leaders of the nine majority-ruled states of the region gathered in Maputo for the first annual meeting of the Southern African Development Coordination

Conference (SADCC), formed in the belief that through cooperation they could take an independent path to development. Mozambique would take overall responsibility within SADCC for transport, and re-establish its traditional role as the main port for four inland states (Malawi, Swaziland, Zambia and Zimbabwe). This had been disrupted with the closing of the Rhodesian border and with Rhodesian attacks on Mozambican infrastructure, shifting much of this traffic through South African ports even though they were much farther away than Mozambican ports. Major developments would rehabilitate and upgrade Mozambicans ports and railways, helping to link the SADCC states and provide an important source of revenue to Mozambique.

SADCC's founding declaration stressed that "future development must aim at the reduction of economic dependence not only on the Republic of South Africa, but also on any single external state or group of states" (SADCC 1980). It was both a declaration of non-alignment and a commitment to reduce the artificial links with South Africa that had been built by 70 years of colonialism and fifteen years of UDI.

The bright hopes of 1980 were never to be fulfilled. Indeed, Frelimo's most serious error was to assume that it would be allowed to pursue a non-aligned foreign policy and a socialist economic policy. The mistake was to assume that it had a real freedom of choice. In retrospect this was naïve in the extreme. But in 1980, who would have predicted the events of the coming decade?

2 Dreams Shattered: 1981-83

It is difficult now to recall the optimism and joy of 1980 in Mozambique. It was not to last. The beginning of the 1980s brought a convergence of factors which dramatically changed the outlook. The second oil price rise triggered a world recession which hit the prices of Mozambique's exports, pushed up interest rates, and cut off new credit. The worst drought of the century hit southern Africa in 1981–83; even the best-run of countries needed aid. Some of the economic chickens came home to roost, as foreign debts came due before production had increased to pay for them. And some of the social issues began to surface, relating to traditional values, religion, and local languages. The lack of democracy and power and the economic problems led to a growing sense of abandonment in rural areas.

Most importantly, the international political climate changed. Mozambique believed, naïvely as it turned out, that South Africa would not see SADCC as a threat, and that the West would not object to Mozambique's non-alignment. This view was probably encouraged by the government of US President Jimmy Carter, which put strong human rights pressure on South Africa and backed the formation of SADCC. With P W Botha, Margaret Thatcher, and Ronald Reagan coming to power, there was a new hostility to Mozambique and to SADCC.

Destructive engagement

Ronald Reagan was elected president in November 1980. His new policy was vociferous anti-communism and "constructive engagement" with South Africa. Chester Crocker, who became Reagan's Assistant Secretary of State for African Affairs, called SADCC a "folly" and urged the SADCC states to retain their "natural" economic links with South Africa (Hanlon 1989: 41). The US was particularly hostile to the Marxist states of Mozambique and Angola. The South African government of P W Botha, who had become prime minister in 1978, took constructive engagement as a licence for the anti-communist apartheid state to attack the neighbouring Marxist states; US officials did nothing to discourage this view.

On 30 January 1981, just ten days after the inauguration of President Reagan, lorryloads of South African commandos came over the border and raided the Maputo suburb of Matola, killing 13 members of the African National Congress and a Portuguese electricity technician. The South Africans left behind one dead commando, British mercenary Robert Hutchinson, whose helmet was painted with swastikas and the words "sieg heil". It was the end of a brief year of peace, and marked the start of an escalating campaign of destabilization. Commandos made more raids in the following months, including a series in November 1981 severely damaging two bridges carrying the road, railway, and oil pipeline from the port of Beira to Zimbabwe. Two other major raids included the destruction of an oil tank farm in Beira in December 1982, and a dramatic air raid on Maputo on 23 May 1983 in which several suburbs were strafed with special fragmentation rockets (for more detail, see Hanlon 1986a).

But the real devastation was caused by the MNR. It soon became apparent that in early 1980, in the waning days of the Smith regime in Rhodesia, the MNR had not been closed down but had instead been passed on to South African Military Intelligence. Training camps and control centres were established in South Africa. Most of the fighters were young Mozambicans press-ganged into the guerrilla force. Some stayed on voluntarily, liking the life of an armed bandit better than the drudgery of peasant farming. Some tried to escape and many succeeded; those caught trying to flee were executed, which served as a strong deterrent to others.

In a few places the MNR could gain local support, for example from régulos who had been marginalized by Frelimo, or from former Frelimo guerrillas who felt they deserved special privileges for winning independence and who objected to Frelimo's continued puritanism. But in most areas the MNR resorted to terrorism, often involving brutal massacres and mutilations such as cutting off ears, noses, and breasts. Children as young as ten or twelve years old were forced to commit atrocities.

By mid-1981 the MNR had established a base in central Mozambique. Regular flights to the interior and seaborne landings on beaches brought arms, radios, and other supplies, as well as trained men and South African commandos for training and sabotage action. By late 1981 the MNR was active in remote parts of the central provinces of Manica and Sofala, and by mid-1982 it had expanded south into Gaza and Inhambane

Woman whose ear was cut off by Renamo. (AIM: Anders Nilsson)

provinces. The South Africans were allowed to establish MNR bases in Malawi, and in late 1982 the MNR launched major raids into Tete and Zambézia provinces which border Malawi.

The MNR burned villages and attacked schools and health posts. But it concentrated on economic targets, burning shops and factories and attacking road and rail traffic. Drivers and bus passengers were burned alive in their vehicles, or hacked to death with axes, in an effort to ensure people were too terrified to travel. The effect was devastating. Rural commerce, still not fully rebuilt after the Portuguese flight, was shattered; in just two years, hundreds of private shops were burned. Traders were afraid to travel. The destruction of factories and collapse of rural commerce slashed the production and processing of export crops: the cotton, tea, sugar, and cashew nuts on which Mozambique depended for foreign earnings.

`A man-made, South African-made famine'

Destabilization encompassed a broad range of aims linked to taking pressure off South Africa and apartheid. In the 1960s, white rule in Mozambique, Angola, and Rhodesia had created a "cordon sanitaire" blocking the southward advance of majority rule. With the independence of those states, this was replaced in the 1980s by what the South African military called a "cordon of instability". As well as creating a psychological and practical barrier against ANC infiltration, it also turned the attention of neighbouring governments to their own problems and away from those of South Africa. The apartheid state did, temporarily, succeed in exporting its war into the neighbouring states.

Particularly critical were attempts to defend the necessity of white rule, both to foreign governments and to its own citizens. South Africa needed to show that majority rule led to chaos. In 1980 in the neighbouring states, this was manifestly not true. So South Africa set out to cause chaos. Creating famine and widespread disruption was one way to do this. TV pictures of white aid workers helping emaciated black babies underlined the need for continued white rule to prevent the continent from starving. South Africa was also anxious to cut the railways running through Mozambique, both to sabotage the newly created SADCC and to ensure that the inland states remained dependent on South Africa for import and export routes.

By 1982, South Africa's destabilization of its neighbours was openly discussed inside the apartheid state. An important academic paper on the "Destabilisation controversy in southern Africa" argued that "as seen from Pretoria ... black states' political and moral support for the so-called liberation movements, and their clamour for sanctions against South Africa and for its international isolation, are part of a concerted campaign to destabilise the country." The author concluded that it would "be naive to expect the country [South Africa] to renounce the destabilisation option for at least as long as black states remain committed to destabilise it."

"Turning to the means of destabilisation, the field is really wide open", the author notes. And at the top of his list was to curtail food to the target state in order "to cause serious hardship to the population, who would in turn direct their frustrations and fury at the target's regime" (Geldenhuys 1982).

Just this was done in southern Mozambique in 1983. In 1981–83 all of southern Africa was suffering the worst drought of the century. By 1983 the Incomati River in Maputo province was dry for the first time in living memory; it was possible to walk across the "great grey green greasy" Limpopo River. In Inhambane and Gaza, peasants were running out of food. Drought is common in this part of Mozambique. During a drought in the same zone in 1979/80, Frelimo organized a successful relief effort which largely prevented starvation. Clearly, it should have been able to do so again.

But this time was different. By late 1982 the MNR was active in the less occupied, semi-desert areas in the west of both Inhambane and Gaza provinces. Expanding MNR forces burned crops in the fields and destroyed peasant grain stores. Food relief lorries were attacked. Peasants caught trying to flee to Frelimo-controlled areas were brutally killed. In August 1983, as the famine worsened, South African aircraft dropped nine tonnes of supplies to the main MNR base at Tome in Inhambane. But this was not food for the hungry; it was mines to put on the roads to destroy food relief lorries.

For UN officials and foreign embassies in Mozambique the issue became a major political problem. It clearly was, as one US official later admitted to me, "a man-made, South African-made famine". In other words, it was an act of war rather than a natural disaster. To feed the starving was to take sides in that war. And in early 1983, the US, with its policies of constructive engagement and anti-communism, seemed to many to be backing South Africa. So to offer food to Mozambique at that time was to take the wrong side in a war.

Mozambique made its first appeal for food aid for the area in January 1983. It said that a severe drought had existed since December 1981 in southern Mozambique, causing "a partial loss of the 1982 summer crop and a nearly total loss of the 1982 winter crop..... The continuation of the drought up to now has led to a nearly complete failure of the plantings of the 1982/83 summer crop or prevented any plantings at all" (DPCCN 1983). People had no food reserves left, and would be running out soon. Representatives of the International Committee for the Red Cross (ICRC) had visited the drought area in January 1983 and compiled an internal report which said there was already – in January – a crisis in Inhambane. But that report was not circulated to the diplomatic community.

In June 1983, Trade Minister Aranda da Silva called together the foreign diplomats in Maputo to report that in response to the appeal, traditional food aid had *decreased*. Some had been simply relabelled as "emergency aid". The big western donors were refusing or reducing food aid despite the early warning (see Table 2.1). The US did pledge some grain, but so little (by US standards) that it was seen as evidence of continued hostility to the Marxist government. The United Nations World Food Programme (WFP), in which the US plays a key role, was so worried by US attitudes that it would only allow its food aid to go to areas without fighting, even though the need was less. In January, WFP turned down a request for food for Inhambane.

It was the non-traditional food donors, such as the USSR, Italy, Austria, and the Mennonite Church, who stepped in to prevent people from starving. Neighbouring Zimbabwe, itself suffering from the worst drought of the century, had become the largest food donor to Mozambique by mid-1983 (see Table 2.2).

Table 2.1 *Aid grain pledged in first half of 1983 (000t)*

Donor	Amount
Zimbabwe	25
USA	23
World Food Programme	13
USSR	10
Italy	10
Mennonite Church	8
Sweden	8
Austria	7
Australia	4
UK	3
France	2
European Community	2
TOTAL	115

Source: MCI 1983a

Table 2.2 *Delivered aid grain (000t)*
         4 month periods during Jan 1983–April 1984

	Jan–Apr	May–Aug	Sep–Dec	Jan–Apr
Australia	0	4★	0	4★
Austria	0	7	0	0
Canada	17	0	0	14★
Denmark	0	17	0	17★
EC	0	15	42★	0
France	0	2★	0	4★
Italy	7	0	10★	2★
Japan	18	0	0	5★
Mennonite Church	0	8★	0	0
Netherlands	0	0	0	19†
Sweden	0	8★	0	0
UK	0	3★	0	0
USA	0	26	8★	20★
USSR	0	0	10★	0
West Germany	3	4	0	0
World Food Programme	0	5★	3★	28★
Zimbabwe	0	25★	0	0
TOTAL	45	124	73	113
Type of grain:				
Maize	3	84	11	65
Wheat	17	21	42	37
Rice	25	19	20	11

★ = in response to 1983 appeals
† = partly in response to 1983 appeals
all other grain was pledged in 1982

Sources: author, data from Ministério do Comércio Interno, MCI 1983a, MCI 1983b, MCI 1984.

A week after da Silva met with diplomats, ICRC visited Vilanculos, in Inhambane, and this time it circulated to diplomats a report which called the position "alarming" (ICRC 1983). WFP then refused another Mozambican appeal for food for Inhambane. In July the US embassy sent a cable to Washington stressing the need, but still the US and other Western powers would not bend.

Problems come thick and fast

Drought, destabilization, and the world economic recession came just at a time when Frelimo began to face some of the consequences of its own errors. The party had wildly overestimated its own abilities; having won a liberation war on a shoestring and then prevented economic collapse against all dire predictions, it assumed anything was possible. Mozambique lacked the skills to develop and manage many large enterprises, and the gap could not be filled adequately by foreign experts. Some of the state farms, factories, and other projects worked reasonably well. But for most, completion was very late and operation inefficient.

The problem was compounded by a high degree of centralization and planning. Even cooperatives and private factories had production targets set in Maputo. Local initiative and variation was discouraged. Meeting targets rather than profitability became the goal. But Maputo was unable to ensure that tractors, fuel, industrial raw materials, spare parts, and so on arrived on time, so plans became meaningless and productivity fell.

In an attempt to prevent unemployment, Frelimo ensured that all urban workers employed in industry or small businesses retained their jobs, even if they produced relatively little. But many of these firms, as well as many of the farms Frelimo was trying to weld into state farms, had never been profitable in colonial times. They had been subsidized by the state or by private banks, or had been set up largely as schemes to get money out of the colony.

Table 2.3 *The emerging economic crisis (US$ millions)*

	1980	1981	1982	1983
Trade & Services				
Receipts				
Exports	281	281	229	132
Transport	93	82	83	66
Migrant labour	53	64	64	75
Other	25	32	24	24
Payments				
Imports	800	801	836	634
Other	69	87	80	78
TOTAL Trade & Services	–417	–429	–516	–415
Aid & Capital				
Receipts				
Donations	56	57	79	90
Loans	503	718	725	339
Payments				
Interest	6	36	60	88
Loan repayments	139	309	329	296
TOTAL Aid & Capital	414	430	415	45
Errors & omissions	–30	–67	–41	44
GLOBAL BALANCE	–33	–66	–142	–326
Run down reserves	32	69	148	47
Unpaid debt				285
Reserves at 31 December	253	184	37	–42

Source: DNE 1987

Thus, by the time President Machel declared his goal of victory over underdevelopment, clouds were already gathering on the economic horizon. The storm broke in 1982. Mozambique's earnings began to fall sharply just when they might have been expected to increase (Table 2.3). The drought and the widening war cut agricultural production and exports. World recession meant that Mozambique's terms of trade deteriorated; the unit value (or price paid per tonne) of exports fell by 20% in just two years (Unctad 1988 and Table A.2). Thus export earnings fell from a peak of $281 mn in 1981 to $132 mn in 1983.

With the founding of SADCC and the end of sanctions on Rhodesia, Mozambique's earnings from transporting goods for the inland states should have been rising rapidly. Instead they fell from $93 mn in 1980 to $66 mn in 1983 and only $34 mn in 1984. Increasing MNR attacks on the railways cut traffic from Zimbabwe and Malawi, while South Africa tightened its sanctions against Mozambique and nearly ended its traffic through the port of Maputo.

Meanwhile, the new more hostile international political and economic climate meant that Mozambique could not obtain new loans, while it had to pay off past debts falling due. New commercial credits were $277 mn in 1981, half that the next year, and negligible in 1983. Interest payments, which had been only $6 mn in 1980, were ten times that high in 1982. In 1983, interest payments alone were two-thirds of exports. In 1982 Mozambique drew down $148 mn of its reserves; this was nearly the entire reserve, and only $37 mn was left – enough to cover only three weeks' imports. Mozambique was in deep economic trouble (Tables 2.3 and A.3).

Because of the pending financial crisis, Mozambique cut imports of consumer goods from $95 mn in 1980 to $65 mn in 1981 and $53 mn in 1982 (Table 2.4). One result was that the shortage of consumer goods and agricultural implements inputs in rural areas became much more severe. This led to an accelerating "black" or "parallel" market, and to a reduction of official peasant sales of food and export crops, even in the north where the drought was not as serious. By mid-1982 the metical had become virtually worthless in rural areas; trade was by barter and black market. Imports of machinery and equipment for the big development projects continued, however, in part because of export credits.

Table 2.4 *Decline in imports (US$ millions)*

	1980	1981	1982	1983
Food	108	114	116	131
Consumer goods	95	64	53	47
Oil	219	167	213	97
Raw materials	168	200	167	135
Spare parts	57	104	108	105
Equipment	153	151	182	122
TOTAL	800	801	838	636

Source: DNE 1987

Gamble and errors

All governments make economic mistakes, but they are proportionately more expensive for a poor country. If a poor person loses £1, it could mean missing a meal, while if a rich person loses £1000 it will only mean a small reduction in luxury consumption. The same is true with countries. Unfortunately, through inexperience, new governments tend to make more economic mistakes; Frelimo made its share, and they proved costly. With hindsight it is possible to argue that Frelimo's attempt at rapid modernization was foolish, although there were many reasons why it did not seem so at the time.

Frelimo was embarking on a calculated gamble. It decided that it could afford in the short term to provide too few hoes and too little cloth for peasant farmers, and instead build cloth and hoe factories that would provide such basic consumer goods in abundance.

The gamble was that the enthusiasm for independence would carry the peasants through the hard times.

It was a close-run thing. Had it not been for Rhodesian and South African destabilization, enough factories might have opened in the early 1980s to make the gamble pay off. Some of the new state farms were proving profitable and efficient. Textile production by new factories would have jumped dramatically had MNR raids not blocked cotton production, cut electricity lines, and so on.

Even some of the failures, such as sugar mills and a large-scale Romanian cotton project in Cabo Delgado, are being taken on now by transnational corporations (TNCs) in a similar form. The Limpopo valley state farm, which was notorious for its inefficiency, has since been restructured and is run partly as a set of smaller state farms and partly as a TNC-owned farm; both are now productive and profitable. This suggests that the original grand plans were not so ridiculous as some critics now assert. Frelimo's modernization strategy was undoubtedly overambitious, but it may not have been untenable.

There was, however, one fundamental error: Frelimo gave too little support to peasant farmers, who had provided its sustenance during the liberation war and should have been its main supporters after independence. It wrongly assumed that they were largely subsistence farmers who were "self-sufficient" and thus could be ignored until they were eventually integrated into the modern socialized countryside. In fact they were already integrated into the market system, selling export crops and food for the cities and buying inputs and consumer goods. The marketing network had been dominated by Portuguese before independence because black people were rarely allowed trading licences. When the Portuguese fled, the rural trading network collapsed, and Frelimo did too little to rebuild it. There were too few shops and traders to buy peasant produce and too few consumer goods were available in exchange. The marketing network actually expanded in the late 1970s, but by 1981 domestic industrial production had not increased sufficiently to satisfy demand, while the economic squeeze had cut imports of consumer goods.

Many peasant families were also dependent on money from migrant labour, and in the south their problems were exacerbated by the sharp cut in migrant miners going to South Africa. Although urban jobs had been protected, little was done for former migrant workers who no longer had jobs and for young men who could no longer go to South African gold mines.

Social and political problems

Finally, the modernization strategy had incurred certain social costs which were beginning to show. The initial gains by women and men who had been marginalized under the old system vastly outweighed any initial losses. But by the early 1980s there was some discontent about the total abolition of tradition. Women complained that initiation rites, which Frelimo said were purely an instrument of repression, had positive aspects and should have been modified rather than banned. Traditional healers and birth attendants still had a role in society and should have been integrated rather than marginalized. Some régulos had merely been Portuguese tax collectors, but others still had respect and were seen as local elders outside the new Frelimo system. Some churchgoers and polygamists supported the new government but were kept outside the system. Although exaggerated by reactionary forces trying to regain influence, these issues were real enough; it was clear that many people were not ready to abandon all of their cultural traditions.

The rural economic and social crisis could occur because of problems within Frelimo. The increasing urban and bourgeois bias of state and party officials led them to overlook and misunderstand the peasantry. The lack of democracy and regeneration in the party meant that the peasants did not have an adequate voice to press their needs and demands. These problems were compounded by certain side-effects of what had initially been one of Frelimo's greatest strengths, the unity of a leadership essentially unchanged after 1970. Although there were disagreements over individual issues, the Politburo never split into factions; decisions were largely by consensus and a united front was maintained. The united leadership and lack of infighting had immense benefits, but it had two serious drawbacks.

First, where there were deep divisions, decisions simply were not taken. This became particularly serious in the early 1980s, when the Politburo sometimes seemed paralysed and unable to act on the war and the economy. During this period, the degree of collegiate leadership decreased and Samora Machel began to take a more dominant and autocratic role.

Second, the leadership proved extremely reluctant to take in and trust people who had not been in the armed struggle. Political prisoners of the Portuguese, those who had remained in colonial Mozambique, and people who were too young to have fought were rarely fully accepted, even if they were strong backers of Frelimo and its policy. This distrust was at the root of the failure to expand and democratize the party. There also may have been an unconscious fear that new people and new ideas would disturb an increasingly fragile unity based more on old comradeship and shared experiences and less on shared goals and ideas.

Thus the fragile unity of the leadership led to a further centralization of power and an unwillingness to delegate. This was shown strikingly by the appointment of Politburo members to be governors of key provinces in the early 1980s, as well as the continued reshuffling of the same group of ministers; since a new generation had not been recruited and promoted, the same people continued to take decisions even at provincial level. Local initiative was never encouraged.

Fourth Congress

The growing rural economic and social crisis was clearly linked to the rapid spread of the MNR; Frelimo officials realized (but did not admit publicly) that in some zones even if the peasants were not actively supporting the MNR, they had withdrawn support from Frelimo and allowed the MNR to enter unchallenged.

In 1983 the Frelimo Fourth Congress called for significant policy shifts, including decentralization and a reduction in central planning, a reduction in the stress on the state sector, and a more peasant-based development strategy. There was to be a new bias toward "small scale projects which have an immediate effect on people's living standards". There were to be no new projects, and the emphasis was on rehabilitation of already installed capacity. Frelimo had never been anti-private sector, and the Third Congress in 1977 had stressed that "small and medium agricultural proprietors" and "artisans and small property owners" should be supported. But the Fourth Congress called for additional support to the private sector, and said that "the state must encourage the most dynamic businessmen". But faced with the growing black market, the Congress also called for public monitoring of the private sector (Hanlon 1984a: 90) .

The Congress recognized many, perhaps most, of Frelimo's economic errors, and proposed sensible shifts. But it was too late. Had the changes been made in 1981, they would have had an effect and perhaps slowed the spread of the MNR. But by 1983 the growing impact of destabilization made the changes impossible to implement. For example, attacks on the roads meant that it was impossible to get newly allocated resources to the peasants or to start small rural projects.

Internal shifts

The crisis brought significant shifts in the class forces inside Mozambique, particularly as they affected the "aspirants to the bourgeoisie". Most notable was the loss of power by the state group. The modern army with its new officer corps was totally unable to respond to a guerrilla war. Drought, war and the foreign exchange crisis meant that government officials were losing control over the economy; state farm profitability and the completion of several big projects slipped irretrievably from their grasp. Politically and administratively, too, Frelimo was losing control.

The response was a complex mix of populism and authoritarianism. In meetings throughout the country before the Fourth Congress people were encouraged to speak their mind, and they did, sharply criticizing Frelimo for past errors. The Congress itself was very open and was broadcast live on the radio. But it did not extend democracy, so there was no way of ensuring that its decisions were carried out.

Yet Frelimo also showed its authoritarian side. The Congress was delayed for a year in a clear (and unsuccessful) attempt to prevent debate. The local press was prevented from reporting on the war, although I, as a foreign correspondent, was free to do so. Increasingly the army was forcing people into communal villages, which were supposed to be voluntary. There was even a return, in Nampula province, to the colonial methods of forcing peasants to produce cotton (*Tempo* 19 October 1986).

In the months before and after the Congress, Frelimo introduced public executions and floggings; it then launched Operation Production, in which tens of thousands of people without proper identity documents were brusquely shipped out of the major cities with no due process. These authoritarian measures were not even effective; forced villagization and Operation Production only created recruits for the MNR.

In 1984 the Mozambique Women's Organization (OMM) held a special conference to discuss social issues; like the Fourth Congress, its preparatory meetings were open and outspoken, but the actual conference was dominated by President Machel who blocked debate. The party's male leadership had earlier blocked passage of a progressive new family law which would have increased women's rights.

It seemed as if the leadership and state group was trying to compensate for its loss of control by increasingly authoritarian actions. During this period, as goods became short, special shops and access to goods became more important for the state group, and their differences in life style from ordinary people faced with empty shops became more apparent. The gap was not large and the state group was still quite poor by developed world standards, but the gap was obvious enough to cause complaints. Also, the first signs of corruption appeared in this period.

The state was also losing control over the economy, as more and more trading shifted to the black market. An Asian trader was executed for smuggling a truckload of prawns in 1983, a clear warning by the state group to the commercial group not to go too far. But there were many more examples of collaboration, such as state company managers using the black market to obtain food for workers, and district administrators making private deals with traders to allow some illegal trade in exchange for special access to scarce commodities. During the 1981–85 period, many traders became wealthy from the black market.

Before the Fourth Congress, and especially after it, the government began to distribute unused land on state farms to private and family farmers. Officially land was given to those who were said to be able to make the best and quickest use of it: primarily, farmers who had tractors or oxen and were already hiring labour. In Chókwè, this meant the traditionally wealthier families, including a group of Mozambicans who had been able to use migrant mine wages to start the accumulation process, plus a group of 40 Portuguese farmers who remained after independence (Hermele 1988: 53). The other group to obtain land was made up of state officials who had the education and connections to push through their applications; this was the first time that some people could be seen as members of both the state and commercial groups.

Turning to the West

Whatever the internal problems, Frelimo realized that destabilization was the central problem, and that it needed international help to end the war. In practice, that meant reducing the hostility of the Reagan administration.

During the liberation struggle, Frelimo successfully retained support from both the Soviet Union and China, while also obtaining help from solidarity movements in the West. After independence, it tried to adopt a similar non-aligned foreign policy. Mozambique joined the UN and the OAU, but did not join the Lomé Convention, the IMF, or the CMEA (the Eastern bloc Council for Mutual Economic Assistance, also known as Comecon). It announced a socialist economic policy while saying that foreign investment would be encouraged. Mozambique was committed to the Indian Ocean as a "non-nuclear zone of peace" and allowed no foreign military bases.

With the increasing Rhodesian attacks in 1976 and 1977 Mozambique had appealed for military assistance from both East and West. On 30 June 1977 the UN Security Council passed a resolution calling on "all states to give immediate and substantial practical assistance to enable the government of Mozambique to strengthen its defence capability". In the event, only the socialist bloc provided military help – which made it rather unfair for the West to complain later about Mozambique being dependent on socialist military support.

Mozambique built its best relations with smaller states such as Sweden, Italy, the Netherlands, Cuba, East Germany, and Bulgaria, rather than the big powers, but it tried carefully not to close any doors. Mozambique had good relations with the USSR and acceptable ones with the US and Britain.

The election of President Reagan made it impossible for Mozambique to continue to steer this difficult course (see Chapter 4). To the US, Mozambique was a "Marxist Soviet satellite", and South African destabilization was acceptable. To the Soviet Union, Mozambique was merely a "Marxist-oriented" country which would provide no military bases and was too far away to be of much interest. So Mozambique received all of the flak but none of the benefits felt by states in the middle of the East-West conflict.

The first result of the changed mood came soon after the South African raid of 30 January 1981. Mozambican investigators found that South African security and the CIA were cooperating and had penetrated the government much more deeply than Frelimo had feared. A high official of the army, who had blocked messages that would have allowed the Mozambican army to stop the January raid, was an agent. A Frelimo Central Committee member was also found to be working for the CIA (Mutemba 1981). In March, Mozambique expelled six US citizens for CIA activities; the expulsion was on the day a USAID delegation arrived, which served to underline Frelimo anger and drive the message home to the US. Relations with the US hit rock bottom.

Mozambique turned East and applied to join Comecon. Despite backing from East Germany and some other members, the USSR vetoed the application in July 1981 (Hanlon 1981). In the next two years, President Samora Machel made two trips to the USSR. In all contacts, Soviet officials stressed that although the USSR would not decrease its support for Mozambique, it would not increase it either. Furthermore, the officials urged Frelimo to make peace with the US. Southern Africa was in the US sphere of influence, and the only way to stop destabilization was for Washington to put pressure on Pretoria. Much has been made of Soviet attitudes to southern Africa changing in the late 1980s, but for Mozambique the policy was set much earlier.

Frelimo saw Western Europe as one route to the US. Though Foreign Minister Chissano argued that membership in the European Community (EC) Lomé Convention "would provide few [economic] benefits" (*Africa Report* January–February 1983), it became clear that it would have symbolic importance. In part this was because West Germany had consistently blocked EC aid to Mozambique over its refusal to accept the so-called "Land Berlin Clause". This was an arcane dispute over a phrase suggesting that West Germany had authority over Berlin, to which East Germany objected. In 1982 Mozambique accepted the Land Berlin Clause and joined Lomé. In October the following year President Samora Machel visited Britain, France, Portugal, the Netherlands, Belgium and the EC headquarters; his trip was seen as confirming Mozambique's turn to the West.

Meanwhile, in less than a year, five Mozambican ministers visited the US, sometimes privately, to make clear to US officials that Mozambique considered South Africa, and not the US, as the enemy. Relations thawed, leading to visits to Maputo by Frank Wisner and then Chester Crocker. In mid-1983 the US named an ambassador to Maputo, filling a post which had been vacant for three years.

Aid for famine victims

The first fruit of Machel's European tour and the wooing of the US was food aid for the victims of the "man-made, South African-made famine" in Inhambane and Gaza. Two states on Machel's European tour, Britain and the Netherlands, made big grain donations. The US made a set of gestures widely interpreted as giving the OK to food aid. The State Department circulated widely a report from the embassy in Maputo stressing that there was a famine. Deputy Assistant Secretary of State Frank Wisner met President Machel in November and pledged some limited additional food aid. George Rutherford, an epidemiologist from the US Center for Disease Control, visited Inhambane in October and found "exceptionally high prevalence of acute malnutrition." He estimated that 72,000 people had already died (Rutherford 1985). Suddenly, WFP released food requested ten months earlier (Hanlon 1984b).

But it was only after a British TV programme in November showed the extent of the famine and British charities began appeals that Western governments acted. They fell over each other to fly in aid that had been refused ten months before. By December, food was reaching the famine areas. It had required both permission from the US and TV publicity before they would send food to a destabilized Marxist government.

But because of the donors' strike earlier in the year, no maize at all arrived in Mozambique in the last three months of 1983 – just when the shortage was most severe. At least 100,000 people starved to death waiting for the donors to accept Mozambique's turn to the West (See Chapter 4).

Default and Nkomati

In November 1982 Zimbabwe had sent in troops to protect the "Beira corridor" with its vital road, railway, and oil pipeline linking the port of Beira to Zimbabwe. But the Mozambican army was too weak and disorganized to respond adequately to South African destabilization, and Pretoria had been able to spread the war to nine of the eleven provinces.

By the end of 1983 the crisis was severe. Frelimo was totally unable to introduce the essential reforms agreed at its Fourth Congress. Agricultural exports plummeted and attempts to develop local production of consumer goods faltered. With sharply falling exports and increased demand for imports, the government ran out of money and was unable to import even essential goods. Frelimo turned to the West for help, and was rejected. In May 1990 President Chissano recalled that period in a talk to a group of international researchers and diplomats: "Germany said 'Recognize Land Berlin'. And we did. And what happened – no new aid. We only needed $200 million and we went to Washington and Bonn and we could not secure it. But South Africa got a credit [from the IMF] of $1 billion at the same time."

In January 1984 Mozambique announced it could not pay its debts and asked for rescheduling of loans. Its creditors replied with one voice that renegotiation could only take place if Mozambique joined the IMF and agreed an economic package with that agency, so Mozambique applied to join the IMF and World Bank.

Meanwhile, Mozambique started talks with South Africa. On 16 March 1984 Mozambique and South Africa signed the Nkomati Accord. Mozambique agreed to stop supporting the African National Congress, and it did so. South Africa agreed to stop supporting the MNR, and it did so until July, when it began sharply to increase assistance.

In just six months, Mozambique's position had changed radically and irrevocably. It made its play to the West and agreed to accept the West's conditions, joining the IMF and opening itself to Western aid agencies. And it signed a humiliating peace treaty which Pretoria tore up almost before the ink was dry.

But for destabilization ...

Some gleeful Western government officials argued that Mozambique's crisis came about because of its failed socialist policies. And yet, the economy had actually grown during 1977–81. Nor was the default so startling as it initially seemed. At the end of 1983, Mozambique's total foreign debt was $1.35 bn, of which only $285 mn in interest and capital was overdue (CNP 1984b). By international standards, this is tiny. More to the point, imposing mandatory UN sanctions on Rhodesia, and coping with South African sanctions against Mozambique, had cost the country $1.4 bn – more than the entire foreign debt. And by 1983 destabilization was having a devastating impact both on infrastructure and on transit traffic and exports.

There is no doubt that Frelimo's errors played a role in the crisis. On the other hand, Frelimo remained widely popular, particularly for its health and education policies, while the MNR was never able to gain much real support or develop alternative government structures. Despite the growth in privilege and power of the apparatchiks, Frelimo cadres retained a remarkable commitment to build a new and different society. The Fourth Congress showed that ordinary people still had confidence in the ability of President Machel to resolve their problems; their desire was to bring the leaders back into touch rather than replace them with alternatives.

By the end of 1983, the economy was in ruins and people were starving in Inhambane, not because of misguided socialist policies, but because of South African destabilization and the unwillingness of the industrialized world to put pressure on South Africa to stop.

3 One Million Dead

At first, everyone, Mozambicans and foreign donors alike, saw the problem as temporary. The signing of the Nkomati Accord on 16 March 1984 seemed to promise an end to destabilization. There were some rains (and floods) in early 1984, which promised at least a cool season (winter) crop in many areas. In September 1984 the UN Development Programme (UNDP) could report that "the nutritional status of the population is better in most areas than it was six months ago, according to reports received. This is partly due to increased aid and more efficient distribution efforts, but also to the fact that some crops have been harvested in parts of the drought provinces" (*News Bulletin* 24 September 1984). The better distribution had occurred because security was much improved in Inhambane and Gaza provinces; food relief could reach nearly all areas, at least by armed convoy.

In January 1984, the government considered that in the six southern provinces, 1.4 mn people were "severely affected" by the drought, meaning that they needed to be supplied with virtually all their food; another 3.1 mn needed at least half their food. These 4.5 mn "affected" people were more than three-quarters of the population of the southern six provinces. By contrast, the government estimated that in January 1985 only 2.5 mn were affected; the numbers had fallen in all provinces except Tete (RPM 1985).

Full backing from Pretoria

This proved to be a chimera. Under the Nkomati Accord, South Africa promised to stop backing Renamo. But documents captured from the Renamo headquarters at Gorongosa showed that at a meeting in Pretoria on 23 February 1984 with Renamo leader Afonso Dhlakama, members of South African Military Intelligence (MI) promised to continue support "so as to win the war." And they did.

In the three months before the Nkomati Accord, South Africa had sharply escalated its support for Renamo. Hundreds of specially trained guerrillas were infiltrated over the border and dropped by air and sea. Supplies sufficient to last six months were sent into Mozambique. So, for a brief period after the signing of Nkomati, South Africa was able to abide by the accord without seriously discomfiting Renamo.

But in mid-1984, as supplies began to run out, South Africa resumed support at an even higher level than before. By then, Renamo also had high-level political support; the South African Deputy Foreign Minister Louis Nel flew to the Gorongosa base three times in 1985 (Hanlon 1986: 150).

By 24 November 1984, Julius Nyerere, then President of Tanzania and Chairman of the Organization of African Unity, was able to declare: "The South Africans from the very beginning never, never meant to honour that agreement." They were still supporting Renamo. "We understand why the Mozambicans had to sign that agreement. That we understand. We don't like it, but we understand." Nkomati was a "humiliation", he said. "Completely frankly, it is a defeat on our part."

Attack the economy

At the February 1984 meeting, South African MI set out the strategy to be followed after the signing of the Nkomati Accord. According to a Renamo notetaker, MI argued that "Machel can only fall immediately through a cut in the economy and communications routes." A special target was "cooperantes [foreign workers] and other targets of an economic nature".

The "general plan no. 1 of 24 February 1984", presumably agreed at the same meeting, set three goals:
"1. Destroy the Mozambican economy in rural areas.
"2. Destroy the communications routes to prevent exports and imports to and from abroad, and the movement of domestic produce.
"3. Prevent the activities of foreigners (co-operantes) because they are the most dangerous in the recovery of the economy" (Minfo 1985).

Renamo activity increased sharply in southern Mozambique, especially near the South African border; tens of thousands of Mozambicans fled to South Africa to escape Renamo terror. The South Africans had been allowed to set up Renamo bases inside Malawi, and from mid-1985 increasing attacks were made into nearby provinces of Mozambique, particularly Tete. The railway linking Malawi to Nampula city and the port of Nacala was cut, and stayed closed almost continuously for the next four years. Renamo also pushed down the Zambeze River valley, and in July 1985 captured the important sugar town of Luabo. They destroyed the newly rehabilitated sugar mill and held the town for two years.

Victims of a Renamo attack on a bus on the main north-south road in Maluana, Maputo province, on 29 November 1987. Renamo frequently set buses alight with passengers still inside. Such attacks were intended to make people afraid to travel.
(AIM: Sérgio Santimano)

Zimbabwean troops increased their help to Mozambique from July 1985, especially keeping open the road and railway corridor linking the port of Beira to Zimbabwe, and the road between Zimbabwe and Malawi that passes through Tete. And it was Zimbabwean troops that captured the Renamo base at Gorongosa in August 1985.

1986: rapid tightening of the thumbscrew

Late 1986 and early 1987 was a period like late 1983 and early 1984 in which many different things happened very quickly. President Samora Machel was killed. Mozambique finally introduced structural adjustment and the first devaluation, paving the way to agreement with the IMF (see Chapter 7). There was a massive escalation of the war, which created hundreds of thousands of refugees and threatened to slice the country in half. Mozambique and the UN declared a full-scale emergency. The international community responded, recognizing the truth of the *Guardian* headline (25 February 1987): "Mozambique facing full-scale famine". In less than a year, the face of Mozambique and of aid to Mozambique was transformed.

In 1986 South Africa expanded Renamo bases inside Malawi and Renamo forces invaded Tete province to the southwest of Malawi. On 11 September President Samora Machel met with President Banda of Malawi and warned him that he would close the border, cutting Malawi's main route to South Africa and the sea, if Malawi did not stop backing Renamo. The response was a full-scale South African backed invasion of Zambézia province; up to 12,000 Renamo men crossed the border, some in lorries (Hedges 1989: 641). They swept down the Zambeze river and across Zambézia province. Renamo captured most of the small district headquarters towns in Zambézia, northeast Tete, and northern Manica and Sofala. It seemed they were pushing toward the coast hoping to capture one of the two cities with a major airfield: Mocuba or Quelimane. This would have cut Mozambique in half, and provided an airstrip to which South Africa could directly fly supplies. South Africa may have intended to set up an alternative Renamo government which it would then have recognized as the legitimate government of Mozambique.

Assassination?

Tension rose rapidly. On 9 October, soon after the invasions of Tete and Zambézia, South Africa announced further economic sanctions against Mozambique; 61,000 Mozambican miners would be expelled at the end of their contracts and no new miners hired. The action was later reversed, but had the threat been carried out, it would have cost Mozambique $50 mn per year, one-quarter of all its precious foreign exchange earnings. On 7 October the South African Defence Minister, Magnus Malan, made a statement attacking Machel and the pro-government press called for raids into Maputo; on 11 October the Mozambique government issued a communiqué accusing the South African armed forces of preparing to attack Maputo. On 16 October the Mozambican news agency, AIM, published an article warning "that the assassination of the Mozambican leader [Samora Machel] appears to be in the minds of the South Africa generals."

On 19 October 1986, President Samora Machel was killed when his plane crashed inside South Africa. Although the crash was never satisfactorily explained, evidence after the crash suggested that the South African military set up a false navigation beacon and that the pilot thought he was landing in Maputo when in fact he was descending into a mountain just over the border in South Africa. Foreign Minister Joaquim Chissano was named president by the Politburo, and he took over in a smooth and popular transition.

Shocked by the probable assassination of Machel and the sharp escalation of destabilization, Zimbabwe increased its military strength inside Mozambique and Tanzania sent combat troops. By mid-1988, the Mozambican, Tanzanian, and Zimbabwean troops had recaptured nearly all the district towns. Under heavy regional pressure, Malawi was forced to sign a security agreement with Mozambique in December 1986; the following year, Malawi sent some troops into Mozambique to guard the railway to Nampula. It also reduced its support for Renamo, although it did not stop that backing entirely. As Renamo men fled from Zambézia to Malawi, they were taken to South Africa and pushed back across the border into Inhambane and Gaza provinces, where the war intensified again. The invasion of the district town of Homoíne on 18 July 1987 received international press coverage (in part because a US agronomist working for a US church NGO was in the town at the time). Renamo guerrillas massacred 424 people; they even rampaged through the hospital, killing staff and patients, including mothers with new-born babies.

1988–89 stalemate

The security pattern throughout 1988–89 was a complex stalemate. Life was relatively normal in Maputo and the major cities. The Beira corridor was open and had become a focus of development efforts; the railway was carrying increasing amounts of cargo. Nearly all significant towns were controlled by the government. The population around towns grew rapidly, as peasants fled the war; they were often afraid to go more than a few kilometers out of town to farm, for fear of Renamo attack. But there was insufficient land, so many of these people were partly dependent on food aid. Most fled Renamo, but some were also pushed into towns by the Mozambican military, anxious to have freefire zones.

The Mozambican military was increasingly war weary. Companies of crack troops trained by Britain and the USSR were highly effective in pursuing Renamo. But conscript troops were tired, hungry, and poorly trained; they were not anxious to fight. Complaints of corruption in the army increased and became public in the debates leading up to the Fifth Congress in early 1989. Supplies were being diverted and sold, generals were setting up farms, and so on; there were also suggestions that some military commanders were not anxious to end the war because their opportunities for corruption depended on it.

On visits to Mozambique in 1987 and 1988 various people described to me the precise locations of Renamo bases in several provinces. The base that was used for repeated brutal attacks on the main road north of Maputo was well known to everyone in the area. I went to a meeting where a provincial governor unrolled a map and pointed out the location of the main Renamo base in his province, which had been there for more than a year; he clearly showed his frustration that the army was unwilling or unable to do anything about it.

Karl Maier in *The Independent* (15 January 1990) described the position as "two ill-fed and ill-equipped armies stagger around the countryside like punchdrunk boxers." More than 10,000 Renamo men roamed the rural areas, and could attack villages and road traffic. But Renamo could no longer hold towns as it did in 1986–87. Massacres continued, with regular instances of more than 50 people killed. Many main roads were open to normal traffic; some were open to traffic only in military convoys. Many roads in remote areas were closed. The South African-organized invasion of 1986 had failed, but the Mozambican army was too weak and demoralized to defeat a Renamo with continued substantial South African – and US – support.

Renamo losses in 1990

But the pattern shifted in 1990, when two factors changed. First, President Chissano's long-running efforts to shake up the army began to have some effect. Probably more important, however, was that South Africa's new president F W de Klerk, following his meeting with President Chissano in Maputo in July 1989, did restrict South African military support of Renamo. Air drops of supplies were sharply reduced, although not totally ended (*Southscan* 17 August 1990). But ground movements of men and supplies across the South African border into southern Mozambique increased. Sea drops and some infiltration from Malawi continued. And Kenya began to play an important role, providing supplies and training for Renamo. Some supply flights into Mozambique in 1990 came from Kenya via Malawi (MIO 7 September 1990).

This led to a major shift in the war. In the interior of Nampula, Zambézia, and Tete provinces Renamo fell back under Mozambican military pressure. Guerrilla activity continued, but at a much lower level. Roads were reopened; the Nacala-Nampula-Malawi railway resumed operation. Farmers moved back to the most fertile areas of Tete that had been unsafe since 1986.

In contrast, significant Renamo activity continued in coastal areas of Zambézia and in Manica and Sofala provinces. In the south, in Maputo and Gaza provinces which were easily accessible to South Africa overland, Renamo action increased sharply. The roads, railways, and electricity line leading to Maputo were attacked frequently, as South African and Renamo forces tried unsuccessfully to isolate the capital.

Mozambique: *Conditions of Accessibility, February 1990*

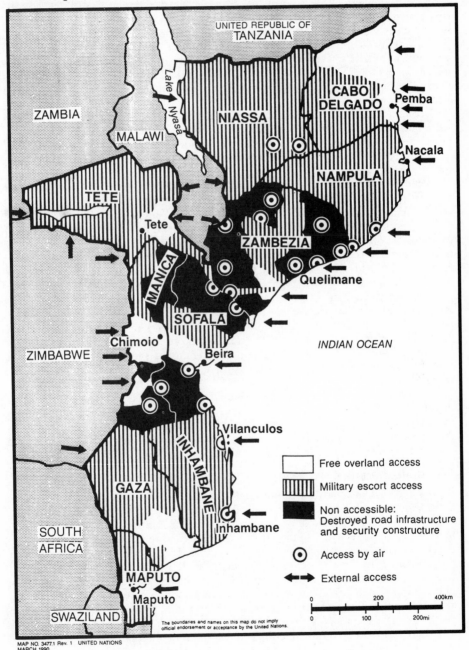

MAP NO. 3477.1 Rev. 1   UNITED NATIONS
MARCH 1990

Renamo support?

It has been argued that Renamo could not have been so effective without having some degree of local support. Indeed, it really needs an entirely separate book to show how it has been possible for South African and other supporters to create a kind of Frankenstein's monster which has no policy or ideology, and precious little local support, and yet can create widespread havoc.

It is impossible to tackle this issue here, but three points should be made. First is the centrality of South African support. More important than Mozambican army weakness was South Africa's continued air and sea drops of supplies, training of guerrillas, and general command and control. This was testified to by many people, ranging from US government officials to Renamo defectors. And it was strikingly confirmed by Frelimo's military gains in 1990 in Tete, Zambézia, and Nampula. These were in precisely the areas where Renamo could only be supplied by air, and it was notable how quickly it collapsed when air support was cut back.

Second, Renamo did have some active support by a few traditional leaders, some of whom may have become warlords. But as Renamo atrocities continued and its military power weakened, there was a steady stream changing sides back to Frelimo.

Third, Renamo has never been able to command any wide popular support. Even where peasants were antagonized by Frelimo's economic policies, they tended to just try to keep their heads down, and only rarely supported Renamo. Alex Vines quotes an old man who said that Renamo "are the locust people. They eat everything – food, clothes, and us – until we have no more. Then they go and eat elsewhere" (Vines 1991).

The World Bank commented that "despite good yields last year in bandit [Renamo] overrun areas of Zambézia, spot nutrition surveys conducted in areas resecured by government forces indicated that level of acute malnutrition (measured by weight for height) approached 50% – largely the result of household food supplies being stolen or destroyed by bandits" (WB 1989g: 38).

The Times of London (23 February 1987), a conservative newspaper not noted for its sympathy with Marxist governments, reported that "Tens of thousands of Mozambican peasants are being held in slave labour camps which anti-government rebels have created as supply bases for an escalating guerrilla campaign" in Zambézia. "Terrified refugees have been running before the fighting in increasing numbers for six months now. But it is only recently that among them have appeared groups who have escaped from the rebels' slave camps."

The Times writer Paul Vallely concluded: "Until now some observers have assumed that the MNR must enjoy a degree of local support in these areas. But the news from the escaping refugees gives credence to the claims of the Mozambique government that the rebels are not supported by local people, and are sustained only by South Africa and other parties intent on destabilising the frontline opponents of apartheid."

Half of the people need food

By the end of 1985, only an estimated 1.8 mn people were considered affected or displaced, and needed some sort of food aid. But the escalating war totally disrupted the economy and caused hundreds of thousands to flee Renamo atrocities and slave labour. In 1986, there was drought in the south again, as well as in Zambézia and Tete where Renamo was making its major push, which increased the suffering. On 22 September the government's Departamento de Prevenção e Combate às Calamidades Naturais (DPCCN, Department for the Prevention and Combat of Natural Disasters, commonly called simply "Calamidades") made a major appeal for food aid, warning that there could again be famine. The number of people at risk had jumped to 3.9 mn, largely due to people fleeing Renamo raids from Malawi.

By late 1986, the government estimated that there were more than 250,000 refugees

Refugee family living under a railway wagon in the goods yard at Moatize, Tete province.

(AIM: Anders Nilsson)

in neighbouring countries and another 1 million inside their own country. (In international agency jargon, "refugees" are only those who cross borders, while those who flee inside their own countries are "displaced".) Another 2.5 million people were "affected", meaning that their ability to produce food was restricted by the war. Typically, "affected" people had lost their possessions in a Renamo raid but had not actually left their land, or could not go out to their more remote fields for fear of Renamo attack. The war had also hit rural production of food for sale in urban areas, which meant many city people were short of food too. All told, 5.7 million people needed food aid – 47% of the population (UNSG 1987).

The plight of 8000 living in a railway yard in Moatize in Tete caught public attention. "Women are sitting underneath railway wagons cooking saucepans of maize porridge for the family lunch. In the shade of disused cement silos dozens of children, using old tyres as benches, are attending improvised schools. Tents are strewn about the yard in apparently haphazard fashion. On bushes wet clothes and blankets are spread out to dry," wrote Paul Fauvet (*Guardian* 2 April 1987). The refugees had fled to Malawi after the invasion of Tete and Zambézia in 1986, and then drifted to Tete when they found Malawi could not feed them. They took refuge in the railway yard, which had been cut off from the rest of the railway network when Renamo blew up bridges the year before. The first to arrive began living in abandoned railway wagons; the rest lived in tents or slept in sheds or in the open. But the yard was safe – it was protected by Frelimo soldiers and was near the road to Tete city.

In May 1987 an NGO worker in Zambézia wrote a confidential report to his head office. "A big Frelimo offensive backed by Tanzanian and Zimbabwean troops has cleared the Zambeze valley of Renamo forces. The offensive has uncovered large numbers of people, mainly women and children, living in pitiful destitution under rebel control, or hiding for months in bush and mangrove, living on wild leaves, roots, and sometimes coconuts and fish, since fleeing from Renamo attacks in 1986. Mass arrivals of these people at established relief centres has put enormous strain on DPCCN and Red Cross facilities. These people are characterized by complete destitution, exhaustion, trauma, and very poor nutrition; most are naked or dressed only in bits of sack and rags."

By early 1988, the UN estimated that there were 700,000 refugees outside the country (which was surely an underestimate because it excluded refugees in South Africa). The UN said 6 million people inside Mozambique needed some food aid. "The war of destruction and destabilization waged by Renamo bandits, together with other effects of South African destabilization, at present dominate all aspects of life – social, economic, and political – in Mozambique" (UNSG 1988). By early 1989 the number of Mozambicans needing food aid had risen to 7.7 million – 50% of the population (*Mozambiquefile* May 1989).

By the end of 1989, the number of refugees outside the country exceeded a million. There were 600,000 to 800,000 in Malawi – a country whose own population is only 8.5 million and which is also desperately poor. Another 100,000 were in camps in Zimbabwe, between 100,000 and 250,000 in South Africa, and 30,000 in Zambia and Swaziland. At least 100,000 refugees had returned to Mozambique in 1988, and a similar number in 1989. In all, more than 60% of Mozambique's population needed help. By 1990, more than 500,000 "affected" people had become self-sufficient because of the success of efforts to provide seeds and tools, but destabilization was creating more refugees (MIO 15 February 1990).

Table 3.1 *People needing help (million)*

Category	1986	1988	1989	1990
Refugees outside Mozambique	.3	.7	1.0	1.0
Displaced within Mozambique	1.0	1.1	1.7	2.0
Affected (production capacity reduced)	2.5	2.2	2.9	2.4
Urban people needing food	2.5	2.6	3.1	3.7
TOTAL	6.3	6.6	8.7	9.1
% of population	47%	47%	60%	62%

Source: Author's summary of various UN and government figures.
The total population of Mozambique (including refugees) in 1990 is probably about 14.7 million, based on a population projection from the 1980 census of 15.7 million, less 1 million dead due to war.

Not 'mindless' violence

A massive increase in aid kept many Mozambicans from starving, but it did not prevent the total collapse of the economy, nor did it help Mozambique pay its debts. Aid flows were tiny compared to the huge cost of destabilization.

One goal of destabilization was the destruction of infrastructure, and the degree of destruction is hard to imagine. I visited the district town of Mopeia in 1988 and walked down the main street. The flame trees were in bloom and neat one-storey houses and shops lined the street. The tailor was sitting on the veranda of the shop, sheltered from the mid-day sun along with his customers and other villagers. Hard at work with his treadle sewing machine, this tailor seemed like thousands of others on shop verandas in towns across Africa.

But this shop was an empty shell and sunlight shone through the missing roof. All that was left was the concrete veranda and its roof which sheltered the tailor. Every door, window, and shelf had been smashed; every roofing sheet had been taken. Every building in town was the same. Renamo rebels had carefully removed nearly every roofing sheet and every door and taken them away. They had meticulously smashed every window in town, and every door or roofing sheet they could not remove. Every piece of mosquito

(*Above*): *Like many other tailors, this one works on the porch of a shop. But this shop in Mopeia was stripped and gutted.* (J. Hanlon)

(*Below*) *Mopeia Frelimo office in December 1988. Renamo stripped the windows, doors, and roofing sheets from every building in the town.* (J. Hanlon)

netting had been slashed. The school, hospital, shops, water tank, electricity generating station, houses, bridges, and vehicles were all destroyed.

I assumed that Renamo had done this in retreat, but I was assured that this demolition job had been done as soon as the rebels arrived. Indeed, having captured and destroyed the town, they set up camp outside it.

Mopeia was a small example of the systematic destruction. Nearly all of the sawmills, tea processing factories, sugar mills, and so on in the entire country were wrecked. Road and railways have been repeatedly attacked; for example, 44% of the entire railway locomotive fleet has been destroyed (*BCG Bulletin* October 1989). This destruction, in turn, has caused major losses in production both for domestic consumption and for export. Mozambique has also lost income due to the neighbouring states being less able to ship goods on Mozambican railways, while it has had to pay the cost of a vastly increased defence budget. Studies for the UN Economic Commission for Africa and for Unicef conclude that for the period 1980-88, destabilization has cost Mozambique an incredible $15 bn (ECA 1989c, Unicef 1989). By contrast, total aid to Mozambique in that period was only $3.6 bn (see Table A.3c).

As we noted in Chapter 2, a key purpose of South African destabilization was to make the population suffer, in the hope that they would "direct their frustrations and fury" against the Frelimo government. By disrupting rural commerce, Renamo was able to exacerbate peasant discontent about shortages of consumer goods, and make it impossible for Frelimo to implement the new peasant bias established by the Fourth Congress in 1983. The so-called anti-communist Renamo guerrillas might have been expected to try to gain the support of local traders, who are the main local capitalists. Instead, shopkeepers became a priority target; repeated and brutal attacks on road traffic made traders rightly fearful to go to rural areas. By mid-1989, about 3000 rural shops had been burnt, destroyed, or forced to close. Private transporters had lost 1500 trucks in Renamo attacks (Frelimo 1989a). In Zambézia alone, 436 shops were destroyed and 36 damaged by

Moamba hospital after 1988 Renamo attack. (AIM: *Sérgio Santimano*)

September 1988; half the shops outside the provincial capital Quelimane were closed, including all the shops in five districts (PZCPE 1988). In some cases, Renamo would loot the shops and distribute some of the goods to local people. But after that, there was nothing. Renamo was blamed for burning the shops. But Frelimo was given much greater blame for failing to reestablish rural marketing structures. (And we see the irony of alleged anti-communist rebels destroying capitalism in the rural areas, while the Marxist government struggled to restore private trade.)

The other target of destabilization has been social infrastructure: schools and health posts and their staff. During 1981–88, 291 health units were destroyed and another 687 looted and at least temporarily closed. Although many health posts were reopened and new units were being built regularly, more than one-third of health units were closed by the end of 1988. In addition, 35 ambulances have been destroyed (Noormahomed 1990). By the end of 1989, 3096 primary schools had been forced to close; this is more than half of the primary schools in Mozambique (MIO 12 July 1990). More than 200 teachers and health workers have been killed. Many have been kidnapped or injured. Indeed, health workers and teachers seemed a particular target for Renamo atrocities, such as cutting off ears, noses, or breasts. Finally, Renamo deliberately attacked patients and students. The way in which Renamo hit the hospital in Homoíne may have been extreme, but it was far from unique; maternity hospitals were particular targets, and in many areas women became afraid to have their babies in hospital. In numerous cases, Renamo would kidnap the entire student body from rural schools, raping the girls and forcing the boys to become Renamo fighters.

The strategy seemed to be to force a collapse of the rural health and education services: by destroying the facilities, by making people afraid to use health posts and schools, and by making teachers and health workers afraid to go to rural areas. The reason for this is clear. When I visited rural areas in the early 1980s, when peasants were already bitterly complaining about Frelimo economic policies, they still saw the vastly expanded health and education services as a victory of the revolution. Whatever else Frelimo had done wrong, their children were not dying so often because of the new health posts, and were going to school and learning to read. Destroying the health and education systems, then, destroyed the last fruits of independence – and with them went much of Frelimo's remaining prestige.

Indeed, why should anyone support a government which cannot protect its people, cannot feed its people, cannot bring them a degree of prosperity, and cannot provide health and education services? Renamo terrorism is often dismissed as "mindless violence" but this is mistaken; it is horrific violence aimed at destroying the last vestiges of Frelimo support.

And in the 1990 debate about the new constitution, Frelimo was increasingly blamed for its failure to end the war. Undoubtedly, destabilization has succeeded in Mozambique.

One million dead

The human cost has been extraordinary. Until 1982 infant and child mortality in Mozambique had been falling rapidly, because of the expanded health system and because of an effective vaccination programme. Births in hospital and monitoring of young children were rising. But destabilization changed that. Health workers such as vaccination teams could no longer go to rural areas, while women were afraid to travel to health posts or have their children in hospital. The number of outpatient consultations reached a high of 0.62 per person per year in 1982 (still very low by world standards). In just five years, this had fallen to 0.35. But this figure conceals the fact that in areas where health services operated reasonably normally, consultations continued to rise, so the fall is totally in areas under Renamo attack. The problem was further compounded by the shortage of medicines caused by the economic crisis. Not surprisingly, infant and child mortality rates soared. Unicef estimates that from 1985 the *excess* under 5 mortality was 140 per thousand. That is, for every 1000 babies born, 140 would die before reaching the age of 5 who would not have died without destabilization. Unicef concluded that during 1980–88, there were 494,000 destabilization-related deaths of children under 5 (Unicef 1989: 40).

In addition, there were many other deaths. Based on figures in a US State Department study (Gersony 1988) and Mozambique government estimates, it seems likely that at least 200,000 people were actually killed by Renamo. Another 200,000 over the age of 5 died of hunger and disease, particularly in the war-induced famines in Gaza, Inhambane, and Tete in 1984 and in Zambézia in 1987. Thus the UN Economic Commission for Africa estimates that in the period 1980–88 at least 900,000 people died in Mozambique because of destabilization (ECA 1989c).

Destabilization remained intense during 1989. If we assume that the human and material costs were the same in 1989 as in 1988, then during the period 1980-89, more than 1 million people died because of destabilization, and the material cost was at least $18 billion (£11 bn).

Even this awful toll does not take into account what many Mozambicans are now calling the "lost generation" – those who have been children during the 1980s. Hundreds of thousands of children have been malnourished during their critical early years and will be permanently stunted, both physically and mentally. Frelimo estimates "200,000 children either do not know the whereabouts of their parents or have suffered the terrible trauma of watching their execution or their death" (Frelimo 1989a). Some have been forced by Renamo to commit atrocities themselves. Others have become homeless street children. Countless others have had little or no education. This is the generation which should have led Mozambique to victory over underdevelopment. Instead, it will be a crippled generation that will have to be supported for life by its parents and children, extending the impact of destabilization well into the next century.

4 The Helping Hand of Uncle Sam

US Senator John Danforth toured famine zones in Africa in January 1984. Shocked at what he saw, he asked for an urgent meeting with his friend Ronald Reagan. He showed the President the photographs that he had taken himself of starving babies in Mozambique's Gaza province. Reagan, too, was shocked and he told the US Agency for International Development (USAID) to do something.

USAID and parts of the State Department were already anxious to support Mozambique for its turn to the West, for opening talks with South Africa, and for helping to push Angola into talks. They had already begun food aid, and encouraged other countries and the UN. But the Danforth-Reagan chat put the political stamp of approval on the aid, and triggered a huge increase in food aid.

Senator Danforth saw starving babies because, in the previous three months, no maize had been delivered to Mozambique. And that was because the US and UN had refused to supply food aid which Mozambique had requested a year before. It is often said that Third World governments are afraid to warn of imminent famine, so the donors do not have enough advance notice of the need for food aid. In January 1983, Trade Minister Aranda da Silva said food would be needed before the end of the year. In June 1983 he said traditional pledges had fallen. And he warned foreign diplomats: "There is hunger now. If we don't get more support there will be hundreds of deaths." And 100,000 people died.

Several years later, a US State Department official in Washington explained to me: "we made it clear to the government of Mozambique that our food aid is political. There are always conditions on aid, although they are often not explicit....To get better relations with us, Mozambique had to demonstrate a willingness to change its economic policies." This was necessary anyway, he said, because "Africans are capitalists; Africans don't like socialism."

Political changes were required too. Mozambique "had to show an independence from the USSR and inject some civility into the relationship with the US". This, he explained, meant that Mozambique should not vote so often against the US in the UN General Assembly, and should not "pillory the US in public for real and imagined sins."

The importance to the US of being respected and not losing face should never be underestimated. US officials are quite obsessed with image abroad, and the US makes clear that freedom of the press does not extend to foreign countries. In early 1983 a US embassy official in Maputo told me that when US Deputy Assistant Secretary of State Frank Wisner met President Samora Machel in December 1982, high on his list of demands was that the Mozambican press curb its criticism of the US. And, crowed the embassy official, this was quickly done.

It is hard to underestimate the power of the US and the central importance of US policy and actions in Mozambique in the 1980s. Mozambique needed the agreement of the US to end destabilization, as well as to obtain international assistance. Throughout this book, US policy, actions, and agencies receive special attention because of their pivotal role.

Three factors characterize the US role, at least as it concerns southern Africa: 1) a sharp rightward shift, 2) splits within government, and 3) privatization of foreign policy.

The new conservative agenda

In the late 1970s, the Carter human rights policy served as a constraint on South African destabilization, while the US was playing a less interventionist role in the world because of its Vietnam defeat. Meanwhile, the socialist bloc provided important initial support to Mozambique.

In the early 1980s, this totally changed. The USSR lost interest in Mozambique, while the new Reagan administration in the US was taking a harder anti-communist line and becoming more internationally interventionist. There was the invasion of Grenada, open and official support for the Contras in Nicaragua and Unita in Angola, and tacit support for South African destabilization. Furthermore, the US was increasingly successful in imposing its policies on the UN, the IMF, the World Bank, and its NATO allies. As we have already seen, in 1983 the UN and several key donors were unwilling to help Mozambique without at least a nod from Washington.

The new conservative agenda was most clearly articulated by the right-wing Washington think tank and lobbying group, the Heritage Foundation. It published thick books entitled *Mandate for Leadership* for both incoming Reagan administrations and the new Bush administration (Heatherly 1981, Butler 1984, Heatherly 1989 – referred to here and by Heritage as *Mandate I, II*, and *III*).

As Heritage itself commented, *Mandate I* "was designed to be a detailed road map to help the fledgling Reagan administration steer the nation into a sound future, guided by conservative principles. In looking back on those early months, Ronald Reagan was to say that *Mandate* gave him and his administration 'special substantive help we'll never forget. ...We've been using *Mandate* to our and the country's advantage.' By the end of the President's first year in office, nearly two-thirds of *Mandate*'s 2000 specific recommendations had been or were being transformed into policy" (Butler 1984: ix).

It is dangerous and unnecessary to fall back on conspiracy theories or to argue that Heritage itself was so powerful that it could tell presidents what to do. Heritage's own description of *Mandate I* as a "road map" is probably correct – it set out in a clear and detailed fashion an existing right-wing agenda which was being formulated by many people, some of whom came to serve in the Reagan administration. As such, its views on Mozambique are descriptions of a central school of thought.

Looking back on the Reagan years, *Mandate III* argued that "Reagan has directed and presided over America's reassertion of its active world role. Previously, the US had been drawing inward and seemed unwilling or unable to exert influence." In part, "the administration has assisted viable Western-oriented movements seeking to topple Soviet-backed Marxist-Leninist regimes." But more important was "reestablishing a willingness to use force", for example in 1983 in Grenada and 1986 in Libya. "The result: US adversaries now hesitate to take actions undermining even peripheral US interests" (Heatherly 1989: 464-7). This is undoubtedly true in Mozambique.

Futhermore, the US had shifted its policy toward developing nations. In particular, "the administration has pressured both developing nations and multilateral financial organizations to encourage an environment conducive to private-sector-driven economic growth" (Heatherly 1989: 467).

Heritage policy for Mozambique

With respect to Mozambique, the Heritage rhetoric has often been extreme. For example in a 31 March 1987 briefing it claimed that Renamo forces "now control 80% of the countryside". *Mandate III* claims that "the Frelimo regime is composed of long-time, hardline Marxist-Leninists; weaning them away from Moscow is surely impossible." It talks of the need to "roll back the Soviet Empire" and says that Mozambique is a "Soviet colony" where "Moscow ...has access to airfields and naval facilities" (Heatherly 1989: 598, 608, 612).

Although totally false, such nonsense should not obscure the fact that concrete Heritage recommendations have generally been followed. And Heritage has targeted Mozambique. Each section of *Mandates* II and III is followed by a list of "Initiatives" for the following year. In both, Initiative 1 for Africa relates to Mozambique.

Presidents Joaquim Chissano and George Bush shake hands outside the White House in Washington, 13 March 1990.
(AIM: António Machave)

Mandate I hardly mentioned Mozambique directly. "Africa is an important part of the Western commonwealth, providing critical raw materials and markets." Therefore the Reagan administration should launch a major programme to make Africa "congenial once again for private investment". Certain specific interventions "must be ironed out on a classified basis" (Heatherly 1981: 583).

It also argued that southern Africa represented "the most productive and economically important part of Africa from the point of view of the West." But its primary concern was with the "White tribe of South Africa" and with its "fear of having South Africa disintegrate into chaos and anarchy – where much of Central Africa headed after the advent of one man, one vote." Thus "South Africa needs both time and a sense of security" (Heatherly 1981: 584).

Mandate II, however, highlighted Mozambique. A key policy goal was to "end Marxist influence in Africa". The top priority for Africa for 1985, even above Angola and Namibia, was to "encourage Mozambique to abandon Marxism." And the report declared that "If, by early 1985, [President Samora] Machel is not decisively moving away from Marxism, then a clear alternative exists through support for the MNR by the United States" (Butler 1984: 357). Although Machel did move toward the West, it was not enough, and the US did escalate its support for the MNR/Renamo.

In *Mandate III*, Mozambique again had a surprisingly important position. "In Mozambique, the new administration should set as its goal direct negotiations between the Frelimo communist regime and the Renamo insurgents to end their 12-year conflict and establish an independent, noncommunist Mozambican government." If Frelimo refused, then the US should openly support Renamo (Heatherly 1989: 616). By 1990 direct talks were under way, and a new noncommunist constitution had been written.

Mozambique was again the target of the top priority action for Africa for 1989 (this time, along with Ethiopia). This was to "set new conditions for US emergency famine assistance", in particular that "food distribution must be allowed to be handled entirely by international organizations and kept separate from the distribution network of the recipient government". As we will see in later chapters, the US did step up pressure on Mozambique for such a change.

Several other goals were set for Africa in general, including "upgrade. the quality of US intelligence on Africa" and "linking US aid to free market reforms in Africa" (Heatherly 1989: 604–7).

Policy divisions and privatization

The new, intensely ideological, and interventionist foreign policy of Heritage and the Reagan administration caused sharp splits within the US government – between Congress and the Executive (the presidency), within the State Department, and between intelligence agencies. This led to oscillations and contradictions in policy, as was shown when Congress imposed relatively strong sanctions on South Africa and at the same time agreed to provide support to Unita, or in a different way by Congress's frequently changing stand on Nicaragua.

In *Mandate III* Heritage admitted that "we underestimated the stamina of liberalism … Liberalism's key bastion is, of course, Congress, but by no means its only one. Indeed, virtually the entire federal government can be viewed as a self-perpetuating preserve of obsolete liberal nostrums."

"Often the State Department, or powerful factions within it, deliberately obstruct executive branch policies. A typical example has been the consistent opposition by State Department careerists to the 'Reagan Doctrine' of support for anticommunist freedom fighters." A key problem is State Department officials' "identification with and sympathy for the policies and culture of the foreign countries in which they have lived and worked" which tends to discourage them from working to further US interests. In some cases, State Department officials "worked hard behind the scenes" with congressional opponents of President Reagan's policies (Heatherly 1989: xiii, 489).

This has undoubtedly been true in the case of Mozambique. But the opposite was also true: Heritage and right-wing elements in the State Department worked with far right Congressmen to undercut Reagan's Assistant Secretary of State for African Affairs, Chester Crocker, and his policy of supporting the Mozambican government.

After its success in obtaining official (as distinct from covert) support for Unita, Heritage launched a campaign to have the MNR/Renamo treated in the same way. It was this which suddenly lifted Mozambique from obscurity in *Mandate I* to the forefront in *Mandate II*. In a June 1986 report, Heritage claimed that "Renamo is establishing a provisional government in the large area of Mozambique in which the resistance movement operates freely." It also alleged that "of all the insurgencies against pro-Soviet regimes anywhere in the world, Renamo's is closest to victory" (Hackett 1986).

In testimony to the Senate Africa Subcommittee on 24 June 1987, Crocker complained that "it is especially ironic that Mozambique got little attention in Washington when it appeared to be firmly committed to socialism, close relations with Moscow, and antagonism toward the United States. Only when Mozambique manifestly changed its course and began to reach out to us and to our Western allies did Mozambique and US policy toward that country become an issue in our own foreign policy debate" (Crocker 1987).

The issue came to a head in October 1986 when President Reagan appointed Melissa Wells as the new US ambassador to Mozambique. She was strongly against Renamo, which she accused of "widespread atrocities". Right-wing senators, led by Jesse Helms, blocked approval of her nomination and pushed for recognition, support, and even food aid for Renamo. The debate became so bitter that the government was paralysed on Mozambique, and proved unwilling even to condemn Renamo's massacre of 424 people in Homoíne on 18 July 1987.

Stephen Morrison, a staff member on the House Africa Subcommittee, noted in mid-1987 that "the State Department reportedly finds itself pitted, seemingly irreconcilably, against Renamo's advocates in Congress and the Defense Department (most notably Under-Secretary Fred Ikle and the Defense Intelligence Agency). Wavering somewhere in the middle are said to be officials of the NSC [National Security Council], CIA, and the White House" (Morrison 1987).

But the kidnapping of a US nurse, the Homoíne massacre, and other Renamo atrocities seemed to tip the balance. After an unprecedented ten-month delay, the Senate finally approved Wells's nomination in September 1987. And on 5 October, President Chissano went to Washington and met President Bush.

Attempts to force recognition of Renamo were finally defeated when the State Department commissioned a study by a former US official, Robert Gersony, who interviewed refugees and catalogued Renamo atrocities. "The level of violence reported to be conducted by Renamo against the civilian population is extraordinarily high," he said. "It is conservatively estimated that 100,000 civilians may have been murdered by Renamo" (Gersony 1988). Speaking at a conference in Maputo on 26 April 1988, Roy Stacey, the US Deputy Assistant Secretary of State for African Affairs, accused Renamo of carrying out "one of the most brutal holocausts against ordinary human beings since World War II." Renamo, he said, had been "waging a systematic and brutal war of terror against innocent Mozambican civilians through forced labour, starvation, physical abuse and wanton killing" (*Observer* 1 May 1988).

By telling the truth about Renamo terrorism, the US State Department did indeed sabotage the Heritage campaign to give Renamo credibility as "anticommunist freedom fighters". So Heritage anger in *Mandate III* is hardly surprising.

Not all of the State Department agreed, however. One section wanted to provide food aid to Renamo, for example. Similar splits occurred elsewhere. During a period when there was heavy (and blatantly false) Renamo propaganda about a possible attack on Maputo, the Central Intelligence Agency (CIA) was dismissing the report as nonsense while the Defence Intelligence Agency (DIA) – US Military Intelligence – was suggesting Maputo was about to fall.

Privatization of foreign policy

Such sharp disagreements caused either confusion or paralysis. One result was an increasing privatization not just of aid work though NGOs, but of the actual design and implementation of foreign policy. The Iran-Contra affair is the most public example of this, where private individuals working for profit carried out foreign activities at the behest of individuals in the intelligence services and in the executive branch of government. The breakdown in central authority over foreign policy caused by the deep ideological divisions meant that it was impossible to stop such semi-private initiatives.

Heritage was deeply involved in this newly acceptable privatized foreign policy. It promoted right-wing rebel movements throughout the world, and provided office space for Renamo in Washington. Other right-wing foundations, church groups, and private individuals – working at least with the guidance and tacit acceptance of parts of the intelligence community – provided direct support, although their exact role in the support of Renamo remains murky.

Africa Confidential (2 December 1988, 7 July 1989) argued that as part of the "world-wide semi-private network put in place by the late CIA director William Casey", he "encouraged his friends to build a network of support for Renamo." At the same time, the DIA set up its own independent network to support Renamo. The CIA built links with the South African Foreign Ministry, while the DIA built links with South African Military Intelligence (MI). MI were the main backers of Renamo in the mid 1980s, and also worked through private business people. (*Weekly Mail* 16 March 1990). The DIA wanted to step up support for Renamo and obtain recognition for it. The CIA wanted to wrest control of Renamo from South African MI and force Renamo to negotiate with Frelimo once enough concessions had been extracted. The CIA shifted increasingly toward this State Department line, especially after the Gersony report and the death of Casey.

Top State Department officials made good use of others' continued support for Renamo throughout the late 1980s. Publicly, and even in private conversation, they condemned Renamo as terrorists. But they delayed putting any pressure on Renamo and its backers until Mozambique had agreed to direct talks with Renamo and to a new constitution which abandoned all references to Marxism. Thus, while Heritage failed to obtain public support for Renamo, it did obtain private support and the State Department used that support to implement goals which had been articulated by Heritage.

"Good for US interests"

US policy has been "good for the people of Mozambique, good for the region, and good for US interests," declared Chester Crocker. "The policy of the Reagan Administration has helped to bolster the conscious decision by the Government of Mozambique to reduce its dependence on Moscow." Evidence of this shift is that "Mozambique no longer votes with the USSR in the United Nations on such international questions of overriding importance to Moscow as Afghanistan and Cambodia." Furthermore, "today the number of Western advisors in Mozambique actually exceeds that of advisors from the Soviet Union and its allies." And "public criticism [of the US] was replaced by more balanced language" (Crocker 1987). With the US basing foreign policy on scorecards of UN votes and hostile press coverage, it is hardly surprising that Mozambique took a more cautious position.

The State Department argued that by backing the government in Mozambique, the US had also "helped to reduce Soviet influence in southern Africa." To back off and support Renamo would give "the Soviets a golden opportunity to get back in the game" (USSD 1987).

Crocker had successfully enlisted the support of first Samora Machel, and then Joaquim Chissano, in pushing Angola toward talks. He saw this as more valuable than did Heritage and the right. "Mozambique has played an important supportive role in US efforts to achieve a negotiated withdrawal of Cuban forces from Angola," commented the State Department. "Mozambique has been a voice for moderation in the councils of the front-line states" (USSD 1987). Crocker went further and declared that "no country in southern Africa has worked more consistently than Mozambique with the United States to further the cause of peace and stability in southern Africa" (Crocker 1987).

High marks for the end of Marx

Relations with the US improved slowly. Mozambique, in becoming the largest recipient of US assistance in sub-Saharan Africa, made a number of political concessions; notably it dropped the word "People's" and became simply the "Republic of Mozambique". Frelimo at its Fifth Congress abandoned its claim to be a Marxist-Leninist party.

Politburo member Jorge Rebelo explained to a meeting of party members before the Congress that "there is the problem of the United States. At a meeting between US Congressmen and President Chissano, the key point was: 'Are you a Marxist? If so, you are our enemy.' The argument used by the reactionary forces is that Frelimo is Marxist-Leninist and so must be destroyed. And the socialist countries say we are not Marxist-

Leninist either. So we are being attacked for something which we are not. Therefore, the new party statutes will not mention Marxism-Leninism, firstly in order to be coherent with ourselves, and secondly so as not to give ammunition to the enemy."

As a result, on 24 January 1990 President George Bush took Mozambique off the official black list of Marxist-Leninist countries. This permits additional aid to Mozambique, as well as US export credits.

Private Support

As this discussion makes clear, the bitter debate was about tactics and not goals. No one in the US government supported Frelimo's socialist goals; all wanted to convert Mozambique into a dependent Western-oriented state. The fight was about how to do this.

USAID budget and policy statements during the 1984–87 period made the US interest clear. "US objectives" in southern Africa included "continued Western access to the minerals and raw materials in the region" and to "support the development of the private sector". Furthermore, the region "offers a largely untapped market for US goods and services" (USAID: Southern Africa Overview FY 1985, Southern Africa Regional FY 1986 & FY 1988).

In Mozambique, assistance was granted "in response to the GPRM [Mozambique government] policy changes giving priority to the private sector." USAID had three "short-term objectives": "humanitarian assistance", "to promote the development of the private sector", and "to promote privatisation". And USAID is pressing the government to implement policy measures liberalizing agricultural prices, increasing private sector participation in production and marketing of agricultural inputs, and privatizing state and intervened companies (USAID Mozambique Action Plan FY 1989).

Mandatory Care

In 1984 the US approved three aid programmes for Mozambique. They were a $40 million programme to supply inputs and equipment to larger private farmers in southern Mozambique, increased food aid, and programmes with two NGOs – Care and World Vision. In practice, Mozambique had little choice but to accept what was offered, because it could not be seen to be quibbling with the US. But Mozambican officials were unhappy with both NGOs, and it is worth exploring their entry into Mozambique in more detail.

Care was originally formed in 1945 to distribute surplus army rations – the famous "Care packages" – to people in war-ravaged Europe. It is now the world's largest private, non-sectarian dispenser of foreign aid. Most of Care-USA's revenue is in the form of agricultural commodities and ocean freight donated by the US government, so it maintains close links with USAID. As part of the package, USAID insisted that Care be involved in food distribution in Mozambique.

The first Care team arrived in December 1983, but an agreement was not signed until October 1984 (Brennan 1985). This long and complex negotiation was a mark of the desire of the Mozambique government to retain some control over the donors, even at the cost of delaying an aid project in time of famine. Initially, USAID had demanded that Care distribute the US food. Mozambique refused.

No foreign agencies were allowed to distribute food, and Mozambique saw no need to permit this, as the DPCCN was successfully coordinating food distribution. Indeed, visiting donors were amazed. In late 1983, Dr Chris Daniel of Oxfam said that Mozambique had "the best local distribution I've ever seen. They've really got their act together."

Some donors, particularly the US, were also demanding better accounting of distributed food aid. And Mozambique, with its severe shortage of literate people, clearly was not up to keeping the detailed records many donors wanted. But Oxfam's Daniel spoke for many donors when he said flatly: "Food is not being diverted. There is no visible falling off lorries as you see in other places. There is nothing like the abuses you usually see."

Mozambique continued to refuse to allow Care to establish an independent food distribution system as it normally did. Finally Care's director for Mozambique, Terry Jeggle, developed a compromise. Care would create a Logistic Support Unit (LSU) within the DPCCN, and subordinate to its director. In what was probably a unique agreement for Care, it agreed not to operate as an independent relief agency and not to fly its own flag, but instead to work within government as advisers.

This was not what Care and USAID wanted, but both were so anxious to have Care on the ground in Mozambique that they had to accept. The compromise was an indication that Mozambique's position with respect to donors was stronger than was normally assumed.

But as an evaluation later pointed out, working inside the government did have the advantage that Care gained influence over government departments and could help to shape relief assistance policy (Brennan 1985). As we will see in Chapter 8, Care took a dominant role in food distribution, in some instances causing the disruption of competing state structures.

As well as being opposed to the idea of independent food distribution, some in the Mozambican government were unhappy with Care on security grounds. The expulsion of CIA agents in 1981 had made it much more difficult for the US to gain an accurate picture of military activity in Mozambique. Some high Mozambican officials believed that Care had CIA links. Care always denied this, but it does seem likely that the US security services could have made use of information that Care collected as part of its role in the DPCCN. Because it needed to know what areas were safe for food distribution, and because of USAID demands for ever tighter monitoring of food distribution, Care inevitably collected detailed information about the war. Care staff went to places that US diplomats did not go, and were legitimately able to question Mozambicans about the most remote places. Other foreign aid workers said that Care staff interviewed them not just about food and security, but also asked detailed questions about local Frelimo and government officials as well as about parastatal bodies like Agricom.

A Care official told me in 1987: "We know a lot about the war – about the movement of people, attacks, accessibility, which roads are open, and so on." Much of this material was never distributed to other donor agencies or even to the Mozambique government; it just remained in the files of the Care office on the ground floor of a block of flats on Av. Filipe Samuel Magaia in central Maputo.

Care officials need not have been "CIA agents", and may have tried to distance themselves from the intelligence services. But they needed the information to do a good job: for food distribution, for monitoring, and to gain power in bureaucratic infighting with other agencies (as discussed in the next chapter). And that information was available, at least covertly, to US embassy staff and the intelligence services. So the presence of Care may have helped to fill the intelligence gap caused by the expulsion of the CIA earlier. There is no way of knowing if US government pressure on Mozambique to accept Care, and then its pressure on Care staff to collect more detailed information, was purely on humanitarian grounds or if there was a subsidiary intelligence motive.

The Care programme in Mozambique was always small and unusual by Care standards. Care-USA spends over $300 mn per year in 37 countries, and normally does development projects and food distribution itself. The Care programme in Mozambique is officially run by Care-International, which is a loosely structured association of 12 national Care groups. But Care-USA is by far the largest national Care, and the Care world-wide headquarters is the same building on First Avenue in New York City as Care-USA. In practice on the ground in Mozambique, other national Care groups such as Care-Canada append their country name, while the word "Care" is used loosely, even on documents, for both Care-USA and Care-International.

World Vision

World Vision International (WV) is a right-wing, anti-communist Christian body which was already controversial in the early 1980s for use of aid as part of its evangelism, and for its links with repressive military regimes in central America (*New Statesman,* 12 April 1982). "We analyse every project, every programme we undertake, to make sure that within that programme evangelism is a significant component. We cannot feed individuals and let them go to hell", explained World Vision's President Ted Engstrom in 1982 (Hancock 1989: 9).

Now one of the largest and wealthiest of international NGOs, WV raises much of its money through expensive, professional, and tear-jerking advertising campaigns. But a US affiliate of WV does receive some money from USAID, and it has unusually good connections within the more conservative elements in the State Department. A US diplomat who had been in the embassy in Maputo told me: "World Vision had clout back in Washington. They could wheel and deal inside the State Department, and we in Maputo had no say."

USAID often insists that some food aid be distributed through NGOs, and it pays some of their administration costs. USAID contracts can be quite profitable to NGOs, which apply to USAID for the contracts. For the 1983/84 fiscal year (FY 1984), all US food aid went directly to the government. But for 1984/85, USAID and the Office of Foreign Disaster Assistance (OFDA, part of the State Department) switched some of the food to NGO distribution. This was done in some haste, and the World Vision Relief Organization (WVRO) was the only applicant.

Under normal circumstances, Mozambique would never have admitted WV, both because of its anti-communist views, and because of Mozambique's opposition to foreign church bodies distributing food. But if it rejected WV, then Mozambique would have lost more than food aid. It would have offended both USAID and the US Congress. Even worse, the US right was falsely accusing Frelimo of suppressing religion. Any rejection of WV, or any other church aid, would have led to orchestrated hysteria in the US about Marxist repression of religion. So Mozambique had to accept WV.

Many of the NGOs arriving in Mozambique were enthusiastic to expand their operations and help Mozambicans. and some ran faster than the government wanted (see Chapters 8 and 16). Government officials had continuing difficulties with WV. Initially, WV was assigned to Tete province. It had wanted to set up feeding centres, but the government prohibited it from having any direct contact with the general public at local level. Instead, WV brought maize from Malawi only to central DPCCN depots. Later it was allowed to distribute to individual villages. Still later, it was allowed to expand to development and relief projects in Manica and Zambézia provinces — again partly with USAID funding.

In its initial project, WV flew 773 tonnes of maize from Malawi to Tete; the controversial airlift was criticized by some as unnecessary when other donors were able to bring in 4273 tonnes by road and rail (*News Bulletin* 13 August 1984). But it generated a lot of publicity, and WV quickly brought in a crew to make a promotional film about it.

From the start, WV began its missionary activities. Large numbers of bibles and religious books were brought in with the sacks of grain; missionaries came in under the guise of relief workers and even came in illegally over the border from Zimbabwe. Some WV staff openly criticized the government. A proposal for a health project called the Ministry of Health "negligent" and "incapable". A few WV staff privately suggested to Mozambicans that they would be better off if Renamo took over the government.

Another struggle was to prevent WV from setting up independent structures which competed with government ones. The government barred WV (and all other aid groups) from operating child sponsorship programmes, a major form of international fund raising but which Mozambique felt was divisive because it privileged an individual child in a poor community. The government also prevented WV from setting up an independent mission health system. But it had to agree to WV distributing USAID funded "agpaks" – boxes of seeds and tools, with WV instruction booklets not cleared with the Ministry of Agriculture. The booklets included bible quotations and the suggestion that people listen to the WV radio station broadcasting from a neighbouring country; they probably had little impact, however, because they were too complex for illiterate villagers.

In several other countries, it has been reported that some WV staff had a technique of trying something on, then temporarily retreating if their hands were slapped. In some instances, WV pushed as hard as it could, then dismissed the staff member who had offended local officials (*National Catholic Reporter* (US) 23 April 1982). This also occurred in Mozambique. In several cases WV simply started projects or announced that is was to do so, then withdrew them when told these projects contradicted government policy or competed with actions by other NGOs. When a WV staff member was caught badmouthing the government or going against explicit government instructions or using aid to proselytize, the WV local director would apologize profusely, saying the person had exceeded their instructions and would be dismissed. But it never changed the anti-Frelimo mood of the WV presence.

Like Care, World Vision started in the US and became transnational. World Vision International (WV) actually runs the projects in Third World countries, and has a budget of over $200 mn per year. The various national World Vision organizations give money to WV for these projects. World Vision USA (WV-USA) is the largest national organization; it has established a separate body, WVRO which later became World Vision Relief & Development (WVRD), to obtain and distribute US food aid. WV, WV-USA, and WVRD all have their headquarters in Monrovia, California.

US policy is increasingly to "channel both food resources, and emergency and outreach grant funds to encourage US non-governmental organizations to implement relief and rehabilitation activities." In addition, "all PVOs will be encouraged to get involved in development activities, especially in the fields of health and agriculture" (USAID Budget Submissions FY 1989, 1990). This is not dissimilar to the priority action set out by Heritage in *Mandate III*. By FY 1990 NGO funds had risen to $10 mn and NGOs were expected to handle $15 mn of food aid. The three main channels for USAID funds are Care, WVRD, and the Adventist Development Relief Agency (ADRA) which is an agency of the Seventh-day Adventist Church.

A Note on the US Government

For non-US readers, it may be useful to detail the structure of the US government and its agencies which deal with Mozambique. The US concept of "separation of powers" means that there are three branches of government: legislative (Congress), executive (the presidency), and judicial.

Congress has two parts, the House of Representatives and the Senate. The Senate must approve appointments such as ambassadors. Both must approve legislation and aid budgets. Each has its own foreign relations committee, and each of these has an Africa subcommittee.

The Department of State comes under the executive branch; it tries to set foreign policy, administer aid, etc. Six bureaux within the State Department cover the various regions of the world. Mozambique comes under the Bureau of African Affairs, which is headed by the Assistant Secretary of State for African Affairs (a third-tier position under the Secretary of State and Deputy Secretary of State). During the Reagan administration, this was Chester Crocker; during the Bush administration this has been Herman Cohen. Crocker's personal assistant, Robert Cabelly, and his Deputy Assistant Secretaries of State for African Affairs, Frank Wisner and Roy Stacey, also worked on Mozambique.

Also within the State Department is the Policy Planning Staff, which has its own African section. The White House has its own staff, some of whom are foreign policy advisers. These sometimes come into conflict with the Bureau of African Affairs.

The Agency for International Development (USAID) is an "agency" of the Department of State. The Office of Foreign Disaster Assistance (OFDA) and the Food for Peace (FFP) Office are both "offices" of USAID.

The National Security Council (NSC) is part of the executive branch of government. During the early 1980s, the NSC director for sub-Saharan Africa was Fred Wettering, who during 1975–77 had been CIA station chief in Maputo.

The US fiscal year (FY) runs from 1 October to 30 September, so FY 1991 ends on 30 September 1991. USAID budgets are normally submitted 18 months before the start of the FY.

The Aid Invasion

5 Free Beer?

Mozambique was always very sceptical about foreign aid, as was shown in President Samora Machel's comments on possible European Community aid: "What are the interests of the EC in this? In my view we are not dealing with a public charity — they must have a definite interest. What is it? As soon as someone says to me 'we are going to give you \$5 million', I reply: 'In exchange for what?' I don't think they will give us something for nothing. God does it. God is good for that. But the EC? Its vocation isn't to carry out distribution, as if it were serving free beer" (*Afrique-Asie*, 7 July 1980).

At the same time, Mozambique recognized the need for outside help. Most of all it needed help to keep the economy and government functioning after the flight of the Portuguese. The biggest need was for sympathetic skilled people, because the levels of education and experience were so low. Teachers were particularly important.

Second, Mozambique wanted assistance to speed its development and transform the backward, skewed colonial economy. This involved a range of development projects, as well as training and technicians.

Later, Mozambique needed assistance to cope with a series of droughts and floods and with the effects of the war in neighbouring Rhodesia. This meant food aid and help with rebuilding destroyed infrastructure.

To some extent Mozambique expected aid as a form of international solidarity; some individuals and countries would want to assist one of the small number of Third World nations choosing a development path intended to benefit the whole of the population and not just a small elite. Also, Mozambique hoped for aid in response to its imposition of UN mandatory sanctions on UDI Rhodesia. But Frelimo was fully aware that good will and solidarity would not be enough, and that the interest of the "donor" should also be addressed.

Investment was seen as better than aid; the best projects were those which also benefited the foreign partner. President Machel argued that Mozambique had sufficient natural resources for foreign countries and TNCs to be able to profit from the country's minerals and tropical agricultural products; yet their developments could also be non-exploitative, so that Mozambique benefited as well.

To Frelimo, non-alignment and maintenance of sovereignty meant not relinquishing control of the development process. Thus it was anxious not to enter into a traditional aid relationship, as the a client of a particular group of wealthy donors. The argument of this book is that this stance was unacceptable to some major Western states and helped to provoke destabilization. The refusal to accept aid was not the only issue, nor even the most important. But the end to destabilization required an end to non-alignment; accepting the normal patron–client aid relationship was an essential part of that.

The who, why, and how of aid

Before looking at the changing role of aid in Mozambique, it is useful to establish some general distinctions as to why aid is given, how it is given, and who gives it. The Organization for Economic Cooperation and Development (OECD – the group of industrialized countries) defines foreign aid as "official development assistance" which consists of grants and loans made on concessional terms, and intended for the "promotion of economic development and welfare." Thus the very definition sees aid as a way of speeding development (Riddell 1987: 81). On the other hand, charitable appeals for the Third World usually highlight the need to keep people from starving. It is sometimes useful to distinguish three different purposes of aid:

1. *Development:* The traditional role of aid, this includes training, improvement of services, and expanding the productive sector.
2. *Maintenance:* Less obvious than development aid, this involves keeping the country functioning for an extended period, until it is eventually self-sufficient. With Mozambique in the late 1970s, it included food aid, support for running camps for Zimbabwean refugees, and technicians to fill gaps caused by the departure of the Portuguese.
3. *Emergency relief:* The subject of the classic aid appeals, this is urgent assistance in response to drought, cyclone, or any other unexpected event. It involves food, medicines, housing, transport, and staff to keep affected people alive, and is assumed to be of short duration.

As well as looking at the purpose of aid, it is also useful to distinguish four different *kinds of aid:*

1. *Money:* Cash grants or soft loans which go by a wide range of names, including import support and balance of payment support. Often cash is tied to purchases in the donor country, or linked to a particular development project.
2. *Material:* Normally food which is surplus in the donor country, this also includes used clothing, medicines, vehicles, and machinery.
3. *Technical:* Permanent staff as well as consultants and visiting advisers.
4. *Project:* Support for a specific project, ranging from a large dam to a small cooperative. Normally this is a package involving the first three kinds of aid, but with a very precise target.

Normal definitions of aid exclude three categories: direct investment and commercial loans (treated as "non-concessional financial flows" in Tables A.3 and elsewhere), as they do not have a grant or soft loan component; military assistance, as it does not promote development; and debt rescheduling and forgiveness, which does not involve "new" money going to the Third World.

There are three different *sources of aid:*

1. *Bilateral:* Given directly by one country to another.
2. *Multilateral:* From UN agencies (including the World Bank and IMF), the African and other development banks, the European Community (EC), the OPEC Fund, etc.
3. *NGO:* From private, non-government organizations like Oxfam and Care specifically formed to provide aid, as well as from churches and solidarity organizations.

Multilateral agencies and NGOs receive much of their funding from donor governments, and in that case are defined as aid "channels". Some of this is bloc grants. Some is for specific projects, in which case the UN agency or NGO is acting as an intermediary or a contractor for a donor government.

Finally, there are four forms of *administration of aid:*

1. *Recipient government:* The assistance is given to the Mozambican government, which administers it, subject to certain accounting requirements. This includes food given

to the DPCCN or the Ministry of Commerce, donor-funded technicians working for government ministries, and balance of payment support.

2. *Donor:* The donor government, NGO, or UN agency has a presence on the ground and actually distributes the food, cares for the sick, or carries out the project. Staff work for and report to the donor, not the Mozambican government.

3. *Third party:* The project or distribution is carried out by a local or foreign NGO or company on contract to the donor.

4. *Mixed:* Staff employed by an NGO or other donor work under Mozambican government supervision and often with government staff. This is common, and can produce effective cooperation; but it also leads to dual responsibility and authority, and conflicting chains of command.

None of these categories is clear-cut, and nearly all purpose-kind-source-administration combinations seem possible. There are both emergency and development projects, while technical personnel can be engaged in training (development), filling in for departed Portuguese (maintenance), or dealing with the effects of an emergency (relief) – sometimes all at once. Cash grants may be assigned to a particular development project or to buy emergency food. And so on.

But these approximate distinctions have been made because major changes took place from 1984, not only in the amount of aid, but also in its form and purpose. During the 1975–82 period, most aid to Mozambique was for development and maintenance, while by the end of the decade, emergency relief and financial credits (maintenance) dominated. The use of aid channels increased and government administration of aid decreased. These shifts are the subject of many of the controversies discussed in this book.

$14 per head

In the initial years of independence, Mozambique received significant aid, but below the average for African countries. Total aid in 1981 was $170 mn (£85 mn), or about $14 (£7) per person. This compared to $23 (£11.50) per person in 1981 for aid to low-income sub-Saharan Africa as a whole, and over $30 (£15) per capita to Mozambique's five majority-ruled neighbours (UNDP 1989b). Aid in 1981 included 137,000 tonnes of grain, about 11 kg per person, which was typical for low-income sub-Saharan Africa. No fewer than 50 other countries received more aid. (Aid to Mozambique is summarized in Tables 5.1 and 5.2, and various Tables in Appendix 1.)

Countries where Frelimo had support during the liberation war began assistance programmes. Sweden was the largest donor, and in the period around 1980 more than half of Western bilateral aid came from four countries: Sweden, Denmark, Norway, and the Netherlands. (These four, plus Canada and Finland, form the "Like-Minded Group".) Several socialist states were important donors (USSR, East Germany, Bulgaria, and Romania, as well as Hungary, North Korea, and China). Small programmes were also started with Italy, the US, the UK, and other Western states. There were a number of development projects which involved capital and technology, such as an East German textile mill, a Romanian cotton plantation and a Nordic paper mill (Hanlon 1984a: 83).

During the 1977–81 period, Mozambique was able to arrange soft development loans from Brazil, France and elsewhere. It was a period in which international banks were still encouraging Third World countries to borrow, and Mozambique also obtained commercial credit. Mozambique's key role in the founding of SADCC in 1980, and growing concern over apartheid in some European countries, also generated increased assistance in the early 1980s, particularly for the rehabilitation of ports and railways.

All this initially confirmed Frelimo's view that it could obtain foreign capital while remaining non-aligned, having economic relations with West as well as East, and staying outside the IMF and EC Lomé Convention.

Skills

The desperate shortage of skills caused first by Portugal's own underdevelopment and then by the flight of the Portuguese at independence meant that a high priority was put on training and technicians. Nearly 5000 Mozambicans have graduated from special schools in Cuba and East Germany, and the socialist countries sent hundreds of teachers, doctors, agronomists, and other skilled people to Mozambique (Frelimo 1989a). The Commonwealth and Western governments such as Italy also sent skilled people.

UN Security Council resolutions calling for support to Mozambique because it was imposing sanctions on UDI Rhodesia led the UN to establish quite a large presence. The UNDP budget in Mozambique was one of its largest in Africa during the early 1980s. Other important agencies included the UN Children's Fund (Unicef), the office of the UN High Commissioner for Refugees (UNHCR) which assisted with the estimated 100,000 Zimbabwean refugees in Mozambique, the UN Industrial Development Organization (Unido), and the Food and Agricultural Organization (FAO), which includes the World Food Programme (WFP). All sent foreign experts to assist Mozambican development.

A number of organizations in Western countries which had supported Frelimo during the liberation war sent technicians to Mozambique after independence. Known as cooperantes (literally "cooperators"), they were people who had been part of the solidarity movement and who had a useful skill. Many were red and expert. Although recruitment was organized through the solidarity groups, cooperantes were employed by Mozambican government ministries and assigned to jobs – for example, to a rural hospital or secondary school, or within the ministry itself. They typically had a two-year contract and were paid wages similar to Mozambicans; this was in contrast to UN staff and workers on bilateral projects, who were normally paid European salaries.

All cooperantes were skilled people, normally recruited to fill specific posts. Mozambique excluded the unskilled "volunteers" who flood into many developing countries. There was no Peace Corps or VSO programme. Mozambique also excluded the traditional NGOs such as Oxfam.

Technical assistance also came from a few other developing countries such as Tanzania. In addition, Mozambique took in a sizeable number of refugees from Chile, Brazil, East Timor, South Africa, and elsewhere; many were technicians who were hired as cooperantes. Some were paid with Nordic aid funds.

Food aid

Mozambique has always been a large exporter of agricultural products, and, surprisingly, a *net food exporter*. The colonial authorities developed plantation crops (sugar, tea, sisal, and copra), cotton as a peasant forced crop, and cashew as a peasant crop. Portuguese peasants were brought to Mozambique to grow food for the cities, but it was never enough and colonial Mozambique always imported grain, vegetables, and other food.

After independence, several factors caused a sharp fall in food production. The flight of the Portuguese broke the marketing network that had purchased maize, cassava, and other peasant food crops; white peasant producers in the colonatos (settlement areas) like Chókwè also left, which reduced vegetables and rice for the cities. Frelimo only slowly reestablished the marketing and urban food production, and the shortfall had to be made up through imports (which, in turn, put a premium on increasing export production to pay for further food imports).

These problems caused a sharp increase in grain and other food imports from 1978. Nevertheless, the value of food exports remained greater than the value of food imports. But the worst drought of the century, coinciding with Renamo attacks on food stocks and agricultural production, finally ended that. Food exports fell drastically and in 1983 Mozambique became a net food importer for the first time (DNE 1985).

Because of Zimbabwean refugees and the structural problems in food production, donors provided an average of 140,000 tonnes per year of grain during the 1978–81 period, and the government imported 190,000 tonnes per year commercially – compared to 120,000 tonnes per year at the end of the colonial period. The EC was the biggest donor in 1978. In 1979 and 1980, the US was the biggest grain donor; this was during the Carter administration, and food aid was immediately halted when Reagan took office. The Like-Minded Group was the most consistent grain donor in this period (Table A.4).

The power to say no

To ensure that foreign help supported national policies and development strategies, Mozambique exerted a high degree of control over which foreign agencies worked in the country and over what they did. Assistance was employed in a controlled, organized way. Priority was given to solidarity organizations and countries which had helped Frelimo before independence, and which the party now felt it could trust. Everything was done in the form of accords and contracts – with countries, UN agencies, and individual cooperantes. There were no NGO offices (other than for solidarity groups which had sent cooperantes) and no freelance aid workers. All projects were under the direct control of Mozambican ministries.

Mozambique had power over donors precisely because it could say no. It could, and did, turn away potential donors (particularly NGOs) and individual projects, and was able to set the terms of the discussion.

Until it fell behind in foreign debt repayments in 1983, it was able to refuse to supply detailed national accounts to foreign countries, and to withhold information on the size of its foreign debt and to whom it was owed. Its non-membership of the IMF meant that there was no collective pressure on Mozambique to produce accounts, permitting a secrecy which increased its power in negotiations with donors. But the donors were not accustomed to being treated with such a lack of deference; they extracted their revenge later.

So long as Mozambique paid its bills, it could fend off demands to look at the books; once it was bankrupt it could no longer do so. When Mozambique could say no to donors, it could set the terms of their participation; when it faced famine, it had to accept donor terms.

And the need for foreign help was real. Mozambique required money and large amounts of food to prevent starvation and collapse. Faced with disaster on an unprecedented scale, it also needed vehicles, seeds, medicines, and so on – as well as technical assistance to run a much larger relief effort than it had ever attempted before.

Suddenly Mozambique was the mendicant – not just for material support, but for political support to end a rampant terrorism which was destroying the fabric of the nation. Mozambique's leaders could no longer talk about mutual self-interest and cooperation between equals; destabilization dramatically and suddenly shifted the balance of power.

No extra food or money

Once the gates were opened, donors poured in. Despite the aid invasion of 1983–85, however, Mozambique remained substantially worse off than it had been before. Aid only partly filled the gap caused by the financial crisis. In particular, commercial grain imports were curbed, and increased aid never filled the gap. Thus, despite the drought and famine, grain imports during 1980–86 remained consistently below the 1979 peak. Indeed, grain imports actually dropped in the two crisis years of 1983 and 1986, reflecting both political pressure and the fact that it takes six to 18 months after a pledge for grain to be delivered.

Similarly, increased financial aid flows failed to compensate for the ending of credits and other non-concessional flows; aid merely helped to pay off debts. During 1982–86 less money flowed into Mozambique per year than in the peak year of 1981. The situation was made worse because export earnings continued to fall due to war and drought.

The increase in aid did not bring Mozambique up to the aid levels of neighbouring states, which also faced drought but were not suffering destabilization. Why was this? In part, as noted in Chapter 3, the improvement in the weather and the signing of the Nkomati Accord in 1984 made it seem a short-term crisis. But the position worsened substantially in 1985. In the jargon of the aid agencies, "August–September 1985 designates a period from which there was an increase in emergency conditions predominantly derived from conflict-induced circumstances in areas of the country not previously affected by drought" (Jeggle 1987). Yet even this did not increase food aid, and food imports continued to decline. Financial aid rose slightly.

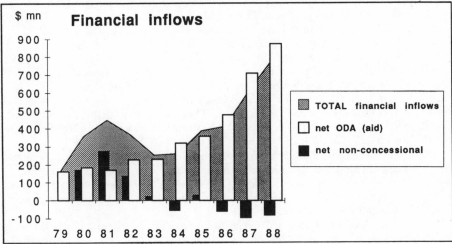

Source: Data from Appendix Table A.2c

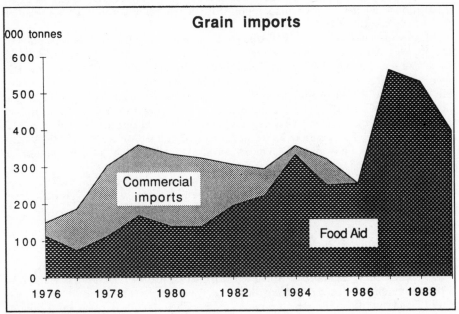

Source: Data from Appendix Table A.4a

The continued low levels of aid, despite strong appeals by Mozambique, must reflect Frelimo's continued attempts at non-alignment. Although Mozambique was negotiating with the IMF and with creditors, it still did not have an agreed IMF programme and still had not made enough pro-West shifts to satisfy the donors. Creditors had agreed in 1984 to partial rescheduling of about half of debt repayments due in 1984–85. But Mozambique failed to pay the other half. In 1986, Mozambique was due to pay $490 mn (£294 mn) in interest and repayments; creditors refused to reschedule without a full deal with the IMF, and again Mozambique could not pay.

1986 turning point

The rapid events of late 1986, notably the death of Samora Machel and the sharp increase in destabilization, seem to have shocked both Frelimo and the donors. The 1986 invasion of Zambézia and Nampula provinces hit particularly hard, because these were the richest agricultural zones. In December 1986, two British NGOs, Oxfam and Save the Children, launched an emergency appeal for Mozambique. "The situation is the most worrying in Africa," said Tony Vaux, Oxfam's emergency officer. At a press conference in February 1987, Bill Yates, Oxfam's head of campaigns, said Mozambique was on the brink of an Ethiopia-scale famine. It needed help "in weeks rather than months" to avert "a man-made disaster." He stressed that "Zambézia, the richest province in agricultural production, is virtually at a standstill today.... There is mindless destruction of people and their living environment. It is an awful side-show to the convulsion building up in South Africa itself" (*Guardian* 24 December 1986, 13 & 25 February 1987).

On 27 February 1987, the UN Secretary-General, Javier Perez de Cuellar, promoted the UN Resident Coordinator in Maputo, Arturo Hein, to be UN Special Coordinator for Emergency Relief Operations (UNSCERO). De Cuellar also launched a special emergency appeal for $332 mn (£200 mn) in additional aid; a special donors' conference was held in Geneva on 31 March.

On 22 April 1987 FAO launched an appeal for Africa in which it said that "the most important cause of concern is the serious and deteriorating food supply situation in Mozambique." As well as the problems caused by the war, the FAO noted that grain production was generally down in southern Africa due to abnormally dry and hot weather in the early months of 1987.

Meanwhile, talks with the IMF, World Bank, creditors, and bilateral donors continued. During 1985 and 1986, the IMF had sent five delegations to Mozambique and the World Bank had sent 22. The Economic Rehabilitation Programme (PRE), Mozambique's own version of structural adjustment, was announced on 14 January 1987. On 30 January the metical was devalued from 40 to the US$ to 200 to the US$ (from 66 MT to £1 down to 330 MT to £1). This was enough, at least initially, to satisfy the international agencies. In May and June 1987 Mozambique finally signed agreements with the IMF and World Bank. This permitted a rescheduling that year of Mozambique's debts with the "Paris Club" of government creditors and the "London Club" of banks and other private creditors.

Subsequent UN-sponsored emergency donors' conferences were held each April: in Maputo in 1988 asking $338 mn (£203 mn); in New York in 1989 asking for $362 mn (£217 mn); and in New York in 1990 when the target was $136 mn (£82 mn).

Aid doubled

Donors were clearly satisfied. Both financial and food aid were twice as large in 1987 as in 1985, and financial inflows finally exceeded the 1981 level. Official aid rose again in 1988 to $875 mn (£525 mn), of which 9% immediately left the country to pay debts. In 1988 Mozambique received 1.9% of all the aid given to the Third World by OECD, OPEC, and multilateral donors. It now ranked twelfth among the world's aid recipients

Table 5.1 *Importance of Mozambique as an aid recipient*

Year	Rank as aid recipient	Total aid		Donated grain	
		$ mn	$ per capita	000 t	kg per capita
1981	51st	171	14	137	11
1985	27th	359	27	249	19
1988	12th	875	62	527	38

Source: OECD and Appendix 1

Table 5.2 *Major aid donors ($ mn)*

Donor	1985	1986	1987	1988	1988 as % of total
Like-Minded Group	119	195	268	275	29%
Italy	95	110	135	160	17%
Socialist bloc	130	134	77	114	12%
IMF/World Bank	5	24	41	69	7%
UK	11	32	45	64	7%
EC	nd	nd	73	64	7%
USA	61	53	76	52	5%
Other UN agencies	43	43	49	46	5%
Others	79	101	139	116	
Overall TOTAL as reported by donors to UN	542	692	902	960	
(Aid as defined by OECD	359	477	710	875)	

Notes:
1. Information as reported by donors themselves to the UN. This is nearly $200 mn per year more than the OECD accepts as "official development assistance"; OECD underestimates socialist bloc aid, but that only accounts for a small part of the difference. Thus many donors are exaggerating their aid by inflating prices and by including non-concessional funds.
2 OECD, World Bank, and UN figures all disagree.
3. Like-Minded Group = Nordic states (Sweden, Norway, Denmark, and Finland) plus Canada and Netherlands.
Source: Tables A.2c and A.3b in Appendix 1

Table 5.3 *Response to emergency appeals ($ mn)*

	1987	1988	1989
Requested	332	338	362
Pledged			
against appeal	248	269	222
other	89	39	44
Portion of request covered by pledges	75%	80%	61%

Notes:
Pledged against appeal = money for items in the emergency appeal.
Other = money for emergency items not requested by Mozambique.

Source: Table A.5a

and fourth in sub-Saharan Africa. Aid was equivalent to an incredible 70% of gross domestic product (GDP), one of the highest rates in the world.

Frelimo's traditional, pre-independence friends remained the major donors. By 1988 Italy had emerged as the biggest, followed by Sweden and the USSR (see Tables 5.2 and A.3b). The Like-Minded Group was still the main donor; socialist bloc aid remained substantial.

In the second tier, however, was a new group of donors: the UK, EC, IMF/World Bank, and the US. The US has a political impact out of proportion to the size of its aid. By 1987/88 Mozambique had become the largest recipient of US aid in sub-Saharan Africa. It had built a large new embassy and USAID office in Maputo, and in 1988/89 USAID staff doubled from 5 to 10. But sub-Saharan Africa has never been a high priority for US assistance. Mozambique received 0.6% of US aid, and ranked only 22nd among its recipients. The US in 1988 was only the eighth largest donor; it gave little financial assistance, and three-quarters of its aid was surplus food, making it the largest single donor of grain (Table A.4c).

The 1990 emergency appeal was less than half previous ones, reflecting several political changes. First, the World Bank had finally gained control of the rehabilitation part of the emergency appeal (see Chapter 13). Second, "donor fatigue" was setting in and Mozambique took this into account. The lower appeal "reflects a sad, battered `realism' in respect to what donors will in fact be willing to pledge and to deliver", commented Professor Reginald Green (1990a). But this was wrong on two counts. First, the government had cut back its appeal too far, and was forced to admit only four months later that its request for food aid had been "clearly insufficient". Nevertheless, there was a sharp drop in donor response; food and transport pledges were well below even the low figure initially requested, and the UN warned there was a serious danger of famine. Some sources cited donor weariness, but others saw it as pressure on Mozambique to make further concessions to Renamo in the sporadic peace talks (*Africa Confidential* 6 April 1990, MIO 12 July 1990, *Guardian* 1 October 1990).

Do conferences generate support?

The four emergency donors' conferences undoubtedly increased publicity. But there is considerable dispute as to whether or not they increased the amount of aid, and some fear that they may detract from Mozambique's more fundamental needs.

One of the biggest problems is that at conferences, donors sharply inflate the real value of their aid. Thus donors often pledge food aid as amounts of money rather than volumes, and then set their own values. In 1988 West Germany claimed its maize was more than four times as costly as apparently identical EC maize, while Italy claimed its rice and wheat was worth twice as much as similar EC grain (Table 5.4).

Zimbabwe was offering white maize (preferred in Mozambique) delivered to Beira at $150–175 (£90–105) per tonne, dearer than the EC price but cheaper than virtually all other donors. Mozambique and the UN complained that donors were including in the price subsidies paid in their own countries. In other words, payments to their own farmers were being claimed as aid to Mozambique (UNDSPQ 1990: 19, 44).

Donors often pledge the same amount twice or even three times. At the April 1988 conference, donors pledged aid they said was worth $270 mn (£162mn). By mid-year, however, it was clear that only $213 mn (£128mn) in *new* assistance had been promised at the meeting; the rest was donors promising again grain and other goods pledged the previous year, but which had not yet arrived. And some donors later failed to confirm some of the money they had pledged. At the 1989 conference, pledges publicly claimed by donors to be $352 mn (£211 mn; *DPCCN Newsletter*, April/May 1989) turned out to include only $222 mn (£133 mn) of new money in response to the appeal.

Nevertheless, pledges did increase after the March 1987 Geneva conference, although only for delivery in 1988 and later. Nearly 600,000 tonnes of grain was promised, well up on previous years, but still only two-thirds of the 890,000 tonnes the March 1987 appeal said was needed.

Table 5.4 *Donors' claimed price of grain, 1988*

Grain	Donor	$/tonne	Multiple of EC price
Maize	West Germany	530	4.6
	Italy	297	2.6
	Denmark	292	2.5
	Canada	217	1.9
	USA	183	1.6
	UK	180	1.6
	World Food Programme	129	1.1
	EC	115	
Rice	Italy	500	1.9
	Japan	260	1.0
	EC	260	
Wheat	Italy	300	2.3
	Canada	270	2.1
	USA	205	1.6
	EC	130	

All donors of more than 10,000 tonnes of grain. Values as claimed by donor in statement to Mozambique government.
Source: *Priority Requirements* 28 October 1988.

The UN reported that in 1987 "there was not enough food to distribute to accessible people, and in some places the available [lorry] fleet of the DPCCN could not be used to full capacity. Furthermore, by October 1987, the late arrival of large quantities of food created a crisis situation in many provinces" (UNSG 1988).

The government estimated that traditionally about two-thirds of the population were subsistence farmers who produced most of the their own food plus a small marketed surplus. "The emergency has caused a 50% drop in output of the subsistence sector; it can no longer feed itself nor produce the surplus needed to feed the urban areas", the government reported at the end of 1987. By then, 90% of the country's marketed foodgrains were imported (CENE 1987b).

In December 1987, in preparation for the next appeal, UN Special Coordinator Arturo Hein warned the government of the need to have "an image of credibility". He said that "we must be truthful in our estimates and avoid the risk of increasing the number in the false belief that we will get more aid. On the contrary, we will only get more aid if the international community can believe that our appeals correspond to reality." For the April 1988 conference, the government lowered its sights, and asked for only 710,000 tonnes of grain. But Hein was wrong. With a lower target, pledges fell as well, to 531,000 tonnes.

In April 1989, there was a consensus that substantially increased numbers of people needed help (Table 3.1). So Mozambique increased its appeal to 765,000 tonnes of grain. Perhaps, too, the government began to realize that donors never provide enough and numbers must be inflated. But that didn't work either; pledges fell to 491,000 tonnes, and deliveries also dropped sharply (Tables 5.3 and A.4). In August 1989, Cooperation Minister Jacinto Veloso called a press conference to warn that the lack of food aid meant that food shortages would reach "alarming proportions". In the six-month April–October period only 159,000 tonnes of grain had actually arrived in Mozambique; at a press conference on 6 November 1989 Veloso warned that food shortages were then "critical". At a national meeting on the emergency in January 1990, Veloso called donor response "feeble"; he said that relief workers had been forced to cut the already inadequate rations in many areas, and the nutritional status of the population was gradually worsening. The UN reported a "dramatic drop" in food aid. Clearly "donor fatigue" was setting in.

According to the UN, the "poor" response to the 1989 appeal has "resulted in increased levels of malnutrition in large segments of the population." There is an increase in malnutrition-related disease. Nationwide, 17% of children showed growth faltering. WFP considers a normal ration to be 2150 kcal (kilo calories) per day. Mozambique calculates its requests for aid on 1500 kcal. But the low levels of donations meant that many displaced people were receiving as little as 600 kcal per day. In some districts, there were signs of famine (UNDSPQ 1990: 4, 17, 19).

The fall in aid came just when needs were increasing. The military position had improved substantially in some parts of the country in 1988 and 1989. Military convoys were able to reach towns previously accessible only by air. And the railway west from Nampula to Cuamba and Lichinga reopened. This increased the amount of food that could be transported. But there was no food to carry.

During 1988 and 1989, 200,000 refugees returned from neighbouring countries. UNHCR set up a programme for them, but donors would not contribute, so it stopped; the refugees continued to return, however. And officials began to consider how they would cope with a million returning refugees once the war ended.

Crises in Italy, USSR

Financial crises in two of Mozambique's three biggest donors, Italy and the USSR, were causing problems in 1989 and 1990, suggesting that non-food aid might also be falling. Because of domestic confusion, Italy had promised Third World aid far in excess of its budgets. The expenditure freeze started in late 1988, although officials denied the existence of the freeze until well into the next year. Of $50 mn (£30 mn) pledged in response to the emergency appeal in April 1988, half was cancelled or delayed, including 120 lorries. Although desperately needed for emergency food distribution, none of the lorries were delivered that year or the next; about 50 were delivered in 1990, and the rest scheduled for 1991. As Guglielmo Colombo in the Italian embassy in Maputo admitted, "a commitment for an emergency which is honoured only two years later is not for that emergency." At the April 1989 donors' conference Italy pledged nearly $60 mn (£36 mn); some turned out to be delayed promises from the year before, and Italy could never be pinned down to sign a contract for much of the rest. In 1989 and 1990 total Italian aid was expected to fall to half its 1987–88 levels. In 1988 the USSR provided $28 mn (£17 mn) in oil products (UNDP 1989a: 206), more than half of Mozambique's needs, and substantial other assistance. With the crisis in eastern Europe, Mozambique had to search for other sources of oil; many Soviet, East German, and other socialist teachers and technicians also returned home, creating serious gaps in the university and elsewhere.

NGO invasion

A notable change in the late 1980s was the increase in number and power of NGOs. The number of NGOs rose from 7 in 1980 – all traditional solidarity organizations – to 70 in 1985 and to 180 in 1990 (Adam 1990: 27; Encontro April 1990). NGOs are discussed in more detail later (see Chapter 17). In Mozambique their main role has been as emergency contractors. In 1989, non-Mozambican NGOs handled more than $70 mn (£42 mn), but of this only $6 mn (£4 mn) was money which they had raised from appeals and members. The other $64 mn (£38 mn) came from governments. UN agencies such as

Unicef and UNHCR also became major aid channels. In 1989, UN agencies other than the World Food Programme spent $15 mn (£9 mn), of which only $2 mn (£1 mn) came from the agencies' own budgets; the rest came as government grants. The significance of this was two-fold. First, NGOs and UN agencies were largely acting as contractors and not independent donors. Second, governments were using NGOs and the UN, rather than the Mozambican government, to administer $77 mn (£46 mn) in aid – more than a quarter of all emergency aid and three-quarters of non-food emergency aid. The government said this was making "coordination, monitoring and control more difficult" (CENE 1989b: 40).

The Italian-funded and built Pequenos Libombos dam, shown here under construction, will provide water for irrigation and for the city of Maputo (AIM: Alfredo Mueche).

By 1990, a significant amount of food aid was also being channelled through NGOs. The US, UK, and EC were outspoken in stressing their preference for sending aid via NGOs rather than the government. Furthermore, a significant portion of the aid via NGOs and the UN was for goods and projects Mozambique had not asked for at all. Donors were giving money to UN agencies and NGOs to do things the Mozambican government did not regard as priorities, while not giving money to the government for areas it considered more important.

Meanwhile, Mozambique's creditors were rescheduling its debts but, for the most part, not forgiving them. Furthermore, much of the new aid was in the form of loans. So the debts and unpaid interest continued to build up. By 1990, Mozambique was more than $5 bn (£3 bn) in debt – more than three times the level when it defaulted in 1984.

People, not Numbers

It is easy to get lost in the numbers – not just the mountains of dollars, lorries, and grain, but the literally hundreds of thousands of lives that have been saved by emergency aid. And it is easy to become immersed in the minutiae of aid battles, as I will later in this book, because they are central to the future of Mozambique. But at the core, aid and development are about *individual* people who survive and improve their lives, or who become impoverished and perhaps die.

Survival in Mopeia

I visited Mopeia in October 1988 (See Chapter 3). Renamo rebels had been driven out six months before by a joint force of Mozambican and Tanzanian troops. Refugees had poured in. When I was there, the rains had just begun; having built their traditional wattle and daub houses, people were planting their crops. Under appalling conditions, they were rebuilding their lives.

Five classrooms had been created – one was in a gutted shop that had been roofed, another was in a grass-roofed mud building, and so on. Teachers in tattered clothing were teaching even more ragged pupils. But those five classrooms were full; three shifts of pupils every day were learning to read, add, and build a new life. The health workers proudly showed me around their rebuilt hospital. In the tiny pharmacy, the shelves had been pulled down and destroyed by Renamo, but the medicines were in neatly labelled boxes carefully arranged on the floor. Patients still had to lie on mattresses on the floor. But the hospital was well organized and spotlessly clean, and the staff were proud of what they had already done to provide care.

In many ways, Mopeia seemed a microcosm of rural Mozambique. Life for these Mozambicans seemed largely determined by foreign forces. Renamo's invasion had been organized by South Africa. Renamo was expelled with the help of Tanzania and Zimbabwe. For the people of Mopeia, food, clothing, drugs, and seeds had come from bilateral donors. An NGO had given the roofing sheets to repair the school and hospital. Indeed, the small plane that flew us to Mopeia had been chartered by an aid agency. Of the six of us on the plane, four were foreigners and only two were Mozambicans; the only way that government officials could visit was courtesy of aid agencies.

Mopeia was attacked again by Renamo in October 1989, and all the rebuilding and replanting destroyed. What little furniture there was in the hospital was destroyed and all the drugs were taken; the make-shift schoolrooms were ransacked. The tailor described in Chapter 3 saved his sewing machine only because he stuffed it in a sack and buried it. When Renamo was expelled, the people and the donors started again.

Not passive victims

If it is easy to get lost in the numbers, it is also sometimes all too easy to see Mozambicans as helpless mendicants being kept alive by benevolent aid agencies. Despite all the aid and aid workers, it is first and foremost Mozambicans who are keeping their countrymen alive. When we visited Mopeia, there were no other foreigners there. It was clearly Mozambicans themselves who were rebuilding the houses and planting crops under difficult circumstances. It was the Mozambican teachers who were struggling to rebuild their school and conduct classes.

Foreign assistance *is* important – for food, tools, seeds, and so on. But the most important help is informal support from friends, relatives, and even strangers. And most official support comes from Mozambican agencies like the DPCCN.

More important, most Mozambicans are not dependent on aid for survival. War directly affects perhaps half the population. The other half continues something resembling a normal existence. Despite the war, development continues. Roads are being built; factories are being rehabilitated; farms are being developed. All over the country, Mozambicans are struggling to overcome the ravages of war and colonialism, to build something better for themselves and their children. They have goals and a vision of what a better future might be.

At its best, aid assists and strengthens those Mozambicans who are building or rebuilding. Aid provides the tools.

Angelo and development

Consider my friend Angelo, who works for the railways. Held back in colonial times because he was black, he rose quickly in the railway workshops after independence. Then he went back to school when he was 40 years old. A modest man who lived with his family in a house he built himself, Angelo studied at night by the light of a paraffin lamp. With a mix of Bulgarian, British, Dutch, and Mozambican teachers at the Industrial Institute, he struggled for his engineering qualification. Then he was made head of the railway workshop. With technical assistance from India, Italy, the US, Romania and probably several other countries, the workshops rebuilt locomotives and wagons repeatedly damaged in Renamo raids, and kept the trains running. Two of Angelo's children went to secondary school and university in Cuba, and received an education that it would have been impossible to get in Mozambique.

Of my friends, Angelo is perhaps the best evidence that aid can contribute to development and self-sufficiency in a Third World country. He and his family are building a new and better Mozambique, and they have been significantly helped by foreign aid. The money spent on them is an investment that will pay dividends for years to come.

War and famine grab the headlines, because that is what we want to read about. The articles about Angelo and tens of thousands of others struggling to develop Mozambique are put aside, to be read next week or next year. But when destabilization and starvation finally come to an end, it will be the development experience of the past 15 years that will determine Mozambique's future course. That is why the donors and the government are engaged in such an intense struggle for control.

6 Why is there a Problem?

When there is a major natural disaster, such as a flood or hurricane, it is considered right that everyone should stop their normal activities to help the victims and prevent mass starvation. In a war, priorities are very different – as well as helping the victims, it is essential to keep the economy going and actively pursue the war. This is especially true in the context of modern low-intensity warfare, where the goal is to destroy the target state's economy and to create huge numbers of victims who will put a strain on the target's limited resources. Timescale is important, too. Natural disasters are over in weeks or months; wars can last for years.

This contrast in how we respond to continued suffering intentionally induced by war and random suffering caused briefly by natural disaster lies at the heart of the confusion about assistance to Mozambique. And it is why donor assessments of the cause of the problem became so important.

It is possible to see five different responses, some of which were adopted at various times by the same donors. Some donors initially refused to help because they understood that helping the victims of war is to take sides in that war. Other donors explicitly backed Frelimo and saw help to victims as a way to support Mozambique against a war of destabilization. Still others chose to help both sides, thus remaining neutral and prolonging the war. Some donors decided that supporting the Mozambican government and economy was to take sides in the war, but helping the victims was not, so they tried to pretend it was a natural disaster – saving lives but disrupting the economy and war effort in the process. Finally, some donors pretended that there was no special problem at all.

The confusion was heightened because of the overlapping causes of the crisis: drought, destabilization, world recession, and Frelimo's economic policy mistakes. Different donors gave very different weight to different aspects of the problem.

Most donors at least accepted that Mozambique was in a deep crisis of a special sort. But their own politics and their analyses of the causes influenced their assistance. There were two key areas of confusion and disagreement. First, was war the problem, and if so, what was the cause? Second, was this a short-term problem where normal first aid would suffice, or was this a long-term problem requiring non-traditional solutions?

A group of European MPs who visited Mozambique in November 1988 assessed the problem this way: "The Mozambique emergency is unusual because it is not a natural disaster where it is only necessary to provide food and tents until the flood waters recede and people can rebuild. Instead, Mozambique faces a permanent structural emergency in which South Africa uses state terrorism to try to destroy Mozambique's economic base.

This means continued destruction and continued refugee flows, and it means massive rebuilding. Thus Mozambique has tried to link 'emergency' assistance to rehabilitation. On the whole, donors have proved unable to cope" (AWEPAA 1989).

Labelling the cause

"Mozambique's children die every day so that apartheid may live", declared two directors of Africare, a US NGO (*International Herald Tribune* 28 April 1988). "If any country can be said to have been bombed back into the stone age, it is Mozambique", commented Richard Dowden, Africa Editor of *The Independent*. "Mozambique's suffering could easily be ended by an end to the war ... but behind the MNR looms Pretoria, its backer and arms supplier. It is in South Africa's interest to keep Mozambique weak and divided" (*Independent* 13 & 25 February 1987).

"Renamo and its campaign of terror bear overwhelming responsibility for the human crisis within Mozambique today", according to the US House Select Committee on Hunger. Famine "was caused not by drought or poor agricultural policies, but was instead the result of Renamo's destruction of rural life and food production". South African Military Intelligence have "used Renamo as a key element in its strategy of regional destabilisation" (HSCH 1987).

Not everyone agrees. The dissenting report of an Australian parliamentary delegation which visited Mozambique in 1988, said African nations "must diminish their obsessive concentration on the South Africa 'scapegoat' as the excuse for all their problems." Indeed, the then President P W Botha was making "modest, domestic, humanitarian advances" and "conciliatory diplomatic contacts". Furthermore, "no evidence was presented to us of South African government disruption being a major cause of this poverty." Rather, poverty is caused by the "dictatorial, oppressive, Marxist government" (PCA 1989: 45, 47).

The contrast between these two attitudes is summed up by the phrases used to describe the causes of the war. To those like me and the European MPs quoted earlier, who put the primary blame on South Africa, the war is due to "destabilization" or South African "state terrorism". To those like the dissenting Australian MPs and the Heritage Foundation in the US, there is a "civil war" going on in Mozambique.

Among those who use the phrase "civil war" are USAID's Office of Foreign Disaster Assistance (OFDA 1987: 23), and Médecins sans Frontières-France (MSF-F) (Pecoul 1990). Both are associated with the right and are seen as hostile to the Frelimo government.

OFDA referred to the "civil war" and was careful not to blame outsiders. It said "the famine in Mozambique has certainly been exacerbated by this renewed insurgent activity. Food convoys have been ambushed, roads have been mined, and grain warehouses have been burned to the ground. By 1985, insurgent activity replaced drought as the primary cause of hunger in Mozambique" (OFDA 1987: 23).

Save the Children-UK carefully touched both sides by referring to a "civil war waged by the South African backed ... MNR guerrillas against President Chissano's government" (*Guardian* 28 September 1990).

Care has taken a cautiously divided view. In its first evaluation in September 1983, Care argued that the security problem was created both by "raids by South Africa" and because "discontentment with this system has led to a number of underground movements" (Care 1983: 4). But by 1987 the first head of Care in Mozambique was arguing that "there would not now be a disaster emergency ... were it not for the motivated and externally supported destructive actions that have occurred since late 1985" (Jeggle 1987).

The World Bank, undoubtedly the most important single agency in Mozambique, showed the widest swings in opinion. A World Bank official told me that, as the name states, it is a "bank", so it could only go into a country where the problem was strictly economic. If the problem was military or political, then the World Bank shouldn't be there at all. Thus, in Mozambique, it was necessary to "assume" that the problem was basically economic and that the normal prescription could be applied. This kind of Alice-in-Wonderland attempt to redefine the problem is so central that all of Part III of this book is devoted to it.

But then, in June 1990, the Bank's chief economist for Africa, Stephen O'Brien, told a Maputo press conference that the ills of the Mozambican economy were largely due to "the very severe impact of the destabilization which has taken place over the past decade" (*Mozambiquefile* July 90). It was probably the first time that a high World Bank official had ever uttered the word "destabilization".

Avoiding 'politics'

In 1983–84 there was a general reluctance by donors to blame the war and South Africa for the famine. That would have been "political", so drought was usually cited. There were several reasons for this, at least in the UK. British charities are not allowed to be "political". But this was also a very useful excuse. People will give money to feed starving black babies so long as their racist and charitable instincts overlap; that is, so long as they think that the problem is caused by native incompetence and stupidity – either the inability of black people to protect themselves against drought, or due to "civil war" and "black-on-black violence" – and black babies are being helped by kindly white nurses. NGO fund raisers argued to me that if they said black babies were starving because of the conscious actions of a white government which was supported by their own government, then people would be confused and not give – it would suddenly become "political" and not a case of doing good works.

Faced with the restrictions on charities and the problems of fund raising, even the February 1987 joint appeal by Oxfam and Save the Children in Britain was cautious. The joint advertisement said that the crisis was "a result of rebel military activity" (*Independent* 25 February 1987). Oxfam's appeal leaflet had the standard pictures of starving and ragged people on the front, and the stress was that "over four million people in Mozambique face destitution". In much smaller print, it also said that the "MNR with backing from South Africa, are terrorizing many parts of the country" and it quotes Unicef that more than 140,000 children had died in Mozambique and Angola "as a direct or indirect result of South African backed rebel activity". But the advertising tried hard to make the problem look like a natural disaster, and to encourage people to see it as similar to the famine in Ethiopia.

Later Oxfam retreated even from this. In mid-1990 when it was under investigation from the Charity Commission for the apparently "political" action of calling for sanctions against South Africa, it launched a campaign on Mozambique with a picture of a black child headed "His silence speaks volumes." The advertisement said: "Nine year old Francisco withdrew into complete silence after Mozambican guerrillas forced him to participate in his parents' murder." The reason was "the war that continues to tear Mozambique apart". This time there was no mention at all of South Africa. But the campaign ran at a time when the media were full of pictures of so-called "black-on-black violence" in South Africa, and it only served to reinforce the image of black people massacring each other and unable to survive without charitable whites to help and govern them.

Other British NGOs were more outspoken. An International Voluntary service advertisement recruiting cooperante engineers for Mozambique led off with: "The current threat of starvation in part of Mozambique is just one result of South Africa's destabilization of its neighbours" (*Guardian* 25 March 1987). The Homoíne massacre in July 1987 also helped to tip the balance. Roland Hodson, Chief Executive of the British NGO Action Aid was in Mozambique at the time and visited survivors of the massacre in hospital. In a letter in *The Times* (7 August 1987) he said that "the fundamental cause of the hunger, the thousands of arms and legs blown off, and the thousands of deaths, is the arming of Renamo" by South Africa. Two months later Action Aid launched a campaign provocatively headlined "Mozambique: we *can't* stand back any longer" which explicitly blamed the "South African-backed MNR".

Another British NGO, Christian Aid, launched a postcard campaign in 1988. It provided postcards saying "Stop the Killing. South Africa *Please* stop supporting the MNR in Mozambique" and suggested they be sent to the South African embassy in London. Christian Aid explained that it was working with the Christian Council of Mozambique, but that "time and again our efforts are destroyed by vicious attacks. Farming projects are ransacked, food convoys ambushed, and development workers murdered."

As the former emergency coordinator, Dr Prakash Ratilal commented: "the best contribution that the international community can give Mozambique is to continue putting pressure on the bellicose apartheid forces to stop destabilising Mozambique" (Ratilal 1990b: 166).

Aid to Renamo?

Food is often a weapon in war. In 1983, South Africa was trying to combine drought and military action to create starvation, in the hope that peasants would "direct their frustrations and fury" at the Frelimo government (see Chapter 2). In 1987, the position was different. First, many donors were more sympathetic to the government, while the US was sending out conflicting messages. Second, South Africa supplied weapons but not food, and the drought and Renamo's own destruction meant that there was hunger in Renamo camps. Third, Frelimo was sending food through in military convoys.

Two issues were hotly debated: Should Renamo receive food aid? And should donors help protect food convoys from Renamo attack?

His
silence speaks
volumes.

It's a cry for help.

Nine year old Francesco withdrew into complete silence after Mozambican guerillas forced him to participate in his parents' murder.

He's now in a centre for traumatised children. It's somewhere to live but it's not a home.

Children like Francesco are usually cared for by surviving members of their families and communities. But the war that continues to tear Mozambique apart

has forced hundreds of thousands of people to flee their homes, abandoning everything.

If they are to have a chance of being able to look after themselves without relying on handouts, it is vital that Oxfam supplies seeds and tools, so planting can take place in October.

If Mozambicans have a good harvest next year, their future will hold more than suffering and uncertainty. Please give as much as you can today.

☐ I enclose a cheque/P.O. made payable to Oxfam for: (Please tick) ☐ £___ ☐ £10 ☐ £15 ☐ £30 ☐ £50

Name Mr/Mrs/Miss/Ms_____(Please use block capitals)

Address_____

Postcode_____ Send your donation to: OXFAM, FREEPOST, Oxford OX2 7BR. (No stamp needed.)

BREAKING THE CYCLE OF POVERTY OXFAM

Or donate by credit card, phone 0865 56916

Oxfam works with poor people regardless of race or religion in their struggle against hunger, disease, exploitation and poverty, in Africa, Asia, Latin America and the Middle East, through relief, development, research overseas and public education at home.

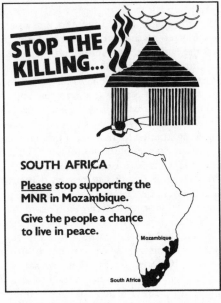

STOP THE
KILLING...

SOUTH AFRICA

<u>Please</u> stop supporting the
MNR in Mozambique.

Give the people a chance
to live in peace.

Mozambique

South Africa

(Above): Christian Aid postcard to be sent to South African Embassy. (Left): Does this Oxfam ad reinforce the image of black people killing each other?

By 1987 most agencies were citing Renamo and South Africa as the root of the problem. But some were trying to feed Renamo. Zimbabwe was forced to close a remote border crossing with Mozambique when it found an NGO taking food across to give to Renamo. In another incident, Mozambique had asked an NGO not to deliver food to a particular town because it could not be defended; the food was delivered anyway, and as soon as the lorry left the town was raided and the food taken. Mozambican officials are sure it was simply a circuitous way of getting food to Renamo.

The Senate Minority Leader Robert Dole called for food aid to be given to Renamo. The *Wall Street Journal* (11 May 1987) supported this, saying that "[US]AID is denying supplies to millions of people whose only crime is that they do not live under the control of a brutal dictatorship." OFDA gave $1.2 mn (£700,000) to the ICRC on the clear understanding that it should be used to provide food to Renamo-controlled areas. This was at a time when the US Deputy Assistant Secretary of State, Roy Stacey, talked about Renamo causing a "holocaust". Foreign Minister Pascoal Mocumbi made an unusual public attack on what he called manoeuvres in the US to give food aid to ICRC for distribution in Renamo-held areas, which Frelimo "rejected absolutely" (*Noticias* 24 & 25 November 1987).

ICRC has never been popular with the government in post-independence Mozambique. Some ICRC staff were seen by Frelimo as unsympathetic, racist, and arrogant. The parastatal news agency, AIM, openly criticized ICRC; one report quoted a comment that "these guys from ICRC think they can give orders to anyone" (Gumende 1989). High Mozambican officials, including the late President Samora Machel, rejected ICRC's statements that it was impartial and helped the victims of both sides in any conflict. These officials claimed that ICRC did not help Frelimo during the liberation war while it assisted the Portuguese, yet it now wanted Frelimo's approval to help Renamo.

Frelimo officials also accused ICRC of being publicly critical of Frelimo, but never of Renamo. On 31 July 1985 an ICRC plane was shot at by Renamo forces attacking Luabo; the plane had flown without government permission, and officials said that if permission had been requested ICRC would have been told the attack was taking place. After the attack, ICRC suspended its operations, including those in parts of the country not affected by the war. It punished Frelimo for a Renamo attack, and implied that this was the fault of the government; Renamo was never blamed.

Under pressure from the US, ICRC was in turn putting increasing pressure on the Mozambican government to allow aid to Renamo areas. ICRC even tried to get EC Foreign Ministers to issue a statement appealing to the Mozambican government to allow aid to Renamo zones, but the ministers refused.

The ICRC was one of several agencies operating airlifts to isolated villages, but it suddenly stopped them on grounds of "security", although other donors continued to fly to the same places without difficulty. ICRC seemed to be trying to make the government dependent on it in order to force the concession of being allowed to help Renamo. Privately, ICRC officials stressed that assistance could go to government zones only if ICRC could be "neutral" and help Renamo too (not a condition imposed on the Portuguese 20 years before, Frelimo claimed).

ICRC's sensitivity on the issue was shown in February 1988, when ICRC President Cornelio Sommaruga visited Mozambique. He first stopped in Lusaka, where he told a Reuters reporter that he was flying to Mozambique to try to persuade President Chissano to allow ICRC to fly into Renamo zones, which would then allow ICRC to resume its airlift to government-held zones. On arrival in Maputo, Dr Sommaruga was questioned about this, and he denied even talking to the journalist. The indignant Reuters correspondent in Lusaka later said that Dr Sommaruga had given him an on-the-record interview in the Hotel Pamodzi in Lusaka.

In the end, however, the pressure worked. ICRC was eventually given government approval to fly to Renamo zones – so long as the government was told in advance, to avoid incidents like the one in Luabo. But problems continued. On 1 June 1990 two ICRC officials went to a prearranged meeting with Renamo in Zambézia to organize a food delivery; they were kidnapped by the Renamo people they were meeting. For several days ICRC refused to admit they were missing, and never admitted that Renamo had kidnapped them.

Protect or Retreat?

As destabilization increased, development projects being built with foreign assistance were attacked and sometimes destroyed. Several foreign technicians were killed. At first, donors simply pulled staff back to provincial capitals or Maputo. In some cases projects were halted. In others, donors were prepared to pay Mozambicans and others to work on the projects even if their own nationals were not allowed to go there.

The thinking of 1983 was still evident: donors were nervous about being seen to take sides in the war. For some, it was a "civil war" and they would simply wait until it was over. Others noted that South Africa had particularly instructed Renamo to "prevent the activities of foreigners (cooperantes) because they are the most dangerous for the recovery of the economy" (see Chapter 3). Thus to withdraw from development projects was actually to take the South African side in a conflict which was definitely not a "civil war". But they were extremely reluctant actually to help Mozambique to protect those projects.

Britain was an important exception. In 1985 it became the first NATO country to provide military help to Mozambique, training groups of Mozambican troops at the Nyanga centre in Zimbabwe that it was already using to train the Zimbabwean army. Several Mozambican officers also attended courses at Sandhurst, the British military academy. With both Mozambican and UK government approval, the British company Lonrho started training and equipping its own forces to protect its projects in Mozambique. The only other exception was a Swedish NGO, which launched a private fund-raising campaign for "non-lethal" equipment.

Mozambique asked other donors to follow suit but, ever-mindful of donor sensitivity, it said nothing publicly. Donors, too, seemed afraid of what head offices and the US would think (although the US State Department had quietly encouraged the British initiative).

In August 1987 Sweden brought in Maurice Strong to look at the situation. A respected former UN official, his "confidential" report was widely circulated. It was important because it articulated the feelings of many concerned donors and legitimized the discussion. In reports to their head offices, embassies and donor representatives could cite the "confidential" Swedish-funded Strong report.

"Mozambican officials made it clear that their need for assistance to defend vulnerable population, the transport corridors, and other strategic development infrastructures and projects from terrorist attack is their most immediate priority. There is considerable frustration on the part of the government at the inability or unwillingness of donors to provide even non-lethal assistance, particularly as it is universally acknowledged amongst donor representatives that this is a priority need."

"It is paradoxical that despite the almost complete unanimity within the donor community in agreement with the Mozambican government that this is its most urgent need, and that which would represent the most cost-effective investment by donors, there seems no evidence, with the exception of the UK military training programme, of any movement towards meeting this need." Strong concluded that "the case for non-lethal security assistance is a compelling one and I am convinced that those governments genuinely committed to assisting Mozambique can no longer escape facing up to it."

Strong argued that Mozambican officials were making a good case for incorporating security measures into development projects which were vulnerable to attack. Mozambique was "very flexible" about how this would be done; projects could use their own security personnel, or by arranging for Mozambican forces to do the job while being maintained and supplied by the project managers.

The Strong report totally changed the climate. At the annual SADCC conference in Arusha in January 1988 donors were vying with each other to be first to link security to project aid. Financing of economic development projects must "include the necessary security factor for guaranteeing their defence", said Luis Yañez–Barnuevo, the Spanish Secretary of State for International Cooperation. Spain had already agreed a pilot project for agricultural development which included a unit of rural guard to be trained in Spain. And, he added pointedly, "the potential of this formula was acknowledged shortly afterward by the European Community itself." In the EC-Mozambique memorandum of agreement signed in November 1987, explicit mention was made of local security conditions, with the EC agreeing to include in the financing of its development projects an amount to cover the costs for the personnel entrusted with ensuring their protection.

At the SADCC meeting D Frisch, Director General for Development of the EC Commission, declared: "We cannot do agricultural development in Mozambique without taking a minimum of measures to protect the area. We are ready to support the troops who are necessary to support these projects. We can provide food, shoes, clothing, and spare parts, but we would not go further than that."

Underlining the new mood shown at the SADCC conference, at the signing of an accord with Sweden and Finland to fund a container terminal in Beira, Transport Minister Armando Guebuza could publicly challenge them to "include a component of defence" in the project.

By the end of 1989 a range of Western countries were providing some form of security help: training (UK, Portugal, Spain), military software such as radios (UK, France, Canada, Italy), and non-lethal items such as lorries, food and fuel (EC, Sweden, Norway, Netherlands, West Germany) (*Mozambiquefile* March 1990; AWEPAA 1988: 22).

Donors had come to understand that protecting projects in Mozambique against Renamo was no different from protecting projects in many other parts of the world against armed robbers. "In Mozambique, protection is simply part of the running costs", explained the EC representative in Maputo, Dr Francisco Santa Clara Gomes. "We provide protection because we don't want to waste taxpayers' money."

Protecting food convoys

Protecting food aid convoys was often more controversial than training troops and protecting projects. While some donors fed Renamo, it prevented food reaching the hungry in some Frelimo areas. Relief lorries were destroyed by mines and ambushes, and drivers killed. EC representative Gomes estimated that in 1988 the EC was losing 10% of its donated food to Renamo attacks.

Table 6.1 *Food aid lorry attacks*

	1987	1988	1989
DPCCN & Red Cross lorries destroyed	32	40	37
Drivers & assistants killed	15	23	5

Sources: CENE 1988b: 15; Ratilal 1990a: 137; Newman 1990: 9; UNDSPQ 1990: 48

Nevertheless, giving food to the troops, even those protecting food distribution, was anathema to most donors. Sitting beside the pool of a Maputo hotel, an NGO worker who had been organizing an airlift told me how impressed he was with the honesty of local officials. The NGO had a rule that no food carried on its plane could be given to soldiers, and the district administrator knew this. The soldiers were there to defend the town (and the food distribution) against Renamo attack, and they, too, were short of food. The administrator actually received a black eye successfully defending the food against the hungry soldiers, the NGO worker said proudly. The soldiers eventually went house to house to beg a share of the food from the local villagers, but none had been given directly to them.

Putting together food convoys became a nightmare for the Mozambicans. Most of the agencies which had donated lorries to the DPCCN had imposed regulations that their lorries could not be used to carry soldiers, and they checked often enough that the DPCCN had to be sure this rule was carried out. But the army did not always have vehicles of its own to go with the convoy. So soldiers would ride on top of sacks of grain on the acceptable lorries – those belonging to private traders or donated by an agency turning a blind eye to the carrying of troops. But sitting on top of sacks made them ideal targets for Renamo, and gave them no protection if they wanted to shoot back. Not surprisingly, the army was reluctant to accompany this sort of convoy; sometimes soldiers demanded bribes or stole goods in exchange for risking their necks sitting out in the open perched precariously on top of the piled sacks of grain.

Under these circumstances, convoys ran irregularly, often dependent on the whim of a military commander. Zambézia, where most districts were accessible only by convoy, shows the problem. In the first eight months of 1988, there were regular fortnightly convoys on the main road from Quelimane to Mocuba and Lugela, but in the whole period there were only 12 other convoys; Mopeia was reached four times and Ile only twice.

In several provinces Agricom, the state marketing board, and the DPCCN established their own forces. The soldiers were given food and a few perks such as soap and sugar. Some DPCCN lorry drivers were given bullet-proof vests and walkie-talkies for communication with the soldiers. Thus, in those areas, DPCCN and Agricom were not dependent on army convoys. They set their own schedules and could go into some rural areas where private traders would not go because of the risk of attack.

The April 1988 emergency appeal by the UN Secretary-General specifically called for "additional protected escort transport" to go with food convoys (UNSG 1988). Mozambique then launched a campaign to fund 130 steel-plated lorries to give soldiers some protection and allow them to fire back at Renamo, reducing the likelihood of attack. The chassis are imported and the bodies are built in Mozambique, at a total cost of around $75,000 (£45,000) per vehicle. By 1989 there were 12 such trucks operating with food convoys in southern Mozambique. None were attacked, although Renamo attacks on other food convoys continued at the normal level (UNDSPQ 1990: 8).

Private armies

Protection forces open more of the country to commerce and something like normal life. But the proliferation of what are, in effect, private armies, may also be dangerous. These armies are under the command of business people, transport operators, and foreign private companies. And there is a loss of sovereignty in giving Lonrho or an Italian dam contractor a tract of land and allowing them to establish a private army to protect and control it. Indeed, it smacks of a return to colonialism.

Suffering Must be Seen

Perceptions of Mozambique's emergency shifted slowly, as a food aid seminar in April 1987 at the Institute of Development Studies at Sussex University in England showed.

Discussing Mozambique, "concern was expressed at the apparent initial lack of attention that was being paid by the Western media to the strong political dimensions of the present situation. The comparisons (felt to be erroneous by participants) between the situation in Mozambique and the Ethiopian famine that had been made repeatedly by journalists and certain NGOs were felt to be partly responsible" (Clay 1987: 33).

In 1987, journalists arrived expecting to find starving babies, as in the Sahel and Ethiopia (and, for that matter, Inhambane) in 1983. UN and government officials were continuously forced to stress the differences; there was widespread malnutrition but no

Man displaced by Renamo builds a new house in Chiweza, Gaza province (AIM: Joel Chiziane)

starvation, precisely because of the success of assistance efforts. Indeed, the absence of starvation meant that journalists and visiting delegations were always pleased if they happened to be visiting a refugee camp when a group of new arrivals struggled in from the bush. They looked ragged and hungry as starving people "should" look, and they made good newspaper photos and good stories for reports to head office.

The replacement of starvation by chronic malnutrition underlined that this was, in the words of the European MPs, a "permanent structural emergency". It was "structural" in two different senses. First, rather than resulting from natural disaster, the emergency had a structural cause, in apartheid, and would continue as long as destabilization continued. This also meant that many – perhaps most – of the victims could not simply go home when the flood waters receded; they had to rebuild their lives in a new secure place. But it was also "structural" in a second way. A target of destabilization was "structures" – physical infrastructures like bridges and schools, commercial infrastructure such as shops, and social infrastructure, notably government services. The suffering was exacerbated and extended by the destruction of these structures.

For both the donors and Mozambique, the special kind of emergency created new demands. First, and most bizarrely for the flying disaster specialists, it became possible to plan ahead – to say with some certainty what the "emergency" needs would be some months in the future. Second, rebuilding physical, commercial, and governmental structures became the most important way of relieving and preventing suffering. Third, the long duration of the emergency and its basis in a war of destabilization made it essential that normal life and even development go on in parallel with it.

In the event of a flood or even an unusual drought, it is reasonable to demand that donors and the recipient country divert all available resources to keep the victims from dying. But that is only practical for a short time. Mozambique's decade-long disaster requires a quite different approach: relief must stimulate the economy rather than disrupt it. This so contradicted the normal first-aid thinking of emergency donors that many were genuinely unable to understand.

Talk but no cash

In 1987 the Mozambique government defined a policy that refugees should be resettled, either in new villages or in existing villages and towns, even if they expected to return to their old homes when security conditions permitted. To fail to do so would be to create long-term dependence on food aid and a "spirit of apathy and resignation" while they waited. Within six months the displaced should be assigned a plot of land and be building a house. There should be help to establish a water supply, shop, school, and health post. Initially people would need free food, as well as tools and seeds (CENE 1987a).

Donors applauded Mozambique's desire to help people stand on their own feet and not become dependent on aid, but they were less ready to back their rhetoric with money. They proved unwilling to fund anything related to rehabilitation and development. Donations "which contribute to the recovery process at family level have not been forthcoming in sufficient quantity, and the international response has focused largely on short term relief", the national emergency commission, CENE, noted at the end of 1987. "This type of response is increasingly at odds with the focus of the Government of Mozambique's policy on addressing the needs for the relocation and rehabilitation of displaced people in new productive areas as a high priority" (CENE 1987b).

The March 1987 Geneva appeal contained various projects of this sort but few were funded. Dr Ratilal told donors at the April 1988 Maputo conference that only 3.5% of the value of donations in response to the 1987 appeal was "to develop agricultural activities and the water supply programme, which did not facilitate the stabilization of the displaced; only a small part of the displaced started production to respond to part of their needs."

Of $5.4 mn (£3.2mn) requested for water projects to improve the health standards of affected people, only $2 mn (£1.2 mn) was provided. "International response in the health sector was mainly concentrated on short-term provision of medical supplies", noted the UN Secretary General's appeal the following year, "while the much more complex process of rehabilitating the severely affected health network, necessary to restore access to basic health care to millions of Mozambicans, has received little support" (UNSG 1988).

There was little support for agricultural projects. Donors were unwilling to help strengthen the provincial agricultural directorates that had to design and implement resettlement projects for returning peasants. With the erratic rains and ever-present threat of drought, there was also a need for small-scale irrigation projects, but most donors were strongly opposed; even the irrigation of vegetable patches was seen as too capital-intensive.

Confidential meeting

The initial failure of donors to accept the new line led Mozambique and the UN in 1988 to try to change the entrenched thought patterns of aid bureaucrats and planners. The first step was an unusual closed meeting at the British Foreign Office's private conference centre at Wilton Park, 1–4 February 1988. This brought together US, UK and other European government aid officials as well as UN, NGO, and Mozambican officials. Dr Ratilal told the meeting that it was necessary to reorient aid away from "meeting short-term acute emergency requirements to a more carefully planned and necessary linkage of emergency and rehabilitation activities." South African backed terrorists "have forced five million people, who lived on subsistence agriculture, from the land. Now they depend on imported food." The goal of aid should be to make these people self-sufficient again. And the meeting participants agreed on the need to shift away from simple handouts and more toward self help (*Times* 6 February 1988).

"The prevailing assumption of earlier relief operations was that development aid would be provided only after emergency help." But meeting participants accepted that "experience has now shown that the way in which emergency help is given can be crucial in determining how successful long term rehabilitation will be."

The UN Secretary General's appeal document for the April 1988 donors' conference underlined these points. It stressed that "the Mozambican context combines aspects of emergency, rehabilitation, and development simultaneously, resulting in a long-term crisis with deep structural roots. The objective is thus to tackle the combined aspects of the emergency by using the aid provided in a manner which directly addresses some of its structural causes." This required "strengthening infrastructure [and] attempts to ensure local productivity". Each of the government's projects "have the combined objectives of relieving the current emergency, redressing the setbacks caused by the prolonged war of destabilization, and, in so doing, laying the foundations for future development" (UNSG 1988).

No development

Donors did not accept the new line. There was little support for integrated rural development projects for resettled refugees. Donors were even unwilling to provide tools for housebuilding. In health, there were medicines and family kits for refugees, but little support for rebuilding health posts. Many donors said they wanted to help children but there was little interest in school building.

Donors provided only 24% of the funds requested for health in the 1988 appeal.

Health Minister Dr Leonardo Simão said that Mozambique had hoped to rehabilitate 247 rural health posts and centres with money from the appeal; but this aspect of the appeal had received "minimal" donor support, so only 2% of the work had been done (MIO 19 January 1989).

In the 1988 appeal, Mozambique announced the setting up of a materials fund to help prompt rebuilding without making special appeals and waiting a long time for a response. For example, the fund was used to buy a pump for a small-scale irrigation programme in Benga, in Tete, which would allow people to move from the refugee camp in the railway yard at Moatize and settle at Benga. In the first six months, only one donor responded. It provided a substantial amount of materials such as water tanks and roofing sheets made by companies in the donor country. No donor was prepared to put up money (CENE 1988b).

The April 1989 appeal noted that "pledging demonstrates a tendency to respond to needs in 'traditional' terms – that is, to fund requests for expendable items such as basic drugs, but not to assist in the rehabilitation of essential infrastructure and services." UNDP tried to underline Mozambique's goals with a brochure entitled "Rebuilding Mozambique Through the Emergency Programme". But again the appeal for rehabilitation help fell on deaf ears. In November, Cooperation Minister Jacinto Veloso warned that critical underfunding of rehabilitation would compromise efforts to resettle people, meaning that more food aid would be needed in future years. But donors still did not respond.

Emergencies cannot be planned

Despite paying lip service to the concept of "structural emergency" which could be planned for, donors never really understood. Ratilal tells of asking for help for a food airlift to try to prevent starvation, and being told that people had to be dying for lack of food before a request could be made for airlift funding (Ratilal 1990a: 147).

In 1988, Mozambique tried to present an appeal covering two years instead of one, because of the time and cost of preparing annual appeals. But donors would only deal with an emergency one year at a time, and did not pledge for the second year. The unique exception to this narrow thinking was WFP. Like nearly all donors, WFP had two distinct categories of assistance, "emergency" and "development". Emergency donations could only be approved for a four-month period. But in 1989, because of what was happening in Mozambique and several other countries, WFP created a new third category of "protracted emergency". This allowed long-term planning, and WFP was able to pledge 75,000 tonnes of emergency grain with delivery spread over 18 months – which permitted Mozambican authorities to plan ahead as well.

One of the most striking aid irrationalities was the conflict between those who wanted to prepare for future disasters and those who were helping people hit by the present one. At a national emergency meeting in October 1988, the Unicef representative Marta Mauras said that early warning systems such as weather forecasting should be strengthened, so that it was possible to plan for future droughts. This was particularly important because a number of meteorological stations in remote areas had been destroyed by Renamo. The April 1988 appeal had included a request for funds to meet this need, but no one was prepared to pay.

No link

Mozambique called for the traditional division between emergency and development aid to be broken down. At pledging conferences, donor representatives always gave strong support to Mozambique's attempts to link the emergency with rehabilitation and development, and many promised help. But when they returned home, they were rarely able to back up those promises with money. Mozambican officials, ever polite and anxious not to offend, argued that it was a problem with budgets. Governments had a separate purse for emergency, and could not shift it to anything they saw as development. It also reflected divisions within aid agencies, where the emergency desk often does not talk to the development officer.

Dr Ratilal in his book *Mozambique: Using Aid to End Emergency* admits that "few organizations, institutions, or international agencies make any systematic link between relief, economic recovery, and development activities." Yet "clear distinctions between the various sorts of problems can really only be made in the abstract, and then not very well" (Ratilal 1990a: 215).

"Experience demonstrates that funds for relief are easily mobilized as long as the suffering can be seen, photographed, and filmed. But after the first aid for the disaster, it is hard to obtain donor funds for rehabilitation or reconstruction of the means of sustaining life. And help for gradually eliminating the causes of the disaster is almost non-existent", notes Ratilal (1990b: 156). When he writes of "experience", it is his own.

In 1990, Mozambique and the UN finally abandoned all attempts to link emergency with rehabilitation and development. The April 1990 appeal included only relief items.

Not just blinkered bureaucrats

It was not simply a case of narrow-minded bureaucrats. There were bitter disputes over the use and control of resources (discussed in Chapter 8) and over the use of aid to force policy changes. And there were genuine disagreements over how best to help.

At the Wilton Park conference Mozambique argued that "donors should work through local government in an attempt to strengthen it, rather than operating in parallel. In the short run, this may slow down aid work, but would mean that when agencies leave, their working methods may have been adopted by local staff." Otherwise, Dr Ratilal warned, donors will be asked for food aid year after year because Mozambique will never be allowed to become self-sufficient (*Times* 6 February 1988).

This simple statement has two controversial points. First is the need to strengthen government capabilities. Some donors strongly oppose this, and use aid to weaken the government.

Second is asking donors be willing to "slow down aid work" in order to build up local capacity for long-term development. Many donors dismissed this out of hand as cruel, and said that suffering individuals must be helped now and at all cost – even at the long-term cost of Mozambican development.

From some, this was sheer hypocrisy. Several governments had been willing to see 100,000 starve to death in order to force policy changes in 1983. They were still using aid to force policy changes, and to weaken rather than strengthen the Mozambican government.

But among sympathetic donors, there was much angst over the issue. A friend from an NGO spelled out the irreconcilable conflict: "If I know that essential medicines won't get on the airlift unless I take them to the airport, what should I do? People may die if I don't. But if I do, we will never develop a system to get the medicines out; local officials will assume that I have taken on this responsibility and that I will do it in future."

The problem is real. Mozambique is underdeveloped and needs aid precisely because people are poorly educated, ill-trained, and inexperienced. The 15% adult literacy rate at independence means that people with two or three years of primary schooling are doing jobs that would require a fistful of O-levels in England, or a high school diploma in the US. Often they have been plugged into the job without formal training because no one else was available. However sincere and hardworking, they lack the wisdom that comes from experience. We too easily forget how many basic office, management, and planning skills we picked up in clubs, parties, and political organizations; how we were able to make our mistakes at college or university, or in a job where our errors wouldn't harm people. Mozambicans have little of that – one of the marks of a colonial heritage and of underdevelopment.

The lack of education and broad experience tends to make people slower, less flexible, and reluctant to take risks. This is a problem in an emergency like Mozambique's which demands creativity and flexibility. It *does* often take longer to get things done in Mozambique than in New York. The need is to support and train the officials who have the responsibility, and to help them to do their job better, rather than simply bypass them.

The matter is further complicated because Mozambique has its share people who are lazy, stupid, incompetent, and corrupt. I think this is actually less of a problem in Mozambique than in many places. Indeed, queuing in the bank in London, or trying to deal with the US government, I am reminded that officials in Britain and the US can be incompetent and obstructive as well. When we are abroad we idealize the level of efficiency at home.

The racism and paternalism of many aid people, especially in NGOs, is something to behold. Aid workers assume that because they are from the developed world, they have a level of "common sense" that Mozambicans do not have, and which qualifies them to make decisions even when they don't understand the problem. They assume that their limited experience running clubs or whatever really does qualify them to run multi-million pound aid projects. Mozambicans are assumed to be stupid and ignorant even about their own country. Some see Mozambicans as being uppity in expecting to play a controlling role instead of being passive and grateful victims.

Donor governments with clear political goals have played on this mix of arrogance and humanitarianism that characterizes so many aid workers. Such donor agencies have encouraged aid workers to reject the Mozambican line, to construct parallel structures, and to help individuals at whatever cost to the Mozambican system as a whole. In practice, then, well-meaning aid workers have often become pawns in a much more complex battle for political and financial control, and in attempts to weaken the Mozambican government.

7 Keeping Shops Open

"While acting to save lives is vital, the focus of emergency operations should be on two fundamental elements: establishing a basic and effective distribution network and developing household capacity to produce food." Central to the first of these is the "need to recuperate the commercial network," argues former emergency head Prakash Ratilal (1990a: 212).

As Prime Minister Mario Machungo explained, "the objective of destabilization is to paralyse our productive base, destroy our economic fabric, and create social instability" (C&D June 1990). To keep people alive while further rending the economic fabric is unintentionally to support the goals of destabilization.

The problem is not simply one of rescuing individual families from starvation. It is also necessary to maintain, rebuild, and strengthen the commercial and social infrastructure, to ensure that the rescued families do not remain mired in subsistence or dependent on charity forever. And it is vital to rebuild and revitalize those structures which were dedicated to a development strategy which benefited all Mozambicans and not only a privileged minority.

In many parts of the country, food aid plays a central role. It is dominant in terms of sheer volume, in terms of keeping people alive, and often in proportion to local production. Food aid can totally destroy the existing marketing and transport system, creating a rural chaos much worse than that caused by the flight of Portuguese traders in 1975. Or it can be used to support and build that system, so that normal marketing and trading is able to replace aid when normality finally returns.

For some donors, feeding the starving takes such a high priority that all else is swept away. Not one second of time nor one grain of maize can be diverted from this goal. But such a single-minded obsession with keeping people alive also creates long-term problems which keep these people dependent on hand-outs for years to come. It is also highly inefficient and often destroys structures and systems which could be helping to feed people more effectively. At its core, there is an arrogance in the view of some donors that they should descend like a *deus ex machina*, sweep all existing institutions and organizations to one side, and take over the feeding of the starving.

The government stressed that a "priority" of the emergency programme "will be the rehabilitation of the commercial network in the rural areas, mainly handled by private traders, [with donors] providing support in infrastructures, materials and transport, with the aim of reestablishing within two to three years a fully operational network able to meet the needs of the rural population, and avoid unnecessary free distribution" (CENE 1987b). Indeed, this has always been Mozambique's goal.

Destroying marketing in Inhambane

This issue was shown particularly starkly in Inhambane in 1985. Mozambique had never intended that the DPCCN would have an independent transport capacity; rather, in emergencies it planned to draw on the private and parastatal transport fleet normally used for agricultural marketing. In Inhambane, food aid was being carried to rural areas by Agricom, the parastatal marketing board, using lorries which had been donated by three different countries. The first problem was that the DPCCN did not have a transport budget, so it could not pay Agricom, which therefore was building up a deficit. This was partly resolved by a donation of second-hand clothing; it was agreed that half could be sold locally, and the money given to the DPCCN to pay for hiring lorries.

Inhambane is a normally dry province with trees adapted to the conditions. Thus, even though people had no food, they were able to gather tree crops: coconuts, cashew nuts, and mafurra fruit, which is used in soapmaking. Some sawmills also continued to operate. Thus some people had money and could buy food; others were refugees and had neither money nor food. Agricom carried food to rural areas, where it was sold or distributed free as necessary; on return trips, the lorries carried timber and cashew, as well as mafurra for the soap factory in Inhambane city.

But all this changed with the arrival of Care, at the end of 1984. According to people working in the province at the time, Care tried to displace other agencies which were already involved in food distribution. One provincial official told me: "The first thing out of their mouths when Care arrived was 'We have a lot of money. We can help you. But you have to do what we say'."

Agricom was indeed short of fuel, batteries, and tyres, and Care began to supply fuel. But it insisted that lorries using Care fuel had to return empty, and could not bring back cashew and other products. Agricom continued to carry small amounts of clothing, hoes, and so on along with the food. And it carried return loads, saying it still had to pay its drivers and pay for its lorries, and furthermore it had a responsibility to maintain marketing. Care argued that the time taken to load for the return trip delayed the supply of food to the starving, but few in Inhambane accepted this view.

Care insisted that its Logistic Support Unit (LSU) have an independent transport fleet, even though the Mozambique government was staunchly opposed to creating two completely different transport fleets for commercial and free food. Finally Care went to the governor and threatened to withdraw. Seeing no choice, the governor took all new lorries away from Agricom and gave them to Care's LSU, leaving Agricom with only four ancient trucks. Care was paying partly in foreign exchange, so some Agricom staff moved over to work for Care.

Care was convinced that feeding the hungry was the highest priority and must override all other considerations. And Care believed that this could best be done by a single organization, with foreign experts playing a key role. Care had considerable world-wide experience to draw on, but not everyone agreed with it. And the cost was high.

Now the lorries whizzed down the highway passing women sitting patiently at the roadside beside their piles of mafurra. Without mafurra, the soap factory closed, and the donors had to bring in soap. Unable to sell their produce, local peasants ran out of money and became dependent on food hand-outs. With no new lorries, Agricom's marketing network collapsed, so when the rains finally came there was no stimulus to resume production.

Who Carries the Food?

Many donors sent food and other goods as far as Maputo or Beira, and simply assumed that the government would distribute – totally ignoring the devastation of the economy which had caused the crisis in the first place. Perhaps the most extreme case was drums of used clothing that arrived labelled only "Jesus Loves Mozambique – Larry Jones Evangelical Mission" (Brennan 1985).

In a "normal" emergency, the Third World country is expected to cover local costs and put vehicles and staff at the disposal of the flying rescue teams. Similarly, development projects normally assume that local costs will be covered by the recipient and local staff will be provided. There are both social and practical reasons for this. Donors see that local contribution as a gesture of good faith and commitment; their attitude is quite rightly one of "why should we help if the recipient is not interested enough to contribute?" Second, many developing countries have underused trained people, and they can contribute non-convertible local currency. Unfortunately, the long-term and comprehensive nature of the crisis meant this was not true in Mozambique. Skilled people were in very short supply, and aid represented such a large portion of GNP that even local currency was not available. This problem was made much worse by structural adjustment (see Part III) and by conflicting donor policies.

WFP calculates the transport, handling, and storage costs for food inside Mozambique as \$85 (£50) per tonne (UNDSPQ 1990: 43). Mozambique simply does not have that kind of money, and the continued donor refusal to provide local costs caused serious problems. According to the former emergency head, "a shortage of funds to cover transport, often at provincial level, has left clothing, blankets, domestic utensils, and soap lying in warehouses while those who need these items continue to suffer unnecessarily" (Ratilal 1990a: 140).

And donors who were happy to give food were reluctant to give the lorries to transport it. Each of the March/April emergency appeals included a major component for transport, but it was often ignored or given a low priority. The April 1988 appeal asked for 730 vehicles (203 for the DPCCN, 200 for the Ministry of Trade, 206 for private traders, and 121 for use in the ports to speed unloading). Italy initially pledged 200, but that was never confirmed because of Italy's aid crisis. All other donors together promised only 135 vehicles. By February 1989 only 23 trucks had actually arrived; in that same period, Renamo destroyed 37, according to Cooperation Minister Veloso.

The April 1989 appeal admitted that "although the food aid received was inadequate to meet the basic needs outlined in the 1988 appeal, even this partial quantity exceeded the country's actual capacity to distribute" (UNSG 1988; C&D February 1989; *Mozambiquefile* March 1989). The April 1989 appeal was scaled down, and so was the response. Mozambique asked for 359 trucks; donors promised 89. Of those, 58 were from Sweden to the Mozambican government, 29 were from other donor governments to NGOs, and 2 were from an NGO's own budget.

By September 1989, most of the lorries promised 18 months before in response to the 1988 appeal still had not arrived. DPCCN Director Salomão Mambo told a press conference that "the number of trucks blown up or otherwise destroyed is greater than we have received," so that the DPCCN actually had fewer operational lorries than at the time of the April 1988 appeal. In Zambézia alone in the first 8 months of 1989, Renamo destroyed 13 of the DPCCN's 64 lorries.

Which lorries?

Mozambique wanted lorries to be in the hands of traders, both private and parastatal, who did agricultural marketing. But the donors demanded a separate DPCCN fleet. A high Mozambican government official told me: "We had no choice. The donors made clear they would only give lorries to the DPCCN and not for commerce." And Care insisted on its own LSU fleet, with an entirely new set of garages and workshops.

It was a period when the rhetoric from the US and IMF was all about supporting the private sector, when their advisers were saying that owner-drivers made better use of lorries, and when the US even had a programme to sell tractors to private farmers. Yet it was "Marxist Mozambique" that wanted lorries to go to private traders, and the big donors who wanted the lorries to go to a big and inefficient state operation. At each appeal, Mozambique would say the DPCCN cannot grow any larger, but the donors refused to listen.

In 1987, "DPCCN received 233 trucks to ensure the free distribution of food supplies. The commercial structures which distributed four times more food supplies did not receive practically any means of transportation", noted Dr Ratilal. This was particularly serious considering that at the same time donors were giving food to be sold and not for free distribution. One result was that "although the 'non-affected' had money, they could not buy any food, and this generated an artificial emergency situation", Ratilal added.

In the March 1988 appeal, Mozambique proposed a hire-purchase system under which the private sector would buy the lorries in local currency, and in exchange agree to carry food and non-food items for the government at the official rates. "It is considered that the sale of trucks to private traders will result in a better penetration of the rural areas increasing the distribution and so stimulating trade at grass roots level." Again, in 1989 Mozambique asked for lorries for commercial food transport. Of the major donors, only Sweden responded; those countries which claimed to be promoting the private sector did not.

There were two successful exceptions to the general donor lack of interest. One was an NGO which agreed to give lorries to a trucking company in Mocuba, Zambézia, which was linked to the railways, and which operated a highly efficient service taking cargo from the Quelimane-Mocuba trains. The other was the Swedish-funded Transcarga. Created in 1988, Transcarga had a fleet of 37 large lorries to carry goods from the port of Beira to Tete, and in emergencies through Malawi to Niassa. Each lorry was assigned to a driver, who would buy the vehicle over several years, and then become a private transporter.

No money

The problem was not simply a shortage of lorries, nor just a shortage of foreign currency. In addition, there was a desperate shortage of local currency, because of the impact of the structural adjustment programme (see Part III). The massive devaluations had vastly increased local costs, while much of the emergency programme budget was limited by the general government spending limits imposed by the IMF. "This was compromising urgent relief work", admitted Cooperation Minister Jacinto Veloso (MIO 15 February 1990). In Nacala, the port periodically stopped the DPCCN from removing commodities because of outstanding unpaid debts (Newman 1990: 28).

The government always intended that DPCCN should hire lorries and use other means of transport, but it never had a sufficient budget for this. Donors refused to pay for local transport, saying that the government should at least pay that much, but structural adjustment meant the DPCCN never had a sufficient budget. The DPCCN's use of its own donated lorries was not affected by the budget cap, which led to foolish inefficiencies.

In Zambézia, the army had been protecting the road from Quelimane to Mocuba, but it eventually reopened the railway, which could carry much more cargo. This should have been a boon to the DPCCN, but it was not. It had no money to pay railfreight, whereas it did not have to pay to use its own lorries. So it could only send food to Mocuba when it could persuade the army to run a special convoy; and opening the railway did not improve food distribution, as it should have.

Finally in June 1989 CENE tried to solve both problems by formalizing what had already been going on quietly and encouraging the DPCCN to carry goods commercially. On trips out to districts up to a third of the cargo of food lorries would be commercial cargo, and wherever possible on return trips DPCCN lorries would collect grain, cotton, cashew and other peasant crops, as well as firewood and building materials. Earnings from this would then be used to pay DPCCN expenses (CENE 1989a).

In 1989, the DPCCN/LSU began to make use of contract truckers. The parastatal Camionagem de Maputo (CDM) carried 23,000 tonnes of food and relief items on the Maputo-Gaza convoy; Transcarga handled 2000 tonnes and private truckers in Nampula carried 2000 tonnes. Truckers were mainly state-owned because private traders were not willing to risk their lorries in insecure areas, and no donor would provide insurance. In some instances, however, contract truckers proved much more expensive. CDM quite rightly charged for the time spent waiting for convoys to be formed, which greatly added to the cost. (Newman 1990: 11)

The politics of road transport

By 1988 "privatization" was the key word, and the US had come around to some of the original Mozambican thinking on food aid distribution. The 1988 evaluation of Care support of the LSU said that LSU should be "providing transport services for agricultural marketing" as part of the "transition from emergency to recovery". This "will require occasional pushes from the outside" (Berger 1988: iv). Indeed, the evaluators seemed unaware that it was only "pushes from the outside", namely Care itself, that had separated food aid distribution from agricultural marketing in the first place. (It was also a classic example of the lack of institutional memory which is so common in the aid industry – because they do not know what went on before, consultants can be very proud of reinventing the wheel.)

In setting up the 1988 Care evaluation, USAID specifically requested the consideration of "privatization". Not surprisingly, the evaluation calls for the DPCCN to sell at least part of its fleet to the private sector, for donors to provide lorries to private traders rather than the DPCCN, and for the DPCCN to contract them to carry emergency cargo. The evaluation fails to explain how to persuade donors which provided lorries to the DPCCN instead of the private sector in the first place to allow the sale of those lorries. It also ignores the Mozambique government's continued attempts to get donors to provide lorries for the private sector. And it does not explain where the DPCCN will get the money to hire transport; indeed it supports privatization precisely as a way of reducing USAID funding (Berger 1988: 50, 66).

There is a genuine confusion here. On the surface, it seemed as if US officials had supported Care's efforts to take control of food distribution in a way that led to the disruption of agricultural marketing, then pushed to reverse that position. In fact, there was a mix of humanitarian, bureaucratic, and political motives. Many Care staff were genuinely anxious to feed the starving at all cost, and were convinced that the only way to do this was to take total control of all available transport – as their contract told them to do. Also at work was the bureaucratic imperative to expand as rapidly as possible.

But there is also an attack on Mozambican structures here. The US was hostile to Frelimo and particularly hostile to state marketing boards like Agricom; therefore embassy and USAID officials supported Care's takeover. Thus a two-stage process evolved – first destroy the alternative state-based structures and replace them with a Care-dominated state organization, then privatize. Clearly, transferring transport to a company like CDM was not the answer, because it was a state-owned company.

The politics of privatization are shown by the Care evaluation. The Ministry of Commerce and Agricom have already been working with local small traders, especially in rural areas, to help them buy lorries as a way of stimulating marketing at the district level. Typically, these are small operators with only one lorry. The evaluation dismisses this policy as selling lorries to "less efficient but politically acceptable transporters". Instead it calls for the lorries to go to "large transporters with three or more trucks" and normally more than ten. There are only about 15 such operators, largely based in Maputo and Beira and generally operating only on main roads. They have already shown an interest in using the vehicles in international trade (Berger 1988: 55–59). Some Mozambicans had a very cynical view of this proposal. First, they pointed to the social and racial implications: the larger operators tend to be white or Asian, while the smaller traders are more often black. Larger operators were more likely to have been in business in colonial times, and supporting them could be seen as part of the process of reinstituting colonial economic structures. Second, small traders who had had lorries and shops destroyed by Renamo would be more likely to support Frelimo if the government helped to re-equip them. The experience of Chile seemed relevant: there, it was the larger private transporters who went on strike as part of the US overthrow of Salvador Allende in 1973.

Road or air?

Mozambique is a big country – the size of Britain and France together – with a relatively small population. Flying over provinces like Zambézia which are densely populated by Mozambican standards one crosses vast tracts of unpopulated woodland. This ideal bandit country makes it almost impossible to root out Renamo completely. After the 1986 invasion, the joint Mozambican-Tanzanian-Zimbabwean force retook the main towns, and refugees flooded into (and were pushed into) those towns. This continued in 1988 and 1989 as the government recaptured more towns. Initially, the only safe access to many of these isolated towns was by air, and relief supplies had to be flown in.

This is an expensive process, as a small plane can only carry three tonnes of cargo. In 1989, more than 400,000 people received 12,300 tonnes of airlifted food, at a cost of $8.4 mn (£5 mn) – nearly $700 (£400) per tonne (UNDSPQ 1990: 8, 51). Donors provided only $7.2 mn, so the government of Mozambique had to use $1.2 mn of its own scarce foreign exchange to keep these people alive.

As security improved, it was increasingly possible to reach these towns by road, at least in convoy. But the roads were in poor condition, and Renamo had destroyed many small bridges; passage was slow and difficult at the best of times and impossible during the rains. As well as being hard on the vehicles, slowing down to ford small streams made strings of lorries sitting targets for Renamo attack.

So Mozambique asked donors to help repair roads and bridges, at much less cost than continuing the airlift. The 1989 appeal asked for $12.4 mn (£7.4 mn) for road repair, but donors offered only $2 mn (£1.2 mn). Road building, it seemed, was development, which had to be programmed years in advance and come from the normal aid budget; it could not come from the emergency budget. Zambézia province had a disabled bulldozer which could have returned to roadwork with just a few spare parts and a mechanic, but even that was considered development and not emergency. Airlift costs continued to be well above expectations purely because roads and bridges were not repaired. Donors continued to fund airlifts, while complaining about the cost and admitting that it would be cheaper to repair the roads.

Or by sea?

Mozambique has a long coastline. Most of the biggest towns and many smaller ones are ports, and about a third of the population can be reached by sea or river. Furthermore, sea transport of bulk cargoes like grain is cheaper than road and very much cheaper than air. Mozambique has two state-owned coastal shipping companies, Navique and Transmaritima, and it seemed only logical to build up coastal shipping capacity.

But this did not fit with normal donor thinking. The appeals always included requests for boats and for port improvements, but there was little response. On the ground, Care officials forced the LSU to concentrate on road transport, perhaps because their experience had been gained largely in places like Sudan and Ethiopia where coastal

Loading sacks of aid maize flour on to a landing craft in Quelimane, to be transported up the coast to Pebane (J. Hanlon).

shipping is not significant. WFP did prioritize coastal shipping, but insisted on hiring and running its own boats.

By 1989 donors did begin to accept the logic of the government attitude. Funds were provided to allow Navique to hire (and in one case to buy) boats, and some upgrading of ports began, speeding up the loading and unloading of cargo and thus increasing the utilization of the existing boats. A new WFP head reversed previous policy, ended direct charter arrangements, and instead made contracts with Navique and Transmaritima. Port equipment and barges that had been operated by WFP were passed on to the Mozambican companies.

An unusual arrangement was worked out in Sofala province, where owners of ten private boats were given spare parts and other equipment by a bilateral donor to rehabilitate their boats, and carried emergency food to pay for the equipment.

Efficiency or racism?

Mozambican government officials, notably Dr Ratilal, were anxious to use the transport of emergency supplies to build up local capability. Not only did they want to help rebuild the local economy, but they also wanted to build local capacity to deal with emergencies when they were less popular with donors and less help was available. Thus they wanted Navique to do the coastal shipping and the national airline LAM (Linhas Aéreas de Moçambique) to do the airlifts. In this they received strong support from Mark Latham, who became WFP operations director in Maputo in 1990: "The way to go is to build up local capacity and systems and work through that. Transport is not our function."

But most donors preferred independent boats and wanted Air Serv for the airlifts, allegedly on grounds of efficiency. In practice, however, it often seemed that they preferred to deal with people from the developed north rather than Mozambicans. This was a complex mix of racism and arrogance (and black Americans can be at least as condescending and arrogant to Mozambicans as white Americans). And it is notable that use of Navique increased precisely when the donor providing development assistance to Navique insisted that it be put under the management of a coastal shipping company from the donor country.

Can the Hungry Pay?

Mozambican ministers have always been very worried about aid dependency, and the development of a hand-out culture. They tried to avoid this by selling as much food as possible and keeping the market functioning. This was not unreasonable. In periods of drought or flood, people often have cash savings even when they have run out of food stocks, and are prepared to buy if food is available at a reasonable price. Even the displaced and affected sometimes have money. In refugee settlements there are civil servants like teachers who have a cash income. Thus Mozambique always put priority on channelling food aid into the commercial network.

There are two other reasons for this. First, much food aid goes to the towns and cities, where supplies have dried up because of the collapse of peasant marketed production. These are people who have jobs and normally pay, so it is foolish to give them free food. Second, Mozambique wants to keep refugees on the land in rural areas and reduce urban migration. Therefore, the government does not give free food to anyone in towns – even to refugees who have moved in with relatives. And in rural areas, it tries to ensure that there is free food for those who need it, and food in the shops for those who can pay.

Many donors want to give free food, even in cities. The Mozambique government had largely controlled distribution, but as NGOs gained power this was less true (see Chapter 17).

Donors are very rigid about whether or not their food aid can be sold, and the balance varies sharply from year to year. In response to the 1987 appeal, donors pledged 99% of the request for food to be sold, but only 36% of the requested free food for the DPCCN. (UNSG 1988) This left the DPCCN and the refugees short of food. In response to the 1989 appeal, donors pledged 83% of the request for maize needed for free distribution, but only 36% of maize for marketing, leaving the cities short (*Priority Requirements* 30 April 1990). The "continuing decline in nutrition levels in urban areas" is probably due to this shortfall, warned the UN (UNDSPQ 1990: 6, 32).

Another problem is that most food aid programmes are linked to the donor's own surpluses, and not what Mozambicans need or want. Rice is eaten by the middle class in Maputo and a few other cities, but not much elsewhere, so it is never high on the list of requests; the requests are always overfilled. Wheat is not grown in Mozambique but is always available from donors, which encourages the shift from maizemeal to bread, thus creating a permanent import dependence. In Africa white maize is preferred, compared to yellow maize in the US and Europe. A number of donors, notably WFP and the EC, buy surplus white maize from Zimbabwe and donate it to Mozambique. Others, however, donate surplus yellow maize. The US actually shipped surplus US yellow maize to South Africa, trucked it through Zimbabwe which at the time had 1 million tonnes of surplus white maize, and then sent it on to Mozambican refugees in Malawi. A USAID official admitted that they hoped Mozambicans "will acquire a taste for American yellow maize" (Thompson 1990).

A bit of sugar in the tea

People cannot survive only on grain, and Mozambique has also asked for beans, vegetable oil, sugar and other foods. Donors have not been sympathetic, because these are not surplus in their countries. Sugar causes a particular problem. From colonial times Mozambique was a major sugar exporter, and considerable amounts were available locally, so poor people became accustomed to using sugar as a source of energy as well as for brewing. Renamo destroyed three of the five sugar mills and disrupted production at the other two; production fell from 115,000 tonnes in 1980 to 35,000 tonnes in 1986, which is just half of local demand (UNSG 1987). Mozambique asked for quite small amounts of sugar, but eventually had to use balance of payments support to buy sugar on the world market because no one would donate it.

Donors did, however, send Mozambique food it did not ask for – and without asking if it was wanted. One donor sent tonnes of surplus tinned tomatoes, despite the fact that tinned tomatoes are one of the few things still produced in Mozambique. Wine has been sent as part of emergency relief, and was no doubt much appreciated by the foreign aid workers and Mozambican officials. Frozen pork was sent to a predominantly Muslim zone (Ratilal 1990a: 149). One donor sent special high energy biscuits without asking the Mozambicans. They were neither needed nor popular with refugees, who needed bulk food instead of high protein; they did prove popular with the middle classes as biscuits with tea, however. Surplus dried milk was always popular with donors, even though Mozambique always tried to discourage it; this has ended since the European "milk lake" dried up.

Wrong place or wrong people?

One of the most depressing sights in any emergency operation is food in the wrong place; warehouses full of food in a zone of relatively well-fed people while somewhere else the hungry sit waiting in front of empty stores. Sometimes it is simply bad planning, but more often it is a problem with donors.

Delays in supplying so-called emergency food are much longer than is generally realized. Although shipping times are not great, no emergency food arrives sooner than six months after it is promised. Most takes a year, and 18 months is not uncommon. Delivery time is also highly inconsistent and unplanned. Shiploads arrive unannounced or without explanation do not arrive when they are supposed to. This makes it virtually impossible to plan, and leads to a hand-to-mouth existence. In Maputo, bread often runs out because wheat shipments are inexplicably delayed.

At the same time, donors often insist that their aid go to a particular place – usually the place where food was short when the appeal was made. Despite government and UN appeals, the problem became worse as donors specified geographic targets for a larger proportion of food (Cene 1989b: 17).

One donor took a year to send urgent beans and cooking oil to Zambézia. By the time they arrived other donors had filled the gap and there was already enough to last eight months; the biggest problem was a lack of warehouse space and the new beans (as well as unwanted dried milk from another donor) took up scarce storage space. Eventually the unwanted oil was quietly swapped for maize from the commercial sector, because free maize was in short supply, and the maize was distributed to refugees.

In other cases, donors change the destination of food without telling the government. One donor bought maize in Zimbabwe and was supposed to send it to Tete where it was desperately needed; instead it was sent to Gaza in the south, where it was not needed and there was no handling or storage capacity.

Some donors insist that certain grain is either free or for sale. It is not even overall quantities, but specific sacks of maize; sometimes Mozambique is not even allowed to transport maize which is free and maize for sale on the same lorry. The effect is that shops may be full while refugees wait for the DPCCN free food which never arrives, or the DPCCN hands out free food while people with money wait in vain to buy.

A similar problem comes about because IMF-imposed financial restrictions mean that the DPCCN cannot buy food even when it is available. War is not everywhere, and the 1988–89 rains were good in the north, leading to a good harvest. Agricom bought substantial amounts of maize and other crops from peasants, but the war and lack of transport sometimes meant it stayed in warehouses.

In early 1990, one donor reported that newly arrived displaced people in Lugela were hungry, while the nearest DPCCN warehouse, in Mocuba, was empty. But a few yards away there were hundreds of tonnes of food stored by a private trader, which the DPCCN had no money to buy. No donor would give it funds. So it was appealing to NGOs which had funds for transport to organize a shipment of DPCCN food from much farther away.

Food swaps

The obvious answer is to swap, but some donors are horrified at the idea; such swaps are sometimes reported as "corruption". Finally, in 1989, a few donors began to relent and the DPCCN was able to swap nearly 5000 tonnes of maize with Agricom. In general, Agricom maize was taken a short distance to refugee camps, and in exchange Agricom was given aid maize in cities where they put it into the normal marketing system. Both the DPCCN and Agricom saved money on transport; refugees had food more quickly.

Buddy Dodson, the food programme officer in the US embassy, told me that each such swap required special approval in Washington – which was rarely forthcoming because "we wouldn't swap good US corn for poor quality Agricom grain." There is a certain irony in this, because in Mozambique donated US yellow maize is considered very inferior to Agricom white maize.

And swapping maize for other food is totally out of the question. In Pebane there were thousands of refugees in need of food. It is not a good area for growing maize or rice, but it is a traditional fishing zone. The fishermen had stopped work because Renamo had cut the road to Gilé, the traditional market, and the refugees had no money to buy. The DPCCN had no money to buy, either. It asked donors if it could give grain to fishermen in exchange for fish which would, in turn, be given to refugees, but they refused – their food was only to feed hungry refugees, and not fishermen, who were not displaced. Similarly, the DPCCN wanted to trade aid food for salt produced in saltworks along the Zambézia coast; this would have created jobs and the salt was much in demand by the refugees, but donors were not interested.

The one exception was the World Food Programme. Its Maputo office developed a programme which drew enthusiastic support from both the Mozambican government and WFP headquarters in Rome. In Inhambane WFP used aid food to stimulate the economy, helping to rebuild the marketing system that had been broken by Care's singleminded stress on food distribution. Maize, sugar and cooking oil were provided to local traders who took them into rural areas to trade for mafurra and cashew, and for high quality maize that could be used as seed. In coastal areas in 1989, 2100 tonnes of aid food were traded for 550 tonnes of dried fish. The fish and seed were in turn given to refugees elsewhere. Cashew marketing doubled, because private traders were willing to go into dangerous areas, which meant that people the DPCCN would not have reached received food. The programme had been worked out with the encouragement of the local governor, but some donors were not told because they wanted the food to go directly to peasants without any intermediaries.

Money, not food, for work

Many donors encourage "food for work" programmes, under which free food is given to refugees and others as payment for road building and other work. The government staunchly opposes this, arguing that people should always be paid for work. Yet again, the "Marxist government" supports the market and the "capitalist US" and other donors try to undermine the market.

The government argues that if people are given money, they can use it to buy food if they want, but they can also grow food and use the money to buy other essential goods such as clothing. If food is genuinely short in an area, which it often is, then the aid food should be put into the normal marketing system and people should be paid a wage which allows them to buy the food. Also, government officials feel that "food for work" is demeaning and creates a charity consciousness which makes people accustomed to hand-outs.

In this, the International Labour Organization (ILO) and WFP have been allies of the government. For labour-intensive road-building projects, ILO and WFP have a contract with the parastatal road-building company, ECMEP. ILO provides an expert to teach ECMEP staff to direct the work and WFP provides food which is sold to the workers at official prices. ECMEP pays the minimum wage in cash, and keeps the revenue from the food to help pay the project costs.

WFP's "Food Bank" was another imaginative solution to the problem. Under the "Food Bank" donated grain and other items were sold to enterprises to be sold to their workers at official prices – through local shops and cooperatives or directly at the workplace. One advantage of the system was that the enterprises already had transport, and could collect the food from the port, so little additional administration was required. Funds generated from the sale of the food were not used by the enterprise for ordinary expenses, but to employ additional workers, pay bonuses, and carry out rehabilitation.

The "Food Bank" served several purposes. Food shortages sometimes lead to absenteeism and other problems with workers in industry, who not surprisingly take time off work to search for food to feed their families if they cannot buy it. So the first goal was simply to keep existing workers working. The scheme was also intended for agricultural projects, for example to expand export crop plantations, to develop new farms in the green zones around cities, and for reforestation. The "Food Bank" was a mechanism to use food aid to pay for road works and well digging without actually exchanging "Food for Work".

But donors did not like it. WFP headquarters in Rome refused to back the idea, because it was not strictly "emergency", and WFP in Maputo got the "Food Bank" going by diverting food from other projects. In the April 1988 appeal 130,000 tonnes of grain were requested for the "Food Bank"; only 18,000 tonnes were pledged and none arrived during 1988. In 1989, pledges fell to 12,000 tonnes, and the Food Bank was abandoned the following year.

Rebuilding the Local Economy

One of the South African goals was to "destroy the Mozambican economy in rural areas" (see Chapter 3). The Mozambique government sees it as a priority to rebuild the rural economy, as part of its continuing development efforts, as part of the Economic Recovery Programme (PRE – see Part III), and as part of its attempt to regain support in rural areas. And it hoped to use assistance for the "permanent structural emergency" as a way of doing so.

One of the biggest successes has been a programme to provide seeds and hand tools to refugees. In the three years 1987–89, 1 million people received 4 million tools and 26,000 tonnes of seed. Many became self-sufficient because of this. In 1989 Agricom purchases from the family sector were the highest in eight years, which was attributed to the seeds and tools programme (UNDSPQ 1990: 18). A wide range of donors participated, and most worked through Mozambican state companies – Agricom for the tools and Semoc for the seeds.

No consumer goods

But the donor goal of the seeds and tools programme is peasant self-sufficiency; marketing is not seen as a humanitarian issue, even though it also provides food for the hungry. At the end of 1983, the Ministry of Trade put forward a project to ask donors to support rural commerce. At the time, a ministry official explained to me that half of all shops were in the cities serving perhaps one-fifth of the population. The ministry wanted to encourage private traders and shopkeepers to return to rural areas and rebuild rural marketing. The 24 most productive districts (out of a total of 115) had been selected as priorities. For those districts, donors were being asked to provide consumer goods Mozambique could no longer afford to import, so there would be something to exchange so as to stimulate peasant production; they were also asked to fund lorries for the private traders. These were seen as three-year projects involving $1 mn (£600,000) per year per district – really quite a modest suggestion. The USSR sent substantial quantities of consumer goods, as well as supplying most of Mozambique's oil after 1983. But the big Western donors were not interested; they were unwilling to provide any money to Mozambique until it signed an IMF agreement. In the end, three European NGOs each took a district. (The irony was that the "capitalist" West was refusing to support private traders, while the Soviet Union and left NGOs did.)

In the first district where an NGO provided consumer goods in the 1984 marketing campaign, marketed production doubled. Still bilateral donors were not interested. Surprisingly, even the Nordics refused. The 1982 annual report for the joint Nordic agricultural assistance project (Monap) stressed that "the lack of consumer goods and implements to be sold in rural areas is probably the single most serious problem, besides the drought." A year later, the annual report noted that "the continued lack of consumer goods is otherwise [after the drought] the single most hampering factor in the marketing process" (MA 1983, 1984). Yet Nordic governments refused to allow Mozambique to transfer money from other activities to provide consumer goods for marketing.

In a truly heartrending letter, Mozambique asked one of its Nordic donors to transfer funds from a less important project to provide consumer goods in Tete province. "In the north of the province it rained normally and was a good agricultural year. But excess production which could go to the areas of starvation [in southern Tete] are going in large quantities to neighbouring countries [Malawi and Zambia] where the peasants can buy essential consumer goods." The Mozambicans wanted to buy basic goods – soap, used clothing, sewing materials, and some carpenters' tools – to be traded for food. The proposal was rejected in a brief two paragraph note.

An NGO in that country was one of the three which had taken on a district, and had expected, as usual, to receive support from its government. Unexpectedly, the government said no. So the NGO joined with others and collected used clothes, which were sent to Agricom to sell in the district. These used clothes caused peasant and cooperative marketed production to triple over three years; cassava marketing jumped ten-fold while bean and peanut marketing quadrupled; Agricom actually had storage problems.

Local buying

The government stressed that *most* people in the country were not affected by the war, and that in most areas industry and commerce still existed. But the economy was hit by the effects of the war, and many factories were not producing because of lack of orders. So donors were asked to buy locally whatever they could.

There were several notable successes. One NGO which had been bringing in clothes for refugees in Zambézia switched to importing the cloth from Zimbabwe and having the clothes made up by Favezal, a factory in Quelimane. The factory had been running at only 25% capacity due to lack of raw materials, and it took on additional workers and produced clothes for 50,000 refugee families. Distribution was handled by the DPCCN.

The NGO provided all of the scarce imported inputs, such as needles and thread. It paid for the work partly in meticais, and partly by providing an extra 10% of cloth to the company, which made it into clothes which it sold locally. After that proved successful, the NGO began buying the cloth from Textáfrica, a textile mill in Chimoio. Also, at the request of DPCCN officials, some cloth was distributed directly to district towns, where local tailors made up the clothes. Thus, as well as providing relief to refugees, the NGO also stimulated the local economy. Its donation worked twice.

A similar success occurred with the Maputo agricultural implements maker Agro-Alfa. In competition with Brazilian and other firms, it won an international tender from the International Fund for Agricultural Development (IFAD) for 2500 maize mills and 1000 maize shellers to be provided as aid to Mozambique. Such a contract is particularly important because it counts as an export, and some of the hard currency earnings can be retained to buy raw materials and spare parts for domestic production. Another IFAD order was won only after a struggle; in 1988 IFAD announced a tender for 500,000 knives for Mozambique to be delivered in less than a year. Agro-Alfa did not have the production capacity and could not even bid. But after some pushing from Agricom, which was to distribute the knives, IFAD reluctantly agreed to split the contract; Agro-Alfa won a tender for 50,000 knives which it was able to produce more cheaply than other bidders for the remaining larger contract.

The government has tried to use aid to stimulate local production of goods which will be needed by the donor agencies. Thus local seed production has been expanded, and a small private company in Maputo, Octavio Jesus Cardoso, was given help to tool up to produce a high-quality hand pump for installation in rural areas. Under pressure from government, donors did increasingly buy local pumps and seed. In all, more than 20 local firms benefited from donor purchasing (CENE 1988b: 14).

But many donors resisted the use of local industry because it was more difficult – precisely because Mozambique is an underdeveloped country in need of assistance. Thus it is not always simple to find out what is, or could be, produced in Mozambique. When a manufacturer is found, it will normally need an advance of hard currency to import the raw materials and spare parts. And few Mozambican companies can prepare tender documents that will satisfy the big international agencies – Agro-Alfa is an exception precisely because it is part of an industrial development assistance package from one of the bilateral donors.

The big donors flatly refuse to deal with Mozambican companies because they cannot do the required paperwork. A UN official told me: "We are importing fishing nets that are available locally. I can walk into Equipesca here in Maputo and buy nets. But we need quotations, and Equipesca just can't cope." The small donors and NGOs often do not want to "waste" time. One NGO coordinator told me: "My head office will not allow me to buy locally. It is more time-consuming and our job is to help poor people, not stimulate local industry. And if we hired someone to do local buying, it would increase our overheads, which would look bad to the people giving us money. Furthermore, they want to keep control of buying decisions at head office."

The result is that donors import goods which are made locally, competing with local production and putting people out of work. Agro-Alfa also provides a good example of this. It installed a forge and planned to produce 500,000 peasant hoes per year. But donors flooded the market with 3 million hoes imported from China, at a price of $1 (60p) each – less than the cost of the steel, alleged Agro-Alfa officials. This will satisfy the market for several years to come, so it did not even try to start production. Similarly donors imported 25,000 ox ploughs even though Agro-Alfa produced them; four years later there were still unsold ploughs in the warehouse. As part of its private sector support programme, USAID imported tractors already equipped with harrows and ploughs; Agro-Alfa makes them, but USAID would not buy the local version because Agro-Alfa is a parastatal company.

In another instance, $2 mn (£1.2 mn) had been set aside to import hand tools, but the major import noted above meant it was not needed. Mozambique asked that the money be shifted to allow the import of raw materials for Mozambican companies to produce consumer goods to trade for the food the peasants would produce with their new hand tools. But the donor refused, and the money was never spent.

The World Bank, which is supposed to be helping Mozambican companies, is sometimes one of the worst offenders. It ran a conference in Mozambique in 1988 and brought everything from the US. The invitation list was telexed to the US, where the printed invitations were prepared and sent back to Maputo by courier. The headed notepaper was printed in the US, even though Mozambique has a relatively sophisticated printing industry. Even the drinks were brought in. A Mozambican official added: "they also brought their own interpreter from English to Portuguese, so they could talk to us, but no one to translate Portuguese to English, since they didn't think we would have anything to say to them. We hired an interpreter locally, with higher qualifications, for a third what they paid to bring one to Maputo."

In some instances there have been bitter battles. As part of its shift to the market economy, the government has spun off a number a state enterprises as companies – state-owned but required to survive in the market place and earn a profit. Several well-drilling companies have been established in this way. In one province, an NGO provided the provincial drilling enterprise with money to allow it to rehabilitate its rigs, and the new company developed a record of successful and inexpensive wells. An NGO agreed to fund drilling in refugee resettlement camps in the province, but insisted that it bring in a rig from Zimbabwe. The government refused, saying that donor money had just been used to rehabilitate local equipment and it should be used. The NGO brought a Zimbabwean rig to the border, and began to claim loudly that Mozambique was unwilling to provide water for refugees; it also took a local director for a weekend in Zimbabwe to persuade him of the merits of the imported drilling rig. Finally, after ministerial intervention, the contract was split, half going to the Mozambican enterprise and half to the Zimbabwean. In the end the Zimbabwean firm did such a poor job that it was replaced by another Mozambican company, which had also been helped with aid money to repair its rigs.

In another instance, an NGO helped to set up seed production in a province badly hit by Renamo activity. A different NGO agreed to buy seed to give to local refugees, but did not trust the first NGO and refused to order seed from the project. Instead it imported seed which flooded the market so the small local seed farm could not sell its production.

In general, Mozambican officials will only complain privately about this. But in a rare outburst, CENE actually identified and criticized two big donors. In a booklet on the emergency, *Rising to the Challenge*, CENE called for donors to stimulate the demand for domestically produced goods. And it noted that "use of domestically provided services offers another area of potential demand stimulus by the agencies involved in relief work. The 'family kits' distributed to families adopting orphaned or displaced children, and 'agpaks' for farmers in the accommodation centres are currently being assembled abroad. The type of service could be acquired locally" (CENE 1988a). The use of names in this way was pointed, because Unicef distributed "family kits" and WV distributes "agpaks" (CENE 1988b).

8 Disaster Tourism

The interaction of aid with the war, commerce, and social and political life are in part issues of the control of aid. The previous chapters show that Mozambique had at least partly lost control of the aid process in the mid-1980s.

Detailed consultation and tight control had been the hallmarks of aid in Mozambique in the 1970s. Project, technical, and financial assistance from individual countries was always negotiated and agreed in a bilateral commission. There was a separate commission for each partner and each was chaired by a Mozambican minister. These joint commissions negotiated in detail all economic and development assistance (but not military cooperation which was organized separately and came almost entirely from the socialist bloc). The UN and solidarity groups which sent cooperantes normally responded to Mozambican needs and requests.

Mozambique used the system to set its own development strategies and gain foreign support for them. This close relationship led in many cases to mutual trust and respect, and did allow foreign partners considerable influence and power – sometimes much more power than they would have in a traditional aid relationship. Because of the shortage of skilled Mozambicans, cooperantes and other foreign workers often found themselves in policy-making roles in ministries, or as *de facto* heads of schools or projects. Mozambique allowed this to happen, and sometimes encouraged it; such a strict prior screening of people and projects had occurred that Frelimo felt confident that agencies and individuals working in Mozambique were in sympathy with its goals and work methods.

There were, inevitably, many mistakes made, including inappropriate courses and unsuitable projects. For example, Mozambique accepted Nordic advice that it should build an inappropriately sophisticated sawmill and particle board plant. East and West European donors and UN advisers all continued to support Frelimo's big farm bias. The structure ensured these were joint mistakes, which both the donor and the Mozambican government had agreed to.

The government created two structures to deal with foreign assistance. The National Directorate of Cooperation was established in 1976, just one year after independence, and it was to deal with technical and development assistance. It was part of the National Planning Commission. Its status was increased to that of a Secretariat of State for Cooperation in 1983. In addition, each ministry usually had an office to deal with foreign cooperation.

Emergency assistance was channelled through the DPCCN. It had been set up during the floods and drought of 1980, and was also within the National Planning Commission.

Its main task was to keep a close watch on the climatic situation and provide better warning of natural disasters. But it was also to be involved in distribution of emergency assistance and coordination of foreign emergency aid. Food aid, however, was largely organized by the Ministry of Internal Trade.

Controlling the vultures

The crisis of 1983–84 meant that this carefully constructed edifice collapsed. Mozambican officials had no experience of the freewheeling and freebooting international aid community that descended like vultures smelling a dying animal. By late 1983 the delegations were flooding unchecked into Maputo from international organizations, bilateral donors, and NGOs. Journalists, TV crews, and researchers joined the torrent. Each potential donor had to see starving babies for themselves; each expected to talk with a government minister, irrespective of whether their help was to be millions of dollars or a few old clothes. Delegations normally consisted of several people, who often expected to be put up at the best hotel in Maputo; some complained about the vagaries of the air conditioning and that the food was not up to international standard. Most demanded cars and translators. They expected to be flown to Inhambane, even though there was no scheduled air link. And looking at starving babies is hard and thirsty work, so all expected to be fed and watered during their brief stay in Inhambane.

Mozambique knew it had no choice. It was dependent on press coverage and on the first hand reports of the visitors if it was to attract food and break the *de facto* aid boycott. But it meant that the few available light aircraft that should have been flying food and medicines to Inhambane were in fact carrying tourists. Overstretched local officials who should have been trying to care for refugees flowing into the camps spent their time caring for foreign visitors, and using their few cars and jeeps to transport the gawpers. In Maputo, ministers and directors who were extremely busy trying to run a government spent endless hours patiently going through the same litany with each group.

As the northern winter deepened, the number of delegations increased. A UN official told me: "It was embarrassing. Some missions who came were totally unqualified, uninformed, and unprepared. We gave them up-to-date reports, which they didn't even read. They insisted on talking to a minister, who told them what was in our report. Then their report would consist entirely of government-supplied data and be identical to our handout.

"In January several UN agencies who had nothing to do with famine relief telexed us to say they were sending fact-finding missions. They did not ask, they just told us they were coming. Oto Denes, who as UNDP Representative was also Resident Coordinator of UN activity in Mozambique, was furious. He fired off a telex to the UN Secretary General asking him to stop sending so many UN missions. And he sent replies to everyone planning to send a mission with a detailed report compiled jointly with the government, and saying that if they wanted more information they should ask. The missions stopped, and no one ever asked for more information."

The NGO landing

Next came the flood of donors planning to set up on the ground, particularly in Inhambane. The shock troops were the NGOs. Some came on their own, some through governments and the EC, and some under UN auspices. Church groups, largely excluded in the past, were prominent in the first wave. All wanted office space and housing in Maputo and facilities in the provinces – immediately. Failure by an overworked official or minister to respond to a donor demand was taken either as further evidence that Third World governments do not want to help their own starving people, or as proof of cupidity.

Some NGOs set out for the provinces with virtually no liaison with the government.

In several cases an agency set up a project that duplicated something another agency was already doing. Some tried to bypass the government health and food distribution system. By early 1984, one NGO had already been expelled from Inhambane for refusing to cooperate with the government. Dissatisfied with the available infrastructure, the NGOs began to establish alternative systems. For example, Mission Aviation Fellowship set up an airline, known as Air Serv, especially for the donor agencies.

Others tried to work through the government, but this was a slow and frustrating process. The government had no experience of NGOs, and was surprised by the large number that arrived. It had no idea how to sort out those with useful skills and expertise from the young, enthusiastic, and often inexperienced volunteers pitching up on its doorstep. And it had no idea how to slot them into its very structured thinking.

Meanwhile the presence of bilateral donors, the UN, and the IMF and World Bank was increasing rapidly.

Dazzled by the headlamps?

At first, Mozambique lost control of the aid process. Like an animal dazzled by car headlights, the country seemed paralysed and did not know which way to turn. Neither Frelimo nor the donors were worried about long-term structures, because everyone felt that the problem was relatively short-term.

And dealing with the donor onslaught was simply not a priority for Frelimo. The war was the first priority, and the Nkomati Accord promised peace, or at least breathing space to regain the initiative. The second priority was dealing with the IMF and World Bank, and finding an economic programme acceptable to them. Linked to both was the need to satisfy the Reagan administration and the West.

Only with the increase in destabilization in 1985 and 1986 did Frelimo and the donors realize that this was not a short-term problem but a "permanent emergency". Frelimo moved to regain the initiative. It developed a framework to monitor and regulate the plethora of foreign agencies, and eventually asserted a surprising amount of control over the aid invasion.

But the donors had moved faster, using their early freedom to carve out fiefdoms and establish their independence from the government. Some set out consciously to undercut government policy and undermine the very fabric of Frelimo's social contract with the Mozambican people.

Several different bodies, both UN and bilateral, often pretending to act through government structures, tried to take control of donor coordination. There were bitter bureaucratic battles for dominance over the aid process with infighting between the UN and bilateral donors, among bilateral donors, between UN agencies, between the government and the donors, and sometimes between groups within the government.

Within Mozambique, there was a need to balance emergency and development aid and financial assistance linked to structural adjustment, as well as to clarify the relative roles of local and national officials.

What Role for the UN?

In early 1984 UNDP took an important role in coordinating donors, ensuring they worked within government structures but also informally taking on the role of preventing overlaps and suggesting where NGOs might best work. In March, UN Coordinator Oto Denes issued a joint appeal for international assistance, and began issuing a monthly *News Bulletin* which was circulated to the donor community and Mozambican government officials "to provide as much up-to-date information as possible" on relief and rehabilitation assistance. He also hoped that publicity in the *News Bulletin* would stimulate competition between donors, and thus generate more aid. UNDP established a coordinating group in which donors met regularly with Mozambican and UN officials; Denes hosted a series of sectoral donor coordination meetings, for example in health and transport.

Initially donors (and the government) concentrated on Inhambane and Gaza provinces, probably because they were more accessible from Maputo. But in early 1984 it became clear that there was also a crisis in Tete province, where at least 100,000 refugees had fled across the border to Zimbabwe. There had been no rain in three years, and MNR/Renamo activity had cut off relief supplies (Smart 1984; *News Bulletin* 27 March 1984). The UN organized a special meeting on Tete.

Several of the UNDP people were sympathetic to Frelimo and built a good relationship with the government, so Mozambican officials were prepared to allow the UN temporarily to take on a coordinating role. This continued until the end of 1984, by which time most of the major donors had established a presence.

But UN efforts to coordinate aid were hampered by the inexperience of the UNDP team, most of whom were newly arrived in 1983. The problem was compounded because Mozambique was considered a hardship posting because of the war, the lack of night-life in Maputo, problems with children's schooling, etc. For some UN agencies Maputo became a dumping ground for people who could not be sent elsewhere; Mozambique did not often get the best or most experienced UN people. Most of the UNDP staff were new and did not know UN policies and procedures. Matters were made worse because none had any experience of disaster coordination.

Denes appealed to the UN in New York for advice and help, but none was forthcoming. One former UNDP official commented: "It seemed like the UN had no institutional memory, and that it had learned nothing from previous disasters in Ethiopia and elsewhere. We screamed for a year but received no help." The UN did send a consultant who organized a week-long seminar on long-term planning and coordination to prevent famines in future natural disasters; it would have been useful a year later, but at the time Mozambican officials were too busy dealing with starving people and demanding donors to make any effective use of the seminar.

Finally, there was intense inter-agency competition, particularly within the UN "family". For example, UNDP had difficulty obtaining food data from WFP, which was also part of the UN system. Different UN agencies brought in competing consultants to look at the same problems. In an extreme case, an NGO team arrived under the general auspices of the UN, and two different UN agencies entered a bitter battle as to which would control the project. The dispute was never resolved; after two months sitting in the Hotel Polana in Maputo doing nothing, the team left in disgust.

Similar problems were adding to the affliction of drought elsewhere in Africa. In late 1983 the UN in New York asked its African missions to send regular "situation reports" (sitreps). As far as Maputo UN staff could see, nothing was done with these sitreps. But in March 1984 UN Secretary-General Perez de Cuellar was concerned enough to set up a special office in Nairobi, which in December 1984 became the Office for Emergency Operations in Africa (OEOA). It was supposed to coordinate the activities of other UN agencies, but the big traditional agencies such as Unicef, FAO, and UNDP saw OEOA as a competing agency and refused to cooperate. There was already an agency, the UN Disaster Relief Organization (Undro), set up for the same purpose several years before but also throttled by inter-agency competition. Not only did OEOA compete with the big agencies, it also competed with Undro, and it never had a chance. OEOA was never of any use to Mozambique; it was abolished in October 1986.

Finally, in mid-1985, Undro did send two people to set up a special emergency operation, but by then Care had taken control. In mid-1985, too, Arturo Hein became the new UNDP representative and UN Resident Coordinator. Initially the emergency was not his priority, and the UN system allowed Care to take the lead. In December

1986 there was a major press campaign by British NGOs about the growing emergency (see Chapter 3). Oxfam and Save the Children sent a telex to the UN Secretary-General's Office urging him to take the lead in alerting the world to the famine and to appoint a high-level special emergency coordinator, like Kurt Jansson who had been Assistant Secretary-General for Emergency Operations in Ethiopia in 1984–86 (*Guardian*, 24 December 1986).

Perhaps surprisingly, the US was also putting pressure on the UN to take a higher profile. In January 1987 the outgoing US ambassador, Peter de Vos, declared Mozambique a disaster area. In February, USAID urged UN Secretary-General Perez de Cuellar to appoint a special emergency coordinator (Stacy 1987). "Ethiopia seemed finished and the Sahel was OK, so Mozambique seemed a good next stop for the 'disaster circus'", one of the many UN consultants who visited Mozambique during this period told me.

UN officials in New York wanted to know why it was NGOs and not the UN which was taking the lead. Abdulrahim Farah, UN Undersecretary-General for Special Political Questions, was sent to Mozambique to investigate. He called for the UN to appoint a special representative at Assistant Secretary-General level. Farah also urged a special donors' conference. The Mozambique government was not enthusiastic about the pledging conference, because it feared that a special emergency meeting would divert attention from higher priorities such as debt rescheduling and more general economic assistance. But Farah pushed and Perez de Cuellar agreed, so the conference went ahead on 31 March in Geneva.

But Perez de Cuellar resisted pressure from the US and Farah for a new high-level representative. The appointment of Jansson over the heads of local UN officials in Ethiopia put many noses out of joint there; his appointment was also fiercely opposed by the heads of FAO and UNDP (Jansson 1987). Suggestions for a similar appointment in Mozambique drew fire from all the competing bureaucracies and from UNDP head Hein. This opposition overrode demands from Farah and the US, and on 27 February Perez de Cuellar simply promoted Hein to be UN Special Coordinator for Emergency Relief Operations (UNSCERO). This was lower status than Jansson had in Ethiopia and Hein was not initially given any extra staff. So the UN never played the key role in Mozambique that it had in Ethiopia.

Not only did Hein fail to coordinate aid to Mozambique, he had difficulty controlling his own fractious UN staff in Maputo. In particular, he was in conflict with two key agencies which were theoretically under his control: Unicef and WFP. UNDP did not control the funds for either, and there were deep personal and bureaucratic conflicts. Hein and Unicef head Marta Mauras were both from Chile and home conflicts seemed to have struck new roots in Maputo. In Maputo, Mauras was rapidly building an independent empire which led to her promotion in 1988 as head of the Unicef Africa Section. WFP representative Dieter Hannusch dismissed Hein as too pro-government; he felt WFP should be "independent", offering advice rather than a sympathetic ear.

Maurice Strong, visiting Mozambique in August 1987, also looked at the UN. Strong had been Executive Coordinator of the unsuccessful OEOA, but he had been much more successful as a fixer in a variety of important UN and development roles (Jansson 1987: 18). In his confidential but widely circulated report, Strong was caustic about the "lack of UN leadership" over the emergency, which he attributed partly to Hein but largely to "the lack of adequate headquarters support and resources". Hein's appointment as coordinator "was not accompanied by the kind of increase in status required to assert effective leadership over other local heads of organizations and agencies." He concluded that the government and donors were getting on with the job, and there did not seem to be any "real need at this point for overall UN leadership."

Perhaps stung into action by Farah and Strong, Hein in his quiet way did eventually serve a useful role in building donor support for the government. He once told me: "I always consider it my role to support the government." He did this through his presence at government-run meetings, and by throwing the UN's weight behind government analyses and appeals at donor conferences. In this way, Hein did give the government significant additional credibility with the donors. In addition, he stressed that Mozambique was very different from Ethiopia in both the cause and the nature of the emergency, and thus had to be treated differently.

Former emergency head Prakash Ratilal commented that "one of the most valuable contributions from the United Nations to the emergency programme revolves around the perceived role of the UN as an intermediary between the international community and the government" (Ratilal 1990a: 179).

Bringing Donors into Line

The Mozambican government did finally move to reassert control over the emergency. Under some pressure from Hein and various donors and consultants, Cooperation Minister Veloso announced a new structure for handling the emergency on 27 April 1987. A new Comissão Executiva Nacional de Emergência (CENE – National Executive Commission for the Emergency) was created. Veloso was chair, with trade minister Aranda da Silva as his deputy. Ministries of Agriculture, Health, Transport, and Defence were also represented on CENE.

CENE was to take direct control of the management of the emergency. Dr Ratilal, deputy minister of trade and thus already da Silva's deputy, was named CENE Coordinator and was in charge of day-to-day operations. The DPCCN, which had formally been under the National Planning Commission but in practice had run emergency coordination itself, was put under CENE and under the control of Ratilal.

The change was an essential step in reasserting control over donors and coordinating donor efforts. Although there was still a division between emergency and development aid, both in donor offices and in Mozambique, all donor contacts were now with the Ministry of Cooperation.

Dr Ratilal moved quickly. Within a month he had established two regular weekly meetings. On Saturday morning a technical committee met, bringing together port and transport officials and others to break bottlenecks in aid distribution.

Weekly meetings with government

But it was the Monday morning meeting of the Comité Operacional de Emergência (COE – Emergency Operations Committee) which proved key. Ratilal and a dozen of the main donors sat around a big table, with other donor representatives present. Donors reported on problems such as lack of food or seed in areas where they were working, and aired complaints. Ratilal tried to solve problems and resolve disputes, and pressed donors to respond to particular emergency needs.

COE soon became *the* donor forum. All the major donors participated, including the USSR, which played an active role in the emergency. NGOs participated as equals with the UN and bilateral donors. By October, Hein was attending all meetings, which put the UN stamp of approval on government coordination of the emergency. Hein sat on one side of Ratilal and the new DPCCN head, Salomão Mambo, sat on the other; this underlined to all donors that there were no alternative channels – they could not bypass the government by going through Care or the UN.

At a typical Monday meeting, Ratilal, Hein, and Mambo would be joined at the main table by representatives of three UN agencies (UNDP, WFP, Unicef), four or five donor countries (typically Canada, Italy, Netherlands, US, and USSR), two NGOs (usually Oxfam UK and Save the Children UK), and the Mozambican Red Cross. In addition there were 20 to 30 other donors, as well as up to 10 Mozambican ministry and agency staff – a varying group which at times included commerce, agriculture, meteorology, customs, and ports representatives.

Ratilal became quite sophisticated in using the meetings to ensure voluntary donor cooperation and participation in Mozambican goals and policies. Inevitably donors had their own small group meetings to discuss various issues, but they never created an alternative coordination system. By forcing donors to air their complaints in public, he reduced the normal diplomatic and cocktail party gossip and backbiting about aid. Many of the exaggerated stories about Renamo actions, port tie-ups, corruption, etc. suddenly evaporated, because an embassy official could hardly claim at a party on Saturday night that the emergency programme was in chaos and then not raise the matter at the Monday morning COE meeting.

One reason this happened was that Ratilal used the meetings to free bottlenecks and resolve questions. For example, if a donor claimed to have goods stuck in the port, then Ratilal would summon a customs official to the following week's meeting to find out why, and would demand (and get) action.

At the same time, COE meetings became the way to resolve disputes between donors. Indeed, Hein's inability to control WFP and Unicef meant that it was only at COE meetings that agreements could be forced between the various UN agencies. The sometimes angry exchanges between donors, for example about who was at fault for a failed or duplicated delivery, made the government look much more reasonable than the donors – and also prevented the donors from continuing their fight through rumour and innuendo.

Ratilal also used COE meetings publicly to embarrass donors who were not cooperating, and force them into line. For example, when one donor was funding an airlift and only allowing food from his own country to be carried, Ratilal regularly challenged him at the meetings, so that the whole donor community knew. Similarly it was made clear to the whole donor community who was not participating fully, and whose donations were arriving late.

During this period, the government increasingly urged donors to select a specific district, rather than work all over the country. According to Ratilal, "better results are obtained when limited resources are applied to a relatively limited area for integrated rehabilitation and recuperation" (Ratilal 1990a: 188). Initially this forced donors to accept government goals and support more of the needs of the district, rather than concentrate on one target group as they would have preferred. It also allowed the government to keep a better check on them, though in some districts it had the side-effect of the donor becoming more powerful than the government.

Counting starving heads

Over a period of months, donors were drawn in to helping to establish government policy, which they then had to support. As Dr Ratilal commented at one COE meeting: "If a decision is taken and the donors agree, then they are incorporated." This was clearest in the fraught issue of just how many people were displaced and "affected", and what portion of them were in secure enough areas actually to receive aid.

It was clear that numbers could only be rough estimates, and several of the more hostile donors claimed that Mozambique was exaggerating the totals in order to get more aid. (By contrast, some of the more sympathetic donors complained that Mozambique had failed to realize the need to inflate the numbers, precisely because donors assume they are inflated and only give half what is asked for.) Peg Clement, Care information coordinator, actually wrote an article in *New African* (October 1987) in which she complained about the Mozambican government's inability to provide accurate data. She went on to admit that the apparently precise figure of "2,479,355 affected people" which she "proclaimed to the world" was just the product of guesswork and estimates – a damning admission considering Care's self-created key role in the emergency.

WFP prepared a regular fact sheet, "Food Balance/Mozambique" for the Commerce Ministry, which distributed it to donors, journalists, and others. Secretly, WFP prepared a second version of the document, which looked absolutely identical except for three changes: at the top it said that it was confidential, at the bottom the Mozambican logo was replaced by the WFP logo, and the numbers of people needing food aid were substantially reduced. For 1987/88, the WFP version said that only 1 million people were to receive emergency feeding, compared to 3.2 million on the commerce ministry edition; that reduced the maize needed by more than 300,000 tonnes, and may have accounted for the shortfall in donations.

The first Care evaluation had admitted that "food donations are insufficient to meet the needs of Mozambique in any case" (Brennan 1985). In 1988 that was still true, and because the numbers in need were so much greater than available aid, Ratilal concluded that it did not matter if the total was 5 million or 4 million in need of food, so long as it was agreed by the donors. So he manoeuvred the donors into setting up an evaluation mission and establishing their own number. WFP was included, but at first USAID refused to participate because it knew that it would have to accept whatever figure was agreed and could no longer complain privately that the government was faking the figures. By openly challenging USAID officials at the COE meeting, Ratilal embarrassed them into participating. The process worked, at least in public. The donors came up with a number very similar to the government one, and could not carp about it.

Private sniping

Ratilal did curb some unjustified criticism, but hostile donors continued to snipe in private or at a distance, trying to undermine Mozambique's credibility. For example, in an otherwise unexceptionable article on mortality among the displaced published in the prestigious medical journal *The Lancet*, two staff from MSF (France) add the sentence that "civil war does not permit the distribution of food, which is largely locked in the port of Maputo, the capital" (Pecoul 1990). The use of the phrase "civil war" suggests the political views of the authors; the claim about food "largely locked in the port" is blatant nonsense. This would never have been said publicly in a COE meeting.

Similar problems occur with the US embassy. Inevitably visiting journalists (like myself) and NGO and donor tourists stop in at the embassy, where we are briefed. An official from one of the major NGOs noted that even when the US was involved in establishing the number of people needing help, they privately rejected it. The embassy official told the NGO person that the Mozambicans "give us a number [of people needing food]. OK, we listen. But it's just a number. We just give what we want to give."

Hostile donors also tried to inflate claims of corruption and shrinkage in food aid distribution. From the first, USAID and some other donors put on heavy pressure for better accounting of where donated food was going. A UN official told me: "A lot of it was part of the general criticism of Africa which was common then. Also there was a lot of suspicion in Washington, London, and some other Western capitals that food was going to the army. On the ground, Western donor representatives said that Mozambicans were very honest – little aid food went to the black market or the army. Even a US embassy official admitted to me: "How much can you expect from semi-literate people? In fact, the distribution is very good. They may not know precisely how many sacks, but at district level they know who is getting the food and it is the right people'."

But as the emergency dragged on, Mozambique's rigid honesty and puritanism did begin to crumble. Significant corruption did arise throughout Mozambican society – an issue discussed at greater length below and in Chapter 19. But it never reached the levels claimed by US officials.

A US embassy official claimed in a briefing in early 1990 that more than half of food aid was being diverted. Later the US embassy became more brazen and circulated what became known as the "50% report". It presented a series of calculations which purported to show that only half of the US yellow maize donated for sale actually went to intended recipients. The rest was diverted to other purposes, and "it is likely that a sizeable portion of this amount is sold on the parallel market." This led the embassy to conclude that "it will be difficult for donors to continue providing the unprecedented levels of commercial food assistance to Mozambique if food cannot be confirmed to reach the intended beneficiaries" (USAID 1990a). The report was circulated at a time that food donations for the commercial network were falling, and must surely have undermined the confidence of other donors in Mozambican government integrity. But soon after the report was circulated, an embassy official admitted to me that the calculations had been done without discussion with the Mozambicans, and were wrong. Indeed, he said, most of the maize could be accounted for. But by the time I left Maputo several weeks later, the embassy had not circulated any correction or retracted its report.

Diversion of food aid was used by the US as a justification for the decision to channel all free food through NGOs. At least one of the NGOs encouraged this by claiming that a shipment was not properly delivered if there was even a small error on a waybill – an impossible criterion when most people dealing with waybills had only two or three years of primary school. In March 1990, all the US-funded NGOs were called to a meeting in the US embassy, a staff member of one of them told me. The high loss alleged by the first of the NGOs was stressed throughout the meeting. The embassy official said it was necessary to "rationalize" the emergency programme, with one US NGO per zone, and that "we have lots of money to spend on this." The NGO staffer told me: "It was like something from a bad movie, with the embassy man in front of the map dividing up Mozambique, saying to each of us 'we want you guys to apply for provinces A, B, and C.' It sticks in my mind because he said one province was to be divided, and he told my NGO to apply for half that province."

Yet USAID's own evaluators said that "there are so few reports of significant leakage with commodities" that major changes were not needed. Although highly critical of Care (see below), the 1988 report precisely opposed what USAID wanted to do. A formal end-use verification system would cost in excess of $1 mn (£600,000) to set up and not be worth the cost. Much simpler would be a "formalized random spot system" using NGOs already on the ground, it suggested. But it went on to stress that even if NGOs are used to spot check food distribution, "the [evaluation] team cautions against OFDA supporting the creation of costly parallel structures by other NGOs." Even for US food, the DPCCN and not NGOs should do the distribution (Berger: iv, 48).

This was the "wrong" answer, so USAID ignored the advice of its own evaluation team.

Who Cares?

As Chapter 4 made clear, the United States and US organizations play a pivotal role. In its attempts to ensure food distribution and satisfy its contract with the US government, Care tried to dominate the emergency and control other donors. But some donors and some Mozambicans distrusted both the motivation and the competence of Care; they tried to marginalize it without offending the US.

The DPCCN had never been intended for the large-scale relief operations which Mozambique genuinely needed. And, whether justified or not, there was strong donor pressure for better accounting. By late 1984 Care had begun to establish the new Logistic Support Unit (LSU) which was intended to satisfy both of these demands. The original agreement was for Care to have a quite limited role. It was to help to establish an LSU which would receive, store, and distribute food and other basic goods to disaster victims. The LSU was to be involved in port clearance, the establishment and maintenance of a lorry fleet, food distribution, and monitoring and verification of distribution. Care was to train local staff so that after four years the LSU would be run entirely by Mozambicans.

Care's actions, however, suggested that it and USAID had a very different agenda. Terry Jeggle, who was Care director in Maputo from March 1984 until February 1987, saw Care "acting as honest broker in response to the needs of the international donors on one hand and participant Mozambican institutions and recipients on the other" (Jeggle 1987). Care dominated the LSU and began to dominate the whole food aid distribution process.

A US Office of Foreign Disaster Assistance (OFDA) evaluation of Care said that "clearly, Care's role in coordinating donor inputs, and even governmental activities, is substantial." It quoted a UNDP official's view that "Care is our main source of information on donations." And it went on to say that Care "has not permitted its responsibility to the [Mozambican government] to retard its efforts to meet its obligations to the donor community", and that it should "substantially up-grade" its efforts to meet its commitments to the government (Brennan 1985).

But donor and Mozambique government disquiet was already growing. The evaluation warned of the danger of "usurping the government's own role" and of the need "to convince local authorities that the donor's interest is in furthering the government's own objectives."

Despite these warnings from its own evaluators, the 1986–88 contract between Care and the OFDA is much broader than Care's agreement with the Mozambican government. The OFDA contract says that "Care will manage and coordinate all requests and receipt of emergency relief assistance ... to the 5.7 million people in need of assistance." Of ten "activities" defined in the contract, only three relate to setting up a Mozambican-run LSU. The other seven call for Care (and not the LSU) to clear goods through the port, maintain warehousing, "manage or coordinate all available land, air and sea transport at the disposal of DPCCN", and "establish and maintain inventory accountability of assistance received" (Berger 1988: B1).

Not making themselves redundant

To be sure, the emergency became much more serious than seemed likely in 1984; covering the whole country instead of just half, it made Care's task of establishing the LSU much more difficult. Nevertheless, Care's official job of setting up the LSU and leaving within four years received a low priority.

Indeed, structures were established which seemed to suggest that Care was in Mozambique for the long haul. The new LSU was not in the DPCCN offices, but rather in the Care offices. Initially Jeggle and the deputy director of the DPCCN, Salomão Mambo, were co-chairmen of the LSU. Care always referred to the unit as "Care/LSU". Staff thought of themselves as working for Care and not the government. In addition to the normal Mozambican civil service salary, Care gave LSU staff what was known as a "food basket" – an extra $70 to $100 (£40-60) of imported food and household commodities monthly, purchased in hard currency. This would make it much harder for the government to take over the LSU later, the first evaluation warned (Brennan 1985).

Care continued to introduce more complex computerized monitoring systems which were beyond the capability of Mozambicans with low skill levels, so that they remained dependent on expatriate staff. It might be better to halt the expansion of the system and "focus increased attention on making what exists work better", commented OFDA's second evaluation of Care's activities. It also concludes that "the vertically integrated LSU, with its 20 expatriates and 400 trucks, has clearly been the 'tail wagging the dog'" (Berger 1988: 41,46).

This second evaluation was in June 1988 when Care's four-year term should have been coming to an end. Not surprisingly, it concluded that "it is clear" that the government of Mozambique "cannot support the LSU on its own and that the LSU cannot yet operate without sustained expatriate involvement, preferably that of Care" (Berger 1988: 71).

No training

But as Care made itself indispensable, there was growing disquiet in the Mozambican government, the donor community, and even in parts of USAID about Care's competence and the quality of the job it was doing. For OFDA it was to monitor aid flows, while for Mozambique it was to train local staff. The 1985 evaluation said monitoring was "inadequate"; in part, this was because it had failed to set up a training programme – thus failing to satisfy its obligation to Mozambique. The failure of some staff to gain any fluency in Portuguese, and Care's failure to appoint a training officer, meant that not much training took place (Brennan 1985).

Despite the advice of the 1985 evaluation, the second evaluation noted that Care had still failed to establish a training programme or hire a training officer. This "highlights the view of training as 'something we need to do when we get the time'" (Berger 1988: 38). Other donors began to train provincial DPCCN staff.

Care finally established a training unit in 1989; Care's information officer was given the new job of being management training coordinator. Five years after its arrival in Mozambique with the purpose of doing logistics training, Care finally began what it admitted was the "first logistics training of its kind in Mozambique." The training unit also brought in a computer specialist, who started to simplify the computer systems (Newman 1990).

No monitoring

Perhaps because of the lack of training, Care had not been very successful in accounting for food distribution, despite its brief from OFDA. A joint donor-Mozambican team which went to Sofala province in September 1989 commented that "in spite of the presence of Care at the provincial level, we saw no evidence of any effective monitoring" (Macaringue 1989).

I met one local Care representative in late 1988 at a provincial airport while I was waiting for a plane. The representative told me that they had been in the provincial capital for eight months, but, as they had no prior logistics experience, that time had been spent learning about logistics from the Mozambican staff they were supposed to help. Only recently had this person realized that the monitoring systems were not very good – which was surprising as there had been another Care person there for two years previously. After eight months, the new representative had not established any formal training schemes.

In that particular provincial capital, a system had been established in which sacks of grain were carefully counted as they were loaded on to lorries and then when they were unloaded, to ensure no sacks went astray. But local staff soon realized that there was no count to see that the number of lorries that left the quayside with sacks of grain was the same as the number that arrived at the local DPCCN warehouse. Drivers took at least three entire truckloads of food which they sold to private traders. For Mozambique this was new; the 1985 evaluation of Care said that although end-use monitoring of food aid was poor, "there has been virtually no evidence, nor even suggestion, of corruption at the lowest levels" (Brennan 1985). But a truckload of grain is worth more money than these drivers had ever seen; the new economic policy (see Part III) was creating hardship for them and their families, and the temptation was just too great.

Promoting corruption?

By failing to establish an adequate monitoring system, Care created a climate which encouraged corruption. This was underlined in a remarkable criticism of Care in a joint government-donor report on corruption in the emergency. Such reports are normally very circumspect, but this one names Care. It stresses that Care's technical assistance agreement was precisely supposed to minimize such problems. LSU "is equipped with computers and adequate working equipment. It has a reasonable number of staff, including the Care advisors as mentioned above. However, its level of functioning does not appear to be in proportion to the resources available." Care had failed to organize regular checks of goods in warehouses or control of reception of goods, and had not studied monthly reports from provinces to compare what is received with what is dispatched ("Executive Summary" 1990).

Despite the widespread acceptance of the problems with Care, it proved impossible to dislodge, change, or sideline. One frustrated high UN official said simply that "the US embassy protects Care". It was running the LSU because the US had insisted, and any change would require US permission. While insisting that it keep its central role, the US embassy made good use of the failures of its own agency.

It is argued throughout this book that donors have used aid to weaken and break the Mozambican government, and this was a classic case. The US insisted that Care play a key role in food distribution. By action even if not intent, Care then damaged the state marketing system and undermined the state food aid distribution system, opening the door to widespread corruption. Then the US embassy used Care's failure to organize the LSU to argue that food aid should be distributed by NGOs and not the LSU and the DPCCN. Finally the US gave much more financial support to conservative religious NGOs to handle food distribution outside the government network than it had given to Care to monitor food distribution within government.

Because USAID was so dominant in its funding, Care is not a typical NGO. Indeed, the 1988 evaluation even recommended that OFDA "treat Care more as a technical assistance contractor than an NGO" (Berger 1988: iv). Other donors were displeased by a US agency taking such a central role, and later with Care's ineptitude. So donors sent a string of consultants to Mozambique to advise on better ways to structure the emergency. For five years, Care used its role at the heart of the LSU and the DPCCN to maintain a high degree of control, and to block other donor agencies from monitoring and influencing food aid distribution.

Airlifts

The issue finally reached a head with food airlifts, which technically came under LSU and Care. A series of reports showed that they were being badly managed, and criticisms became more public and outspoken. The government's mid-year evaluation of the emergency noted in a section on Care, that "the lack of management in the airlift operations was evident" (CENE 1989b: 13). A report of a mission to Sofala said simply "it had not been possible to find out who exactly has been in charge of the airlift." Care had not established any system to ensure that food was flown to where it was needed, and the report concluded that $230,000 (£140,000) had been wasted airlifting food where it was not needed (Macaringue 1989).

Care had again failed to introduce systems to monitor distribution, creating an open invitation to corruption. Recommendations made by interagency missions, were not implemented. One of the major problems was Care's road transport bias, and its unwillingness to assign additional staff to the airlift.

Yet in April 1990 Care refused offers of staff from other donors. At a meeting with high UN and Mozambican officials, Care stressed that it had the exclusive contract to support the LSU. Care's OFDA contract made it responsible for "all available land, air, and sea transport". The following month, one of the major donors said that it would no longer fund airlifts unless there were non-Care monitors. Fear of offending the US led to a complex arrangement according to which the UN would provide up to four people. Funded by a bilateral donor, they would be provincial representatives of the UN and CENE, and be attached to the provincial emergency committee rather than the LSU. Such is the importance of not stepping on American toes.

How much power?

From Care's arrival, there was a conflict between the view of many Care officials that the best way to ensure efficient food distribution was for Care to take an ever more central role, and the view of many donors and Mozambican officials that Care was overextending itself. Care officials successfully put forward the argument that Mozambicans and not the UN should call meetings and issue reports. UN officials considered this simply a trick to allow the US to take control of emergency aid, but with no support from New York, UNDP was not able to maintain its leading role. At the end of 1984, the new LSU took over. Meetings were chaired by Amós Mahanjane, director of the DPCCN, or by deputy director Mambo. A new *DPCCN Newsletter* replaced the UNDP *News Bulletin*. But the process was really controlled by Care officials, not the Mozambicans. The new newsletter was prepared by Care staff and issued with a cover letter from the DPCCN.

A Care official told me that Care had engineered the removal of Amós Mahanjane as director of the DPCCN (he later became ambassador to Malawi) and his replacement by Mambo. "We had problems with Mahanjane. Talking to him was like having an audience with the President. Mambo is a lot more accessible to us, because we know him as a person." As co-head of the LSU, Mambo had worked in the Care office.

The creation of CENE and the subordination of the DPCCN to it sharply reduced Care's dominance. A Care official told me that Ratilal's appointment had been orchestrated by the UN, and complained that Care had not even been consulted. The official admitted that after CENE was formed and Ratilal appointed, some Care staff unsuccessfully tried to force donors to work with Mambo and not Ratilal.

But those Care officials failed to undermine Ratilal. The LSU was treated as an operational arm of the DPCCN and did not even have a seat at the main table of COE meetings. The weekly COE meetings replaced Care's *DPCCN Newsletter* as donors' main source of information. Unicef provided assistance to the DPCCN to set up an information and planning office. Finally, in November 1988 the information section of the LSU was moved out of the Care offices and into the DPCCN offices, which were in the same building as the CENE offices.

Decentralization and Development

The prominence of CENE and Dr Ratilal's new dominance of the emergency raised fundamental questions, and also caused friction within the Mozambican government. The emergency generated at most $250 mn (£150 mn) per year in aid, and probably much less new money since some would have gone to Mozambique anyway. This is compared to total assistance approaching $900 mn (£540 mn). Yet the emergency was dominating donor and press interest and was overwhelming the much more critical question of economic restructuring, which demanded much more aid.

Despite the emergency, major development projects were under way, including large dams and port and railway rehabilitation. And a structural adjustment programme had been agreed with the IMF and World Bank (see Part III). As part of that package, the World Bank took over donor coordination for non-emergency assistance.

The World Bank and IMF are formally part of the UN. Under a document of 18 February 1986, "Guiding Principles for Aid Coordination Between the World Bank and the UNDP in Sub-Saharan Africa", the two state that they "have decided to strengthen their collaboration on aid coordination." Under the agreement, the World Bank chairs

"Consultative Groups", which are annual meetings with representatives of the IMF, World Bank, and the main donors. The Mozambique consultative group meets at the World Bank European Headquarters in Paris. The first meeting was in July 1987; from 1988 meetings were held each November.

Finding a structure for cooperation

Although Mozambique maintained very tight control over aid in the late 1970s, it was done in an *ad hoc* way. This worked when aid flows were relatively small, donors were sympathetic, and there was a post-revolutionary consensus on at least broad development goals. But ten years after independence, this proved incapable of dealing with large volumes of aid, hostile donors, and internal divisions and disputes. While the donors were coordinating their side, Mozambique worked to organize its end to retain some power.

Cooperation Minister Jacinto Veloso admitted in a speech in 1989 that "we lacked a global vision of cooperation. We lacked an integrated and coherent policy, and we were not able to identify needs and priorities." There was no clear structure for cooperation, nor any agreement as to which government departments were responsible. And there was no control and evaluation (C&D December 1989).

The system was a free-for-all in which ministries and secretariats dealt directly with donors and often ignored the Cooperation Ministry. Although it increased the power of individual ministers and directors, it increased the power of donors even more, because they could play ministries off against each other and more easily force policy changes in exchange for aid.

In ten years, cooperation systems were restructured five times. Officials seemed to feel that if only they could find the right organogram, everything would be fine, when the problems were much more basic ones about power and resources. Finally, as part of a major government reshuffle in April 1986, President Machel created a new Ministry of Cooperation to take over from the former secretariat of state. And he appointed Veloso as minister.

But this, if anything, exacerbated the problem, because it created yet another body with responsibility for aid. Under structural adjustment and in dealings with the IMF, the finance minister was dominant. The National Planning Commission still existed and had a role, albeit a diminishing one as central planning was down-played. Food aid was the responsibility of the trade minister, and Prakash Ratilal was a deputy minister of trade when he was put in charge of the emergency. And the commissions that dealt with bilateral aid, and which were headed by ministers, also had power.

One key decision, however, was not to create a new super "Emergency Ministry", as had been done in some countries. "We decided not to create parallel and autonomous structures to deal with emergency. Emergency is part of the problems that Mozambique faces and the effort for its solution is essentially made in the framework of existing structures", Dr Ratilal explained (Ratilal 1988).

Appointing Veloso cooperation minister should have resolved the problem, because he was a member of the Politburo. This gave international cooperation a much higher profile, and he had higher rank than the finance and trade ministers. But the former security minister had many other jobs; he played an active role in various discreet international negotiations, including the Nkomati Accord. And Veloso was not a "hands-on" minister; he often left the new ministry to drift.

During the following three years there were a series of studies (invariably funded by competing donors) of how the new ministry should be structured. The problems were both political and practical. At a practical level, Mozambique lacked the skilled staff to undertake detailed coordination, monitoring, and evaluation of aid – if it could have done those things, it would not have needed so much help. So there was a need to set up a structure which was simple enough to function, but which still improved the government's ability to monitor and regulate aid flows. On a political level, the new ministry could not compete too directly with other fiefdoms.

Is CREE the answer?

In May 1989 the government created a Comissão de Relações Económicas Externas (CREE – Foreign Economic Relations Commission) and redefined the role of the Ministry of Cooperation and of individual ministries. CREE is chaired by the prime minister; members are the governor of the Bank of Mozambique and the ministers of finance, planning, cooperation, and trade. These are the big guns, and if they agree on policy no one can dispute their decision.

Following the establishment of CREE, a new National System of International Co-operation was defined in late 1989. The Ministry of Cooperation sets policy and norms, monitors projects, collects more detailed information on aid than existed in the past, evaluates proposals from individual ministries, and monitors and evaluates projects being executed. The minister of cooperation now chairs all bilateral donors' commissions, which will bring them under tighter control.

CREE is the decision-making body, and with the advice of the Ministry of Co-operation will try to make rational allocations of available aid to projects proposed by individual ministries and approved by the Ministry of Cooperation.

Although the new system will increase coordination and central control, it retains a high level of decentralization. Cooperation secretariats in individual ministries and secretariats of state control the actual execution of projects. They also identify possible future projects.

The new system will require the good will of the people who are losing power over resources – something which cannot be guaranteed. It will work only if the Cooperation Ministry has enough good people to play a role that both donors and ministries find useful.

Questions have been raised about the new system, however. It is much too elaborate, with 26 sections and departments. One normally sympathetic donor official dismissed it as "just a bureaucratic paper chase overloading an already non-functioning system." It fails to create any strategy or priorities.

The shortage of money and skilled people means that many sections are one-person operations. When these people are good, the system runs. Inevitably, some have proved weak and disruptive; some seem more anxious to use their contacts with foreign donors to improve their own life style and status, and to arrange foreign trips and alcoholic lunches at the Hotel Polana.

In practice, it remains unclear if the Ministry of Cooperation serves any useful function at all. Perhaps its job would be better done by the planning and finance ministries.

Emergency squeezed

The key question is whether any system can end the infighting which so much foreign money generates. The traditional unhappiness in some quarters about a special high profile role for the emergency resurfaced. In a May 1988 government reshuffle, Dr Ratilal lost his title of deputy minister of trade. His full time job as coordinator of CENE did not change, and he kept the car and other status symbols of a deputy minister, but it was clearly a demotion in protocol terms.

The UN Special Coordinator, Arturo Hein, pressed the government, and even President Chissano, to make Dr Ratilal a deputy minister of cooperation or deputy minister without portfolio, but this was never done. Hein argued that while Ratilal's good standing with the donor community inside Mozambique did not need to be reinforced by a title, visitors from abroad expected to talk to a minister and not just a coordinator.

It was always argued that Dr Ratilal had not been demoted at all, and had simply lost a title long since inappropriate, but no one believed this. The exact reasons for the demotion were never made clear. Probably, it was to demote the role of the emergency in general and to lower the status of Dr Ratilal, whose popularity with donors had elevated his standing compared to others involved in aid. Race and Dr Ratilal's Asian origin may have also played a role. This was a period in which some elements in the emerging black bourgeoisie were arguing that their advancement was being blocked by too many whites and "Indians" in high places.

Ratilal's drop in the pecking order had two internal consequences. First, he no longer had higher status than provincial governors: one governor, for example, was then able to stop him investigating allegations of corruption in aid distribution. And Ratilal lost some of his authority over the DPCCN, whose officials rapidly began to reassert their independence. He resigned as coordinator in July 1989.and was not immediately replaced. The deputy minister of agriculture, Alfredo Gamito, took the post as acting coordinator until he was made a governor.

The emergency was de-emphasized further at the end of 1989 when the rehabilitation component was shifted to the World Bank and the Finance Ministry, completely outside the ambit of cooperation. The Economic Rehabilitation Programme (PRE) became the Economic and Social Rehabilitation Programme (PRES). The World Bank, displeased that more than $250 mn (£150 mn) per year in emergency aid was outside its control, and not discussed in the Consultative Group, agreed to provide funds for rehabilitation if the emergency programme was cut back. The April 1990 appeal thus asked for much less money, to be used for relief only. Rehabilitation and food aid for the market were both dropped from the appeal. It was decided that there should be no separate emergency appeal in 1991.

It was a major about-face, amounting to an acceptance by the World Bank that destabilization is the central problem, and that there is a structural emergency. But it was also the final defeat by the donors of Mozambique's attempt to link emergency with rehabilitation and development.

Baloi named

On 23 February 1990 Oldemiro Baloi was named deputy minister of cooperation and coordinator of the emergency programme. This gave the emergency post the status it had lost two years before, but meant it did not have a full-time coordinator. Baloi had previously been assistant director of the coordinating unit for import programmes in the Ministry of Trade, and thus had substantial experience in dealing with donors. Now he took an active role in the Cooperation Ministry, substituting for the often absent minister, chairing bi-lateral commission meetings, and taking tighter control over the running of the ministry. Initially he delayed taking on the emergency, which gave space for DPCCN officials to sabotage Baloi's position there by effectively dismantling the coordinator's office staff. As the year went on, however, Baloi reasserted control over the DPCCN.

Beyond Maputo

One of Frelimo's persistent weaknesses has been the inability to decentralize. It consistently failed to define the role and competence of local and provincial government. Even with the demise of central planning, key decisions were taken in Maputo.

Provincial governors have a protocol status below deputy ministers but above secretaries of state (although at various times Politburo members have also been governors, giving them a much higher status). A provincial director of, say, education or agriculture, serves as part of the governor's provincial cabinet. Thus the provincial director is subordinate both to a minister in Maputo and to the governor. It has never been clear how much authority a governor has over development projects and emergency activities in his province. A provincial governor told me: "All decisions with bilateral donors are made in Maputo. Sometimes, the first I know of a project in my own province is when I read about it in *Noticias*" (the Maputo daily newspaper). The new system appears to strengthen the Maputo-centred nature of cooperation, at least with larger projects and bilateral donors.

However, in deciding not to set up a new all-embracing emergency ministry, Mozambique did take a cautious step toward decentralization. The national structure of CENE and COE were reproduced at provincial level, although with substantial variations. Most provinces have a provincial emergency commission. Rather than automatically appoint the holder of a particular post as emergency coordinator, someone was usually chosen from among the best available people in the province; in some provinces it was a party official, in others the provincial planning director, and so on. Each province has a DPCCN office, subordinate both to DPCCN Maputo and the provincial emergency commission. Similarly, each ministry is expected to create an emergency office within the ministry.

Thus CENE was to have a small staff, and would be abolished after the war ended. the DPCCN would continue to have a role in natural disasters. Otherwise, sectoral ministries would carry out their normal roles: food for sale would be distributed through commercial channels; in camps with displaced people the Ministry of Education would establish the schools, and the Ministry of Health the health units, etc. Special emergency funding would be used to strengthen the capabilities of existing ministries. At provincial level the same process would be followed – a small office for coordination with provincial directorates of health, education, trade, etc. taking on the appropriate responsibilities.

What Kind of Economy?

9 The Road to Structural Adjustment: 1982-86

Frelimo's struggle to maintain control over the economy is the subject of Part III of this book. This chapter looks at Frelimo's three-year unsuccessful battle to find a middle way. Frelimo wanted to do three things at once: follow at least a modified socialist path, correct genuine economic problems, and make enough changes to satisfy donors. It failed. Chapter 10 looks at some of the reasons why structural adjustment was unlikely to work in Mozambique. Chapters 11 and 12 look at the impact of adopting the IMF/World Bank structural adjustment package. Faced with growing suffering and the failure of its policies, the Bank in 1990 in effect admitted that it had been wrong and Frelimo had been right on some points. Chapter 13 considers the World Bank's attempt to turn back and go forward at the same time. Finally, Chapters 14 and 15 consider specific areas of conflict: the role of the state in the economy, and the nature of the development path.

'We Had no Choice'

Once the economic collapse began in 1982, the descent was rapid indeed. By 1983 Mozambique had no foreign exchange. It could not pay its foreign debts, and imports plummeted. There were shortages of fuel, consumer goods, and medicines; industrial production fell, largely due to shortages of imported raw materials. At first, Mozambique would not publicly admit the crisis, but it became clear that in October 1983 President Samora Machel was touring Europe with cap in hand. The tour was a diplomatic success but a financial failure. The President received warm support for his turn to the West and the proposed talks with South Africa, and he also received significant emergency assistance. But he was told in no uncertain terms that money would only be forthcoming when Mozambique had an agreement with the IMF. By the end of 1983, Mozambique had opened informal talks with the IMF and World Bank.

Frelimo still tried to go it alone. On 30 January 1984, Mozambique effectively declared bankruptcy and defaulted on its debts (as neighbouring South Africa did a year later). It asked creditors to reschedule these debts, deferring principal and interest due in 1983–86 until 1991–98 (RPM 1984). The creditors turned up their noses at the offer, and pointed to the IMF.

The donors, too, pointed that way. "Even our friends who had supported us during the armed struggle started to shut the door, saying you must have a programme with the IMF," a minister told me. "We had no choice."

In January 1984 Senator Danforth was showing his photos to Ronald Reagan, who approved a major emergency effort. President Machel had meetings with a string of major international capitalists, including David Rockefeller, Harry Oppenheimer, Lord Jellicoe, and Tiny Rowland. On 16 March Mozambique and South Africa signed the Nkomati Accord. On 18 April the Council of Ministers agreed to open formal negotiations with the IMF and World Bank. On 27 April the People's Assembly (parliament) rubber-stamped a plan for the coming year which stressed the need to gain "the confidence of the creditors" and pointed the way down the road required by the IMF.

'Spirit of getting things for nothing'

But in presenting the plan to the People's Assembly, Finance Minister Rui Baltazar stressed that "it is in our own interest, as well as that of our creditors, to clean up our economic situation and make our economy more viable".

The crisis had come on very quickly, and there had been a dramatic reversal in state financing in 1983. Revenue fell while expenditures on defence, subsidies, and salaries rose sharply. For the first time, the government had a current account deficit.

Baltazar stressed the need for tighter control over state-owned and intervened companies. Some parastatal companies, notably fishing, textile sales, insurance, and the lottery, continued to show a profit, earning $70 mn (£45 mn) in 1983. But loss-making companies such as the sugar mills were building up large deficits. In 1983 bank financing of the economy was an incredible $342 mn (£206 mn). In effect, this was simply printing money and the money supply doubled in three years. At the same time, the value of consumer goods on sale in 1982 had been only two-thirds the 1980 level because of the squeeze on imports. The result was a vast surplus of cash in the economy, which promoted a rapidly growing black market. (Hanlon 1984c; WB 1989d)

Whatever the causes of the crisis, it was clear that something had to be done to control the money supply. The plan called for sharp cuts in government expenditure in the following year, 1985; necessarily this was to entail wages cuts and substantial redundancies in government departments and parastatal companies (Hanlon 1984c).

Managers of state companies were to be given more freedom but much tighter budgets. Stress was laid on the shortages of foreign exchange to import raw materials. State farms should remember that "the most advanced technology is generally the most expensive, especially in foreign exchange." Local technology should be used and the areas farmed should be reduced to what can be better controlled and farmed with fewer resources. Similarly, craftspeople should make consumer goods with local materials, such as shoes from old tyres.

Finally Baltazar made a somewhat obscure statement, that it was necessary to end "the persistent spirit of getting things for nothing". This will not have meant much to his audience, but the phrase was used in a confidential paper then circulating which said there were to be charges for health and education, including prescription charges. In fact, there were already token charges for health and education. The Frelimo Third Congress in 1977 had stressed the importance of health and education, with the stress on expanding basic services, notably literacy and primary health care. Services should be genuinely available to everyone, but Frelimo never said they should be free; indeed, it had always been common practice for people to save some money for medical expenses and this was still considered reasonable. So there was no principle at stake.

The content of the speech seemed both reasonable and necessary. But it was the tone of the speech that was ominous. As I commented at the time, its Thatcherite spirit would "not seem out of place in the UK or US" (Hanlon 1984c). In fact, the tone of that and similar speeches reflected division and confusion. Not all ministers were happy with the new line, and few really understood its implications. Some of those who did not agree or did not understand had trouble justifying the changes to the people, and responded to even sensible questioning by being paternalistic and authoritarian.

In the event, the debate within the government and between the government and the IMF continued for some time, and it was three years before some of the proposals were actually implemented.

Mozambique formally joined the IMF and World Bank in September 1984. This led to the first rescheduling agreement the next month with the Paris Club of OECD government creditors. It was actually quite exceptional that the Paris Club was prepared to negotiate even a limited rescheduling with a country which was an IMF member but still did not have an agreed IMF programme (IMF 1987). OPEC debts were renegotiated in early 1985. These renegotiations covered only debts already in arrears, plus those falling due in the near future which were clearly not going to be paid. So this did not get Mozambique off the hook.

The struggle commences

The initial talks between the government and the IMF and World Bank started from very different premises, and it sometimes seemed they were talking about different countries. Mozambique stressed that there had been real per capita economic growth between 1977 and 1981, which was better than in the late colonial period. There had been a government current account budget surplus in the early 1980s. The 1982-83 crisis was caused by drought, destabilization, and a cut-off of aid and credit. Rain and the Nkomati accord would solve that. Thus Frelimo's economic policies were fundamentally sound. The biggest problem was the delay in completion of various large development projects, due in part to destabilization, and thus the need was for short-term bridging finance until these were on line. Of course there were structural problems, but these related to the colonial inheritance, the costs of imposing sanctions against Rhodesia, and the impact of South African destabilization.

Central planning, *per se*, was not a problem; rather there were "errors and shortcomings of cadres who must gain experience in economic administration and management during the process of transformation of economic and social structures" as well as "the natural weakness of the state's administrative structures." Thus the state intended "to improve and render more operational and efficient the state apparatus for the management of the economy" (CNP 1984a: 37, 53).

The government announced its Economic Recovery Programme. This stressed support for family agriculture "through the provision of tools and equipment and a supply of consumer goods for commercial exchange in the countryside." Spare parts and inputs would be given preferentially to import-substituting industries, especially those which produced agricultural implements, hand tools, clothing, and foodstuffs. Mineral exports were to be promoted. And private entrepreneurs would be encouraged (CNP 1984a: 51).

On its side, the IMF could only see a crisis caused by state control of the economy, an explosive growth of the money supply, excessive management of foreign exchange, and too few exports. Its initial demands were sweeping: a virtual end to all controls and denationalization of virtually all economic and social sectors – health, education, property, and industry. The ration system in Maputo and Beira had to be ended. The metical should be immediately devalued from the official rate of MT 40 to the US$ to the black market rate of MT 1500 to the US$.

Officially the IMF and World Bank are concerned with different aspects of the economy and negotiate separately with member countries. In practice they were often in Maputo together, and in the same meetings. The annual Economic Policy Framework Paper (WB 1987a, 1988a, 1989a) is a joint IMF/World Bank/Mozambique government document. Quite sharp divisions were to emerge within the IMF and between the IMF and World Bank, but they tended to be over the speed of implementation of the programme and not over its merits.

A central problem for all negotiations was the lack of data. The lack of trained people meant that the government had never built up an adequate picture of the economy, and statistics were often questionable. Thus a first, reasonable demand from the IMF was that teams compile much better basic information. This delayed organization of any sort of programme.

But a more serious problem was the lack of knowledge of Mozambique on the part of IMF and World Bank staff, and their assumption that Mozambique was just like any other African country. This was quite widespread. I once met a World Bank official at the Polana Hotel in Maputo on a Saturday, when he had just arrived from another African country. He knew nothing of Mozambique, but said he had a lot of literature with him and would spend the weekend reading, so by Monday he would know enough to advise the Mozambicans. After all, he explained, the problems in Mozambique were the same as everywhere else. But the solutions were not: one Mozambican official complained to me that successive World Bank delegations would demand totally opposite and conflicting solutions to problems.

The first 18 months was spent trying to reach common ground. At the same time Mozambique began introducing a range of its own reforms. The first experiment with the free market had already started in early 1984 when the government responded to a *de facto* charcoal traders' strike by allowing a completely free market in Maputo for firewood (a competing fuel). The effect was dramatic and prophetic: all available vehicles, including private cars, drove out to rural areas and firewood poured into the city. But the price was high; firewood to cook one day's meal for a family cost more than the daily minimum wage for a worker. And, as was to happen repeatedly later, the market did not "work" – prices remained high even as market stall holders sat behind mountains of unsold firewood.

In 1984 the government also introduced a variety of measures to stimulate agriculture. State farms were not abolished, but a review of them was launched with the idea of retaining only those likely to be profitable; this recognized the fact that many state farms were made up of abandoned settler farms which had also been unprofitable in colonial times. Some of the bigger state farms were broken up. Part of the Limpopo complex at Chókwè was given to a foreign company, Lonrho; parts were given to peasants and local cooperatives; and parts were broken into smaller, more manageable state farms. At the same time, efforts were made to stimulate smallholder production through the supply of inputs and consumer goods, the distribution of land, and changing land title regulations to give families security of tenure. And, as the UNDP later candidly admitted, "private farmers who use wage labour and modern machinery are encouraged by being given priority access to new inputs and improved marketing facilities" (UNDP 1987c).

New efforts were made to encourage private owners to take over smaller firms owned by the state or run by it (intervened) after their owners abandoned them at independence. This built on an attempt that had been going on since 1980. As President Machel said in a speech the following year, "the Mozambican state cannot go on selling needles, and managing shops, garages, and taxis" (AIM January 1986 supp.). A new foreign investment code was introduced.

A variety of other measures were also introduced in 1984. One was an export retention scheme, under which exporters were allowed to keep some of their hard currency (foreign exchange or "forex") earnings to import raw materials and spare parts.

A year later, in May 1985, the first significant economic changes began. On 11 May the Council of Ministers announced further liberalization of regulations on business. More companies were allowed to import and export directly (rather than through state trading companies). The 1984 export retention scheme was liberalized to permit the use of some of the money to pay directors and workers in forex or goods bought in forex. State-owned companies were formally removed from the government apparatus, and managers were told to treat them as businesses rather than part of the civil service, while continuing to take account of government policy and objectives.

On 14 May Edward Jaycox, World Bank vice-president for Eastern and Southern Africa, arrived for a five-day visit with a World Bank team which was to make its first major report on the Mozambican economy. While in Maputo, Jaycox announced the World Bank's first loan to Mozambique, of $45 mn (£27 mn) for spare parts and raw materials for industry.

The week after Jaycox's departure, the government announced that fixed prices for maize, beef, and chicken were to be doubled, both to the producer and the consumers. Price controls were ended on fruit, vegetables, duck, and rabbit. The first steps had been taken toward policies announced a year earlier.

The government also decided to give new priority to consumer goods to support agricultural marketing. Using aid funds, consumer goods were to be imported directly from India, China, the USSR and East Germany; raw materials for local factories were also to be imported.

Finally in June 1985, six months late, the government announced the plan and budget for 1985. There was a major increase in military spending; health and education were cut by 15%.

The big stick

Neither the donors nor the IMF and World Bank were satisfied, although they did accept that Frelimo was making a start. Thus the November 1985 World Bank mission involved some hard bargaining.

In a briefing note to the Mozambican government, the World Bank underlined its powerful position: "Mozambique is also going to require increased cooperation and support from the international donor community. But the extent of assistance that can be expected will depend to a considerable extent on the perception that the Government is making bold and determined efforts to solve the country's problems.... Adoption of a comprehensive program would serve as a convincing demonstration of the Government's willingness to undertake reforms to revive production.... This would almost certainly improve the prospects for inflows of concessional aid, both from the Bank and other donors. It could also provide the basis for regularization of Mozambique's external debt situation, facilitating the resumption of normal commercial credit relationships" (WB 1985a).

In less diplomatic terms than usual, the Bank was pointing out that essential foreign aid and debt rescheduling were conditional on a comprehensive structural adjustment agreement with the IMF and World Bank. The Bank accepted that "continued disruption of production and transport by 'armed bands' ... would dampen the effects of such measures." But it argued that Mozambique had to take action any way, just to convince the donors of its sincerity. Truly, Mozambique had no choice.

And the Bank made its position clear. "Mozambique's economic situation is now critical. While this situation is largely the result of factors and events outside the Government's control ... reversing the decline of the Mozambican economy will require a comprehensive and sustained effort by the Government to correct existing distortions and imbalances, improve the efficiency of resource use and provide more powerful incentives for producers, especially those of export commodities" (WB 1985a).

"Major changes" are required in the exchange rate. The free market in fruit and vegetables is merely "a cautious step". Price increases are needed to "soak up some of the excess liquidity in the economy." "A fiscal and monetary program must include strict ceilings on government expenditure." Subsidies to state farms "must be drastically reduced". The government must outline a programme for the "disposition" of state enterprises. As a bank which puts the highest priority on repaying debts, the World Bank insisted that top priority go to reviving production of export goods (WB 1985a).

The Aide-Memoire agreed after the November meeting revealed that the Bank had not gained as much ground as it hoped. "The Government indicated, however, that it did not think that the mission had adequately taken into account the effects of South Africa's destabilization efforts ... on the Government's ability to take measures that might have an adverse effect on living standards. However, it affirmed that, within its basic socialist framework, it would proceed along the path toward greater economic efficiency." And government rejected further price liberalization, noting that initial price liberalizations had not increased production, "and the middlemen, rather than farmers or consumers, appeared to have been the prime beneficiaries" (WB 1985b).

Building up to PRE

That was nearly the last time anyone talked officially about a "basic socialist framework". In April 1986 Rui Baltazar was replaced as Finance Minister by Abdul Magid Osman, who was much more sympathetic to the IMF. And in July 1986 the Politburo forced President Samora Machel to accept a reduction in his own power and appoint a Prime Minister who would take more direct control over the running of the government and economy, while President Machel would concentrate on restructuring the army and winning the war. The new Prime Minister was Mário da Graça Machungo, one of the few economists in the Frelimo leadership. A member of the Politburo, he had been planning minister from 1980. He also served as governor of Zambézia from 1983 until early 1986, and tried out some of the economic reforms there, including the free market in fruit and vegetables.

Also in July 1986, the government presented the IMF with an outline of what was to be the Programa de Reabilitação Económica (PRE – Economic Rehabilitation Programme) – its structural adjustment programme. (WB 1990c: 4) In the following months, conditions in Mozambique deteriorated rapidly. When the joint World Bank–IMF team arrived in Mozambique on 10 November to talk about the proposal, it met a Mozambican leadership battered by an impending famine, escalating war, and the apparent murder of a much-loved leader.

This initial programme did not satisfy the IMF, whose Executive Board on 17 November "expressed deep concern" at "the limited progress made in implementing corrective policies." Measures taken so far were merely "initial steps [which] fell short of the major policy reform that was required" (IMF 1987).

After ten weeks of negotiations, the World Bank team said it "has been impressed by the Government's determination to proceed with the policy changes", but that "these measures will, however, need to be accompanied by more fundamental changes" (WB 1986).

The Bank demanded "fundamental changes in the pricing and allocation system" including an end to price controls, "greater emphasis on support for private sector activities", more rapid devaluation than proposed, fewer restrictions on foreign currency, changes in credit policy, and consideration of closing down heavily indebted enterprises. The Bank also warned that Mozambique was expecting too much aid, and that "substantial cuts are needed" in the proposed imports programme (WB 1986). The Bank team then returned to Washington where it intended to "prepare, together with the IMF, a draft of the Policy Framework Paper setting out the proposed program."

Unilateral action

Instead of waiting for the paper, Mozambique took the dramatic and perhaps unprecedented step of announcing its own structural adjustment programme. Prime Minister Mário Machungo presented PRE to the People's Assembly on 14 January 1987, and introduced it over the next month – without IMF/World Bank approval.

According to the government: "The broad objectives of the programme are to:
a. reverse the decline in production;
b. ensure a minimum level of consumption and income, especially for the rural population;
c. reduce domestic financial imbalances;
d. strengthen the balance of payments position; and
e. lay the foundation for economic growth.

More specific aims are to:
a. increase agricultural production for domestic consumption, export, and agro-industries;
b. increase industrial production to support agricultural marketing, for import substitution, and to stimulate the development of exports …
c. rehabilitate physical infrastructure …
d. increase international rail and port traffic; and
e. mobilize external resources and allocate them to priority sectors" (RPM 1987).

PRE involved a wide range of actions:
- Devaluation to one-fifth the previous value, from $1 = MT 40 to $1 = MT 200. The black market rate at the time was $1 = MT 1500. (In terms of sterling, the devaluation was from £1 = MT 66 to £1 = MT 330. The black market rate was equivalent to £1 = MT 2475.)
- Consumer prices were increased: basic food and water and electricity prices doubled; beer, cigarettes, newspapers, bus fares, postage, telephones and a wide range of similar items tripled (that is, increased two-fold); and a few items including soap and paraffin (kerosene) for lighting increased five-fold or more.
- Fewer prices were to be regulated. Only essential consumer goods and the main crops were to have fixed prices; for others, guidelines would be set and prices could be determined by companies within those rules.
- Wages were increased by between 50% and 100%. New wage rules encouraged bonuses, incentives, and profit sharing, and permitted greater differences between high and low paid.
- Private employers and the state were encouraged to sack unneeded workers "wherever possible"; the state should redeploy underused staff if possible.
- Prices paid to farmers were increased: maize was tripled, peanuts and beans increased four-fold.
- A special MT 3 bn marketing fund was established to ensure that consumer goods reached the countryside, to stimulate peasant production.
- The tax structure was reformed and a more broadly based income tax introduced, with rates between 6% and 15%; state employees remained exempt from tax. Price rises on beer and cigarettes were largely due to excise duty increases. Total tax income was significantly increased.
- Rents were to be substantially increased. (All rented housing was state-owned, and there were no legal private landlords.)
- Higher charges were announced for health care. (There was also no private health care.)
- The state budget was made more transparent and included all subsidies, many of which had been hidden as bank credits. Price subsidies for the year were set at MT 7 bn ($35 mn, £21 mn after the first devaluation) and subsidies to state companies at MT 14 bn. Limits were imposed on the size of the budget and the current account deficit was capped at MT 30 bn.
- Bank credit regulations were sharply tightened and credit would no longer be used as a hidden subsidy to private and state companies. Interest rates increased substantially

(although still to less than the rate of inflation, meaning that real interest rates remained negative).
* Aid funds were to be directed less to development projects and more to the purchase of raw materials and spare parts for local industry. However SADCC transport projects, particularly the Beira corridor rehabilitation, continued to be encouraged.
* New legislation was planned to encourage national and foreign private investment.

In introducing the PRE, Prime Minister Machungo said that "as regards reactivating production, priority will go to the agricultural sector, and to the family sector in particular. Economic recovery must begin in the countryside."

A key issue was to remonetize the metical; increasing amounts of trade were being conducted in rand or by barter. Dr Machungo explained that "by making the metical a scarce resource we intend to give our currency value."

Machungo admitted the failure to control the black market. "The fight against the illegal market must be waged principally by economic means", he said, and the new pricing policy "should staunch the current flow of excess and illicit profits into the pockets of racketeers."

Machungo put great stress on increasing productivity and better workplace organization. He said that labour productivity was only half what it had been in 1980, largely due to lack of raw materials and spare parts; in an average eight-hour working day, useful work is carried out for only three hours. "Businesses must be viable and the criterion for assessing their value to the national economy will be profitability." Managers will be more independent, but they must make their businesses efficient. "Directors of companies must take responsibility. They cannot say 'I have nothing to do with this, I received orders from above'."

"Broadly speaking, there is an attempt to avoid the lowering of workers' living standards by the range of measures proposed. The basic aim is to staunch the decline of recent years, which could become worse if appropriate steps were not taken", the Prime Minister concluded (AIM, MIO various issues early 1987).

The PRE was being introduced at a time of upheaval. The new president, Joaquim Chissano, was remodelling the government. Zimbabwe and Tanzania had increased their troops in Mozambique and were beginning to push back the Renamo invasion. But the food crisis caused by the war was worsening. In December British NGOs had launched a famine appeal for Mozambique; in February the UN highlighted the crisis and held an appeal conference in March. The eight months from September 1986 to April 1987 were probably the most fraught and fluid in the history of independent Mozambique.

Whose programme?

Ministers loudly and repeatedly claimed that the PRE was Mozambique's own programme, and had not been imposed by the IMF and World Bank. That was at least partly true. The World Bank had sent eight missions to Mozambique in 1984 and 14 in 1985; the IMF sent five delegations over the two years. Clearly Mozambique knew full well what was required of it. But the PRE was introduced without IMF clearance, and fell short of IMF demands. IMF and World Bank officials were genuinely surprised and taken aback by Mozambique's action. They had been outflanked, and in the main were forced to accept the programme Mozambique had written.

There were several very different reasons for IMF acquiescence. First, the IMF was under some pressure to agree its first programme with a socialist developing country, and show that the way to joining the West was through structural adjustment. This increased Mozambique's power, and ministers made good use of their limited leverage. In part, too, the IMF and World Bank saw Mozambique as a model for Angola, which was considered more important because it was wealthier. For their part, the IMF and World Bank were not quite sure what they were doing, so they were willing to make initial concessions while they gained more knowledge and felt their way.

The IMF also accepted implicitly that the South African destabilization made a full programme impossible initially. Finally, and perhaps most importantly, it was clear that Mozambique would require an IMF programme for decades; any concessions made to get Mozambique involved could be recuperated later.

The IMF and World Bank laid the groundwork for increased future influence. The World Bank put people into the Bank of Mozambique (where the IMF also posted an 'adviser'), the Ministry of Finance, and the National Directorate of Statistics. These people served an important training and technical assistance role, but they also kept the World Bank and IMF informed of Mozambican data and policy, and kept Mozambique informed of Bank and Fund demands. The World Bank began its donor coordination and exerted increasing influence on the donors when it called the first meeting of the Consultative Group for Mozambique, in Paris in July 1987.

On the Mozambican side, it was clear that some sort of radical adjustment was required. Falling productivity, the rapid growth in the money supply, and the burgeoning black market could not be allowed to continue unchecked. Thus, although details of the initial PRE package might be debated, there was little dispute with the broad outlines – particularly the emphasis on the rural areas. The devaluation, for example, seemed about right to bring the real local cost of goods to a level comparable to that in neighbouring countries.

And Frelimo had won some significant concessions. The PRE said little of privatization and accepted the continued subsidization of state industry. All social sectors remained state-controlled. Key prices were still controlled. The ration system continued. Lower interest rates were maintained for small producers. In other words, many of the key tenets of a socialist economy were still intact. Frelimo also thought it had resisted pressure to reduce government spending and cut services, but this proved a false hope.

Fundamental changes?

Nevertheless, there were disputes as to how radical the new shifts were. The new Foreign Minister, Pascoal Mocumbi, stressed to socialist ambassadors that Mozambique had not abandoned its socialist goals. "Socialism does not mean that the national product should be distributed for free", he said. The former health minister pointed to the new health charges, which were designed to recover money from employers (see Chapter 15); Dr Mocumbi stressed that no one would be denied medical treatment simply because they could not pay.

Prime Minister Machungo argued that the PRE did not represent a new economic policy, but was simply the implementation of guidelines set by Frelimo at its Fourth Congress in 1983. He summarized these guidelines as: "pay wages to those who work, don't pay those who don't work, rationalize the labour force." He said that the PRE "seeks basically to reward good organization and good management. We have to end the situation where everyone, good and bad, has the right to wages, and receives wages, working or not."

But the World Bank had a different view. "Both the macro and the sectoral policy measures incorporated in the ERP [PRE] represent a major intensification in the process of economic reform in Mozambique. While the conceptualization of the reforms is broadly in line with the proposals of the 1983 Party Congress, the detailed program differs substantively from the Government's earlier Economic Action Program (1984–86) in that it addresses – in a more fundamental fashion – the critical macro and sectoral issues" (WB 1987b).

Mozambican ministers tried to argue that PRE was not really a standard structural adjustment package. UNDP made the most sensible compromise when it called PRE a "structural adjustment and economic rehabilitation programme" (UNDP 1987c).

Further demands

For the most part, the IMF and World Bank accepted the PRE, and the "Economic Policy Framework 1987–89" issued in May 1987 was not significantly different. The most important further concession was an additional devaluation. In June Mozambique was forced to cut the value of the metical in half, to just 10% of its former value, at $1 = MT 400. This was followed by a wage increase of only 50%. The Bank admitted that total wage increases in 1987 were "considerably less" than official price rises.

In addition, Mozambique agreed to reduce the number of items for which prices are fixed from 44 to 36 by mid-year, to 32 by the end of 1987, and 28 by July 1988. Whereas the PRE had maintained government expenditure, the IMF insisted on a 20% reduction in real terms in non-defence spending. Mozambique also had to promise further easing of foreign exchange controls from 1988. In particular, individuals and traders were to be allowed to import up to $500 (£300) of goods without a licence if they had the foreign currency (WB 1987a, 1987d). The World Bank also talked of "substantial cuts in public sector employment" and significant further devaluations (WB 1987b).

In the short term, this satisfied the donors and creditors. At the end of 1986, Mozambique owed $3.2 bn (£1.9 bn), of which $700 mn (£420 mn) was arrears. In May the London Club of international banks agreed to reschedule $250 mn (£150 mn) in arrears. In June the Paris Club of government creditors agreed to reschedule $360 mn (£220) in arrears and 1988 maturities, with grace periods of five to ten years, terms considered by the IMF to be "relatively favourable" (IMF 1987). Nevertheless, this meant Mozambique would have to continue the battle to reschedule debts falling due after 1988, when it was obvious that it would be unable to repay anything for several more years. And Mozambique remained concerned that interest rates on many loans were still linked to commercial interest rates, which have remained high and which impose a continued drain on Mozambique's very limited foreign exchange earnings. By the end of 1988, only two countries had agreed to lower interest rates: Italy (1.5%) and the USSR (no interest). Even after debt relief, actual debt service payments in 1988 were estimated at 58% of export earnings, and this was likely to become worse as interest payments on rescheduled debts grew.

In June the IMF put its seal of approval on the programme by agreeing a $16 mn (£10 mn) structural adjustment facility. The World Bank agreed a set of loans worth $45 mn (£27 mn) in May and a $90 mn (£54 mn) second rehabilitation credit in August. In July the first Consultative Group meeting raised some additional donor support.

The socialist bloc accepted the necessity of the programme and also increased its support. The USSR promised 370,000 tonnes of fuel and Rouble 70 mn (then $90 mn, £54 mn) worth of consumer goods and raw materials.

10 Is Mozambique a Special Case?

Structural adjustment is based on a package of des: deregulation, devaluation, denationalization, decreased government deficit, decreased demand, and deflation. This is called "economic policy reform". The package assumes that the crisis is caused by overregulation, mismanagement, profligacy, and excessive consumption. Resource allocation should be determined by prices and the market, rather than planning and equity considerations. The dogma of socialism should be replaced by the dogma of the free market.

Frelimo accepted the need for reform, but only as part of a larger package. It saw the crisis as brought on by war and colonialism as well as mismanagement, and put its emphasis on growth and increased production. It looked for a "third way" between rigid central planning and crude free market capitalism (See also Chapter 20). "The government is committed to a strategy which places primary emphasis on rural development and which combines a strong effort toward poverty reduction with liberalization measures designed to promote freer markets and economic growth" (RPM 1989).

As the programme was being implemented, there were a series of struggles over the nature of the problem (see Chapter 6), the appropriateness of structural adjustment, and even the impact of the programme. For the most part, the IMF and World Bank pushed for an ever-freer market and more belt-tightening; the high cost of adjustment is simply the bad taste of an essential medicine. Frelimo stressed that the war made a totally free market inappropriate. It pointed to the immense suffering being caused, and stressed the need for growth.

In general, the IMF deals with macro issues and the World Bank with micro policy. In Mozambique, the IMF sets the exchange rate and devaluations, and determines limits on government expenditure and credit. The World Bank deals with all other matters: it coordinates donors, does the studies, and has permanent staff in Maputo. Although the Fund is technically the senior agency, the Bank takes the lead in Mozambique (in contrast to some other countries).

Although the Fund and Bank agree on free market dogma, the Bank (prodded by Unicef and other agencies) has become increasingly concerned about the social impact of adjustment. This has led to some disputes between Bank and Fund on Mozambique, and, as noted in Chapter 13, to the Bank's increasing acceptance of some of Frelimo's arguments.

What really happened in 1986?

Both sides accepted that people had money but little to spend it on. Put simplistically,

Frelimo saw the solution as increasing production so people had something to buy, while the IMF and World Bank saw the solution as raising prices so that people did not have excessive money.

What happened in 1986 and 1987 was important to this argument. In 1986 there was a brief period in which the Frelimo line was followed, and the economy was stimulated with only partial "reform". In 1987 the full panoply of PRE/structural adjustment was added. Thus 1986 was the test of the Frelimo line, and 1987 the test of the IMF view. Not surprisingly, the two sides disagreed on what occurred.

1986 boom

Frelimo consistently argued that the core of the economic crisis was not policy errors but the shortage of foreign exchange which had become serious from 1982. The colonial industrial base had been highly import-dependent, and post-independence restructuring had only begun. All vehicles are imported, so transport was hit hard and commerce and industry were grinding to a halt. Without spare parts, equipment which broke down or was damaged by Renamo raids could not be repaired. Raw materials were not available either because they were imported or because the lorries which normally carried them were out of commission, so even machinery that was still operating was not used to capacity. At the same time, peasants were not going to produce for the market if there was no one to buy their crops or no consumer goods to spend their money on, so officially marketed farm production fell.

From 1983, Frelimo had been appealing – not very successfully – for consumer goods and spare parts to stimulate commerce. The very act of joining the IMF and opening negotiations in mid-1985 was enough to release substantial new grants and soft loans. In 1986, imports increased by 28% ($120 mn, £72 mn). Half the extra money went on imported consumer goods, and the other half on raw materials and spare parts for both industry and agriculture (DNE 1988: 52).

The import programme was a dramatic success. Industry, both large and small, expanded production. Suddenly shops were full and people could buy. For the first time in five years, goods did not disappear from shops the day they arrived; suddenly there were no queues. And as goods were available across the counter in the normal way, the importance of the black market decreased.

GDP increased in 1986, despite the fact that no structural adjustment programme had been introduced. But there was a dispute as to how much; the IMF reported a 2.6% real increase (IMF 1987) and the government reported a 1.5% increase (RPM 1988). But the World Bank alleged that the changes had "proved insufficient to reverse the economic decline" and claimed a 2% decrease (WB 1988a: 2, 34). It kept recalculating this figure, however, and later admitted to a 0.9% rise (WB 1990c: 8).

Peasant agriculture always lags behind, and only the 1986 cashew marketing campaign was affected by the extra consumer goods; cashew sales were up one-third. For other crops, the changes of 1986 were only reflected in marketing in early 1987. At constant prices, family sector marketing increased 80% in 1987. Peasant sales of maize, rice, cotton and beans were all up dramatically (DNE 1988: 32ff). Some may have been increased production, but a substantial amount must have been produce that had been sold or bartered on the black market in previous years.

1987: more boom, then bust

In 1987 loans and grants allowed a further 18% increase in imports, which in turn caused GDP to increase by 4%. The World Bank admitted that this "modest recovery in output" reflected "a pickup in light industrial activity as a result of increased imports of inputs and spare parts" (WB 1988d). It was imports, not policy reforms, which boosted production.

The 1986 growth was before devaluation, which meant that in practice imported goods were artificially cheap; this probably had a distorting effect. But for a short time people spent their limited savings on scarce consumer goods which had not been openly available for several years.

Two sharp devaluations in January and June 1987 took the metical to one-tenth its former value. Mozambican officials agreed to the first, but not the second, which was considered excessive. Because they came so close together, it is difficult to distinguish their relative effects.

What is clear is that the combination of more consumer goods and devaluation remonetized the metical; there were goods to buy in local currency and people were no longer forced to barter or use rands or dollars. The black market rate of the metical fell drastically; after the second devaluation the black market rate was $1 = MT 800, half the former rate and only double the official rate. An IMF official admitted to me that the IMF had never expected the parallel rate to fall, and that it would have been catastrophic and unnecessary to go immediately to an official rate of $1 = MT 1500 as the IMF had initially demanded.

But the two large devaluations in 1987 triggered massive price rises, which threw the boom into reverse. After the first devaluation, wages in Maputo rose 70%, from an average of MT 5000 per month to MT 8470. But average prices rose 200%. Even the cost of the basic ration in Maputo increased 85%, leaving less money to spend on other goods, which were themselves much more expensive. The June devaluation saw wages rise 50% and prices increase 100%. (IMF 1987) Producers and traders had serious difficulty calculating their new costs, and tended simply to raise prices in proportion to the devaluation. Competition did not lower prices.

Frelimo had underestimated the size of the black market, erroneously assuming that peasants and others had simply kept money under the bed or buried in the ground. In fact, ordinary working people ran out of money much more quickly than the government expected. Suddenly there were unsold goods in the shops. Artisans, who in 1986 received raw materials and could sell all the buckets or baskets that they made, found themselves in 1987 with unsold stock. AIM noted that "some industries are facing difficulty selling their products." AIM also commented on something which was widely remarked: the black market just a year before had been goods diverted from controlled channels and selling at well above official prices; by late 1987 it was increasingly made up of stolen goods selling at below official prices (AIM November 1987 supp.).

The World Bank admitted from the first that "many people in urban areas may be affected adversely" due to prices increasing more rapidly than salaries, and because "urban unemployment is projected to increase significantly as a result of rationalization of the public sector" (WB 1987b). They were right on the first count, but not on the second; urban unemployment rose, but not due to dismissals. Civil service employment did decline by 10% by mid-1987 (WB 1988d). In Maputo the biggest source of new unemployed were refugees coming in from the rural areas and miners and others expelled from South Africa.

For several years there had been a drift away from urban industry and commerce (and even to some extent the civil service) as workers abandoned their jobs due to low and irregular salaries and the apparent lack of a viable future. Thus, in Maputo, at least, private companies found that increased raw materials allowed them to use the remaining workers that they kept on through the lean periods, so there were fewer sackings than expected.

The biggest lay-offs occurred on the state farms (WB 1988d). Thus the initial impact of the rationalizations hit hardest in rural rather than urban areas, just the reverse of what was intended. This was to be a marker of things to come.

Imports or free market?

When imports were again available, commerce and industry restarted – before PRE and with only limited policy changes. Thus what was promoting economic growth was increased imports to stimulate the economy. Policy changes were only secondary to this. But free market policy changes were essential to push donors to provide money. So the real purpose of policy reform had less to do with the needs of Mozambique and more to do with IMF doctrine and the demands of donors.

The contrast between 1986 and 1987 went to the heart of the policy dispute. The World Bank dealt with this by ignoring 1986. At first, it said GDP had continued to fall in 1986. When this was clearly not true, it always grouped statistics for 1982-86, said to be the period of decline. In this way, it tried to give the impression that growth began with PRE in 1987. But government reports always stressed that growth and recovery began in 1986, which was before the structural adjustment programme was agreed.

Rotten tomatoes

The World Bank repeatedly tried to claim that improvements were due to its free market policies even when they were not, and they seemed prepared to distort the evidence to do this. One example was a study of fruit and vegetable marketing in Maputo.

Frelimo had ended fixed pricing of fruit and vegetables in May 1985, in part as an experiment. The Bank was so convinced that Mozambique would learn free market truths from this, that one of its conditions for the second loan was that the government must undertake a study of fruit and vegetable marketing and the impact of price liberalization (WB 1987d). Then, when the conclusions turned out "wrong", the Bank simply presented highly selective versions of those conclusions which supported their own view.

The study (Francisco 1987b) found that 30,000 tonnes of fruit and vegetables were sold in Maputo in 1984; this fell to 29,000 t in 1985, rose to 36,000 t in 1986, and fell again in 1987 back toward 30,000 t. (Other reports indicated a further fall in 1988.) Initial free market prices were similar to the previous black market ones; prices then rose less rapidly than inflation, but faster than consumer purchasing power (which was falling precipitously in this period). There was a major shift toward private production: in 1984 state farms provided 58% of commercialized vegetables in Maputo, the private sector 37%, and family and co-op 4%; by 1986 it was state 18%, private 64%, and family and co-op 18%.

The study notes that price liberalization took place in 1985, leading to no increase in production. In 1986 there were several changes: USAID sold trucks to private farmers, the government and various donors provided agricultural inputs, Lonrho took over a major state farm and produced substantial quantities of tomatoes, and several state farms were attacked by Renamo. This led to a shift in production from state to private sector, and to an overall increase in production.

Thus the study concludes that although price liberalization was useful, inputs and equipment supplied to the private sector by USAID and the government were much more important.

The study also concluded that traders wanted to deal in low volumes and high mark-ups. They used the free market to keep prices high. In times of abundant production, retail prices were kept high, while wholesale prices where pushed down to increase profit. Retail profit margins were "very high" and retailers earned a "substantial" part of the price; on turnovers as low as 15 kg of vegetables per day, retailers could have an income larger than the average national wage. The 1987 fall in production reflected both a decrease in purchasing by consumers who could no longer afford vegetables, and the withdrawal of many producers because wholesale prices had been pushed down.

The exception was the state wholesaler Hortofruticola, which had a 30% share of the fruit and vegetable market. It operated profitably with high volumes and low margins. As well as operating as a wholesaler, it established its own market stalls and even street-corner stands. Hortofruticola charged much lower prices, and when it began to sell a product, private traders were forced to reduce their prices as well. "The strategic action

The parastatal fruit and vegetable wholesaler Hortofruticola set up stalls like this on Maputo street corners in a successful campaign to lower retail prices (J. Hanlon).

of this company is actually fundamental in stabilizing the market, in dynamizing commercial circuits, in lowering consumer prices, and in promoting competition between different agents in the market", according to the study.

It concludes that "for the laws of the market to function in a dynamic and progressive way, the state is called to intensify its support and participation." It recommends giving extra resources to Hortofrutícola. And it says the state should establish programmes of research and extension to help producers extend the growing season and increase production.

This conclusion was shocking and unacceptable to the World Bank. In private discussions with me, a World Bank official flatly rejected the view that traders were making excess profits. The official went on to say that state enterprises are *always* less efficient than private, and that Hortofrutícola could not possibly be profitable and must be subsidized by the state. Hortofrutícola director Belmiro Baptista flatly denied this. They made money, he said, because volumes were so much larger. One person on a street stall sells 300 kg per day, compared to 15 kg for the typical market trader. Despite having had six lorries destroyed by Renamo, Hortofrutícola bought and hired trucks out of profits and without state subsidy. "As a state company, we have a clear social role to try to keep prices down. But we must make a profit, and we do." Bulk trading is higher risk, and he pointed to the irony of a state firm being prepared to take a risk when private traders refused to do so.

Baptista cited the case of tomatoes in 1988. Early in the season, the wholesale price was 250 MT/kg and private traders sold at 800 MT/kg. The wholesale price fell to 200 MT, but the retail price stayed at 800 MT. As production increased, the wholesale price fell to 30 MT/kg, but the private retail price was 220 MT/kg – allowing an eight-fold profit. Consumers could not afford many tomatoes, and producers found they could not sell to market traders, so lorryloads were left to rot. "We stepped in and bought truckloads at 30–50 MT/kg, and sold retail at 100 MT/kg. We made a massive profit, and brought the price down."

The World Bank responded by presenting highly selective and distorted summaries of the study that reflected its own preconceptions. For example, in one of its "Mozambique Policy Framework" papers (WB 1988a: 13) it said the study showed that "private-sector production responded significantly to the improved market incentive structure", which is not at all what the study said. It went on to note that the study "found no evidence of monopolistic practices", which is true, but irrelevant since the study found that cartelizing had kept prices high. And it simply ignored the main conclusions of its own study – that price liberalization played little role, that Hortofruticola should be supported, and that the general state role should be "intensified".

Adjustment in Time of War

"During World War II in Europe, every country intervened in the market. But the IMF tells us we cannot. They say 'this is our money', and we have to listen."

"We asked for help to rebuild after our war. After World War II, the US had the Marshall Plan without anything like structural adjustment. But the Marshall Plan was for white people in Europe, not for Africa."

"They think that what works in Ghana is also applicable in Mozambique. But the situation here is different, because of the war. Aggression destroyed the base of our economy. But they insist we must follow the same prescription. I have never accepted this and I have fought it very strongly. But in the end we have no choice."

These quotes come from Mozambican government ministers, speaking off the record in private discussions, as they compared their own position to Europe during and after the Second World War. Frelimo has a tendency to exaggerate Mozambique's uniqueness, and some of its problems are common to all countries faced by unpayable debts and falling world commodity prices. Nevertheless, both IMF and World Bank officials admitted to me that Mozambique *is* unique, and that they had no other experience of a country undergoing structural adjustment in time of war.

There are three separate issues. First is the "war economy" and the need for unusual economic actions during a war. Second is rebuilding after the war. In the shifting war in Mozambique, however, reconstruction and war go on in parallel. Indeed, physical reconstruction is an essential part of rebuilding the economy, while reconstruction is also an important aspect of gaining popular support. In practice, structural adjustment goes against the needs of a war economy and of the reconstruction period, however much they overlap. And that points to the third issue: does war create special conditions which mean that structural adjustment cannot work?

Is there a 'war economy'?

"No war is won just by soldiers on the battlefield", declared Prime Minister Mário Machungo. "To win the war we must produce.... Every country at war finds ways of combining war with production. We cannot separate one thing from the other." (*Noticias* 16 February 1987) The Frelimo Politburo in a communiqué on 5 March 1986 stressed the importance of "the war economy".

In 1940 Maynard Keynes wrote a paper for Britain on "How to Pay for the War". In it he argued for a strongly managed economy to mobilize resources to finance the war without excessive hardship. This meant compulsory savings, wage and price controls, subsidized basic rations and family allowances. This is just the opposite of what has been pressed on Mozambique: reduce management of the economy, end wage and price controls, end subsidies, and cut family income.

A similar problem occurs with reconstruction. Under the Marshall Plan, resources poured in to help reconstruct Europe. Although aid is pouring into Mozambique, it is for survival and repaying debts, and seldom for reconstruction. Indeed, the Bank discourages repair and rehabilitation of war damage, both to keep down government expenditure and because, as a Bank official told me, "we are not building bridges to have them blown up."

False assumptions

"Countries give us a prescription they would never use themselves. They are using us as a laboratory to see if their theories work", a government minister told me bitterly.

There is no evidence that structural adjustment actually works anywhere. Indeed, the Economic Commission for Africa suggested that structural adjustment was harmful; it found that in a sample of African countries, those with adjustment programmes had shown a 1.5% per year annual decline in GDP, while those without had shown 1.2% growth. Furthermore, growth rates declined after countries adopted adjustment programmes (ECA 1989b; *Africa Recovery* October 1989). Indeed, in 1990 IMF and World Bank officials were reported to be "a bit conscience-stricken" about the failure of structural adjustment in Mozambique's neighbour Malawi, which started one of Africa's first adjustment programmes in 1981 (*Financial Times* 10 April 1990)

Furthermore, the World Bank and IMF had never before tried structural adjustment on a country at war, so Mozambique represented a two-fold experiment. As Chapter 13 shows, the Bank is beginning to admit the failure of its experiments. But Mozambique pays the price. As Arne Disch of the Norwegian aid agency Norad comments, the World Bank imposes its policies but takes none of the risk. Mozambique must repay the loans whether or not structural adjustment works, "while the Bank can simply mumble 'sorry about that' and try to come up with another panacea – also funded by loans.... The Bank should be willing to consider its proposals as bets, and thus willing to forego the payback if the bet fails" (Disch 1989).

Resources to the countryside?

The Mozambican government, the IMF, and the World Bank all agree that a central goal of PRE or adjustment is to transfer resources from the city to the countryside and to stimulate rural agricultural production. In principle, the countryside must be the basis of development because it is the source of food, industrial raw materials, and most exports, as well as the home of the bulk of the population. The theory, upheld by a broad consensus, is that peasants and small private producers will produce more if they are given higher real producer prices and more consumer goods, and if rural markets work better. Higher real producer prices in the short term require a transfer of money from urban to rural areas, even if this means taking money from the poor to give it to those poorer still.

After three years of pursuing this line, the Bank now admits the "apparent incongruity of a rural, agricultural-based strategy in a period of extensive rural insecurity" (WB 1990c: 60).

How can marketing work in a country where the marketing structure and peasant production have been a very specific target of attack? Refugees do not have the means to produce even their own food, let alone respond to market signals; marketing is erratic and peasants are unsure if they can sell their production and if consumer goods will be available; damaged roads and bridges make marketing difficult; and private traders, who are a target of the South Africans, follow a natural strategy of risk aversion.

It remains unproven that the unfettered free market is the best way for a country as poor and underdeveloped as Mozambique, especially in time of war. The best free market strategy is to stick to safe urban areas, or to deal in high profit items on the black market.

Reducing support for Frelimo

In a war, it is crucial for the government to retain popular support. Yet when Mozambicans have made tremendous sacrifices due to the war, PRE seems to punish rather than reward them.

Privately, one person from the World Bank made an explicitly political argument to me that Frelimo would actually would gain support through PRE. Frelimo has support in urban areas but has lost support in rural areas, he argued, and thus resources should be transferred to rural areas to regain that support. But others see it in exactly the opposite way — that structural adjustment is undercutting Frelimo support in urban areas. PRE creates unemployment and suffering, which promotes crime and banditry which Renamo can claim and perhaps even encourage. The hungry and unemployed are vulnerable to the blandishments of any anti-Frelimo group, be it religious or political. Indeed an IMF official admitted to me in deep confidence that he wondered about the wisdom of encouraging the sacking of workers. A World Bank report actually warned that "by increasing consumer prices past the ability of a significant proportion of the urban population of Maputo and Beira, government may open itself to other problems that could affect its constituency" (WB 1990a: 87).

Even in rural areas, the IMF-imposed cuts can only inflict further damage on health, education, and other government services already under attack by Renamo and South Africa, which further weakens support for Frelimo. And in practice, the inflationary effects of the repeated devaluations have hit people badly in rural areas; only the better-off, who have substantial capital or cash reserves, can hang on to the upward price escalator and profit from it.

The ostrich position

The IMF and World Bank avoid the contradictions between war and adjustment by pretending they don't exist. World Bank and IMF staff know that, while the war continues, promoting rural areas is what one of them called an "Alice in Wonderland policy". One IMF person admitted: "incentives for farmers are meaningless when you have terrorism." He concluded: "It's a holding action. And it must be so long as that regime is beating on them."

But they do have to satisfy their chiefs in Washington. And their strong free market beliefs assure them that what they are doing is building the future. "We take a long term perspective and look at fundamental issues in the economy. Mozambique's management of the economy has been very inappropriate. And it has not just been specific issues like the exchange rate, but central planning, state enterprizes, and all the market rigidities", one official said. "We are addressing the critical variables. Market oriented policies can lead to the restoration of production. The programme is good if it pushes out the least efficient producers."

In part, it goes back to the debate of Chapter 6: Why is there a problem? To the World Bank, war is only one of a variety of factors, and is less important than "past policies". Thus "insecurity continues to be a constraining factor in the responsiveness of the economy" and destabilization is a "persistent exogenous constraint". But the key to solving economic problems remains "a shift in the system of management from one based on administrative and central allocation of resources to one based on market forces." (WB 1988b, 1989b). In 1987 the World Bank said that despite the security problems, "the maintenance of elements of a command economy in a war situation ... will inevitably dampen the impact of the reforms" (WB 1987b).

The IMF sometimes simply ignores the problem. In one paper it argues that real incomes of city dwellers have declined "even as the potential real income of rural producers has increased substantially" (IMF 1988a). But the urban decline is real while the rural potential cannot be realized because of the war. As the IMF admits in another paper, "effective demand was reduced in urban areas because wages had not risen commensurately with sale prices. In rural areas, despite the large positive effects of increases in farmgate producer prices, purchasing power in some areas had suffered as a result of the security situation and drought" (IMF 1987).

The only answer is faith. "Under prevailing conditions, the economy's response to even these strong policy initiatives will probably not be sufficient to yield a sustainable growth and balance of payments outcome in the program period. Nevertheless, the reform and adjustment measures provide a framework for more effective utilization of both domestic and external resources in support of structural and institution changes which, once the security situation improves, can lead the economy to sustainable growth" (IMF 1988a). Structural adjustment will "establish the conditions for a return to higher levels of economic growth once the security situation and other exogenous constraints have eased" (WB 1988a).

Bank and Fund views that Mozambique is partly a "holding action" have led them to moderate structural adjustment policies slightly. They have not pushed for full deregulation, especially in rural areas; they have accepted some state allocation of goods and some continued price controls; and they have quietly accepted the continued state subsidies for industries that would be viable in peacetime. A typical comment is that "in view of the current insecurity in the countryside, as an interim measure, the Government will need to retain some direct administrative control over certain key products to ensure that minimum levels reach all regions and sectors of the economy" (WB 1987a). But they cannot always get support for this in the more doctrinaire free market climate of Washington. In the following reports the Bank and Fund reduce their acceptance of such controls, so that by 1988 they talk only of "some limited controls" (WB 1988a).

But the war cannot be ignored or turned into a subsidiary or minor issue; it is the core issue. Prime Minister Machungo told donors at the 1988 conference in Paris that PRE "tries to find a response to a difficult and complex situation created by the systematic destruction of human lives and economic and social infrastructure by terrorist actions of armed bands which are the agents of the apartheid regime." Sten Rylander, for the Swedish delegation, stressed that "we continue to have the firm conviction that the present difficulties and sufferings facing the Mozambican people are primarily caused by the sabotage, ravages and terror actions committed by the South African backed MNR." The Mozambique government continues to argue "that the principal obstacle to growth and development has been and continues to be rooted in the political situation in the region" (RPM 1989). And the government stresses that losses to date due to the war are four times the accumulated debt.

Adjustment with growth

Mozambicans argue for an alternative policy. "I insist that if there is a case where adjustment must be accompanied by economic and social growth, then it is Mozambique", Finance Minister Magid Osman told donors in Paris in November 1988. This is because of "Mozambique's unique economic situation and overall because of the level of destruction."

"The government is committed to a strategy which places primary emphasis on rural development, and which combines a strong effort toward poverty reduction with liberalization measures designed to promote a free market." Agricultural policies are intended to stimulate smallholder family production. The link between industry and agriculture is repeatedly stressed, as is marketing as the connection between the two. The growth of family agriculture is dependent on sufficient consumer goods to exchange. Industrial rehabilitation will concentrate "on facilities to produce textiles, shoes, and other consumer goods in rural areas" (RPM 1989). The construction sector is seen as important for employment creation and to provide low-cost housing, so the rehabilitation of the building materials sector (cement, bricks, tiles, stone) will be encouraged. In the short term the need is still to increase capacity utilization through the import of raw materials and spare parts. In the longer term, the goal is to restructure away from import dependence to more use of local resources, but that will require imported machinery.

Improving marketing is much more an issue of improving transport – both lorries and roads – than of disputes between private and public. The government is committed to supporting a growth of private trading, while ensuring that there is never a local monopoly which can sabotage the whole project by worsening the terms of trade for rural people so as to increase their own profits. That means the state, through the parastatal marketing board, Agricom, must always have a presence in the market.

The government's initial priorities in allocating resources, particularly forex, in industry are: produce consumer goods for rural areas; produce agricultural tools; produce food for domestic consumption; contribute to tax revenue (beer and cigarettes); import substitution; and support export sectors (RPM 1987).

The government warns that there "is clear evidence that a lack of basic social services and adequate income causes the productivity of many, if not most, Mozambican workers to be far lower than it could be." (RPM 1989) "Employment generation is also a requirement of sustained economic growth." Therefore Mozambique's investment priorities will be "rural development, poverty alleviation, and employment generation."

11 Devaluation, Inflation and Recession: 1987-89

The World Bank argues that "inherent" in the PRE "is the recognition that the closer integration of the Mozambique economy into the international economy is essential, with domestic industrial and agricultural production being exposed both to the incentives and disciplines of international markets" (WB 1987b). Central to a more "open" economy is the elimination of all international trade barriers. Mozambicans should be able to buy goods abroad as easily as they buy inside their own country, while foreigners should have open access to Mozambique.

One part of this is making the metical a fully convertible or "hard" currency, like the D-Mark or franc. In most countries of the world, as in Britain until the 1960s, US dollars and other foreign exchange (normally shortened to "forex") is in short supply and is allocated in some way by the government to potential travellers, importers, and investors. Ending this system involves three steps.

The normal first step is to ensure that exports and other foreign earnings generate enough forex. This is one of the goals of PRE, but the free market theorists argue that by jumping ahead to the second and third steps, the market guarantees the first.

The second step is to establish the correct exchange rate, or "value", of the metical with respect to the US$. This is not easy even for major currencies; within a five-year period in the early 1980s, the US$ to UK£ rate doubled, and much of the debate about Britain joining the European Monetary System is about the "value" of the UK£.

The final step is to make hard currency freely available and not to allocate it administratively. The free market should determine who imports and what is imported.

Is exchange rate the key instrument?

The relative importance of exchange rate compared to other financial issues is a central part of the debate between the government and the Bank and Fund. In 1988 the World Bank said that "the exchange rate will remain a key instrument to attain the objective of PRE", requiring further "substantial" devaluations (WB 1988c). In 1989 it set "three key areas where further reforms are critical". Number one was "the management of foreign exchange".

A minister involved in the negotiations told me that "the only thing the IMF knows is devaluation. It's their main objective." The IMF insists on reaching a "market rate" for foreign exchange and eventually having a free market in foreign exchange.

There had been two big devaluations in 1987, from MT 40 to the US$ to MT 200 in January and MT 400 in June. In 1988 there were further devaluations, to MT 450 in

January, MT 580 in July, and MT 620 in October. The first big devaluations proved very disruptive, and Mozambique wanted to make smaller ones more often. Initially the IMF insisted on big jumps, but then it became divided within itself on this point. So from the beginning of 1989, the government imposed regular smaller devaluations at the beginning of most months, reaching MT 830 by December 1989 and MT 1050 by early 1991. (Overall that is a devaluation from £1 = MT 66 to £1 = MT 1730.)

The government was anxious to continue devaluing only at the rate of inflation, but the IMF forced faster devaluations. A minister argued to me that the IMF has already pushed too hard for devaluation, and that the metical is now undervalued. I certainly found that items with a high local content, like food, cost me much less that I would pay in Britain, even changing money at the official rather than black market rate.

One of the IMF's main justifications for devaluation is that it stimulates exports and reduces imports. But the minister argued this does not work with Mozambique. "If we are not exporting more tea or coal, it has nothing to do with the exchange rate and everything to do with the war. The problem is to increase production and remove transport bottlenecks. But they don't understand – or don't want to understand."

How important is the black market?

Inevitably, if forex is allocated by some mechanism, there will be people who do not receive an allocation and who are prepared to pay substantially over the odds. This creates a black market. The two main sources of black market hard currency are migrant workers from South Africa, who have rand to sell, and foreign workers and diplomats, who have dollars. This parallel market is quite open, and as a white foreigner I was often asked in shops if I wanted to change money. The rate is well enough known and consistent enough for the US embassy (and no doubt many others) to publish a regular report with the black market rate.

The parallel market in foreign currency is actually quite small and big demands for forex can cause sharp jumps in the parallel rate. In May 1990 the US$ parallel rate suddenly jumped 20% as less than one planeload of Muslims tried to obtain hard currency for their air fares to go to the haj. Government ministries buying office furniture can push up the rand parallel rate (because desks and so on are imported semi-legally from South Africa).

In 1986, a dollar on the parallel market was worth at least 20 times the official rate. But after the first two devaluations the parallel rate unexpectedly fell to just double the official rate. It remained roughly double after each subsequent devaluation.

The Fund and Bank argue that the existence of the parallel market for forex shows the need for devaluation. In negotiations they say they want to get the official rate to be 70% of the parallel rate, compared to the normal 45–50%. (South Africa has what is, in effect, an official parallel rate, with the "commercial" rand rate averaging about 70% of the "financial" rand rate.) But the unchanging link between official and parallel rate led the Fund to complain that "the stated program objective of a substantial narrowing of the gap between the official and parallel market exchange rates has remained elusive" (IMF 1988b). This creates a permanent cycle: the IMF says the parallel rate is too high and forces Mozambique to devalue, so the parallel rate goes up, and the IMF demands another devaluation, independent of any other assessment of the "real" value of the currency.

In fact, for several reasons the parallel rate is not a "real" value. First, and most important, growing differentials in income mean that demand for luxury goods will continue to outstrip the reasonable availability of forex for such purposes, and this will always fuel a black market. Second, in most developing countries traders are trying to smuggle hard currency out of the country, which creates a parallel rate and market. Third, and most important in Mozambique, the IMF is itself fuelling the parallel market. The IMF insisted that traders be allowed personally to import up to $500 (£300) worth of goods for resale, without a licence, so long as they already have the forex. Most of this money comes from black market currency deals in Maputo, and it ensures that a parallel rate exists. Clearly the IMF knows this, because when the plan was first mooted, the World Bank said it was intended for "the recycling of parallel market proceeds" (WB 1986).

In practice, then, the differential seems to be about what would be expected for smuggling money out of the country and for bringing in goods from neighbouring states.

Forex auctions?

The IMF and World Bank stressed their desire "for shifting towards a system under which the price of foreign exchange would serve as a main allocative instrument" (WB 1989b). They repeatedly tried to force Mozambique to introduce a forex auction. Under this system there is a weekly or monthly auction, where business people bid, in meticais, for US dollars. This is supposed to establish the "market rate" of exchange. After the fiasco of such auctions in Zambia and elsewhere, many Mozambican and donor officials could not believe that the IMF was serious. But it was, and strong pressure was brought to bear during talks in 1988. Indeed, in 1988 a World Bank official told me confidently that there would definitely be an auction the following year. But Mozambique resisted.

Again in December 1989 the IMF negotiating team in Maputo demanded an auction. After a stiff fight, the IMF team finally conceded that an auction was inappropriate, and an agreement was signed. Then, in an action unprecedented with respect to Mozambique, the IMF refused to recognize the agreement and sent a different team in February 1990 to demand an auction. After days of hard bargaining, the second IMF team also agreed that Mozambique need not have an auction. A minister involved in the negotiations commented: "When Washington sees that a negotiating team understands the situation in a country, it changes the team. A team leader who defended our position was removed, because they have certain parameters and policies they must follow."

The experience in Zambia was clear. The system worked badly even in a narrow technical sense. And it was a social and developmental disaster. The price of forex was pushed up by traders importing luxury goods for the wealthy, because this was where the quickest profits were to be found. In contrast to IMF predictions, industry did not use the system to import raw materials and spare parts; indeed, traders found it more profitable to import South African goods in direct competition to locally made goods. Thus the auction hit industrial development, and benefited the rich at the expense of the poor.

Mozambican officials repeatedly pushed for a compromise of a dual exchange rate or "second window", such as is used in South Africa and several other countries. This involves one rate set by the Bank of Mozambique for official transactions, and a second "tourist" or "financial" rate set by the market. IMF officials vociferously resisted any form of dual exchange rate; government ministers argued that there was a *de facto* dual rate in any case, and failing to legalize and regulate it simply encouraged corruption.

Finally, after the IMF conceded in 1990 that it could not force Mozambique to accept a forex auction, it allowed the legalization of the black market. Licensed private dealers (and special Bank of Mozambique exchange bureaux) were able to buy hard currency from foreigners and others with cash, and sell it to Mozambicans. As the government had always said would happen, legalization brought the second rate down – from $1 = MT 2200 for the illegal black market rate to $1 = MT 1800 for the new legal second rate at the end of 1990 – because there was open competition rather than clandestine dealing.

Free trade?

As well as pushing for an auction, the IMF and World Bank also pressed Mozambique to end import restrictions and allow companies to import whatever they wanted. Some tariffs and import surcharges would be allowed, but there would be no licensing, no quotas, and no assignment of imported goods for priority uses. This is the so-called "non-administrative allocation" of forex.

Mozambique considers this to be totally ludicrous, especially with a war on and most forex controlled by donors in any case. Indeed, the Bank admits that in 1987, 75% of forex was for uses "determined by previous commitments (tied import programs, project aid, and debt service obligations)." Of the rest, a third went to essential imports. So at best only "15% of imports could be considered 'free' foreign exchange which could be allocated non-administratively" (WB 1989b).

Nevertheless, in 1988 talks with the World Bank actually broke down for two months because of demands for what it calls "a more open trade regime". Finally the Bank accepted the compromise of a pilot programme, called Sistema Não-Administrativo de Alocação de Divisas (SNAAD – system for non-administrative allocation of foreign exchange). There would be no licences for a handful of very important items: spare parts for heavy vehicles and construction and agricultural equipment, plus parts and key inputs for the garment and shoe industries. The costs of those items would be paid from a World Bank credit; a ceiling would be applied to how much any one applicant could use, and the whole programme would be limited to $25 mn (£15 mn) per year.

Mozambique was satisfied because it had limited the programme to areas in which the availability of forex would benefit the economy most and have a positive social and economic impact (unlike the Zambia auction); furthermore, the World Bank had agreed to provide more money for this course of action. The Bank was satisfied because its foot was now in the door; it intended to force Mozambique steadily to expand SNAAD. Indeed, in 1989 the Bank was hoping "donors would channel an increasing proportion of their external assistance through the SNAAD" (WB 1989b). This was in clear conflict with Mozambique's own goals.

Pushing Up the Cost of Living

Devaluation, supposedly a response to inflation, is itself inflationary in a country like Mozambique where so much is imported. This puts further squeezes on living standards and on industry.

In pushing ahead with PRE without prior IMF agreement, the government made significant gains, but it also made one critical mistake. Government economists badly underestimated the cascade effects of devaluation. After the first devaluation, all imported goods cost (in meticais) five times more. There are few things to be purchased in Mozambique that do not have a very high import content, which means that all costs – government and private – went up substantially with the devaluation. Not only did the direct cost of imported goods like fuel and medicines go up, but there was a related rise in the price of locally made goods. This inflationary spiral was much more serious than the government expected.

It was clear from the early talks that the IMF would force Mozambique to impose tight spending limits. So when the government introduced PRE, it increased food subsidies and some other spending to cover the first devaluation, then announced a curb on further expenditure. Unfortunately, the government's underestimate of the knock-on effects of devaluation meant that its caps on government deficit, parastatal subsidy, consumer subsidy, and credit were all much too tight. This was made much worse by the unscheduled second devaluation (June 1987), which increased the inflationary spiral dramatically,.

The government's own costs, of which a large portion is wages, rose more rapidly than expected. Tax revenues, of course, rose as well. But the amounts that the government had allowed for the budget deficit proved to be too small. State companies suffered a similar costs and wage squeeze. Food subsidies could not be increased to accommodate the vastly increased costs of imported grain. Businesses needed to borrow much more money than expected to cover their vastly increased cash flow needs; despite restrictions commercial credit was hitting the ceiling even before special programmes were introduced to extend credit into rural areas to help marketing and production.

In private, an IMF official admitted to me that he had been surprised at the low levels Mozambique had chosen for food subsidy and deficit ceilings, and that higher levels would have been acceptable if Mozambique had pressed for them. Indeed, he seemed a bit embarrassed about forcing Mozambique to stick to the lower erroneous level. But the IMF never backed down.

By late 1987 when negotiations opened with the IMF and World Bank for the 1988 programme, there were open disagreements as to what was happening to the economy. The government estimated that inflation in the first year of PRE was at least 166%; the World Bank tended to support the government, while the IMF initially felt it was much less, but eventually admitted to 125% (IMF 1988a). A minister in one of the economic sectors told me that in his opinion, most of the inflation in 1987 was due to devaluations.

The impact on living standards is discussed in more detail below and in the next chapter. But one of the most important effects was the way in which the devaluations interacted with other parts of the PRE to cut government spending, particularly on subsidies and social services.

Spending cuts

Because the state budget was capped, devaluations and rising costs forced cuts. By 1988, spending on health and education was sharply down. Health expenditure was less than $1 per capita compared to $4 in 1981, while education spending in 1988 was only a third of the 1982 figure (WB 1990c: 165; DNE 1987, 1989). "The provision of health and education services has been severely affected," admitted the Bank and Fund in their 1989 "Economic Policy Framework" paper. This is because of a "contraction of aggregate real recurrent expenditure" and because "the share of allocations to health and education has declined" (WB 1989a).

But the Paper stresses that this is "consistent with macroeconomic objectives" (WB 1989a). This is probably the first time that the Bank and Fund admitted that it was policy to cut health and education. In part, this admission may have reflected increasing disquiet by some Bank staff at the magnitude of the cuts. One Bank report admitted that in health "present recurrent cost allocations by the government and foreign donors are not sufficient to maintain a reasonable level of service in the sector". In education, "budgetary resources are extremely limited and below what is necessary to provide reasonable levels of service. Parents' contributions … are high when compared to existing wages". Nevertheless, "unit costs for primary and secondary education are already significantly below those of African countries because teacher salaries are low and because the provision of materials and supplies is very minimal" (WB 1988c). Luckily for the government, no one quoted this report when teachers struck in early 1990.

The Bank's own "Public Expenditure Review" concluded that "essential expenditure included in the current budget … appear to have been squeezed to very low and perhaps dysfunctional levels, and a case can in fact be made for permitting real increases to resume in spending on recurrent goods and services and on social welfare."(WB 1988c).

It is truly amazing. The IMF and World Bank have knowingly imposed policies which their own advisers say are "dysfunctional", and which are destroying the health and education service, in direct opposition to Mozambique's own goals.

Ending subsidies

The government's error was probably to express its subsidy and budget caps in MT rather than in real values, because with each devaluation the value of the meticais was less.

Having already agreed such a dramatic cut, Mozambique was further forced by the IMF to cut total subsidies from MT 21 bn in 1987 to only MT 15.5 bn in 1988, and allowed a rise to only 22 bn in 1990. Due to devaluations, real subsidy was cut to a third, from $74 mn (£44 mn) in 1987 to $29 mn (£17 mn) in 1988 and $23 mn (£14 mn) in 1990, at average rates of exchange for each year. Subsidies fell from 9% of GDP in 1986 to 2% of GDP in 1989. Subsidy to state industry was cut from MT 14 bn in 1987 to MT 12 bn in 1988 and fixed at that rate thereafter. Thus real subsidy to industry fell from $50 mn (£30 mn) in 1987 to $23 mn (£14 mn) in 1988 and $13 mn (£8 mn) in 1990 (IMF 1988a, WB 1990c).

The government did have some freedom of manoeuvre left from its original PRE. Although both total and state enterprise subsidies were limited, the government could still shift the subsidies around. By 1988, both the IMF and World Bank were worried about the social impact of structural adjustment, and both had come around to supporting rationing in Maputo and Beira as a way of ameliorating the worst affects of their own programme. In fact, the Bank wanted Mozambique to continue to subsidize the ration, end industry subsidies, and close loss-making factories, no matter what the long-term implications.

But the government was anxious to keep open, and in state hands, industries like cement which would be profitable after the end of destabilization, but which were presently loss-making. Much is made of socialist governments massively subsidizing loss-making state industries. But the World Bank "Public Expenditure Review" concluded that before 1983, state company profits substantially exceeded subsidies. The peak year was 1981, when profits were $84 mn (£51 mn) and subsidies only $18 mn (£11 mn). But with the war and other problems, profits fell and subsidies rose. Nevertheless, in 1987 subsidies to state enterprises had only risen to $33 mn (£20), and of that $18 mn (£11 mn) could be attributed to the war, according to the Bank (WB 1989d: 4, 29). In other words, subsidies that could be attributed to inefficiency had actually fallen (but profits from other state firms had disappeared). The biggest part of the subsidy, $14 mn (£8 mn), went to plantations and factories for three export crops: sugar, cotton, and tea. They were affected both by the war and by falling world commodity prices. The money was used, for example, to keep staff maintaining tea bushes so that production could resume quickly. Other subsidies included $2 mn each to the railways, coal mine, and cement factories. The first two were also important foreign exchange earners in normal times, and were badly hit by Renamo attacks. Cement is a particularly important local industry, and production is down 70% because of Renamo raids on lime quarries and railways to them. Finally, there was a $3 mn (£2 mn) subsidy to the state electricity company, Electricidade de Moçambique (EDM).

What is clear from this is that most subsidy was going to keep alive export industries so that Mozambique could earn foreign currency as soon as the war ended – which would seem to correspond to World Bank goals to expand exports.

It was an example of the World Bank's ostrich approach to the war. While accepting that "many of the subsidies to state enterprises that are attributable to the security problem will have to be continued", the Bank continued to press for "reduction in subsidies, particularly to parastatals" (WB 1989a, 1989b). Indeed, the Bank went further and pushed for an increase in electricity prices in Maputo; because of South African sabotage of the electricity line from the Cabora Bassa dam, Maputo buys its electricity from South Africa at a much higher price than it would pay if the line to Cabora Bassa were open. And when South African commandos blow up the line from Maputo, as they do sporadically, electricity must be produced by an old and inefficient generator in Maputo. EDM estimated that destabilization cost $5.5 mn (£3 mn) in the first four months of 1990 alone (*Tempo* 3 June 1990). Clearly, the Bank feels consumers should pay this cost of destabilization (although a World Bank energy project wants to encourage the use of electricity as a lower cost fuel).

Nevertheless, the government insisted on the maximum subsidy for state industry to cover war-related costs, seeing that as sensible long-term investment, even at the cost of reducing food subsidies. In a speech on 7 May 1988, Prime Minister Machungo made clear what was at stake: "For the state to maintain the level of subsidies necessary to stabilize prices, it would be forced to remove resources from the important fronts of defence and production." Caught by its own agreement to PRE, which was clearly designed to allow this, the Bank was forced to accept. The IMF, however, was anxious to see food subsidies end because this would "value more appropriately" food aid and thus avoid "distortions in incentives for production" (IMF 1988a).

In any case, food subsidies are an extremely complex issue, and a combination of US and IMF policy made it increasingly difficult to subsidize the urban ration. When food is donated to a Third World country and is sold, the recipient country must put the money received – known as counterpart funds – in a special bank account that can only be spent with donor agreement. Each donor has different rules as to how the money is to be collected and spent. Uniquely, the US forces Mozambique to pay in meticais at what the US says is the market price (as Table 5.4 shows, the US claims its maize is worth 60% more than similar EC grain). With each devaluation, the US raises the meticais price of its donated grain, while the subsidy that the government can pay is limited by the IMF cap.

In March 1988, the price of rationed food was increased on average three-fold (that is, to four times its former level). Although wages were also increased, the effect was dramatic. People simply could not afford enough food, and for the first time the ration was being left unclaimed in shops. Malnutrition rose, and seemed set to get worse; in late 1988 the World Bank admitted "a decrease in nutrition levels in the cities is likely (WB 1988b) (see Chapter 12).

By contrast, all other donors (except Japan) allow Mozambique to set the retail price and then pay as counterpart funds only the "net value" – that is, the wholesale price in Mozambique less transport and handling charges (WB 1989g: 65). As wheat is donated mainly by Canada and the EC, Mozambique is able to set the price of bread at half the world market price. This is an implicit 50% subsidy on food consumed more by better-off people (compared to maize). And it is entirely a question of IMF and donor bookkeeping rules. *Implicit* subsidy is allowed but not *explicit* subsidy; if the donor allows a lower charge, that is acceptable, but if the donor requires a full payment, then the extra counterpart funds generated cannot be used to pay a subsidy.

What is most bizarre about the whole exercise is that because of the way IMF and US demands interacted, people could not afford to buy food which has been given to Mozambique "free".

Counterpart funds

As the subsidy discussion shows, the central area of IMF financial control is through its detailed control of the state budget. This, in turn, leads to some quite complex budgetary battles, particularly over aid funds. In some circumstances aid put into Mozambique in such large quantities could be inflationary, but in other cases where it is used directly for rebuilding or feeding people it does not increase the money supply and is thus not inflationary. Both Mozambique and the IMF realize that aid funds can be used to bypass the constraints of structural adjustment, so this adds to the importance of the battle. The use of counterpart funds is a particular area of conflict.

Some donors allow the money to be used to pay the government budget deficit. Some require that the money be used to pay local costs for development projects, which can be a hidden subsidy to government because it can sometimes be used, for example, to pay the salaries of health or agricultural extension workers. Some bilateral donors use counterpart funds to pay the local costs of their NGOs.

But the US, as in so many other places in this book, creates special problems. Foreign agencies are expected to pay for rent and utilities in hard currency. In part, this is to reduce black market currency dealings; in part it reflects the fact that there is a hard currency cost in maintaining buildings and importing electricity; and in part it is an attempt to make the aid industry a useful source of foreign exchange. But the US insists that it pay local costs out of counterpart funds; so the US pays for telephone calls and electricity in meticais even though Mozambique has to shell out hard currency, exacerbating the balance of payments problem.

The US controls billions of meticais in counterpart funds from its inflated-price maize. Initially, it was reluctant to spend the money, but taking that much money out of circulation was highly deflationary, so the World Bank and various donors finally forced the US to agree to pay the budgets of various ministries, notably health and agriculture, with counterpart funds. For the first two years, the money was just handed over to the state. But it was apparent that the US intended to demand policy changes in health and agriculture in exchange for continued funding. One mark of this is that USAID has now established a permanent joint working group with the Ministry of Agriculture, in which the US informs the Mozambicans of its demands and, as imperiously, flies in US consultants to advise on policy matters. Another indication is that USAID was the only bilateral agency, and Care the only NGO, to have representatives on the World Bank food security study team (WB 1989g). The US also wanted to use increasing amounts of counterpart funds for its own purposes, such as funding management buy-outs of state companies.

Normally the US and World Bank work in close alliance, but there are apparently disputes on counterpart funds in several countries. The Bank suggestion that "the use of counterpart funds derived from the sale of food aid should be made more flexible so as to allow government budgetary support for critical areas to be augmented" is directed particularly at the US (WB 1989a).

For 1988 the government estimated that the equivalent of $27 mn (£15 mn) was to be spent from food aid counterpart funds. Of that, $9 mn (£5 mn) went to general government funds (including US funds for the budgets of the Ministries of Health, Education, and Agriculture), $2 mn (£1 mn) to the DPCCN, $3 mn (£2 mn) to projects, $2 mn (£1 mn) to NGO projects, and $11 mn (£6 mn) to agricultural credit. "What seems to have happened is that the new idea of promoting agriculture with subsidized credit has been seized on by almost every donor wishing to restrict the use of its counterpart funds, so that what made sense from an individual donor perspective may have resulted in an over-allocation", noted the World Bank. The possible contribution of "counterpart funds to promoting growth and reducing poverty has not been fully exploited and their administration has been a source of disagreement and confusion", the Bank added (WB 1989b, 1989g).

Mozambique's Ministry of Finance is over a barrel; there is a limit to deficit financing in the state budget and to the amount of money that can come from the banking system. By 1989, counterpart funds were almost as large as total tax revenue. Without some of this money going into the state budget, the government would have to make even further spending cuts. For many people, however, the process seems confusing and bizarre; these are not scarce donor dollars, but local currency collected by the government, and they don't understand why donors should have such power over billions of meticais.

Countervalue

A related problem occurs when donors give goods in kind or through import support to industry. The recipient is expected to pay the local value of the donation, and these are known as "countervalue" funds. At one level it is clearly correct that companies should pay for donated inputs and raw materials, so that they can correctly assess production costs and set prices. Countervalue funds, like some counterpart funds, go directly to the government, and are an important source of revenue. Thus the Ministry of Finance exerts substantial pressure to ensure that countervalue is paid.

But at what level? And by whom? As already noted, tied aid means that imported goods are sometimes twice as expensive as goods on the world market, and directly donated materials often have a vastly inflated official value. That imposes a distortion, because some companies are being asked to pay much higher countervalues for donated goods when other companies which can buy freely on the world market pay less. Very quietly, so as not to offend donors and expose donor corruption, the Ministry of Finance began to allow recipients to pay countervalue at the world market price rather than at the official donor price.

In some cases, devaluation means that goods are too expensive even at the cheapest world price, and the donor intends them to be free or cheap. Countervalue causes problems. The Ministry of Education semi-privatized textbook printing and distribution; the former ministry warehouses became state companies and distribution was done through shops; printing was done by parastatal or private companies. As well as satisfying the ethic of privatization, it genuinely did prove more efficient. However, private and state companies pay countervalue while ministries do not. In order to keep textbooks cheap, all paper is donated. Suddenly, the new companies had to pay countervalue on the paper, and Nordic paper is expensive. Parents could not afford to pay for textbooks, and sales plummeted. Shopkeepers found themselves with warehouses full of unsold textbooks. As with expensive "free" food in Maputo, the complex of IMF rules and devaluations meant that people could not afford to buy "free" textbooks. The crisis came to a head when the donor said that the programme would be ended if the textbook countervalue was not sharply reduced, which eventually happened.

A similar problem revolves around technical assistance. Mozambican companies were expected to pay the countervalue of the foreign salaries of consultants and technicians. One or two foreigners could be costing the company more than the entire local workforce; this cost could never be recovered out of local sales, and companies cannot afford essential "free" technical assistance.

Further demands

Structural adjustment contains many other quite detailed requirements, which are normally tightened year by year. One important one is the restriction on total credit to business. This has caused quite serious squeezes, and some of the larger companies have had difficulty in obtaining the kind of bank overdraft for working funds that would be normal elsewhere. The credit squeeze has limited the rate of industrial expansion and thus made PRE even more deflationary.

The very high rates of inflation mean that the IMF forced Mozambique to charge high interest rates and to try to reach real positive interest rates. The shortage of credit and the high interest rates have made long-term investment of any sort impractical. The government is being forced to end its low interest rates on agricultural loans, which will make it even harder for small farmers to increase production.

Meanwhile there was strong pressure to cut government spending wherever possible, and to increase revenue. The Bank insisted on civil service pay levels being frozen. The IMF insisted that rent increases, which had been promised for 1985 and 1987 and postponed both times, should finally be imposed. And there were big increases in electricity and water prices. This meant housing costs rose in Maputo just as the cost of food jumped.

And taxes were rising; tax revenue was 13% of GDP in 1985–86 and 23% in 1989. "By international standards, this represents an impressive achievement", comments the World Bank (WB 1989b), while also admitting that this taxation level is "already high"

(WB 1988c). Furthermore, the government was forced to shift the tax burden away from business and on to consumers: turnover tax (effectively VAT or an implicit sales tax) was raised from 5% to 10% while taxes on profits and dividends were reduced or eliminated (WB 1989a). Import duties were raised and coverage expanded to include many donations. Suddenly foreign donations were being left in the port because recipients did not have the meticais to pay the duty.

Mozambique did gain a few concessions from the Bank and Fund. For example, the government has won acceptance for its investment strategy, which tries to link industry to agriculture, and which puts particular stress on transport, with "substantial imports of vehicles" (WB 1989a). And the new tariff system will be allowed to contain "protection" for Mozambique's priority industries (WB 1988b).

The World Bank also gave in partly on the issue of price fixing. The government had already recognized that it did not have the ability to control all prices, so in 1986 it limited itself to fixing the prices of key items. Not subject to price control were items like goats where individual buyers and sellers had always ignored official prices, plus industrial goods like batteries that were already so expensive that traders were having difficulty selling them, so were unlikely to inflate the price. Products still subject to fixed price legislation account for a third of GDP. And the Bank has accepted that "some elements of an administered economy would be maintained" because "the present insecurity in some rural areas requires measures to direct important incentive goods to these areas to promote production" (WB 1989b). This is a point which the government has been making since 1983.

The IMF and World Bank have high praise for Mozambique. In various reports they say: "The program is on track." Mozambique has "vigorously implemented" the PRE. It has observed all "quantitative financial benchmarks" set by the IMF, relating to budget, domestic and bank credit, and external borrowing. But they continue to put pressure on Mozambique for further changes, many of them attitudinal. The Bank and Fund wanted Mozambique to de-emphasize the goals of growth and increased production and consumption in the original PRE. Instead they stressed freer markets, further cutting of deficits and subsidies, the need "to enhance efficiency", and the requirement "to restore orderly financial relationships with trading partners and creditors" (RPM 1988; WB 1989a).

How tight was the squeeze?

Mozambique may have been "on track" in implementing IMF demands, but the economy was not "on track". In 1987, growth was only a quarter the level promised in the announcement of PRE. In the first half of 1988 there was a "notable slump" in industrial production, and GDP growth was also less than expected. In part this was due to the lack of spare parts due to delays in donors supplying funds. But it was also due to "lack of demand" and the "constrained financial situation faced by a number of enterprises." It was, the Bank admitted, a "constrained demand situation" (IMF 1988b; WB 1988b, 1988e).

The government privately admitted that it was not just the urban population that was hit, but that purchasing power in the countryside was not rising as predicted. People simply could not afford to buy more expensive consumer goods. When the parastatal Pescom nearly doubled the price of fish, people couldn't pay. In Inhambane Pescom even tried setting up roadside stands, but one-and-a-half tonnes of fish rotted unsold in the cold store (*Notícias* 29 February 1988).

Throughout 1987 and 1988 there was a growing dispute as to just how bad life was for the urban poor, and how much tighter they could be squeezed. The IMF argued that "the *average* level of real wages is declining only modestly in 1987, but it seems likely that the incidence is much greater for lower-income city dwellers". But the IMF had to admit that Mozambique felt that the IMF "considerably underestimated the cost of living increase".

Indeed, in negotiations with the IMF in 1987, "Mozambican representatives believed there had been a reduction in real wages at most levels of employment, and particularly at lower income levels. These poorer segments of the population, they emphasized, were largely dependent on official-market supplies, which now absorbed most of their incomes. Indeed, while the authorities had expected some adverse effect on real incomes, its extent had proven to be cause for concern" (IMF 1987).

The 1987 IMF–World Bank "Economic Policy Framework" paper (WB 1987a) argued after the first two devaluations that "given stable or falling parallel market prices due to tight financial policies and increased supplies, average wages are estimated to at least keep pace with the actual cost of living for the majority of civil servants." In part this was a dispute over what the old black market prices had been. Government ministers who were pushing PRE, as well as the IMF, argued that free market prices were lower than the old black market prices, and thus the overall cost of living did not rise as much as the official price data suggested. On the other hand, people told me that traders tended to put goods on sale at the old black market price, and even sometimes increase them to take notional account of the first devaluation. But it seemed apparent to me that once goods such as fish and vegetables moved from the parallel to the open market, their prices tended not to rise so rapidly. Thus goods entered the free market at a high and very inflationary level; then prices did not fall as predicted, but only rose relatively slowly. This suggests that the IMF has substantially underestimated inflation in 1987, and this affects all of its later estimates of standard of living.

This was all before removal of food subsidies, which the Mozambicans warned would cause "further compression of already low real consumption levels." But the IMF "staff team reiterated that the evidence on price and wage developments in 1987 did not point to a marked reduction in average real earnings." Numerous reports (e.g., WB 1990c) later showed that the Mozambicans were right and the IMF team wrong. In any case, the IMF team had no way of knowing how the poor lived; they stayed in the Hotel Polana and only went to government offices. Indeed, when Dr Michael Irwin walked out of his post as acting vice-president for personnel at the World Bank, he complained that "the Bank staff, living and working comfortably in the Washington area and venturing forth in such a luxurious manner (first-class flight and hotels), are generally out of touch with the realities of poverty" (Irwin 1990).

Disquiet with the official IMF line grew slowly. In 1987 an IMF staff member told me privately (as IMF staff are not normally allowed to talk to writers) that "we have been very chastened. We realize that the bottom has been hurt very badly. This is true, and not just a negotiating point." But the IMF is rigidly hierarchical, and such lower-level views did not modify thinking at the top.

There was an increasingly wide split between the IMF and World Bank. The IMF stressed the need above all else to control the money supply and reduce inflation to below 15%. The World Bank saw Mozambique going into a recessionary spiral and demanded that the economy be stimulated. But the IMF said it was necessary to get the economic structures right before the economy was stimulated. Any loosening of the economy would create runaway inflation, according to the Fund.

At a joint meeting with Finance Minister Magid Osman in December 1987, when there was discussion about ending food subsidies, there was an open split between the Bank and the Fund. World Bank staff argued that people had been squeezed too much; they had no purchasing power and the economy was being pushed into a downward spiral. The IMF said that adjustment should be accelerated.

The split between lower levels of Bank staff, who were worried, and those at the top who sided with the IMF, was shown in a paper which stressed the "potential conflict between the need to maintain the momentum of reform on the one hand and the need to tailor the rate of policy adjustment to the implementation and absorbtive [sic] capacity of the economy on the other." But it stressed the desire to see that "the most important adjustments are completed as expeditiously as possible" (WB 1988e).

Reaching the riot threshold

By 1989 even Bank and Fund staff were becoming worried. The 1989 "Economic Policy Framework" paper points to the "adverse short-term effect on the welfare of some sectors of the population, in particular the urban areas, where further contractions in real wages and employment have taken place."

In October 1989 the Bank warned that "social programs need to be expanded to ensure that the social costs of the adjustment program are not borne disproportionately by the poorest households. This is important in order to maintain the social consensus which has been a key factor in ensuring the determined implementation of the ERP [PRE]. Unlike other countries having to implement comprehensive adjustment programs, Mozambique's does not have the option of relying on significant decline in consumption for increasing investment" (WB 1989b).

It was an honest statement that structural adjustment works by squeezing the consumption of the poor, and that the poor in Mozambique had already been squeezed too hard. World Bank staff admitted in informal chats that the Bank and Fund have a "riot threshold". They continue to press a country until there are riots, and they could not understand why there had not been riots in Mozambique as early as 1988.

A wave of strikes in January 1990 signalled the approach of that threshold. Workers turned the May Day rally into a protest. In the traditional march past a reviewing stand with dignitaries that included President Chissano, engineering workers carried a banner reading "We demand a balance between prices and wages"; the city council workers' banner called for "a drop in the prices of rice, sugar, and bread"; port workers carried placards reading simply "Down with starvation wages".

In Beira, Mozambique's second city, there was a riot in June. In a statement afterwards, the City Council noted that because of PRE, "the cost of living has risen very much, obliging everyone to work and to earn money in addition to their salary" (DM 5 June 1990), a remarkable admission which contrasted with official silence in Maputo.

Near Beira in August, sugar cane cutters at the Mafambisse plantation struck for higher wages. The house of the plantation director was sacked, police killed three strikers, and then the workers set fire to the cane fields (*Mozambiquefile* September 1990).

In December, a group of hungry war-wounded and disabled people raided a DPCCN warehouse in Beira and took meat and cooking oil. Two were arrested, leading to an assualt on the police station by the disabled to try to free the detainees. Police killed one demonstrator (*Mozambiquefile* January 1991).

The threshold had been crossed.

Deputies to the People's Assembly said it was clear, after three years of PRE, that it was not benefiting the 60% of Mozambicans living in extreme poverty. A peasant deputy, Maria Florinda, noted that PRE had filled the shops with goods. But she and other peasants could not buy. "We are tightening our belts too much, and now our bodies are about to be divided in two. We ask the government to look for a way that will permit us to loosen our belts, at least by one centimeter" (MIO 5 October 1990).

12 Selling Cigarettes on Street Corners

The children on the streets of Maputo selling cigarettes one by one are surely the symbol of PRE. In the controlled pre-PRE economy it was never allowed; now, after the free market reforms, anything can be bought on the streets. Before, there was no need for these children to sell; now the tiny amount of money they bring home helps to keep malnutrition at bay.

Certainly, structural adjustment and the market economy have energized Maputo. People do move about more quickly, now. There are goods in the shops. The metical has value; even black market traders no longer demand rand. Stricter competition has increased the quality of locally made goods. And PRE has imposed financial discipline on both public and private companies which had grown accustomed to permanent deficits and endless credit.

PRE can be seen and felt everywhere in Maputo. There are a lot more cars; there are fancy restaurants and night clubs, where it is easy for one person to spend the equivalent of one month's minimum wage on dinner. Informal markets have sprung up on street corners everywhere; women sit behind small mounds of charcoal, piles of cabbage, trays of eggs, cases of South African beer, or charcoal stoves with a few ears of roasted corn.

On the streets are trucks carrying passengers. Known by a thousand names all over Africa, here they are called "chapa-100" after the fare of 100 MT. On the streets, too, are thousands of people trudging to work on foot, because they cannot afford 100 MT (7 US cents or 4 British pence in 1989), when 200 MT per day represents 30% of their wage.

Income gap widens

The widening gap between rich and poor is part of any structural adjustment programme. Minimum wages in early 1989 were 12,000 MT (at that time $18, £11) per month for agricultural workers and 17,000 MT ($25, £15) per month for others. Top wages for government workers (including benefits) were 250,000 MT ($380, £230). Mozambicans working for foreign aid agencies could earn $2000 (£1200) per month. Some foreign workers earned $25,000 (£15,000). Thus the ratio of top to bottom salaries within the government was only 15:1, for Mozambicans as a whole it was more than 100:1, and within the economy it was more than 1000:1.

Monthly wages of 500,000 wage workers registered with the Ministry of Labour in early 1989 (and their $ and £ equivalents at the time) were reported as:

Children selling chewing gum and cigarettes on a Maputo street corner (Oxfam)

% of workers	Range		
40%	under 20,000 MT	under £18	under $30
26%	20-30,000 MT	£18-27	$30-45
30%	30-50,000 MT	£27-45	$45-75
4%	50-100,000 MT	£45-90	$75-150
<1%	over 100,000 MT	over £90	over $150

Only 1550 people had wages over 100,000 MT (Green 1989). The number of high earners is probably underestimated because it may not include perks, such as payments for rent and car, and because private traders and other business people are not included. Nevertheless, it is clear that most wages are very low.

And most Mozambicans do not earn a wage at all. Traditionally, most farmed their own land. In urban areas, many are self-employed or are in the "informal sector", like the children selling cigarettes.

How poor?

"Poverty is pervasive and even by the tightest definitions, affects about 60 per cent of the population", according to the World Bank (WB 1990b). Their source is a widely accepted estimate by Professor Reginald Green of Sussex University's Institute of Development Studies, who concluded that a third of the urban, half of the peri-urban, and more than two-thirds of the rural population lived in "absolute poverty". This is the level at which a family must spend half its income to obtain two-thirds of the necessary calorie requirements, and "growth faltering in children is very common" (WB 1990f: 8).

Donors make a big point of targeting "the most vulnerable" groups. For example, the World Bank wants "supplementary feeding programmes" for the "nutritionally vulnerable groups (such as very young children, and pregnant and lactating mothers)" (WB 1989a). But according to Green "virtually all absolutely poor people must be considered vulnerable. Their margins of living above survival are at best slim – indeed many are not well nourished or healthy enough to work long, hard, or productively. Any negative external event endangers their ever being able to escape from absolute poverty and increases their morbidity and mortality rates." Many who are not already poor are vulnerable to loss of jobs (Green 1989).

Many donors try to target children, and set up special feeding programmes, on the false assumption that Mozambican parents do not feed their children. But the World Bank noted that "children are favoured when problems of absolute food shortage occur. For example, relief workers frequently report that children of families arriving at accommodation centres are better nourished than adults" (WB 1989g: 34).

'Social Dimensions of Adjustment'

By publishing a string of critical reports, Unicef and other agencies forced the World Bank to look at what were called the "Social Dimensions of Adjustment" (SDA) all over the world. SDA became part of World Bank programmes, including the one in Mozambique. But they were always tacked on, and not integral. The Bank failed to modify programmes to minimize the harm done, and instead patched the programme with a charity component. SDA's string of anti-poverty mini-projects has always been an exercise in damage limitation.

As the Bank itself says, "reforms are focused on several key macro-economic policy issues, including the exchange rate, foreign exchange allocation system, trade policies, pricing policy, the budget, and credit" (WB 1989g: 5). But as Reginald Green comments, "food and vaccination imbalances need to be closed just as much as government revenue/expenditure or import/export ones".

The World Bank's SDA identification mission in Mozambique stressed that its "main objective" was "to strengthen the capacity of the government to design and implement improved structural adjustment". This included improved national accounting systems, increasing the ability of the government to carry out policy studies, and "programs to mitigate the transitional costs of adjustment for vulnerable groups". But the SDA project would only address "poverty alleviation in the medium term"; short-term poverty alleviation would be left to the emergency programme and to special donor projects (WB 1988g).

The Rural Poor

Most poor people are rural. Many were poor even before independence, but Green estimates that rural incomes have fallen by a third since 1980, largely due to destabilization. Perhaps half the rural population have been displaced or affected by the war, and are partly dependent on free food. He estimates that PRE has had "a very limited effect" on rural incomes (Green 1989). The World Bank concludes that "in the 1980s war has been and remains the dominant single cause of absolute poverty in Mozambique."

The biggest group of very poor people in the rural areas are those who have had to flee and set up again elsewhere. They are dependent on donations of food and clothing to survive, and of seeds and tools to get started again. Another large group are those who have lost access to farmland, often because plots are in areas subject to Renamo raids, and who can no longer produce enough food. Even for those with enough land, the widespread destruction of transport, commercial, and social infrastructure has lowered living standards.

A survey in late 1989 in rural areas close to 24 district towns showed the extent of poverty (CNP 1990). Average income per person per month was 7100 MT (then $9, £5). The equivalent of 8000 MT was needed to satisfy minimum nutritional requirements, so 70% of the population "is living under the absolute poverty level". Not surprisingly, malnutrition of children "is very high": 26% are underweight and 52% are short for their age, showing chronic malnutrition. The report stressed that these people are much better off than rural people in general, precisely because they all lived within 5 km of a town.

Of the 7100 MT per person per month average income, 2200 MT was the cash value of food the family grew and ate, just 200 MT was marketed produce, and 4900 MT was cash income from wages. A quarter of household heads were officials and half were farm labourers, sources of income less likely to be available in more remote areas. Income distribution was very skewed:

Group	Portion of total income	Average income per person per month	Vulnerability
Poorest 20%	1%	300 MT	
Next 20%	8%	2300 MT ($ 3)	"High risk"
Next 30%	28%	5600 MT ($ 7)	"At risk"
Penultimate 20%	29%	9400 MT ($12)	"Not at risk"
Top 10%	34%	22000 MT ($27)	"Not at risk"

The poorest 40% have so little income that they survive partly on insects, leaves, roots, and hand-outs from others who are somewhat less poor.

Adjustment has an impact

But if the war is an overriding issue, PRE has still had an effect. For the large minority who have mostly avoided the war, impact probably depends on the size of the farm. For small peasant farmers, there are now goods in the shops and an improved trading system, compared to the black market system of the early 1980s. But evidence suggests that terms

Rural people displaced by the war who have fled to the town of Caniçado in Gaza province (AIM)

of trade have deteriorated. Peasant farmers definitely have to sell more crops to obtain salt or cloth than in 1980, and more than in 1987 (Hermele 1990). Many health fees are waived for peasants, but education fees can be quite large for a subsistence farmer. Furthermore, prices of consumer goods and inputs are rising with each devaluation, which means before the peasant is able to sell crops at the new higher price. And private traders are often not following official prices, charging more for consumer goods and paying less for crops. Thus rapid inflation and continued profiteering mean that peasants simply do not have the cash to make essential purchases. There were several instances of peasants not being able to buy improved quality seed which they wanted and knew would raise yields and be highly profitable. This suggests that the average peasant or family farmer is probably worse off under PRE.

Inflation also creates problems for those displaced or affected by the war. Although they receive some help from the emergency programme, many fail to accumulate enough money to acquire hoes, seeds, and so on because the price keeps going up. Thus they can never get back into the system and become productive, independent farmers. The 1989 survey of 24 districts estimates that only 19% of the total rural population are able to buy non-subsidized consumer goods and agricultural inputs. The 70% at risk cited the inability to buy seeds and tools as the second biggest reason for not producing more of their own food; security questions and lack of land was the biggest problem (CNP 1990). Even when they can obtain tools, labour time is the biggest constraint for most peasant farmers; when a woman is already working all of the daylight hours, price liberalization is not going to encourage her to work harder and produce more.

Larger farmers, however, have done well out of PRE. They have received transport and inputs from USAID and other donors, and they have access to credit. They have been given additional high-quality land from state farms. And they have been able to hire displaced people at wages well below the official rates. Some larger farmers have lost tractors, buildings, and even their lives to Renamo. But for many, the late 1980s have been a time of expansion and high profit.

Thus the benefits of PRE have been reserved for a very small group in rural areas, while the conditions of the majority have worsened significantly. The 1989 survey concludes that "the only beneficiaries of PRE in the rural areas are a few professionals linked to the modern sector, such as shopkeepers, high officials, and private farmers" (CNP 1990).

The Urban Poor

Some urban poverty is due to the war. Many people have fled from insecure rural areas; the population of Maputo has increased by 50% in ten years, straining existing services. Living on what was suburban farmland, they have reduced the ability of older residents to produce part of what they eat. Before the era of destabilization, most urban people maintained contact with cousins or aunts in rural areas, and obtained some food from the family farm; this has ended, because the rural family members are often displaced or affected, or the road to the rural area is dangerous. Nevertheless, the main cause of absolute poverty in Maputo is structural adjustment, or PRE.

In the early 1980s, shops and markets in Maputo became emptier and queues were longer. But there was a basic cushion. A rationing system was introduced in Maputo in 1981, followed by one in Beira in 1986. (Maputo and Beira have two-thirds of the urban population.) It was well run and efficient, and guaranteed that people could buy half to two-thirds of essential foodstuffs from their local shop at the official price. Health and education were effectively free. The system applied even to those moving into Maputo from the countryside. It was hardly luxurious, and by the mid-1980s people were forced to turn to the black market for some of their necessary food. But it did reduce the amount of absolute poverty.

With PRE, this changed. It was always intended that urban dwellers should be squeezed so as to transfer money to the rural areas. And urbanites were severely squeezed, even though the rural transfer seems not to have taken place. Devaluation and deregulation pushed up all prices, and wages did not rise as fast.

Initially, the ration was not subsidized, but was made available at a low fixed price (which was, perhaps, artificially low because of the low exchange rate). With the first devaluation in 1987, the ration was subsidized so the poor could still afford it. But this was not continued with further devaluations, even though the prices rose to those the US demanded. Then in 1988 and 1989, the government ended the subsidy to all ration products except maize. By 1989, the price of the ration was 16 times what it had been in 1986, reflecting the 20-fold devaluation.

The official consumer price index (CPI) showed a five-fold increase, but the World Bank admits this did not work for the poorest half of the Maputo population. Green suggests that for poor families, 40% of their expenditure is on the ration, 20% on other food, 15% on wood for cooking, 15% for transport, and the remaining 10% for clothing, shoes, soap, and all other necessities. The ration, fuel and transport costs all rose much faster than the CPI. For the poorest half, the World Bank estimates that prices rose roughly 12-fold,

The crisis in 1988 forced Mozambique to push up minimum wages faster than the CPI, but by 1989 the minimum wage was only nine times the 1986 level, compared to the 12-fold price rise for the poorest half. Thus there was "a real decline in the minimum wage". Other groups, too, were much worse off. Government employees real per capita earnings had fallen by 15%. Even those with above average incomes had real income in 1989 which was "still well below" the 1986 level (WB 1990c: 23ff, A36).

Not enough to eat

The effect of the food price rises in 1987 and 1988 was shown quickly in nutritional levels. In 1981 10% of the babies born in Maputo Central Hospital had low birth weight. This had risen to 13% in 1987, and jumped to 16% in 1988. Even pregnant women were not getting enough to eat.

Admissions of severely malnourished children to the Maputo Central Hospital jumped from 46 in April 1988 to 140 in April 1989 to 283 in April 1990. This five-fold increase overwhelmed the hospital, which had to put two children in each cot (*Boletim Trimestral*, May 1990).

A survey of Maputo households in late 1988 showed that the quantity and quality of food consumed were both directly proportional to income. Under 2000 MT per person per month, each person ate only 6.5 kg of food per month – less than two-thirds of what is considered the minimum. At 4000 MT per person food consumption finally passed the minimum necessary. An income of more than 10,000 MT per person led to food consumption of 20.5 kg per person per month. Furthermore, consumption of more nutritious foods like vegetables and beans rose with income (MC 1988; WB 1989g: 44, 116).

Not surprisingly, the survey also showed that chronic malnutrition was high. Of children less than four years old, 32% were short for their age (compared to 3% normally) and 14% showed growth faltering. The survey found that the main cause of malnutrition was lack of money; there was food in the shops but people could not buy. Malnutrition rates were "very high" when the family income was below 4000 MT per person per month (then $7 or £4, a quarter of the minimum wage) and quite low when family income was above 8000 MT per person.

In eliminating the subsidy on the ration, the government raised wages at a rate that assumed that each worker supported only two other people. This was never admitted to the public, although it was reported by the IMF (IMF 1988). Privately, ministers admitted that a typical Maputo family of seven or eight people could only survive if it had two salaries. Unfortunately, only one quarter of Maputo families have two salaries. Half have one salary; one quarter have none at all. Only about 5% of Maputo residents have access to a plot that allows them to produce a significant amount of their own food. Green suggests that in 1980 only about 15% of Maputo residents were in "absolute poverty" – the aged, disabled, and female-headed households which form a significant portion of the quarter of families with no wage. Green calls this "structural poverty". The jump to 50% absolute poverty in 1989 is largely accounted for by one-wage households. Green points out that many of those households were so close to the line that ending the subsidy on the ration pulled them down into poverty (Green 1989).

Living on the margin, these families depend on quite small extra earnings or savings to stave off malnutrition. Children selling cigarettes, or an aged relative selling handfuls of cabbage, or the wage earner walking to work instead of taking the chapa-100 can all ensure that bit of extra food. And for those on the margin, paying for school books or medicines is out of the question. Health consultations fell by a third in two years.

People cannot even afford water. Of those living in houses with piped water, which are by definition somewhat better off, in 1986 only 19% paid the minimum charge. By 1988, 54% used so little water that they only paid the minimum; they could not afford to pay the new higher prices, and were taking fewer baths and washing their clothes less. This has serious implications for health, Green warns (Green 1989).

Extra income

The World Bank's own health and nutrition study adds that the problem is not confined to families with only one salary. "Since food expenses should not exceed 50-60% of income, even families with two wage-earners could afford an adequate diet only by supplementation with non-purchased food or with additional income from informal sector activities or petty crime" (WB 1990a: 75).

As the Beira City Council admitted, people simply cannot live on their salaries and must supplement their income. Those who can take on extra freelance work. Many of my Mozambican friends do translations or consultancies for aid agencies. Teachers are now allowed to do tutoring outside class hours (so long as they don't teach their own students). Nurses and doctors now have private patients (with a cut of the fee going back to the state health service). Technicians, car mechanics, and other service people are often allowed to use company facilities for private work, to boost their income.

For those who don't have an obviously saleable skill, some form of dishonesty or corruption may be necessary to survive. Drivers use company or government cars for chapa-100. There are widespread reports of thefts by workers, especially of goods that can be resold. And the growing corruption extends to teachers who demand bribes. Even exam passes are for sale in the IMF's new free market.

Workers who don't steal goods will often steal time. They do other things when they should be at their desk or workbench, and one casualty is government efficiency. Sten Rylander of Sweden warned donors at the 1988 Paris conference about "the substantial fall of real wages in the public sector. The potential for improved efficiency of the public sector, and indeed the whole rehabilitation programme, is at risk if civil servants have to look for other duties in order to survive on their salary." And President Chissano admitted in May 1990 that "directors want to do something to make their own life sustainable. So they do their job with just half their mind, or just do enough to justify their meagre salary. So problems which we could solve are not solved. This makes our difficulties worse."

The need to search for a second income is compounded by silent resistance, which is much more the Mozambican way – despite having passed the riot threshold. People simply don't want to do more than they feel they are being paid for, and if they feel their wages are worth only half what they were before, they will find ways of doing only half as much work.

Who to help

Faced with the obvious increase in poverty and malnutrition, donors moved in to try to help. All wanted to target particular "vulnerable" groups. Ration subsidies and other broad approaches were dismissed as "inefficient", whereas targeting would be an efficient way to reach those most in need. For example, it is argued that subsidies go to rich as well as poor, and in extreme cases rich people may feed subsidized food to animals, so subsidies are wasteful. Mozambican officials argued from the first that if the majority of the population was vulnerable, targeting was pointless and broad programmes and subsidies made more sense.

But there was also a sharp political conflict between the concepts of "rights" and "charity". Part of Mozambique's socialist project was to guarantee basic food, health care, and education to everyone. This was demonstrated by the stress on expanding primary health care and adult literacy. The concept of an urban food ration was also part of this – everyone, rich or poor, should be able to buy the basic ration at a reasonable price. The rich may not choose to purchase, but it should be available to everyone as of right.

Under structural adjustment and the new dogma of the free market, this changed. The market should provide for most people, who should be free to buy what they want. For the few who fall by the wayside, there should be charity. Knowing what the impact of structural adjustment would be, the IMF and World Bank insisted from the beginning that there should be a "safety net" for the "poorest section of the population" (e.g., WB 1987a).

Initially, the Bank and Fund wanted to end the ration as a mass programme and replace it with a narrowly focused programme. Eventually, in part because of the Green report, they came to accept the ration as essential, and even called for it to be expanded. But there was still strong pressure for a targeted programme as part of the ration. Unicef proposed that the ration should include a less desirable poor people's food which would be subsidized, but which people would only buy if they were desperate. The World Bank encouraged this, because they wanted to experiment with subsidies on what they called "inferior foods".

Initially Unicef pushed the idea that the ration should include subsidized US–surplus sorghum. Sorghum is eaten in the north, but is not a part of the diet in southern Mozambique, and Maputo residents would not even know how to cook it. The Bank argued that an "inferior food" had to be something that only the poorest would eat and for which consumption would decrease as income increased; unfortunately, people in Maputo are so poor and hungry that consumption of all foods increases with income. Thus "the general opinion that sorghum would not be considered acceptable by many consumers makes it a potentially ideal commodity for a targeted subsidy", commented the Bank (WB 1989g: 119). It was noted, however, that sorghum is used to make traditional beer, and thus including sorghum in the ration would have provided an income to female-headed households, as some women would set up shebeens. Although female-headed households are among the poorest in Maputo and a special target for World Bank projects, the sorghum idea was dropped.

Finally, it was decided in May 1990 that US yellow maize, which was already in the ration and was less popular than African white maize, would continue to be subsidized. Meanwhile, price controls were removed from locally produced white maize. When people had the money, they would pay extra for local maize or rice. But people were of necessity already eating yellow maize and knew how to prepare it, and it would not have the stigma of a totally unacceptable food like sorghum. The US encouraged the idea, but it also insisted that Mozambique continue to pay counterpart funds at the price set by the US, so that the subsidy would have to come from the government budget and be limited to the ceiling set by the IMF. Thus the subsidy on the yellow maize would be relatively small.

Children can't object

School children became a special target, both because they were easy to reach, and because they were popular with donors. Mozambique objected that half of Maputo children were not in school (in part because of IMF-imposed cuts in the education budget), and these were the poorest children. But donors persisted. In February 1990, a French and World Bank sponsored programme was introduced to give protein-enriched bread to 210,000 Maputo primary school children.

The World Bank also pushed an alternative: instead of giving children more food, give them pills that will allow them to make better use of the limited food they do eat. The Bank wanted to give iron, vitamin A, and deworming medicine to primary school pupils. Initially, it proposed a case-controlled study, intervening in two schools and having two others as controls. It argued that deworming would be cheaper than an alternative school lunch programme while having a "similar nutritional impact" (WB 1989f: 143).

The Ministry of Health objected vociferously. It argued that vitamin A was not a problem in Maputo. And it objected to what it saw as a pointless experiment being conducted on Mozambican children. More fundamentally, the Ministry pointed out that deworming was very expensive in terms of time, training, and money, and Mozambique could never continue it without external assistance. Furthermore, without improved sanitation, children would simply be reinfected. Yet other IMF/World Bank restrictions were worsening sanitation; for example the ending of subsidies for latrine slabs had virtually halted a latrine building programme in the Maputo suburbs.

Finally, the Ministry said that 75% of children have anaemia and vitamin deficiency due to lack of food. It would make more sense spending the money on a better diet than on iron and vitamins. The World Bank replied that, although expensive, the programme would improve learning. The Ministry responded that pupils' learning would improve more if the money was spent on text books and repairing school roofs.

The Bank promoted the project for two years, repeatedly putting it into drafts of papers; several Bank delegations had a person whose main role was to push the micronutrient/deworming experiment. Finally, the Ministry of Health said they would accept the programme if it were done in tandem with environmental improvements such as a latrine programme. The Bank refused, and the project was rejected by the Ministry of Health. So the Bank turned to the Ministry of Education, and pushed it to accept the micronutrient/deworming experiment. But Education passed it back to Health, which rejected it again in early 1990.

Cut-price labour

Mozambique argued that, at the very least, the Bank had to take special account of structural poverty. The government called for special programmes to create labour-intensive jobs. And it pushed a system of income transfers or direct payments to the poorest families who did not have enough potential workers. The Bank eventually agreed to both, because, as it admitted, 70% of the extra income of the poorest is spent on food. But some battles remain.

On job creation, the issue is over who creates the jobs and how much they pay. "The objective here is explicitly to create jobs for the poorest, most malnourished groups in the urban population", the Bank argues. "Paying less than the minimum wage is one unfortunate but probably necessary 'self-targeting' device to help ensure that only workers from the very poorest households would be candidates for the jobs created." This is a long-running battle, with the Bank opposed to increasing the minimum wage on the grounds that this will "reduce the demand for labour" (WB 1989g: 93ff, 114). Yet the Bank accepts that people cannot live on the minimum wage. In effect, it is trying to create jobs with literally starvation wages. This is already happening; the Maputo survey showed that 18% of salaried workers already earned less than the minimum wage (MC 1988).

The Bank, naturally, stresses private sector job creation, particularly "micro-enterprises [which] tend to have a greater proportion of low-wage workers." It points to "an explosion of small-scale, private sector activities in Maputo and Beira – street traders, artisans, and the like – with little or no government support." It accepts that the private sector may be slow to create jobs and will need financial and technical support, for example from NGOs. In the interim there will have to be public works projects, but these should be services like rubbish collection which can be privatized.

There are two conflicts here. First, the Maputo City Council had cut the number of dustmen (garbage collectors) and street cleaners from 1200 to 740, because of IMF-imposed budget cuts on the City Council, and rubbish was piling up (*Domingo* 23 October 1988). Will the Council now be allowed to hire them back as part of job creation? Second, the World Bank Food Security Study criticizes the World Bank's own urban rehabilitation programme for being too capital-intensive. If it were better planned it could create an additional 6000 long-term jobs (WB 1989g: 99).

For its part, the government wants to create real jobs with high enough wages to support a family, and it puts priority on infrastructure rehabilitation through the government. It cites the ILO labour-intensive road-building scheme, which pays the minimum wage. It accepts that most jobs will eventually be created in the private sector, but emphasizes the need to create sustainable employment rather than jobs which pay so little that people want to leave them. Rather than further deregulation, the government stresses the need for loans, tools, inputs and raw materials – difficult to obtain when credit and imports are tight due to IMF restrictions.

Income transfers

The Bank has accepted that the poorest 11% will never earn enough, and must be given money. Starting in 1991 there will be pilot schemes giving the equivalent of between $7 and $16 (£4-10) to households with a total income of less than half of one minimum wage, and with a family member satisfying one of four other conditions: over 60 years old and unemployed, disabled and unable to work, malnourished pregnant woman, or severely malnourished child (WB 1990f: 24).

The Bank admits this could be an administrative nightmare since the recipients will change frequently, particularly with respect to the last two criteria. This is because everyone is so poor, and thus "a large proportion of households may fall from time to time into the group defined as most vulnerable (for example, when someone in the household dies, becomes disabled or loses a job, or when the dependency ratio is increased through the birth of a child)" (WB 1989g: 132). Since these people will spend the extra money on food anyway, it would make more sense to subsidize the ration – but that is not politically acceptable.

The core of the problem, according to Mozambican negotiators, was that structural adjustment hurt the majority of the urban population. The World Bank wanted to help just a few groups – the poorest 11% plus some who would get low-wage jobs. And this went directly against the development goals of Mozambique, in part because it was so deflationary. People were being forced to spend increasing proportions of their income on imported, largely donated, food, and less on non-food items, which would make it even harder to generate employment.

Don't Tell the People

The continuing battle with the World Bank and the IMF was fought largely in secret. Inside Mozambique, there was no public discussion about the implications of structural adjustment. There were many reasons for this.

First, and perhaps most importantly in the early stages, the US demanded that Mozambique be a willing and enthusiastic convert from Marxism to the new cult of the free market. Mozambique was so desperate for substantial amounts of foreign aid and for an end to support for Renamo, that it could not be seen to be less than enthusiastic; blaming the IMF simply would not be acceptable. "A market economy was a pre-requisite" for peace, Finance Minister Magid Osman commented later, because "at that time the world was polarized between the two superpowers" and Mozambique could not escape that division (Osman 1989). As the Central Committee told the Fifth Congress, "we are therefore aware that it must be ourselves who consent to the sacrifices" (Frelimo 1989a). Furthermore, the IMF and World Bank prefer maximum secrecy for the negotiations.

Frelimo felt that secrecy increased its power, at least in the first stages of negotiation. During 1985 and early 1986, it clearly hoped to get a deal which took account of the war and other special circumstances, and thus was less than full structural adjustment. When this failed, Frelimo took the gamble of introducing PRE without satisfying some of the key demands of the IMF. This was initially successful; on balance it was a slightly more moderate programme than one fully negotiated with the Fund and Bank. But this required Frelimo to claim the programme as its own, rather than one imposed from abroad.

There was a certain bravado in that claim, but it also corresponded to Frelimo's own attitudes. Foremost, Frelimo could not admit to being forced to change course without a massive loss of face. Frelimo under Samora Machel had also become much more paternalistic, and the Politburo undoubtedly felt that it was acting in the best interests of the Mozambican people. Therefore, in a real sense, it was Frelimo's plan, and there was no place for debate.

Most individuals in the leadership had personal interests in suppressing debate. A few who had opposed the decision to accept structural adjustment, but who still supported collective leadership, did not want to be drawn into a debate on the plan. Others – perhaps quite a large group – were simply too embarrassed to admit publicly the magnitude of the defeat PRE represented, or the scale of suffering they knew would be caused. Finally, as I will argue in Chapter 18, some of the leadership had already abandoned any idea of socialism; there was an element of class- and self-interest involved, and there was no desire to have that discussed. And with no tradition of debate and democracy at a national level, there was simply no pressure for debate.

The isolation of the Mozambican intelligentsia also contributed. They had no experience of other countries undergoing structural adjustment, and little economic training, so they were unsure of even what questions to ask. Many simply accepted that there was no alternative. Frelimo party members were reluctant to question what had become a very strong orientation from the top. So there was no debate within the Party, and no framework for discussion outside Frelimo. When I visited in 1988, there was surprisingly little questioning of PRE, even in private.

But even without experience and a thorough understanding, debate might have helped. Simply by asking "why?" intellectuals might have forced ministers and technocrats to justify their decisions; often hard-pressed ministers did not have time to rethink, and some policies were continued even when the original reason had been lost. Furthermore, even poorly-informed debate might have pushed issues like equity and social justice to the forefront, and raised questions about alternatives.

The lack of experience and debate undoubtedly weakened Mozambique's position in negotiations with the Bank and Fund. The Frelimo leadership was also reluctant to draw on the experience of neighbouring states, or on foreign experts who had advised other countries in adjustment negotiations. This was perhaps due to a mix of embarrassment, insecurity, and a genuine (if naïve) belief that the Bank and Fund would accept

Mozambique's uniqueness. Whatever the reasons, Mozambicans – especially those below ministerial level – went into negotiations poorly armed.

The Bank and Fund had dealt with dozens of other countries and knew what they wanted; the Mozambicans often did not know what to expect or exactly what they should be pushing for. The Bank team would have several people, including a secretary with a computer. After a day of hard negotiating, the Bank team would retire to the Hotel Polana to work late into the night revising its position. The Mozambican team would return to its offices and spend the evening trying to get through some of its ordinary work. Inevitably the Mozambicans missed many of the more subtle manoeuvres of the Bank and Fund, and made concessions they would have resisted had they understood the implications.

Debate suppressed

As time went on, Mozambique came under more rather than less pressure. In public statements, Bank and Fund officials increasingly stressed the importance of national "ownership" of the programmes, and stressed the need for government to adopt these programmes as their own (Marshall 1990). The Bank simply ruled out certain kinds of questioning. For example, the World Bank "Food Security Study" says that "an under-lying assumption throughout this report is that the reform measures taken by the government under the ERP [PRE], including exchange rate and domestic price adjustments, and cuts in subsidies to restore fiscal balance, are fundamentally sound and, indeed, essential" (WB 1989g: 6).

When debate did begin to surface, it was quickly suppressed. For example, in early 1988 as part of the World Bank SDA evaluations, a series of inter-ministerial study groups were set up to consider the impact of PRE, and they were given advance warning of changes planned for later in the year, including the removal of the subsidy from the Maputo ration. After detailed discussion, the Food Security study group concluded that the removal of the subsidy on the ration would seriously worsen the living standards of the poorest, and it called for the subsidy to be retained. When the group reported back, it was told by an angry minister that its conclusion was unacceptable. Its finding was suppressed and its recommendation did not appear in the report on the social impact of PRE.

Later in the year various nutrition surveys showed the seriousness of that impact. One report even warned of "the deterioration of social order"; crime was up 300% as people stole to feed their families (MC 1988). These reports, too, called for a subsidy on the ration; they were not even circulated within the government. One was leaked to me by a sympathetic donor agency, which could not understand why Mozambique was not using the shocking figures in its negotiations with the World Bank.

Perhaps there is no point in opening up a debate which the Bank will not permit. But Frelimo never explained to people even where it had been able to make a political choice, for example that removing food subsidies was related to keeping open certain industries badly hit by the war. Indeed, ministers initially refused to admit this to me, until it was apparent from the documents.

Which is another example of the prevailing secrecy. Embassies have complete sets of World Bank documents, and I have been able to obtain many of them from donors. Mozambican journalists have much more difficulty getting such reports. In effect, Frelimo is allowing foreigners to be better informed about Mozambique than its own people.

The Fourth Congress in 1983 had been a turning point on economic issues. At the time of the Fifth Congress in 1989 the economy was probably the second most important issue in people's minds, after the war. But it was assigned only a small portion of the original discussion paper. Nevertheless, in meetings before the Congress complaints about economic management were raised. These were all shelved when the Fifth Congress was turned into a national unity Congress; divisiveness was avoided in an attempt to gain unity against Renamo. Much more of the Fifth Congress was in secret than the Fourth. Again, there was no public discussion of PRE.

Frelimo argued to the Congress that "it has not been possible ... to precede certain measures with the correct explanation", in part because revealing some measures beforehand "would put at risk the impact they were intended to have." But it had to admit that lack of information "has fomented rumours" and "led to a distorted understanding of the programme, and often an interpretation that PRE is an activity merely at the level of wages and prices" (Frelimo 1989a).

In early 1990, workers took things into their own hands with a series of strikes. All editors and section heads in the Mozambican media were summoned to a meeting and told that under no circumstances could they write anything which "brought PRE into question." Thus they could write about the mismanagement involved in not paying workers their back wages (one of the demands of the strikers), but could not discuss the more fundamental issues of structural adjustment.

Implications for elections and free press

The new constitution which came into effect on 30 November 1990 could change the picture. After a forceful campaign by journalists, the new constitution guarantees "freedom of the press, as well as the right to information." Although this is subject to "the imperatives of foreign policy", the press should now be much freer to debate PRE, and might be able to use the freedom of information clause to obtain World Bank documents.

The move to multi-party elections must also have an impact. The danger for Frelimo is that having proclaimed so loudly that the programme is its own, it will be blamed for the suffering caused. For example, the World Bank has now tacitly admitted that it was wrong to end the subsidy on the ration so quickly. And a 1990 report noted obliquely that "by increasing consumer prices past the ability of a significant proportion of the urban population of Maputo and Beira, government may open itself to other problems that could affect its constituency." In other words, people might support Renamo or at least vote against Frelimo in an election.

The opportunities for a demagogic opposition party are immense. For example, it could simply promise the social services that Frelimo provided in the late 1970s: free health and education and living wages for teachers and nurses. This would bring to opposition ranks health and education workers who have considerable prestige in many communities; if they stood as candidates, they would garner significant votes.

What would happen if a party stood specifically against structural adjustment? Would the US or IMF intervene in the election to warn that aid money would dry up? Indeed, it is hard to see how any democratically elected party could continue with structural adjustment – not just in Mozambique, but throughout Africa. And it does seem that the big Western powers are having second thoughts about exporting multi-party democracy. The in word has become "governance", which is taken to mean good administration rather than democracy. Herman Cohen, US Assistant Secretary of State for African Affairs, said that democracy need not mean Western multi-party systems, and that Mozambique might be able to find an alternative "African solution".

It is noteworthy that the US and EC have proved unable to introduce some of the free trade reforms demanded of Africa by the IMF – because their voters won't allow it. Perhaps structural adjustment is incompatible with genuine democracy.

13 Doubts and Second Thoughts: 1990

The worldwide failure of structural adjustment and the immense suffering it was causing finally led to some rethinking in Washington. At the same time, World Bank officials began to accept that Mozambique was a special case, and the adjustment less than totally appropriate. The new thinking may open more space for Mozambique, but it has also created many new contradictions.

Mozambican leaders, too, are becoming worried about the failures of structural adjustment. In May 1990 President Joaquim Chissano told a large group of foreign visitors: "The readjustment programme must start showing results, or we must take other directions. We are totally dependent on inputs from the outside. If they are not forthcoming in the correct manner, it is no use."

At the end of 1990, Prime Minister Mario Machungo admitted that economic performance for the year had been poor. GDP growth was only 1%, less than in the year before PRE, while inflation was over 30% (*Mozambiquefile* January 1991).

There are two areas of concern: that essential and appropriate aid has not been forthcoming, and that cuts have been too swingeing.

The Aid Trap

Without massive aid, "policy adjustments would be unsupported [and] policy reforms would provoke only a minimal response from the economy, and the transitional costs of the adjustment process could well prove to be insupportable", warned the World Bank (WB 1988b).

Mozambique will need $1.4 bn (£840 mn) per year in grants, loans, and debt forgiveness. Even this is not really enough. "This level of financing would support a growth level of about 4% per annum, which is low considering the base from which the economic recovery has started." Indeed, the Bank admitted that it had selected growth targets based on what it thought donors would provide. "A more rapid rehabilitation and recovery would be feasible, but would require additional inflows of external assistance to finance increased imports." Less money would mean "lower growth or further reduction in the very low level of domestic consumption." And this could have serious political implications, because "the social and political costs of the adjustment process would be greater and more prolonged, and the implementation of further reform could be jeopardized" (WB 1987b, 1988f, 1989b).

In other words, if more aid were not available, people would be squeezed too hard, there would be riots, and the whole structural adjustment package would collapse. And the money is not coming in. In its 1990 "Country Economic Memorandum" for Mozambique, the Bank sets out three scenarios for the 1990s (WB 1990c: 213–9). In one scenario, based on the expected level of donor support, "GDP growth is weakly positive, averaging around 0.5% over the ten years. Consequently, per capita consumption shows a serious decline of over 2% per annum. This factor alone raises the important question of the viability of the program under such circumstances. The social cost of this scenario and the political ramifications would be far reaching."

Another scenario asks what would be needed to get just a per capita 1% per year real growth in GDP – an increase which would mean that it would be at least the year 2030 before living standards returned to 1980 levels. With population growth of 2.5%, GDP growth would have to reach 3.5%. This very modest growth, the Bank finds, requires that "aid levels are greater than currently envisaged." The financing gap reaches $130 mn (£78 mn) per year in the second half of the 1990s, and aid must grow at 5% a year.

This decade-long increase of 5% a year in aid must occur despite changes in eastern Europe and the Gulf, and the likely end of apartheid. The World Bank warns of "the specific danger ... that the donor community would react to the diminution of regional insecurity by channelling its resources elsewhere, or by not supporting the higher potential growth. This would be particularly serious if donors view the 'emergency' as having ended, and therefore terminate their emergency aid programs, and if the financial aid that is politically rather than developmentally or economically motivated were to be reduced."

But even if aid rises at this limited rate, Mozambique will be aid-dependent for decades to come.

Will donors cancel debts?

The current account deficit for trade and services for 1989 was $658 mn (£395 mn). In addition, Mozambique was expected to repay $292 mn (£175 mn) in debts and $159 mn (£95 mn) in interest payments. Interest payments alone were 171% of exports and total debt service was 486% – probably the highest rate in the world. Thus Mozambique needed to find $1109 mn (£665 mn). Of this, it received only $380 mn (£228 mn) in grants. Most of the rest was made up of $275 mn (£165 mn) in new loans, plus $398 mn (£239 mn) in debt relief (mainly simply delaying of repayments), which continue to clock up interest and must be repaid eventually (WB 1990c: A47).

Consequently, Mozambique's debt is rising rapidly and alarmingly, from $1.8 bn (£1.1 bn) in 1983 to $3.2 bn (£1.9 bn) in 1986 and to $4.7 bn (£2.8 bn) in 1989. In 1989 debt was 366% of GDP, which was by far the highest rate in the world (WB 1990c: 47). Of that debt, 85% is to governments, 8% to multilateral institutions, and only 7% to banks. Of the bilateral debt, 44% is to OECD countries, 31% to centrally planned economies, 10% to OPEC states, and 7% to other countries.

Mozambicans will be paying off the cost of destabilization for the rest of their lives, long after apartheid is consigned to the history books and the West has rebuilt South Africa as the region's economic powerhouse.

The World Bank estimates that in the 1990–94 period interest payments alone will be about $230 mn (£140 mn) per year, which will be more than total exports even if exports increase at a quite healthy rate. By 1992 three-quarters of interest payments will not be on old debt, but on new loans and refinancing. Capital repayments will be nearly $300 mn (£180 mn) per year, again well over exports. Even by the year 2000, debt servicing will be greater than total exports (WB 1989b: 26, 1990c: 215).

Despite the Special Programme of Assistance to Debt-Distressed Low Income Sub-Saharan African Countries and other general promises to reduce the debt burden, Mozambique's debt grows inexorably. The Bank admits that Mozambique has, in most cases, failed to obtain concessions such as low interest rates or debt forgiveness from most of its creditors; rescheduling is on non-concessional terms. And new money tends to be loans, or the rolling over of old debts, so the debt burden increases.

The IMF and World Bank are part of the problem. The maximum that Mozambique can be expected to pay in repayments and debt service is only enough to cover IMF and World Bank debts (Green 1990). Indeed the Bank admits that servicing only World Bank and IMF loans "consumes over one-third of total visible and invisible exports plus worker remittance earnings" (WB 1990j: 7). Thus it has told Mozambique that it should only accept grants, and not even take interest-free loans from the Bank's own International Development Agency (WB 1990g: 203).

Inevitably this means using aid money to pay debts rather than for essential investment. It also means that Finance Ministry officials are continuously engaged in debt relief negotiations instead of getting on with other matters. "Even the most favourable debt-rescheduling terms that are likely to be attainable fail to restore external financial viability", the Bank warns. "Debt cancellation ...will be essential" (WB 1990c: xi).

Changes and Contradictions

By the end of the 1980s, even the World Bank could not hide from the suffering it had caused in Mozambique, and in all of Africa. There was a shift in policy at head office in Washington, which was reflected in the World Bank office in Maputo.

Unfortunately, the new thinking recognized the problems without questioning the underlying policies which had caused them. This, in turn, creates new contradictions within World Bank strategy. On the one hand countries were being told to spend more, particularly on education, and to push ahead with democratization. On the other hand, they were being told to follow traditional structural adjustment, which required harsh cuts in social spending like education. And no government could make such cuts if it had to face a genuinely free election. The Bank wants it both ways; at the time of writing the outcome remains unclear.

Globally, the new line is spelled out in two books: *Sub-Saharan Africa: From Crisis to Sustainable Growth* and the *World Development Report 1990* (WB 1989h, 1990e). The Bank points to what it calls donor "faddism". Donors in the 1970s put "a single-minded emphasis on food security and poverty alleviation that undermined export-crop production", while in the 1980s there was "a sharp and simplistic swing of donor attention toward efficiency and away from equity concerns." The Bank is disingenuous in not admitting that it led the simplistic swing; but readers in the aid community knew, and thus surely saw in this bankspeak an unexpected recantation and admission of error. Bank president Barber Conable concludes that there is a need for combining continued domestic policy "reform" (that is, continued structural adjustment) with a new focus on economic growth and poverty reduction (WB 1990e: iii, 133).

Squeezed enough

The new line for Mozambique was spelled out in the "Country Economic Memorandum." It admits that "to date, great emphasis has been placed on the policy reform elements." But "policy reform alone will be insufficient to restore sustained growth." Indeed, "the economic problem in the 1990s is fundamentally one of [increasing] production." "It is a major conclusion that macroeconomic balance depends on the restoration of the productive base, rather than on further reductions in expenditure and living standards" (WB 1990c: iii, xxxi, 62).

The report goes on to say that "further reductions in living standards for the poorest households in Mozambique are no longer a realistic option." The words "further" and "no longer" are key; they represent an admission that, as critics had claimed, reducing the living standards of the poor had been policy. It was "no longer" possible, the report said, "both for humanitarian reasons" and because it was no longer "politically sustainable" (WB 1990c: lxii). The strikes of early 1990 meant that Mozambique had passed the riot threshold, while the decision to adopt a multi-party system meant that Frelimo could no longer be pushed to starve its own people.

The report recognizes the fundamental failures of structural adjustment in Mozambique. "Real income levels in 1990 remain well below those of 1987 [at the start of PRE] and, particularly, 1980–2." Around 60% of the population lives in "absolute poverty". But this suffering has not brought benefits. Export growth has been "disappointing", industrial growth has been "fragile", and agricultural improvement only "modest". (WB 1990c: ii, xiii, 11)

The Bank has finally accepted the central point urged by Mozambican ministers and economists since 1984: that structural adjustment would have a strongly deflationary effect which would create a downward spiral, and that the key problem was not pricing policy but supply of goods. The disagreement was not about the problem, but about the priority actions needed to solve it. Now the Bank itself criticizes "deflationary demand management policies that lower growth". It adds that "the principal constraint is the exceptionally low level of per capita consumption" (WB 1990c: x, xviii).

The Bank also admits that "non-price incentives play an essential role; these include the supply of incentive goods and the provision of the necessary rural and social infrastructure.... The rural supply of consumer goods should be maintained at a high level" to stimulate production. In industry, import substitution should be stressed in order to produce rural consumer goods (WB 1990c: vi). This has been the theme of Mozambican officials since 1982, but donors would not listen because it did not have World Bank backing.

The World Bank also recognized that the concept of cost recovery, which it had pushed so hard, had been counterproductive. The poor simply couldn't pay, so they weren't going to clinics and weren't sending their children to school. In 1988, a typical family with three children had to pay 35% of a minimum agricultural wage or 6% of an average urban salary for books and school fees. This is "prohibitive". Many simply didn't have the money (WB 1990c: 167, 173).

Privatization was still on the agenda, but the state was now acknowledged to have a "key role" in all areas, including the economy.

Spend but don't spend

Like a contortionist, the World Bank has twisted itself into an impossible position on government spending. On one hand, it calls for a continued tight cap on public expenditure. The "tax burden is high" so taxes cannot be raised any further, and should perhaps be reduced, although the government cannot be allowed to go into debt. On the other hand, the Bank points to "the extreme need to increase the recurrent expenditures on the social sectors and on maintenance and operating costs". It notes that "the enhancement of health care services rests fundamentally on the provision of more resources." And it calls for other increases in public expenditure, including "very substantial" investment in rural infrastructure, and government intervention to absorb the cost to the private sector of some of the devaluations (WB 1990c: vi, xl, lii, 21, 186, 200, 212; WB 1990g: 138).

Indeed, every World Bank report calls for increased expenditure on its particular area. "An implication of the strategy proposed in the report is increased public spending to address food security problems" (WB 1989g: i). "Increase resources for the provision of basic agricultural services"; salaries of agricultural extension workers should be increased to improve motivation (WB 1989g: 105, 155). "Improvements in the quality of education necessitate increased expenditures" (WB 1990c: 166).

The contradiction in education was particularly stark. Structural adjustment had cut the education budget from $125 mn (£75 mn) in 1986 to $33 mn (£20 mn) the following year. This is only 2.3% of GDP, "one of the lowest figures in Africa". Yet the agreed programme calls for expenditure to rise only 80% in real terms by the year 2000 – in other words still less than in 1986. And the Bank calls for several expensive new programmes to be undertaken on a "priority basis", including introducing mother tongue teaching in the first two grades, upgrading of all teachers, and special programmes for the "lost generations" of children who could not go to school because of the war. The report admits that "when security is restored, extraordinary demands will be placed upon the education system". Yet a detailed look at the tables in the report shows that the Ministry of Education has been able to meet the World Bank budget cap only by assuming that the number of primary pupils will remain below 1987 levels until 1995, and then rise more slowly than the growth in the number of school age pupils. This assumes, in effect, that *none* of the rural schools destroyed by Renamo will be rebuilt and that the "extraordinary demands" of returning refugees simply will not be met (WB 1990c: 142, 165-180, A111).

Less than half of primary school age pupils are actually attending school. Even in Maputo, there are only places for two-thirds of the children that want to start primary school. And Frelimo admits that over the coming decade, "half of all children aged from seven to 11 years old will still not have adequate conditions to attend primary school normally" (*Tempo* 13 March 1988; Frelimo 1989a) .

The *World Development Report 1990* puts great emphasis on the need to improve education as the key to increasing productivity and reducing poverty. In Mozambique, "only with substantive investment in educational and manpower training will growth be sustainable in the medium term" (WB 1990e: 74; 1990c: iv, 166).

But where will the money come from? "The education system is basically unable to provide reasonable levels of service, either in terms of coverage or quality.... As in health, there is a need for donors to increase recurrent cost financing", argues the World Bank. But the Bank also knows that as it is donors are not coming up with enough money. Therefore, there should be "more donor funding for recurrent expenditures, even at the expense of reduced rehabilitation" (WB 1989b: 20).

The Bank pressed Mozambique to spend even less on investment and repairing war damage, and shift the money to social services. But Mozambique felt that higher levels of investment were essential if it was ever to get out of the aid trap. A government minister told me: "The World Bank argues that we must reduce capital expenditure in order to reduce the budget deficit. But we said to the World Bank that we have to repair war damage to infrastructure. We cannot rebuild our economy without roads in the rural areas."

Indeed, the Bank and Fund's own report admits that "reform of pricing policy is a critical [but] not a sufficient condition for improvement in marketed production [which also requires] an adequate transport system, including roads" (WB 1988a). And the Bank was calling for "very substantial new investment" in rural areas, and was complaining about lack of donor finance for investment projects. A Bank study noted that "lack of financing was apparently one of the key criteria used to suspend projects, some of which appear to be of very high priority (e.g. airport infrastructure and irrigation rehabilitation)" (WB 1988c).

Such contradictions are much more serious because of the centrality of the World Bank. The head of one of the major bilateral donor agencies in Maputo told me: "The World Bank now dominates all thinking, both in government and by donors. Their constant missions dominate policy formulation." Yet the missions often contradict each other. For example, the Bank's Health and Nutrition mission concluded that "consumer prices of the main food staples are currently in excess of import parity prices" (WB 1989c: 17). But the Food Security study team concluded that "consumer prices of maize, maize meal, sorghum and beans would need to be raised substantially, by between 30-60%", to bring them into line with international prices (WB 1989g: 82). Getting prices "right" is at the very heart of the World Bank prescription, yet its own teams cannot agree. Not surprisingly, Mozambique officials are confused.

Not our problem

The World Bank is trying to offload its responsibility on to other donors. And it is pushing those donors in totally contradictory directions, while blocking government expenditures that the Bank itself sees as being absolutely essential.

To compensate for the poverty caused by PRE, the Bank calls for a massive expansion of the urban ration – extending it to two more cities and doubling the amount of maize provided. This would require donors to provide an extra 33,000 tonnes of maize for sale (WB 1989g: 125). Yet the proposal was made when donors were already falling 224,000 tonnes short of Mozambique's request for maize for the market (See Chapter 7).

The Bank also puts forward solutions which donors have already explicitly rejected, such as more grain swaps between the DPCCN and Agricom. And it calls for the DPCCN to be able to sell donated grain and use the money to buy food elsewhere for displaced people. As the Bank says, "money can be moved around, stored, and distributed more cheaply than food." Which is true, but it is a pointless suggestion when, as the Bank itself admits, it violates donor rules (WB 1989g: ix, 55, 134).

The Bank even proposes things which cannot be done under the IMF accounting rules, such as making the subsidy on bread explicit, and paying an explicit subsidy to transporters to cover the additional costs of waiting for military convoys (WB 1989g: 140, 155).

Have it both ways?

There are at least four other areas in which the World Bank is trying to have it both ways: devaluation, food vs exports, the war, and the emergency.

First, the Bank calls for continued "real" devaluations – that is devaluations that outpace the rate of inflation. Yet it admits that past devaluations have been one of the main causes of inflation, increasing urban poverty, and falling rural terms of trade. And these must be resolved if the economy is to grow (WB 1990c: xxiv, liv).

The second contradiction is over export promotion. As noted earlier in this chapter, the Bank in Washington has admitted the "faddist" error of jumping from the stress on food to the stress on exports. But it has not recognized that it made this error in Mozambique. In 1985, after its first visits to Mozambique, the Bank concluded that "a logical place to start is with measures to provide greater incentives to producers and processors of export commodities." Frelimo always recognized that this was not necessarily logical, and pricing policy encouraged farmers to produce food. This continued to make sense in 1990, when aid grain was still more than 80% of marketed supply. At the Fifth Congress Frelimo said that "today the principal aim is to achieve a recovery in food production." Peasant production of export crops "should not displace the priority given to growing food" (Frelimo 1989a, 1989b).

With the introduction of PRE, Mozambique raised the real prices of export crops faster than those of food crops, but still kept the bias toward food – export crops are priced at roughly half of international prices whereas food crops are similar to world market prices. Despite the claims at the top, in 1990 the Bank still wanted further changes in Mozambique to encourage farmers to switch from food to export crops (WB 1990c: v, 30).

Is war the problem, after all?

The third contradiction revolves around the war and the question posed in Chapter 6: Why is there a problem? "First, and foremost, Mozambique is a country at war." And the Bank called on donors to provide "non-lethal military assistance to facilitate movement of food supplies", as well as to protect development projects (WB 1989g: 25, 154).

"Mozambique is exceptional in the depth and comprehensiveness of the current crisis, even in the context of Africa", the Bank admits. There are four reasons for the "extreme poverty in Mozambique". They are the colonial heritage, the war, the "adverse impact" of PRE, and "the economic policy choices of the pre-ERP [PRE] period." And the Bank uses terms that until then had only been used by the government, mentioning, for example, "the boycott of Maputo port by the South Africans". It even admits that in the early 1980s there was a donor strike, and that Mozambique's "policy stance was, moreover, instrumental in provoking a sharp decline in external assistance, which further exacerbated the emerging crisis." That is bankspeak for allowing 100,000 people to starve to death to force Mozambique to join the Bank (WB 1990c: 4, 57, 101, 210).

The Bank notes that economic recovery has been only "modest" and concludes that "growth was certainly affected primarily by the security problem and by the scarcity of foreign exchange and thus of imports." The Bank even talks about the need to maintain "a quasi-war economy" (WB 1990c: xvi, 101).

The contradiction here is that World Bank policy is still committed to structural adjustment and economic liberalization, and the Bank still believes that Africa's problems are largely self-inflicted (*Africa Recovery* December 1989). Thus the Bank is imposing on Mozambique its standard prescription that assumes the illness is the fault of Frelimo and can be cured by narrow economic means, while at the same time admitting this is not so.

What place for the emergency?

The fourth area of contradiction is the "emergency". This has been the one source of foreign funding not under World Bank control, but it has also allowed the Bank to ignore the impact of the war.

"War has been and remains the dominant single cause of absolute poverty in Mozambique. It also results in a certain division of economic policy, with life sustaining and rural rehabilitation programmes largely grouped under the emergency rubric, and financed by special donor appeals, while urban economic and social policy are … responsive to what one normally considered economic actions" under structural adjustment. The emergency programme is "the centrepiece to poverty alleviation" (WB 1990b). This allowed the Bank largely to ignore rural poverty and the impact of the war, and simply assume donors would deal with it through the emergency.

At the same time, however, the Bank repeatedly demanded that the emergency programme be "fully integrated with other government programs financed by the general budget" (WB 1989b). As well as bringing a further renegade sector under World Bank control, it would also cap emergency expenditure.

By the end of 1989 the Bank had decided that "the emergency program is structural in nature and therefore requires integrating with the ERP [PRE]" (WB 1990c: 51). This was agreed at the 1989 Consultative Group meeting. The 1990 emergency appeal was much smaller than before and there was to be no separate emergency appeal in 1991. Rehabilitation and donated grain for marketing were now to be routed through donor programmes controlled by the World Bank. In exchange, the Bank accepted the permanent, structural nature of the emergency, and allowed some of its own money to go for rehabilitation of roads and other infrastructure destroyed by Renamo.

But the confusion remains, with some parts of the Bank still calling for more donor funding to be routed through the emergency programme. The danger is that the reverse will happen: donors will conclude that rehabilitation is now being taken care of by the World Bank and thus there is no longer a need to make donations for the emergency.

By reducing an aid channel outside its control, the Bank may have reduced the total flow of aid funds.

No reward for being right

It is a tribute to the tenacity of Mozambican officials that after five years of struggle they have finally convinced the World Bank of the accuracy of their diagnosis of the problem, and that the solutions put forward in 1982-4 were at least a sensible starting point.

"Mozambique's leadership has been among the first in sub-Saharan Africa to assert that poverty reduction was necessarily central to economic reconstruction and that it must be an integral part of macro-economic policy and project goals, and not ghettoized in a series of peripheral add-on projects. To assert that and to cite the rebuilding of domestic demand as the first priority of a structural adjustment programme in 1986 was an act of vision and of courage," noted Professor Reginald Green. The World Bank "now advances virtually the same analysis. This is a tribute to Mozambique's foresight and ability to stick to its position" (Green 1990).

But it is a tribute to the uncontrolled power of the World Bank that it could provoke a donor's strike by refusing to accept that plan, then turn around and admit Frelimo was right in the first place – without anyone batting an eyelid. Much nonsense is talked of Frelimo's doctrinaire Marxism; how little is said about the immense suffering caused by the World Bank's doctrinaire monetarism.

14 What Role for the State in the Economy?

Privatization and the elimination of the state from the economy are pillars of any structural adjustment programme. In a socialist economy, the state plays a central role. Predictably, this is the crux of one conflict between Mozambique and the donors. Yet, Frelimo always wanted a mixed economy, and never intended that the government should own the means of production. Most factories, shops, and farms now run by the state had simply been abandoned at independence; the few things that were nationalized were taken over for special reasons – the banks because of fraud, the coal mines because of safety lapses, etc. Only land, rented housing, and social services (health, education, law, and funerals) were nationalized as a matter of policy.

Mozambique's mixed economy was thus a hotchpotch. Most sugar mills and tea factories were run by the state but some were still private; some textile mills were state-owned and some private; some factories were complex mixes of private, bank, Mozambican state, and Portuguese state ownership. Frelimo encouraged the completion of the Mabor tyre factory which was under construction at independence: it remains a standard joint venture, partly owned by General Tire of the US. Other new investments were state-controlled by default, because no local or foreign capitalist had the capacity or interest to build large textile mills and other consumer goods factories. Frelimo also encouraged the formation of cooperative farms and shops, and expanded the state agricultural marketing board inherited from the Portuguese.

But if Frelimo never wanted the state to *own* the means of production, it had always aimed to regulate the economy. By the late 1970s, this meant central planning with precise control of prices, production targets, and distribution of scarce commodities. Annual plans were to cover private and cooperative businesses as well as state enterprises. Development policy and new investment were to be decided at national level. Foreign investment was encouraged.

These plans ran into trouble even before they were worked out. The panicked flight of the Portuguese shattered rural marketing and left many factories without managers and "know-how". Instead of planning, Frelimo found itself actually running businesses. "Faced with the confusion created by the massive Portuguese exodus, the only alternative was administrative management accompanied by 'management by campaign', where political mobilizing activity predominated over economic stimuli", explained Finance Minister Magid Osman. "The planned economy arose more from a practice that gradually became theorized, and not from an ideological option" (Osman 1990).

To be sure, the climate of the late 1970s was not sympathetic to private businesses;

they were not forced out of business, but they were not encouraged, either. Indeed, in a few areas which had no private business (communal villages and former liberated zones), new private business was banned. By 1980 the mood of both Frelimo and the private sector had changed. In November 1980 the government began to sell off shops, bakeries, and restaurants. In some cases there was stiff competition for businesses that had been abandoned only five years before. When the rationing system was introduced in Maputo in 1981, food was distributed largely through private wholesalers and shops, and only to a lesser extent through the new consumer cooperatives.

Frelimo's management of the economy worked, in the sense that production recovered in 1977 and continued growing until destabilization began to take hold after 1981. By then the limits of Mozambique's management capacity were also much clearer. With technical assistance it was proving possible to run, reasonably effectively, some of the larger factories and even some of the state farms, for example the tea estates. But skills were

Workers sort cashew nuts in a factory which was abandoned by its owners at independence and is now run by the state (AIM: António Machave).

too thinly spread, and other factories and farms were poorly run. Similarly, it was becoming apparent that Mozambique did not have the capacity to run a complex central planning system, whatever its merits. Finally, it was also clear that too much stress had been put on large development projects, which were taking too long to come on stream and were becoming impractical in any case due to destabilization. This led to a series of economic decisions at the Fourth Congress in 1983 to cut back on central planning and to promote small farmers and small industry. The private sector was openly encouraged, and former restrictions were lifted; the Frelimo Party Programme was rewritten to give more space to the private sector. Nevertheless, the Congress also said that "we must ensure that by 1985 the state controls wholesale trade at national and provincial level and guarantees effective control of the distribution of goods" (Hanlon 1984a: 208). This was not unreasonable considering the worsening war and the monopolistic tendencies in the private sector. Here again, there is a clear distinction between ownership and control; there can be private wholesalers but they must work within rules defined by government.

Thus Frelimo entered its negotiations with the IMF and World Bank with a strong commitment to rebuilding the market and increasing the role of the private sector. Planning and state price regulation were to be reined in. On the other hand, Frelimo remained opposed to an unfettered free market; the state should retain a major economic role, through ownership of key industries and other businesses, by directing development policy, and by continuing to set some prices and exert control over scarce foreign exchange. In speeches to parliament on 27 April 1984, the then Finance Minister Rui Baltazar stressed the desire to turn "state-owned wholesalers into true instruments of government policy", while President Machel stressed that companies were being given more freedom in order to reach objectives set by the state.

Promoting the private sector

The international push for privatization is very strong. The World Bank produced a special paper in 1987 on its "Role in Promoting the Private Sector" (WB 1987c) which sets out its strategy. It says openly that it uses the conditions on structural adjustment loans to promote the private sector by insisting on "studies to help identify divestiture candidates and design sales programs". The Bank also promotes deregulation as a way of promoting the private sector. It argues that "economically rational decisions" should determine investment rather than any kind of policy or strategy.

In the paper, the Bank speaks highly of programmes it is supporting to "withdraw the state from direct involvement in production". "The Bank has also supported programs to rationalize the public sector and reduce the crowding out of private activities by eliminating public monopolies, privatizing public activities, and reducing and redirecting public expenditure." It talks of programmes to help redeploy civil servants into the private sector. And it even argues for "private delivery of public services", especially by contracting out services like customs collection or transport to TNCs.

The Bank calls for "an outward oriented economic policy". Foreign investment should be promoted. As a way to do this, the Bank encourages debt-equity swaps, in which a country pays off debt that it would never be able to repay otherwise by giving parastatal companies to TNCs. For example, Portuguese interests took 43% of the Mabor tyre company by using $4.1 mn of Mozambican debt held by Portugal to buy state shares in the company.

This approach is strongly promoted by the US and the UK. USAID has a Private Enterprise Bureau which launched a Third World privatization campaign in 1986; USAID says privatization is "one of the cardinal pillars" of its work. In 1988 the US President's Commission on Privatization urged that aid from the US and World Bank be contingent on recipients carrying out privatization (*Africa Analysis*, 13 May 1988).

In 1988 Britain and the US, working together, sent instructions to all their Third World missions urging them to identify candidates for privatization, such as railways and airlines (which in many Third World countries were inherited as nationalized industries from the colonial powers). The US and the UK would cooperate at local level, and aid would be available to assist (*Guardian* 3 January 1989).

And William Draper, former president of the US Export-Import Bank who became head of UNDP in 1986, earmarked the role of the private sector in economic development as an area deserving special attention by UNDP (UNDP 1988a).

Weakness of the market

At the start of the structural adjustment programme, the government ran more than 300 production enterprises (not counting shops, restaurants, etc.), of which 200 were industrial. Between 1985 and 1988, 47 medium-size enterprises were sold off and 40 smaller ones were privatized. That was not enough, and the continued "large role of the public sector in the economy" was a "major concern" of the World Bank. The Bank and Fund insisted that by mid-1990 Mozambique have a privatization programme (WB 1986, 1988b, 1989a, 1989b).

But the ambitious privatization plans of the Bank and Fund had to be scaled down. They had assumed a private sector ready and waiting to take over state industry. The World Bank actually sent a short mission to draw up a list of such people. But it was a fantasy; they weren't there. Antonio Almeida Matos, director of the parastatal Companhia Industrial da Matola, told me: "The World Bank doesn't understand what it is doing. They come in here with clichés. When you talk about privatization in Mozambique, you must ask who is going to buy. We still have shops on offer that no one buys. No one is able to take over industries."

The weakness of the market in Mozambique cuts to the very heart of the free market approach. Colonial Mozambique was largely a service economy so it did not develop a large entrepreneurial class. The Portuguese did not allow black business people in most sectors, and many of the white and Asian merchants left at independence. The remaining market has been a direct target of destabilization, and the destruction has been widespread. Furthermore, there is strong evidence that South Africa responded to the economic reforms of 1984 and 1987 by stepping up attacks on the marketing system, precisely to prevent the reforms working. Thus Mozambique's market is structurally weak as well as damaged.

The government has been trying to support the development of private trading in rural areas since independence, and with significant force since 1980. But it admitted that "efforts to sell off state owned rural stores have met with limited success due to the unwillingness of the private sector to invest" (RPM 1989).

Even the World Bank had to admit that "the absorptive capacity of the enterprise sector is limited" (WB 1988b). USAID conceded that the private sector reforms it had been promoting "have had limited success in attracting new investment and in increasing significantly private sector participation in the economy" (USAID 1987b).

Most of the new generation of entrepreneurs have grown up in the state sector, and many of them like it there. "If my company were privatized, I would have a better salary myself, but the enterprise would be no better run", Matos commented. "I don't feel any government interference in the day-to-day running. Knowing the condition of Mozambique, I know I would face the same problems if this company were private or state." And he concluded: "Of course there are state enterprises that are badly run, but there are also private companies which are mismanaged. It depends on the quality of the people available."

Thus the US and World Bank seem anxious to force the best people out of the state sector. They do this in negative ways, particularly by discriminating against parastatals. And they do it in positive ways by permitting much higher private salaries (particularly to attract national directors and other high state functionaries) and by promoting privatization through management buyouts and debt–equity swaps.

Privatization does not mean competition

Privatization has so far rarely succeeded in increasing competition. There are simply too few businesses in any market sector; only a handful of companies make clothing or shoes, there are only a few shops in any town, and even in urban neighbourhoods the number of shops is limited.

Monopoly industrial suppliers are increasing their own profit margins and trying to squeeze those of the traders. For their part, traders tend to reach informal arrangements rather than compete. For example, they do not lower prices of seasonal fruit and vegetables when production increases, but instead push down the price paid to the producer and increase their own margin, making more profit off a smaller quantity of goods. When shortages occur, goods disappear from shelves as traders try to push up prices. Private traders make large amounts of money from black market trading. Thus one effect of decontrol under PRE has actually been to reduce competition.

Mozambique previously had a system of district wholesalers, normally private traders, who had a monopoly but were required to follow state rules and pricing. With the free market this system was ended. In towns, this did increase competition, but in rural areas it had the opposite effect. Instead of several wholesalers moving into a district and competing, individual wholesalers expanded their monopoly to several districts. Indeed, as I found in Pemba when I talked with traders, family and friendship links meant that one closely knit group of people had come to dominate wholesale trade in Cabo Delgado province. This gives traders immense power. In several provinces, for example, traders simply refused to handle school textbooks because they judged the profit too small.

Frelimo demands a state role

Frelimo is anxious to increase the roles of the market and the private sector, but it recognizes how few local capitalists are in the wings waiting to take over from the state. Mozambican capital is mainly interested in quick profits from trade; it is not interested in rural development or in creating productive industry. There is no choice but for the state to take a key role in promoting development, and in ensuring that the market functions.

Many Frelimo leaders feel that Mozambique's practical needs point to a "third way" between rigid central planning and unrestrained capitalism (see Chapter 20). As Prime Minister Machungo noted, "businessmen do not always react to the stimuli of indirect mechanisms of managing the economy, such as interest, pricing, and credit policies." Thus the state must both have a planning role, and actively intervene in the economy (MIO 2 August 1990). "We should not fall into the mistake of thinking that financial measures can solve economic problems," Finance Minister Magid Osman stressed in an interview with AIM. "The state must intervene and must direct resources in order to reorganize the productive sector" (MIO 8 April 1988).

Central government accounts for roughly 50% of GDP and parastatal companies another 20%, which means that "the public sector will continue to represent a very large share of national product for the foreseeable future." Even when resources are redirected away from past misguided investments such as large state farms, "it is important to make public investments, particularly in the areas of services" (RPM 1989).

Frelimo's view of the state role in the economy is not yet reflected in a clear policy. Decisions continue to be made on a case by case basis – but it is apparent that the state is trying to retain certain strategic companies and a presence in some market areas. Also, even the World Bank admits that some quite large parastatal companies "appear to be performing adequately, with good management and sound accounting procedures" (WB 1989d: 36). So there is less interest in denationalizing these.

At the same time, the state has been trying to divest itself totally of small companies, companies which are badly run, and companies which have no strategic role. The result is the continuation of a mixed economy. For example, many state farms will be sold off or the land redistributed, but some will be retained if they can be made profitable and have a social role in supporting small farmers in their area. Some small firms are simply auctioned off to the highest bidder, while others are being sold preferentially to former guerrillas and ex-soldiers.

For larger firms, the government is encouraging mixed ventures. The Ministry of Finance has been proposing a 40% state holding (in order to be able to influence social and policy issues), with local capital, foreign capital, and the management having 20% each (there are no proposals for shares for workers). For its part, the World Bank has finally accepted that local entrepreneurs are in short supply and talks of "mobilizing private participation in public enterprises active in the productive sector" – clearly something short of full denationalization (WB 1989a).

US Leads the Way

For several years US foreign aid legislation imposed the condition that development aid to Mozambique had to go "to the maximum extent practicable" to the private sector. The USAID office in Maputo interpreted this in the strictest possible sense, to mean assisting exclusively the private sector. "The rehabilitation of the private sector remains the keystone of our program" (USAID 1987b). The USAID office defines "private" to include larger private commercial farms and companies, family farmers, and, perhaps surprisingly, cooperatives. It excludes parastatal and intervened companies, other than those explicitly planned for privatization.

USAID's main development programme in Mozambique since 1985 has been a $10 mn (£6 mn) per year private sector programme aimed largely at the private farming sector in Maputo, Gaza, and Manica provinces. The "principal beneficiaries" have been "commercial farmers who employ labour and generally have larger farms." They have been sold tractors, trucks, irrigation equipment, and inputs. Larger family farmers have been able to buy animal traction equipment, improved seeds and fertilizers (USAID 1989).

The official goal of the programme is to "enhance the private agricultural sector's production and income." But the emphasis seems more on the latter than the former. Officially, trucks and tractors were sold to farmers to allow them to increase production. In fact, many have been used for commercial goods and passenger transport. Some can be seen carrying commuters in Maputo. USAID reports note this, and officials say they have no objections because it all encourages the private sector. Indeed, USAID admits that those private farmers who initially received AID lorries "reaped large windfall profits" because of transport shortages. One USAID report estimated that transporters made a net profit of MT 6 mn ($150,000 or £90,000 at the then official exchange rates) in the first year they had a USAID lorry, which was a fortune in Mozambique in 1986 (USAID 1986b, 1989a).

'Principal benefactor'

The US had two quite open political goals. The first was to convince Mozambicans that it was the US and not Frelimo which supported them. One USAID report crowed that "the United States is now seen as the principal benefactor of the Mozambique private agricultural sector" (USAID 1986a).

The second goal was to ensure that potential allies of Frelimo did not benefit. Initially, tractors and other equipment were allocated by the district directorate of agriculture, in accordance with US rules. But the US later insisted that they be distributed through private sector firms. District agriculture directors had required the big commercial farmers to make a commitment to use their USAID equipment to provide services to neighbouring family farmers. A USAID evaluation team was appalled at this – despite USAID's admission that its equipment provided a windfall profit, and despite commercial farmers making a profit on the contract services. The evaluators fulminated: "the farmer shouldn't have to use his investment to help other farmers. Why should the commercial farmer provide welfare to family farmers?" (USAID 1987a: 26) The second reason for taking allocation away from government was only admitted by embassy staff privately. President Samora Machel, before his death, had established a programme of encouraging army officers to retire and establish farms and other businesses. This had the two-fold goal of cleaning out the army and creating a pro-Frelimo group of black businessmen. Retiring officers received preference for credit and equipment such as that from USAID, and US officials were clearly unhappy. They may have felt that the largely Portuguese-owned private firms would give preference to Portuguese and other farmers who had dealt with these firms in the past, rather than the black pro-Frelimo newcomers.

Aid tied to privatization

The US intends to enforce privatization, and aid has been increasingly tied to this. Mozambique has been required to agree programmes with the US for denationalizing 3000 ha per year of state farm land (from specific state farms agreed with USAID), develop private sales and service networks for agricultural inputs, set up a programme to increase the amount of agricultural marketing done through private traders and transporters, and privatize parts of the construction industry. The US said that Mozambique "will adopt the agreed-upon policy agenda as its own program, in effect institutionalizing a policy process in which USAID will actively participate." Aid is conditional on this policy being followed (USAID 1989).

Under the private sector programme, the US imported raw materials for private companies to make tractor tyres, irrigation pipes, and other equipment. But if items were made locally by state companies, the US imported them in direct competition. In one instance, two different firms in Maputo could make a similar pipe, and a US embassy official told me the intervened firm could do it more cheaply; nevertheless US support went to the less efficient private firm.

In one instance USAID had been supplying raw materials to an intervened firm which the US had expected to be privatized, but the government instead decided the firm was strategic and converted it to a full state company. US support immediately stopped. The firm had been very good and the embassy official was sad to see the end of a "very successful project". Similarly all importing was to be done by private firms. Contracts to state importers were stopped because giving contracts to parastatals will only help "to prolong their existence" (USAID 1987a: 14).

Confrontation with the Nordics

USAID's private sector obsession has brought it into conflict both with other donors and with the Mozambican government. USAID is arrogant enough to believe it can intervene in other nations' aid programmes to stop them from supporting state enterprises. The Country Strategic Plan says that "special attention must also be given to the Nordic aid programs to minimize counterproductive reinforcement of parastatals" (USAID 1990b: 69).

Frelimo is not happy with the US bias, but the power of Washington makes it difficult for Frelimo to oppose this directly. Nevertheless, whenever ministers and other officials feel confident that they will not offend the US, they do take a stand. Thus, in a speech in Matola President Chissano criticized US concentration of support on the private sector and called for support for the state and cooperative sectors (see Chapter 22).

Who Controls Food Trade?

Two parastatal food trading companies have been the subject of particularly bitter battles. Agricom is the rural marketing board. Built on a colonial grain marketing board, it expanded to try to fill the gap caused by the flight of Portuguese traders. The other firm is Hortofrutícola, which was discussed in Chapter 10. It is the largest fruit and vegetable wholesaler in Maputo, and also runs market and street-corner stalls.

Both Agricom and Hortofrutícola triggered a hostility in World Bank and US officials that is hard for outsiders to appreciate, and difficult to explain on rational grounds. These two state companies seemed to represent satanic demons which had to be exorcised. Some bilateral donors, too, have the same view; one donor imported hand tools in direct competition to Agricom.

Agricom was formed in 1981 and was soon hit by the worsening war, which pushed many private traders as well as Agricom out of some rural areas, and which sharply increased operating costs. In colonial times there were more than 6000 private retailers in rural areas. By the end of the 1980s, there were about 1700 private shops, 300 consumer cooperatives, and 120 Agricom outlets (MC 1990).

Agricom has a presence in 90 districts and serves largely as a wholesaler and warehouser linking the main cities with the countryside. It buys food crops from retailers and large private and state farmers, and sells them in urban areas and to factories, schools, and the military. Agricom has tried to leave grain purchases from peasants to the private sector, so it buys only 9% of food crops at retail level. But it handles 36% of wholesale trade, including 70% of wholesale maize trade.

Although it never intended to do so, the need to provide consumer goods to exchange for peasant crops led Agricom to become the main wholesale supplier of agricultural hand tools, grain sacks, and clothing (largely donated used clothes) in rural areas. Agricom also handles substantial amounts of donated food intended for sale outside the main cities.

From its founding, Agricom received Nordic and other donor support. But the stress was on technical and material support, and there was too little training, particularly of management. In part due to weaknesses in the Nordic programme, Agricom failed to develop an adequate vehicle preventive maintenance programme. A Nordic official admitted to me that "for ten years we treated this as an emergency programme. We were lazy. We filled gaps and kept it running, but we never provided the support that would create a strong organization. We sent mechanics but not specialists in organizing maintenance." Nevertheless, by the end of the 1980s Agricom and the DPCCN, along with health and education, are the government agencies most commonly seen in rural areas. Agricom functions reasonably well, considering the constraints imposed by the war, and has undoubtedly played a key role in the increase in peasant grain marketing under PRE.

What place for Agricom?

One of the ironies is that the World Bank wanted to abolish Agricom in order to boost the private sector, while in fact private traders think Agricom is essential. The Centre for African Studies of Eduardo Mondlane University found that, especially with high interest rates under PRE and the risk of Renamo attack, traders did not want to hold maize but wanted to sell it on to Agricom as quickly as possible (Adam 1989). In many war-affected areas, only Agricom was willing to risk its lorries to travel into rural zones.

Another study pointed out that the decreased number of private traders meant they had a monopoly in most rural areas. Thus "in large areas of the country, Agricom is actually the only institution which can provide farmers with protection from exploitation by certain tradesmen, or [provide farmers] with a functioning link to the market economy" (Eduards 1990). Thus it became clear that Agricom was necessary not as an alternative to the private sector, but as a means of keeping the free market functioning. Under continued pressure from the government, by 1989 the World Bank had revised its views, and accepted a continued role for Agricom.

In 1990 the Ministry of Commerce proposed to continue the trend by which Agricom would steadily withdraw from retail purchasing of grains, and purchase only in bulk at district levels. It would continue to be a major wholesale supplier of agricultural inputs and consumer goods, and would begin to provide agricultural credit. In this role it would function as a profit-making parastatal company.

It is also proposed that Agricom have several additional roles, for which it would receive a state grant. It would maintain grain reserves at provincial level, both for food security and to intervene if private traders try to manipulate the grain market. It would promote cooperatives and peasant associations and help them to take a bigger role in agricultural marketing. It would be a buyer of last resort, guaranteeing to purchase at the legal floor price, and thus prevent private traders from paying peasants too little. And it would train the retail sector in improved grain storage methods (MC 1990).

Industry

At independence, Mozambique was perhaps the eighth most industrialized country in Africa. Heavy industry included railway wagon manufacture and other metal working, an oil refinery, and three cement factories. There was a substantial agricultural processing sector, both for export and for local consumption. And there was a textile and clothing sector. After independence there was a major expansion of the electricity grid, new textile mills, a large new sawmill, and various other new industries. In general, however, the main effort was to keep industry going after the flight of Portuguese technicians and owners; existing equipment was not maintained and modernized, so that by the late 1980s a great deal of industry was in desperate need of rehabilitation. (Hanlon 1984a: 73)

There were three battles with the World Bank and other donors: over keeping this relatively large industrial sector operating, about maintaining a state presence, and over whether Mozambique should have an industrial development strategy or be guided by narrow assessments of profitability and efficiency.

On the first, Mozambique was relatively lucky, because by 1986 the World Bank had abandoned the narrow deindustrialization strategy it had tried to impose on Zimbabwe and other Third World states in the early 1980s, on the grounds that those countries had a "comparative advantage" in producing raw materials rather than industrial goods. One Bank study concluded that "Mozambique's industrial sector cannot be dismissed as 'inefficient' and therefore be neglected or liquidated. On the contrary, the analysis suggests that rehabilitation is a good possibility for many firms" (WB 1989e). Nevertheless, as the previous chapter showed, Bank policies are in conflict with each other. Deflation and demand reduction have depressed manufacturing, which has grown less than expected. And there remains the conflict between directing donor funds to social sectors or to the rehabilitation of economic sectors.

From the early 1980s, Industry Ministry officials realized that the post-independence heavy industry emphasis was wrong, and they actually hoped for World Bank help in setting a new industry strategy. Instead, the first Bank team simply said that the problems were due to socialism (and not due to war), and that the best thing was to return to the colonial industry pattern and bring back the Portuguese. Not only was this advice offensive, it was also unhelpful.

The initial World Bank credits of 1985 and 1987 contained components for industrial raw materials and rehabilitation, which were used for all sectors of industry. But the credits were conditional on a study of 25 industrial and 15 agricultural enterprises; that the government produce plans to "restructure, divest, or close specific enterprises"; and that a system be developed to rank industries according to "efficiency criteria". These criteria will be based on "higher value added at world market prices". Foreign exchange must be allocated preferentially to the most "efficient" enterprises (WB 1986, 1987d). The World Bank was committed to a $70 million (£40 mn) industrial rehabilitation loan, to be allocated according to the outcome of its studies.

Mozambican officials were unhappy about the World Bank's efficiency criteria on two grounds. First, they objected on principle and wanted development criteria to determine investment. Second, they alleged that the Bank chose a very convoluted way of calculating efficiency, which seemed to show that only private firms were efficient.

The Mozambican government made effective use of foreign help in developing an industrial strategy, and in its battles with the Bank. In particular, it brought a UN agency on to its side. So while the World Bank (itself a UN agency) was doing its narrow efficiency-based studies of Mozambican industry, Unido was preparing an alternative industrial sector study. Unido argued that "top priority must be given to satisfying the basic needs of the people" for food, clothing, tools, etc. These industries should be given priority for rehabilitation, along with export agro-industries plus beverages and tobacco for tax revenue. Later, emphasis should shift to diversification of exports and import substitution (Unido 1987). PRE prioritized industries which make consumer goods and tools for rural areas, produce food for the cities, produce construction materials, make a large contribution to tax revenue, and support exports or import substitution (RPM 1988).

In meetings with the government, the World Bank pushed its efficiency criteria. Mozambique's Ministry of Industry brought its own foreign experts into these meetings, much to the annoyance of Bank officials: they prefer to deal with government officials and ministers who lack the technical competence to challenge them.

Only private manufacturing?

There is a strong regional commitment to mixed economies. SADCC spoke for the entire region when it said that "parastatals, on their own, cannot overcome the daunting challenges of investment, production, and trade facing the region; but the catalytic role they play has tremendous potential to unleash the enormous investment capacity of the private sector" (SADCC 1989). Throughout Africa, private investors have been unwilling to accept the risks of investing in areas which will have the most impact in stimulating development.

A study of Kenya showed that "efficiency levels in public manufacturing are comparable with those in private sector manufacturing, and that quasi-public firms [joint ventures] combining both public and private control substantially surpass efficiency levels in the private sector considered separately. Perhaps even more surprising, public firms are shown to be the recipients of less governmental trade protection than private firms when comparison is made within industries." The relative lack of protection for parastatals is because of "a general unwillingness on the part of many private firms in Kenya to invest in unprotected areas of the economy." In general, publicly owned companies were more efficient and more profitable, so "the scope for privatization to achieve improved performance is limited" (Grosh 1990). This would seem to support Frelimo's stress on a continued role for the state in industry, with a bias toward joint ventures.

Mozambique and SADCC talk about the "enterprise sector" which includes all forms of ownership: state, private, joint, and cooperative. All should be treated on the same footing; the private sector should not receive preferential treatment. In particular, Mozambique has given substantial freedom to managers of state companies – sometimes more than they would be given by a private board of directors. It has also imposed financial discipline, expecting parastatal managers (in industries not heavily affected by the war) to obtain their working capital from banks, just as any business would, and to turn losses into profits.

The Nordic states, with their own mixed economies, tended to support Frelimo aspirations to have a strong state sector. For example, in 1983 Sweden set up a "sister industry" programme linking three Mozambican state companies with Swedish sister firms in the same industry which provided both rehabilitation and training. Two of the Mozambican firms, Electromoc and Eromoto, were profitable at the end of the project (Norrbin 1988). The government hoped to keep both in the state sector because of the importance of the repair and rebuilding of electrical and combustion engines, because domestic rebuilding would save foreign exchange.

The debate with the World Bank over the industrial rehabilitation credit continued for three years. By October 1989 the Bank had dropped its narrow efficiency criteria and said that "the selection of enterprises is being based on a judgement of comparative advantage and contribution to growth" (WB 1989b). The Bank also came to support Mozambique's efforts to promote import substitution industries, especially those producing goods which satisfy basic needs. By the end of 1989 a list of 15 firms to receive funds from the rehabilitation credit had been agreed: 9 state-controlled, 3 joint ventures, and 3 private. These firms were distributed across five sectors: building materials, food, consumer goods, export crops, and packaging for export crops. The government had won at least one battle.

15 Controlling Development

Clean water, better health care, and improved agricultural productivity should be fundamental issues. They are part of that amorphous process usually called "development". In a way, it was a dispute about who controlled development that brought about destabilization, famine, and structural adjustment – the issues that have dominated this book. But out of hearing of the gunfire, out of sight of the refugee camps, and far from the luxury hotels with the visiting experts, Mozambicans are slogging away improving their own lives and those of their compatriots.

In this chapter, I want to look more closely at three areas – water, health, and a particular rural development programme – where progress is being made in spite of all the hardships. In particular, I want to show how they have been affected by war, emergency programmes, structural adjustment, and donor attitudes.

Access to clean water is a basic need, and has always been a high priority in Mozambique. Between 1980 and 1986 only 250 wells and boreholes (tubewells) were dug annually. Then the government's Água Rural (rural water) programme took off: 700 wells and boreholes in 1987, 950 in 1988, and 1050 in 1989. The government estimates that by the end of 1990 one-fifth of Mozambicans had access to safe water, which is defined as living within 1 km of water and having access to 20 litres per person per day (GM 1990). Although 80% of the funding came from donors, the government has exerted effective control over the programme: the management and work was Mozambican.

Teams are being established at district level which can dig wells to a depth of 20 metres, line them (normally with standardized, locally cast concrete rings), and install a hand pump or bucket and cable. Mozambican parastatal and provincial companies have been established to drill boreholes. Água Rural has decided to use the India Mark II hand pump throughout the country. Aid was used to give a private company in Maputo the capacity to make the pump and spare parts.

Mozambique is trying to avoid the worldwide problem of non-working pumps by ensuring that beneficiaries see the well as their own, and accept responsibility for it. For its part, Água Rural must ensure that the well is properly built in the first place and provides sufficient amounts of good water; it must also guarantee servicing in the event of a serious breakdown. Villages are to have water committees, be involved in planning the well, and participate in its construction. Each pump will have someone responsible for cleaning and reporting breakdowns. In each village there will be two or three people with basic hand tools, able to do preventive maintenance and make simple repairs. At district level there will be a technician with a bicycle and a better set of tools. Finally, for every two or three districts there is to be a workshop (with a four-wheel-drive vehicle) with the capacity to dig wells and carry out major maintenance.

The biggest programmes have been limited to three provinces. In Cabo Delgado, a bilateral donor has been running a ten-year, $7 mn (£4 mn) programme, and two-thirds of the demand for wells has been satisfied. In Inhambane and Gaza, the 1983 drought and famine led donors to put up $14 mn (£8 mn) for well and borehole programmes which have now satisfied a third of the need. By contrast, in less donor-favoured provinces such as Nampula and Zambézia, as little as 7% of the need has been met.

Bringing donors into line

Many bilateral donors insist on giving money to intermediaries, notably Unicef and NGOs, rather than directly to Água Rural. Thus there is a continuous struggle to bring donors and their agents into line with the three main requirements of government policy: donors should build local capacity to construct and maintain facilities rather than dig the wells and boreholes themselves; government experts should be involved in choosing the sites; and hand pumps and well-building techniques should be standardized to ensure maximum local input and maintainability.

Some donors and intermediaries resisted, insisting on digging wells themselves in their own way. One NGO initially refused to do reports in Portuguese (or even English). It set up a system of management of the project in parallel to Água Rural; foreign technicians organized the digging of the wells and did not train local staff. An evaluation noted that the total lack of institutional support for Mozambique meant that the project was creating dependence, because Mozambique would be permanently dependent on this NGO to keep the wells functioning (Adam 1987).

Another NGO brought windmills and pumps from their home country; all quickly broke down. One NGO brought pumps and a hand borer from Zimbabwe, despite Água

New wells and handpumps have brought safe water to many people. But who will pay? (J. Hanlon)

Rural objections; this NGO was one of those which was most dismissive of government development efforts. Soon, 38 of its 45 wells did not have water, and many of the pumps were broken. As Água Rural had warned, the hand borer the NGO brought did not dig deep enough, so the wells soon ran dry; the pumps were used on farms in Zimbabwe, and quickly broke down under more intensive village use. Somewhat embarrassed, the NGO finally gave money to the Água Rural workshop for further wells.

A similar incident happened when one of the intermediaries, which had received funds instead of Água Rural, argued that it had been given the money because Água Rural was not competent and that it should ignore Água Rural's advice. So it used the wrong kind of PVC pipe, which collapsed, making a dozen expensively drilled boreholes useless.

Nevertheless, the government has been largely successful in directing funding for water projects toward capacity building.

Hit by PRE

Just as Mozambique had gained control of the programme, and well digging seemed prepared to take off, it was hit by structural adjustment. The most serious problem now is the lack of money to use existing capacity, because of government expenditure limits. For example, in Gaza the provincial water budget was cut from MT 72 mn ($100,000; £60,000) in 1989 to MT 30 mn ($30,000; £20,000) in 1990. This meant that the number of wells dug was expected to fall from 180 in 1989 to only 110 in 1990, although the local teams had a capacity to dig at least 200. The need is for meticais, not donor dollars. A similar problem is occurring across the country. Rigs for drilling boreholes stand idle for lack of funds, or are doing contract work for better-off private farmers instead of providing water for poor peasants.

The other question is paying for maintenance of the pumps, which will cost on average MT 3000 ($3, £2) per family per year. Donors are happy to pay for digging wells and installing pumps, but not for maintenance. The World Bank and other outside agencies argue for user charges, and $3 per year seems a tiny amount of money. But, as Chapter 12 showed, for the poorest 20% of the rural population this would be their entire income, and for the next poorest 20% this would be a tenth of their income. Thus, in practice, the poorest 40% could not even pay this tiny user charge. For at least the next few years, districts will need a mix of local taxation of the better-off and financial support from the national government or donors to pay for maintenance services, as well as for further well construction.

Health Care for All?

Soon after independence, Frelimo nationalized the social sectors of health, education, law, housing, and funerals in an attempt to reduce exploitation, end the narrow urban bias of the colonial systems, and provide basic services for all. In the first five years of independence, Frelimo was widely seen, both locally and internationally, to have made an impressive start. But destabilization and the shortage of human and financial resources had blighted these high hopes by the mid-1980s.

Following the Fifth Congress in July 1989, Mozambique ended the state monopoly of social services. In so doing it was forced to abandon one of the most cherished socialist tenets, and allow the development of two-tier services. There will be better services for those who can pay, are members of the right church or clients of the right NGO, or work for the right company. For the rest, there will be second-class state services. Whatever brave face is put on it, this is the bitterest pill: social services had been the pride of Frelimo's revolution.

Only a small number of Mozambicans live in state-owned permanent housing. Their rents do not even cover repairs, and buildings have deteriorated; there was no money for a house building programme. Now, private firms will be authorized to build housing for sale or rent, and state tenants will be able to buy the house or flat they occupy (MIO January 1991).

The Fifth Congress also agreed to allow the establishment of private schools, so long as they follow the state syllabus. The Congress specifically linked this to the inability of the state to provide places for 40% of eligible pupils, because so many schools had been destroyed by Renamo, and the state could not rebuild them (because of IMF expenditure limits).

'Much better than other African countries'

Of the social sectors, health had the clearest policy, the most politicized workforce, and the most success. Even the World Bank, not noted for its praise of Frelimo, gave the health service a glowing report: "Since independence Mozambique has been in the vanguard in the development of broad-based primary health care and in the implementation of an essential drugs program. A comprehensive health care system was established and preventive medicine was declared a priority and translated into action by a strategy of expanding the network of primary health care facilities and stressing preventive and rural health.... Mozambique has done much better than other African countries....The common problem of excessive concentration on referral hospitals has been avoided, with nearly all investment directed to lower level facilities and over 64% of the recurrent budget devoted to primary care and rural health services" (WB 1989d: 71-3).

Although health and education were threatened alike by war and structural adjustment, Frelimo took a somewhat different view of health. The Central Committee told the Fifth Congress that in education "state action must be complemented by a proliferation of all initiatives" by the private and charitable sectors, and private schools would help to resolve the problem. In contrast, "the National Health System must be preserved and valued by the state for the benefit and well being of the people.... There are today groups that are applying pressure for the privatization of medicine, but this would not solve the situation of the majority of health personnel, nor would it improve the quality of the services.... The nationalization of the health sector was and is a correct option – the only one which serves the working people.... In the actual conditions of our country, the liberalization of medical practice will not increase the quality of health care, even though it can improve the quality of services provided to some people" (Frelimo 1989a).

Frelimo did make some compromises. Companies and social institutions can set up health centres, with specific links to the National Health Service. And as in the British National Health Service, there is now a fee-paying option which provides priority treatment and better facilities. Health staff are now allowed a measure of private practice. But there is no private health sector; changes to the health service have stopped well short of those imposed on education.

Cost of destabilization

The cost of destabilization has been very high. As noted in Chapter 3, the health network has been a particular target of Renamo because it contributed so much to the popularity of Frelimo. Perhaps a third of health units have been forced to close, leaving large parts of the rural areas without any health coverage.

Frelimo has always emphasized primary health care (PHC) and preventive medicine, with a stress on vaccinations and maternal and child care. Thus vaccination teams and maternity hospitals became special Renamo targets. The loss of PHC services in many zones led to a dramatic increase in child mortality; more than 650,000 children under five have died who would still be alive if there had been no destabilization, according to Unicef (1989: 40).

The war has imposed immense additional strains on the health and social services. At least 170,000 people have been mutilated or handicapped by the war; in 1989 it was possible to provide artificial limbs for fewer than 2000 people. More than 200,000 children are orphaned, separated from their parents, or otherwise traumatized by the war (Frelimo 1989a). Widespread malnutrition in rural areas makes people much more susceptible to a whole range of diseases, while the constant movement of displaced people and soldiers exacerbates the spread of AIDS, which will be one of the major health problems of the 1990s.

Just as the demands on the health service increased, the economic crisis forced swingeing cuts bringing recurrent health spending to below the levels at independence (WB 1990a: 105):

Table 15.1 *State expenditure on health*

Year	Health as % of state budget	Per capita expenditure		
		MT	$	£
1975	8.2%	49	1.80	.82
1981	11.0%	149	4.26	1.80
1986	7.1%	140	3.50	2.38
1988	3.5%	360	.68	.39

Health services had never been free, but charges had been low. The Ministry opted for increased charges in an attempt to meet part of its budget through cost recovery. The idea was that employers would be expected to pay most charges, while a wide range of exemptions would ensure that the poor majority did not have to pay. But it did not work that way. Charges were introduced in some haste by the Health Ministry, apparently without sufficient consultation with the Ministry of Finance and other government departments. The system was too complex and inadequately publicized, so no one understood it. Income from charges varied from 10% to 50% of what had been expected. In 1985, user charges (excluding medicines) had earned 3% of the health budget; remarkably, the new higher charges earned no more while causing a sharp fall in use of the system. Frelimo's tradition of democratic centralism, plus the suppression of all debate on PRE, made it impossible for health workers to criticize the charges, or even to propose a simpler and more workable system.

Charges were also increased for medicines, to try to recover more of their cost. But the effect was catastrophic. In 1988, prime minister Machungo told the People's Assembly that income from prescription charges had earned only 5% of import costs. One member of the assembly, Jorge Tembe, told Machungo that the reason was that people were simply not having prescriptions filled because they could not afford them. Tembe said that at one Maputo hospital, he saw a large pile of unused prescriptions (MIO 15 September 1988). Several doctors told me that many patients would only fill as much of the prescription as they had money to pay for, and thus were not being adequately treated. The Ministry of Health (MoH) was aware of the problem. Drug prices for drugs obtained through the health service (which covers about 85% of all medicine consumption) had been increased to account for the first devaluation (from MT 40 = $1 to MT 200 = $1), but were not increased in parallel with later devaluations.

Donor dominance

Mozambique became increasingly dependent on donors to fund the health service, and donors were unhappy with any sector where Mozambique was as strong-willed as it was in health. So bilateral funds were increasingly channelled through Unicef and NGOs, in an effort to reduce Mozambican control. Some NGOs even created a kind of parallel mission hospital system (see also Chapters 16 and 17).

Donors claimed aid of more than $27 mn (£16 mn) for Mozambican health (including drugs) in 1988. The main donors were Italy ($16mn, $10 mn), WHO ($3 mn, £2 mn), and the USSR, Norway, and Netherlands (each about $2 mn, £1 mn) (UNDP 1989a). Other estimates suggest that these figures may be somewhat inflated, the real total is closer to $20 mn (£12 mn). At least 40 donors and agents are involved in the health sector.

By the end of 1987, the MoH was complaining about emergency donor agencies acting without even informing provincial authorities. The International Committee for the Red Cross (ICRC) and Médecins Sans Frontières - France (MSF-F) were cited as particular problems because they had their own planes and flew without informing the MoH and without giving Mozambican health workers an opportunity to accompany them. Some agencies were so anxious to expand that they were moving on to new areas without first consolidating their work in their first location. Nutrition surveys were done without giving the data to the ministry, and in a form which was not compatible (Misau 1987).

Over the next two years, the MoH was able to reassert some control. Unauthorized flights largely ended. Nutrition surveys largely followed MoH format, so that it was possible to compare surveys done in different areas by different NGOs. After much pressure, NGO doctors were increasingly following government treatment norms, for example for TB. The MoH also distributed standardized plans for donors building health posts, and issued an emergency manual (Misau 1989).

But as NGOs and other donors began to cooperate more with the MoH and give it more information, international agencies were increasingly stealing MoH administrative staff by paying them much higher salaries than the government was allowed to pay. One MoH official told me, "we are getting weaker. There are many organizations and so few of us. We cannot give adequate attention to the reports they submit, and cannot give proper feedback."

The man who came to dinner

The US, as always, provides an example of how a donor can outflank the government. In 1987 the MoH asked the US for support for a small blindness control project in Zambézia, involving simple surgery and vitamin A treatments. The US accepted the invitation but rejected the project, and replaced it with one of its own on "child survival". The USAID-Maputo proposal said that the "project would seek to improve primary health care delivery by strengthening the Ministry of Health." This was rejected by USAID in Washington, who said the project had to be implemented by an NGO. In part, this was because of USAID policy to use NGOs for health projects. Also, supporting the government "seems a circuitous route to achieving the objective" of decreasing the rates of child morbidity and mortality (USAID 1989b).

The $800,000 (£500,000) USAID-designed programme was to strengthen primary health care (PHC) by concentrating on four interventions: oral rehydration, immunization, growth monitoring, and vitamin A supplements. The first three are part of the government's own highly praised PHC programme, and could surely have best been carried out by strengthening local efforts. USAID itself admitted that the MoH "currently contains the basic infrastructure for delivering preventing and curative services." But it wanted to concentrate on what it called the "'core activities' of oral rehydration therapy and immunization", rather than on the broader mother and child care of MoH policy.

USAID contracted MSF-F for the project. Although MSF-F was already active in Zambézia province, this seemed an unusual choice. MSF-F was widely seen as being hostile to Frelimo, and had been criticized for failing to cooperate with the MoH. Even USAID had to admit that "critics have questioned the extent to which MSF's assistance has created a parallel system vs. stronger integration with the MoH." MSF-F was not even a US NGO, and it had to get special registration in order even to be eligible for a USAID contract (which was not put out to public tender).

MSF-F seemed uniquely unsuitable. Its staff were normally assigned to Mozambique for only a six-month period, so that they were unable to pick up much Portuguese or learn about MoH policy. Furthermore, USAID admitted, MSF-F was "biased toward curative services" and had little PHC experience. Faced with this problem, USAID "and MSF collaborated on a project design which grafts on the established MSF curative emergency program a preventive health program for children that is consistent with and supportive of MSF program activities." Faced with MSF-F's lack of PHC skills, USAID demanded that another European NGO, which was training MoH staff, should also train MSF-F staff (USAID 1988a, 1989b).

Discussions with USAID staff and reading USAID reports made clear why it was taking such an unusual and complex route when it clearly would have been simpler to support MoH. USAID was trying to design an alternative PHC policy involving NGOs, which it hoped to impose through its control of counterpart funds. One report said that the Zambézia "pilot project is to help develop the analytical basis for an expanded program of US assistance within the next two years." The project was to have frequent visits by US consultants and $330,000 (£200,000) of the money was for a contract with Johns Hopkins University in the US (USAID 1989b). A US official told me it was in part "an anthropological study" of the health care system in Zambézia. "AID is doing the Zambézia project to learn how to get involved in Mozambique." In addition, the US was demanding that its accountant have access to Zambézia's provincial health service accounts, better to understand financial flows.

The project also gave the US its first independent, on-the-ground presence in parts of rural Zambézia that were important in the war and would be sharply contested in the event of an election.

Mozambican officials claim USAID made its first informal agreement with MSF-F without even consulting MoH, and that it was originally planned that MSF-F would act totally independently of the MoH. Mozambican officials bitterly resented this, and the project was delayed for two years as they forced the US to make substantial changes. In the end, it is still a parallel structure, and still duplicates some MoH functions. But now the government has some limited control over policy formulation and the operation of the programme; the MSF-F project director must report to the MoH as well as to USAID; MSF-F officials must work with district directors of health, which had not been envisaged in the original plan.

Which drugs?

Medicines policy had been a Frelimo success, well recognized internationally. In colonial times, pharmaceuticals had been largely unregulated; drug salesmen had free reign, and more than 13,000 products were in circulation with no discussion of need, cost, or effectiveness. After independence, Mozambique moved quickly to a new pharmaceutical policy. It developed a short national formulary containing all the drugs which are really needed. The formulary has been steadily reduced to only 316 drugs plus 27 other items (dressings and laboratory and test materials), and has a corresponding therapeutic guide which shows how the drugs should be used. No drug not in the formulary can be imported without special permission. A hierarchy was established, so that major hospitals can use all the drugs in the formulary, while lower-level staff are allowed to prescribe only those medicines they are trained to use. Finally, two-thirds of medicines are distributed through the national health service, and only a third through shops.

To reduce costs, Mozambique took two steps. First, drugs are purchased and prescribed by generic rather than brand names. Second, a state company, Medimoc, was set up to import drugs for the entire country, by open international tender. Up to 200 companies bid on parts of the tender. Before independence, 95% of drugs came from TNCs based in just five countries; after independence, drugs were purchased from 15 countries. Companies in western Europe remained major suppliers, but only by selling for much less than they did before independence. Many common medicines were purchased at a third of pre-independence prices.

Mozambique also cut back on purchases of sophisticated and expensive drugs of dubious utility, while the drug budget was doubled. Thus there was a massive increase in imports of medicines for common illnesses suffered by people in rural areas. For the first time, ordinary peasants had access to health workers and basic drugs. When I visited remote village health posts in the early 1980s, most had adequate stocks of basic medicines (Hanlon 1984a: 62).

Although Mozambique was one of the first countries to move in this direction, it was part of an international trend backed by the World Health Organization. But the transnational drug companies moved to combat bulk buying and basic drug lists. With Mozambique, they did this through the aid process.

The financial crisis of the early 1980s reduced drug imports from $1 (£ .50) per capita in 1981 to $ .32 (£ .19) per capita in 1984. Spending increased again only when aid became available, as Table 15.2 shows. Mozambique became dependent on donors for 90% of its medicine imports, which has led to a series of struggles.

Starting in 1982, donors began to send actual medicines to Mozambique in response to various emergency, drought, and famine appeals. But it soon became clear that donors were dumping drugs on Mozambique. Some of the donated items were already past their expiry date, or were dangerous drugs which had been banned in many industrialized countries. Values were exaggerated. The most extreme case was an agency which carried out an impressive public relations campaign to announce it was sending $500,000 (£300,000) of drugs; when the drugs finally arrived, it was found that the true value of the donation, at the prices Medimoc was paying, was only $11,000 (£7000) (Cliff 1986).

Initially drugs were sent without any consultation with the government. The MoH took a hard line, and simply threw away anything which was neither in the formulary nor similar to anything in the formulary. MoH officials also worked hard with donors to get them to talk to government before they sent drugs, and preferably to supply cash. In 1983, $634,000 (£420,000) of drugs were sent, but only 37% could actually be used. In 1985, $975,000 (£750,000) of drugs were sent and 74% could be used.

After that, donations in kind fell and donors increasingly provided money. But the money was not given to the government to spend as it saw fit. Under pressure from the transnational drug companies, bilateral donors gave the money to Unicef rather than the government, or they gave tied aid, which meant that drugs had to be purchased from the donor country.

Thus the sharp increase in spending on medicines in 1988 (shown in Table 15.2) reflects an increase in tied aid, according to MoH officials. Mozambique pays up to 50% more for drugs bought from TNCs on tied aid, compared to Medimoc tenders (for which the same companies offer lower prices). Despite spending an extra $3.5 mn (£2 mn) in 1988, fewer drugs were imported than in 1987 (and much less than in 1981).

Drug companies were anxious to undercut Medimoc, but time and again Medimoc was shown to be doing a good job. Even the World Bank grudgingly admitted that "unlike many other such agencies established in Africa, Medimoc has been relatively efficient"

Table 15.2 *Imports of medicines*

Year	$ mn	£ mn	Year	$ mn	£ mn
1977	5.7	2.9	1983	6.1	3.7
1978	5.4	2.7	1984	4.4	2.6
1979	7.9	4.0	1985	5.3	3.2
1980	9.6	4.8	1986	8.6	5.2
1981	11.8	5.9	1987	10.1	6.0
1982	8.7	5.2	1988	13.6	8.2

Source: Misau 1986a, O'Brien 1990

(WB 1990a: 48). Sweden, the Netherlands, and West Germany all gave tied aid and insisted on doing their own procurement; Mozambique objected, and as a compromise the three donor governments commissioned four separate consultancy reports. All four recommended that Medimoc continue to procure the drugs (Kanji 1988). USAID and Italy gave money to Unicef, which insisted on procuring from Unipac, its in-house company. Not only did Unipac prove to be more expensive than Medimoc, it was also much less efficient; in 1986 Unipac took 11 months to deliver urgently needed drugs, made mistakes in the orders, and did not follow packing instructions, so that all the drugs had to be shipped to Maputo and repackaged, further delaying delivery (Misau 1986b).

In response to the very limited amount of money available, the list of 316 drugs in the formulary was cut still further. A list of items necessary to save lives and alleviate suffering was defined as the "vital" drugs list; this included 97 drugs and 6 types of dressing. Of the 97 drugs, 53 were authorized for use at health-centre level and the rest only in hospitals. For use at the lowest level where 85% of all patients are treated, an even shorter "essential drugs programme" list was devised: it consists of 28 drugs plus six other items such as dressings, which are needed for outpatient treatment at primary level. These are packed into kits and distributed to health posts throughout the country.

Italy committed much of the money for the essential drug kits, which created two problems. First, donors were obsessed with primary health care, so there was never enough money for the "vital drugs". The tiny essential drug kit contains only basic antibiotics, anti-malarial drugs, and a few other items. The longer "vital" list contains items absolutely necessary for treating those with war wounds and accident injuries, women undergoing difficult childbirths, and so on. Painkillers are also on the vital drugs list but not on the shorter essential drugs list. Calling the very short list "essential" is actually confusing, and it would have made more sense to call them something like "basic" drugs. "Vital" drugs are absolutely essential to the running of a health service, but do not appeal to donors. Thus there were serious and highly publicized shortages of dressings and medicines in many hospitals. In a war the number of patients referred to hospitals increases, yet care of the injured was sometimes halted because of lack of intravenous fluids and basic surgical material (UNDSPQ 1990: 112).

One normally sympathetic donor wrote to the MoH asking it to find other non-drug uses for money which the donor had reserved for medicines for 1988. This is because "we have a strong preference for primary health care. As we are informed that drug needs at this level are funded by other donors, we inform you that your request for drugs at other levels for 1988 has not been taken into consideration."

The second problem with Italian funding was the sudden cut-off in Italian funding for Unicef in 1990 (See Chapter 16). Italy had been providing $8 mn (£5 mn) for the "essential drugs programme" and for vaccines. Italian officials assured Mozambique that the money would be forthcoming, but it was not. An official in the Italian embassy in Maputo was angry at criticisms of Italy. The money had only been promised verbally; Italy never signed anything committing itself to provide the funds. "We are entitled to revise our programme", he said. In any case, he claimed, a Unicef study had shown that "there is an overstocking of medicines" throughout the country, so Mozambique didn't need the drugs.

In their turn, Unicef and MoH officials were livid. One MoH official said simply: "The Italians are lying to you." A Unicef official said there was no such study, and that there was no drug surplus. Indeed, by mid-1990 there was a "crisis", with health posts running out of medicines and vaccination teams stopping work. The Unicef official said that "the whole programme had been worked out with Italy, and Italy confirmed its pledge in October 1989. If we had known the money would not be forthcoming, we could have tried to approach other donors."

Meanwhile, Mozambique is under strong pressure to liberalize all its imports, including medicines. So far, Medimoc retains the monopoly on non-emergency medicine imports;

nothing can be imported that is not in the formulary and there are no brand-name medicines. But pressure is growing from the free-marketeers in the World Bank, as well as from the pharmaceutical companies, for Mozambique to allow the importation of luxury and brand name drugs. It will be interesting to see if Mozambique can hold the line on something as fundamental as this.

Rural Development

Even before independence, Frelimo realized that the countryside was the key to development. But in the first five years after independence, the policy of "socialization of the countryside" became an increasingly centralized, top-down approach to development that assumed that central government directives could resolve problems. The modern sector was stressed and almost no attention was paid to ordinary peasants. Frelimo also assumed that successful pilot projects, such as the best communal villages and the most organized cooperatives, could simply be replicated everywhere. Too little account was taken of the wide regional variations in culture, climate, and crops. Local initiative was discouraged.

By 1982, faced with growing economic problems and destabilization, as well as the approaching Fourth Congress, Frelimo began to look for more decentralized and popular solutions. The Congress put the stress on the family sector, and government began belatedly to try to support ordinary farmers, particularly by stimulating the market system.

But it was too late. The war and the economic crisis worsened, and donors were not prepared to support the private sector without major concessions, which only came later. Then the NGOs and other donors flooded in, and set up more than one hundred small

rural development projects, each with a different philosophy, methodology, and rural extension strategy. Previously, Frelimo thought it knew best and could tell the peasants what to do; now the NGOs said they knew best and could tell the peasants what to do. Without a clear strategy, the Ministry of Agriculture was totally unable to control the donors. One World Bank mission commented that "donors themselves have tended to pursue their own particular aims without much concern for what might be wider rural priorities" (WB 1990h). The National Director of Rural Development, João Carrilho, accused some donors of being "irrational" in their allocation of resources (Carrilho 1990).

The Priority District Programme

From 1982 the Ministry tried to develop a strategy. In 1987 it established a Direcção Nacional de Desenvolvimento Rural (DNDR – National Directorate for Rural Development). Over the next three years, DNDR developed the Programa de Distritos Prioritários (PDP – Priority District Programme). Government had already accepted that it was impossible to

Agricultural technician Antonieta Ferrão shows local farmers how to cut and use a bamboo measuring stick in order to space cassava plants more accurately. The farmers are gathered in front of the agricultural extension centre in Mieze in the green zone near Pemba (J. Hanlon).

do everything at once, and began to target specific districts. During the 1980s, several lists were compiled, and in 1989 the People's Assembly finally approved the PDP and defined 40 of the 128 districts as "priority" districts to be included in the programme.

The objective of PDP is quickly to re-establish the economic, administrative and social fabric of the priority districts. It should stimulate local production, particularly by the poorest, and thus improve both food security and commercial production of food and industrial raw materials. At the same time, it should increase access to basic social services. The government proposes that the three indicators to measure success of the programme should be: commercialized production, number of children in primary school, and number of people per health post (Carrilho 1990).

Two other aspects are less obvious, but also crucial. First, PDP must strengthen local government, both in terms of increasing the power and experience of elected councils (thus strengthening democracy) and in terms of the full-time administration which must become more skilled and better able to deliver services. Second, PDP should help to reflate the economy by increasing rural consumption and thus stimulating industrial production.

PDP takes into account some of the key aspects of rural development experience in Mozambique. It gives most emphasis to food production by the family sector. But it also recognizes that Mozambican peasants are already part of the cash economy and are not "self-sufficient"; thus two priority aspects of PDP will be restoration of commercialization and the creation of labour-intensive public works projects, such as road building, to provide a cash income. PDP also recognizes that women's time is one of the biggest constraints on increasing production, which means that proximity to clean water and health services are essential.

PDP will stimulate controversy

The PDP is controversial on several grounds. First, it is based on a development philosophy which is no longer fashionable (although the wheel may be turning yet again, perhaps bringing it back into favour). PDP is based on the concept of "development poles", where certain centres become foci of development which hopefully spreads throughout the area. It is also based on "integrated rural development", where efforts are made to introduce a package of measures which reinforce each other. Thus roads are improved to stimulate trade, agricultural extension is strengthened to increase production, social services are expanded in the same area, and parallel institutional development ensures that there are administrators and staff to maintain the new infrastructure.

The World Bank talks of "the now discredited integrated rural development model" but the Fifth Congress actually uses the phrase "district integrated rural development". (WB 1990g, Frelimo 1989b). Integrated development has always been part of Mozambique's socialist goal that development should involve a general raising of living standards, rather than the now fashionable approach of targeting to benefit a select few. In practice, individual donors – NGOs, Unicef, and even some bilaterals – are assigned to one or two districts. Normally, at most one other donor is working in the district. Donors are pushed to do integrated development in "their" district, rather than to help a particular target group such as children, or old people, or the poorest of the poor. Thus the local administrator can push donors to move outside the narrow brief and, for example, repair key infrastructure. The administrator can point out to a donor that wants, for example, to help children that the local warehouse needs a roof if food for children is not to be spoiled by the rain, and that repairing the town water pump will provide the health centre with water, and that there are no other donors in the district who can help.

Second, PDP is by definition selective – some people will benefit before others. The overriding considerations are economic. The main criterion is that PDP districts should have the most potential to benefit from development funding and grow most rapidly. This implies the best natural conditions, relative accessibility, a high population density (to maximize impact, since most of Mozambique is under-populated), and relative security (Carrilho 1990). Priority districts should also already have an economic focus, such as a large state farm. This means that in practice the priority districts are already the better-off ones, so in the short term PDP may increase differentiation. But the choice of the 40 districts also has some political input, notably the inclusion of some districts in every province, and the selection of a few districts in which Renamo has had a strong presence. The priority districts have about 50% of the rural population and 70% of commercialized agricultural production, but only about 30% of those who are displaced or refugees due to the war. Thus the PDP will not provide much help for resettlement.

But the PDP is not selective in the way that many would want. It accepts that targeting of individual programmes is impossible, and it implicitly accepts the political danger of helping to resettle former Renamo guerrillas without giving similar aid to their victims. Thus PDP does not distinguish the poorest of the poor from the extremely poor, and the extremely poor from those who are simply very poor. All of these people need seeds and tools to get started, and need free or highly subsidized access to clean water, health, and education. PDP will try to help all of these in a similar way. This could have later implications for increased class differentiation, and will also annoy those trying to help only the poorest.

Third, PDP involves a high degree of decentralization and devolution of power. In theory, the programme will evolve differently in each district. But at local level there will be coordination, for example to ensure that priority is given to repairing the roads that go to the zones within the district targeted for initial agricultural support. Decisions will be taken at provincial or district level, which means that local government will have more power and a larger budget than at present. Although this has been accepted in principle at national level, there may be some problems in implementing decentralization. Will central government bureaucrats accept the shift of money and power to local level? Will ministries allow themselves to be coordinated? Will donors accept the authority of local officials and councils?

Fourth, PDP accepts that building local government capacity requires the reversal of the flow of trained and experienced people to Maputo. Agronomists, technicians, administrators, and others will have to live and work in the priority districts. And the PDP argues that under PRE, the only way to do this is to give then substantially more pay and better housing and living conditions than they receive in Maputo. They will, in other words, be very wealthy by local standards.

Fifth, PDP involves a delicate attempt to balance public and private. The enterprise sector (that is, public, private, and joint venture companies) will carry out the marketing, road building, well digging, and many other components of the programme. Private entrepreneurs will clearly benefit from the improved infrastructure and increased consumer spending. Thus there will be a need for intervention by the state and by local popular organizations to prevent exploitation: to ensure that peasants get a fair price for their crops and do not become permanently indebted to traders, to ensure that the poor benefit from the roads and wells, to ensure that land is fairly distributed, etc.

Finally, there is the unresolved issue of who will be in charge. What will be the "lead agency"? On one hand is the argument that no new institution should be created. In that case PDP might be run by the DNDR within the Ministry of Agriculture, or perhaps by the National Planning Commission. Others argue that the coordination role requires a new agency, outside any existing ministry. Perhaps there should be a new body such as an Institute of Rural Development headed by a Secretary of State. Some donors want PDP to be a "project" with joint donor-Mozambican administration.

Will the donors agree?

PDP is very much a Mozambican-designed programme. Few foreigners have been directly involved, while a series of meetings and seminars has drawn in governors, provincial and local officials, and technical staff at various levels. This means the programme is not as neatly designed as one drawn up by consultant project designers, but it has a broader national consensus and more chance of working than a donor-imposed programme.

Reginald Green of the Institute of Development Studies calls the PDP an attempt by Mozambicans "to recapture design initiative and operational control from donors and cooperantes", and he points to "the deep distrust of cooperantes' and donors' dominance" (Green 1990b: 25).

"PDP is not perfect. But it is better conceptualized, more contextualized, better linked to political level goals and decisions, more integrally Mozambique's own work, and more likely to be broadly successful in attaining its targets than any previous Mozambican rural development strategic initiative"(Green 1990c: 45).

The government of Mozambique has chosen the PDP as policy. And it seems unlikely that the donors, acting together, could find a better policy. But will large and small donors allow the government to direct their efforts to certain areas and to certain kinds of work? Will donors support government policy, or will they continue to promote a hundred different rural development strategies? This will be one test of who calls the shots.

PDP assumes that no additional donor funds will be available, and thus that donors will redirect their existing funds to PDP. In particular, big donors are being asked to redirect funds from some large prestige development projects into small-scale integrated projects as part of PDP – a switch which may have less direct benefit to companies in the donor countries.

The government wants to manage the programme and wants donors to channel funds through the normal government budget rather than create a plethora of special projects in the priority districts. It wants to avoid the creation of parallel project administrations which bypass the government, and which have been a common cause of failure of integrated development projects in other countries in Africa. Districts should not be "labelled" with the name of a donor, as they often are now.

Furthermore, government officials want to prevent foreign NGOs from being executors of projects in the priority districts. Instead, "NGOs must carry out their activities in a way that reinforces local capacity" (Carrilho 1990). NGOs should be involved in training Mozambicans to increase their capacity to implement projects. Indeed, the lack of experienced local officials means that training will be a vital part of PDP. One official commented, "if NGOs 'do', then local people 'don't' because they don't ever need to learn how."

This view is supported by the Like Minded Group (Canada, Denmark, Finland, the Netherlands, Norway, and Sweden), whose aid representatives in Maputo sent a letter to the Mozambican government arguing that there should "be no direct project implementation by foreign entities (NGOs, UN agencies, etc) within the PDP" (Hermans 1990). But will NGOs agree to train instead of implement?

Donors 'unhelpful'?

So far, donor responses to PDP have been "basically unhelpful", comments Professor Green. Some donors have pushed for a narrow, purely agricultural, technocratic solution. Others "call for a participatory utopia ... and misread the PDP as a hi-tech-bureaucratic parallel authority scheme rather like their own past agricultural sector initiatives in Mozambique, rather than as an attempted transformation based in large measure on Mozambican reaction against them" (Green 1990b: 25).

One set of donors said the initial proposal was too ambitious, so the Mozambicans scaled it down to start in only a few districts in the first year and reach 40 districts only in the fifth year (Green 1990c: 44). Then another set of donors complained that the programme was too selective and should cover more districts from the start.

The US has already said that it "will take into consideration the government priority districts, but the primary emphasis will be to build on the information and experience of

PVOs [NGOs] most familiar with local conditions" (USAID 1990b: 57). In other words, the US will support priorities determined by US NGOs rather than by the Mozambican government.

Donor and Bank driven?

The designers of PDP have worked closely with the World Bank, knowing that the programme would have no hope of success without Bank approval. In what one official called "a convenient alliance", the Bank supports PDP in part because it would like to see funds going through the state budget where they can be more directly controlled. But this has led to a major conflict over the design and control of PDP.

The World Bank and the FAO/World Bank Cooperative Programme are proposing a "Rural Rehabilitation Project" which seemingly would take control of PDP. It is a highly centralized project under a World Bank "Task Manager" with a complex monitoring and review system. The project would "formulate a series of indicative technical strategia [sic] for increasing small farmer income in representative settings". Special "farm models would then be used to confirm the financial attractiveness of each strategy to the intended beneficiaries." The very use of language shows who is in charge. Bank officials would make "rural enquiries *together with* government representatives" and would define "technical models ... *in consultation with* communities in the selected priority districts" (WB 1990h; emphasis added). It is a far cry from the decentralized definition of the PDP, with key decisions being taken at local level. "The impression one gets ... is one of a centralized, donor-driven programme", commented the Like-Minded Group (Hermans 1990). One donor official called it "an external takeover" of PDP: "Mozambicans are simply set to one side while foreigners take over the planning and execution."

But it has been pointed out that the rationale behind the World Bank/FAO project is that PDP will "eventually" need World Bank funding. But initial PDP planning assumed it would use existing donor funding, and would not take World Bank loans. If that view is upheld, then there can be no justification for the World Bank to be lead agency, or indeed to have any direct participation.

Test of intentions?

One government official told me: "The real point about PDP is that it is a way of shifting both government and donor thinking to the rural areas. Finally people are talking about 90% of the people instead of a handful of urban entrepreneurs." Thus it is possible to see the PDP as a two-fold test of good faith and intentions. Is the government really committed to a rural-based development process, despite the increasing centripetal forces exerted by Maputo under PRE? And are the donors prepared to support the government, and will they allow the government to set rural development priorities?

IV Doing Well by Doing Good

16 The Aid Industry

Aid is by far the biggest economic sector in Mozambique, and is the main source of food and other resources for a significant part of the population. To understand the impact of aid on Mozambique, however, it is also necessary to discuss the aid industry itself: its needs, imperatives, and influences.

Worldwide, aid is a $50 bn per year industry. This makes it a medium-sized industry with an annual international turnover similar to that of the machine tool, computer software, or semi-conductor industries (Unido 1989, *Financial Times* 15 January 1991). Donor agencies are major international bodies, and in many ways can be treated as if they were non-profit transnational corporations (TNCs).

The 1970s were a boom time for the industry, with aid doubling every five years: $8 bn in 1970 to $20 bn in 1975 to $37 bn in 1980. But the world economic crisis also squeezed the aid industry, and for the next five years aid flows remained at $33 bn per year. From 1986 aid began to rise again, but at a much slower rate than in the 1970s (according to World Bank figures, which differ somewhat from other sources).

During the palmy years of the 1970s, the industry flourished. But in the 1980s, with real resource flows declining, competition became much more fierce. Aid agencies fought for funds and for control of good projects which would attract funds. The takeovers and mergers of the business world are rarely seen in the aid industry. Two related phenomena do occur, however. Agencies increase their resource flows by forming consortia. And agencies try to dominate and control others by becoming the lead or coordinating agency for a project or, in the case of the World Bank, for a whole country.

Smaller agencies, particularly NGOs, opt for niche marketing. They target aid to children, old people, or the disabled. Or they provide certain kinds of services, as pilots, doctors, or computer specialists. Mozambique was seen as a previously closed market which was suddenly opened, and agencies rushed in to carve out a market share.

The financial flows of the aid industry are complex, and give it a special character. Most of the money comes directly from industrialized country aid budgets which must be regularly approved by national parliaments. They support aid out of a mix charitable instincts and their views of national and group self-interest. Global political considerations play an important role.

For example, Israel is by far the largest recipient of US aid (more than $250 per capita) even though it is already treated by the World Bank as a "high income" country. And "the British government's sudden burst of generosity towards Mozambique can only partly be explained by compassion", according to Richard Dowden, Africa Editor of *The*

Independent. "Britain has been developing a closer relationship with the country to show black Africa that although Britain is not going to impose sanctions on South Africa, it will help the Frontline States" (13 February1987).

Multinational bodies like the UN, EC, and development banks receive their money from member governments. They are not directly controlled by those governments, but must take considerable care not to offend the members. In the 1980s, the US began to play a much more direct role in the running of UN agencies.In general, NGOs also obtain most of their money from governments and usually serve as contractors. But they must raise some of their money from public appeals, and the growth of their sector of the industry is dependent on highly publicized disasters which will trigger public charity.

People

Aid is mainly a service industry – like education, health, or banking – and it employs tens of thousands of people. Many of the people working in the industry are strongly committed to improving the lot of those they work with. Sometimes aid workers support the political goals of their funders; at other times they disagree but accept the political constraints as the price of doing what they see as good work.

As in education or health, many of the workers are relatively poorly paid. But some are highly paid, an example of doing well by doing good. Graham Hancock (1989) calls them "The Lords of Poverty". Dr Michael Irwin became acting vice-president for personnel in the World Bank, and then resigned in disgust at the way World Bank staff were "underworked and overpaid". Citing the high salaries, perks, first-class hotels, and first-class travel, he asks: "is it not hypocritical to prescribe financial discipline and savings for so many developing countries without being more careful how one spends money within one's own organisation?" (Irwin 1990)

Administering so much money necessarily creates international bureaucracies, which are self-perpetuating and have their own internal dynamics. They have the usual bureaucratic imperatives to protect the jobs of employees, and to expand and increase turnover.

Aiding Ourselves

The basis of much charity is the wealthy giving their cast-offs to the poor. And the modern aid industry is built on the concept of distributing unwanted items from the developed world to those who need them in the Third World. The original Care Packages were army rations which were surplus after the Second World War. Food aid is normally giving away surplus production. Oxfam in the UK usefully linked charity at home and abroad: people gave second-hand clothes to Oxfam shops, where they were sold to poorer people, and the money was used for still poorer people in the Third World.

Most of us buy from jumble sales, garage sales, and Oxfam shops. At its best international aid really was, and perhaps sometimes still is, recycling and reducing waste to the benefit of everyone. But it is increasingly a self-perpetuating industry with other goals. For good domestic political reasons, the EC, the US, and other rich countries spend $245bn (£150bn) per year on farm subsidies – five times their Third World aid (*Independent* 11 July 1990). This is partially to pay their own farmers to overproduce. Food aid is a good way of disposing of this surplus and justifying the continued overproduction. But it also creates a demand in the Third World for exotic foods. Maize is the normal staple grain in much of Africa, and it is difficult to grow wheat, but wheat is surplus in the North and is a common form of food aid. People become accustomed to bread, which *is* more convenient than most forms of maize meal, and the country must continue to import wheat even when the food aid ends.

Also, there is a complex pricing issue. On the one hand, subsidized overproduction by developed countries keeps the international market glutted, which keeps prices down. Thus it is often cheaper for countries like Mozambique to import grain than to produce it. Neighbouring Zimbabwe has a regular maize surplus which it cannot sell profitably because of artificially depressed world prices. All of this discourages southern African regional food self-sufficiency, and creates a permanent dependency on imported grain from the North. On the other hand, giving away some of the surplus food reduces the amount on the world market, preventing world grain prices from collapsing completely, and making it more expensive for Mozambique to buy US or European grain when it does not get enough as aid.

Whatever the original charitable motivation of giving away surplus food, it is now a big business which has a very different dynamic.

Tied aid

Most aid money flows back to or through the donor, to suppliers and contractors in the donor country. Except for World Bank loans, all donors tie at least some of their loans and other monetary assistance to purchases in the donor country. Italy and Unicef tie a particularly high proportion of their aid. The World Bank estimates that, worldwide, two-thirds of aid is tied (WB 1990e: 128).

Tying rules are normally specified in some detail in the aid accord, and often in the donor's laws or regulations. The degree of tie varies. It can be all or some defined portion spent in the donor country. Sometimes the tie is relaxed to allow purchases within Mozambique, within SADCC, or even from any Third World country (but not from industrialized world competitors). Aid-trade packages are another form of tie, in which aid is given to support a big export contract.

Some of the ties are informal, and ensure that even officially untied aid is spent in the donor country. Import support and commodity import programmes sometimes must be negotiated in detail with the donor, and negotiations are shorter and simpler if the purchases are to be made in the donor country. If an embassy or head office must oversee purchases, it is always easier to purchase from home suppliers that speak the same language and understand the bureaucratic procedures than to buy from a third country. The EC has an allocation mechanism designed to ensure that all EC members get a fair share of contracts on EC aid, so in some cases recipients are required to select contractors or consultants from only certain countries. An NGO representative in Maputo told me: "Our government gave us money to import lorries for the emergency. Officially we could have bought anywhere, but we imported from one of our own national manufacturers because we knew if we didn't we would have problems the next time we applied for a grant." A country which gives much of its aid untied sometimes puts ties on precisely those contracts which would be easiest to award elsewhere; thus building houses for an SADCC project which could have been done by a Zimbabwean contractor and used some Mozambican fittings was one of the few tied contracts from that donor, so the contractor and all fixtures and fittings came from the donor country. Similarly aid for lorries might be tied, but aid for spares untied – because the spares must come from the same manufacturer.

Once in a while ties can be useful, particularly when they are long-term and linked to development projects. Mozambicans feel that, in the best case, an aid component can encourage a private company to become involved in Mozambique where it would not otherwise be interested. Over time this could lead the company to develop a presence independent of the initial aid, resulting in technology transfer, training, and increased employment. They stress that capitalists grow rich by avoiding risks, and that aid can attract TNCs by reducing the risk.

At its worst (most of the time), tied aid is a nightmare. The Tudor battery factory uses aid from 14 different countries – 13 tied and the other to fill the gaps. To make up a big enough order from so many suppliers, Tudor often must import an entire year's raw materials at one time, leading to cash flow problems. Materials cost more because it is tied aid, raising costs. Each donor releases the money at different times during the year, leading to materials flow problems. One donor official commented to me: "What factory in Europe would accept such conditions?" Inevitably Tudor cannot produce batteries as efficiently as foreign producers with lower raw materials costs and smoother cash and material flows. But IMF and World Bank officials argue that traders should be free to import cheaper competing batteries; companies must compete, and if Tudor is less efficient it should close. Another example is the DPCCN, which has nine makes and 25 models of lorries from seven different countries, creating a spare parts nightmare.

Sometimes tied aid forces Mozambique to import things that are made locally. The Mozambican company Cometal-Mometal manufactures railway wagons, and Mozambican railways are desperately short of wagons. Yet aid ties have forced Mozambique to buy wagons in Spain and Brazil, rather than cheaper locally made ones. Cometal-Mometal was about to lay off workers for lack of orders, until it won a tender for $3.8 mn (£2.3mn) to supply 80 wagons to Tanzania, outbidding European manufacturers for an untied aid-funded project (*Mozambiquefile* September 1990, *Market SE* October 1990).

As this also shows, tied aid is expensive because Mozambique cannot buy from the cheapest supplier. Indeed, when a donor country has only one or two suppliers and they know an item is being purchased on tied aid, they often push up the price – whereas if it was an open international tender, they would probably quote lower. A minister complained to me about one country with a $22 mn (£13 mn) tied import support programme. "They force us to pay $1 mn of that to a consultant to do the buying for us, and we are paying 30% more than if we did the buying ourselves in the same country."

In 1987 Mozambique established the Unidade de Coordinação de Programas de Importação (UCPI), an agency to coordinate donor funds designated for imports. Importers still do the negotiations, but UCPI monitors and assists, in an effort to get a better deal. UCPI also negotiates with donors, in an attempt to get more consistent regulations and procedures. Simplification is also important: UCPI officials complain that World Bank and EC regulations, in particular, make it very difficult to obtain approval. In 1989 UCPI handled $300 mn, and this was increasing.

In 1990 UCPI began a system of doing international tendering, trying to use tied aid where possible. For example, a French firm will bid higher if it knows the contract is for tied French aid, and lower if it is a more competitive international World Bank contract. UCPI now tries to use French tied aid where French firms win international tenders, and other countries' tied aid when their firms win, in the hope of getting lower prices.

Another form of tie is where aid contractors buy goods from themselves or related businesses. Unicef channels most of its orders through the Unicef Procurement and Assembly Centre (Unipac). Goods worth more than $70 mn per year are supplied directly from the Unipac warehouse in Copenhagen; Unipac acts as purchasing agent for another $100 mn per year. It was set up to allow Unicef to benefit from bulk purchasing and to have a huge warehouse so items can be shipped quickly. In Unipac's own phrase: "faster, cheaper, better." But it has not always worked out that way. Unicef admitted that in 1988 only 24% of orders were delivered on time, and that typical delivery time was five months (Unipac nd, Unicef 1990). Mozambique may have been worse than average. Officials found that goods from Unipac sometimes took nine months or more to arrive, and sometimes could have been bought on the world market more cheaply and with quicker delivery than from Unipac. Even the Unicef representative in Maputo, Marta Mauras, admitted that Unipac had been "disappointing" and that some local procurement would have been better (Mauras 1987). In 1989 Unicef allocated $1 mn for purchasing in Mozambique and Zimbabwe, and this was used for construction materials, clothing, seeds and household goods. But the local purchasing programme was reduced again the following year.

In many cases, contractors pay themselves or their associates inflated prices for raw materials. Pipe for one water project was valued at twice the world market price, but the donor would not allow it to be purchased elsewhere. In a similar case when Mozambique became very angry about an inflated price, the donor insisted on the same supplier but finally agreed to "charge" Mozambique's aid allocation only at the world market price and pay the rest of the inflated price out of another part of the aid budget.

Italy

Italy is an extreme example and in many ways a special case. In the 1970s it was a very small donor. But a major shift in public opinion pressed the government to increase aid, while other OECD countries prodded Italy to play its part. A new law in 1979 set up a major aid programme. In 1985 an "emergency fund" was created with the remit of spending 1900 billion Lira (nearly $1.3 bn or £800 mn) on aid in just 18 months. From a position as the ninth largest OECD aid donor in 1980–81, it rose to fifth place in 1987–88 passing Sweden, the Netherlands, Canada and the UK. Aid increased four-fold in just seven years. Italy became Mozambique's largest donor, pledging more in 1987 than in the previous six years combined. Then in 1989 a change in government and developments in eastern Europe brought new priorities, with less money for Mozambique. Finally, a bureaucratic crisis in Rome froze aid to Mozambique altogether.

The 1979 law allowed the avoidance of public tenders by technically giving the recipient country the right to choose the Italian contractor. In reality, however, recipient countries had little choice. The magazine L'Espresso (21 May & 9 July 1989) argued that "hundreds of billion of lira [of aid for Mozambique] have been given through private deals which always favour the same companies and the same intermediaries. Besides, strange consulting companies have sprung up which have links to fixers who turn out to be relatives or friends of high officials in the Ministry of Foreign Affairs." Companies particularly involved are subsidiaries of parastatal groups, which tend to have links with the Socialist and Christian Democrat parties, or members of the Lega delle Cooperative, which is linked to the Communist Party. "No one must disrupt this uninterrupted flow of billions of Lira coming from Italy, and which is due to come back to Italy."

L'Espresso cited the case of a 125 bn Lira ($83 mn, £50 mn) agricultural development project downstream from the Italian funded and built Pequenos Libombos dam near Maputo. L'Espresso alleges that it was agreed in the Italy–Mozambique joint ministerial commission in 1988 and contracts were awarded based on no more than a back-of-the-envelope calculation of costs. Treated as "urgent and extraordinary", as are many Italian aid projects, the contracts were granted without a public tender. Snam Progetti, part of the parastatal ENI, and Bonifica, part of the parastatal IRI, were to oversee, design, and direct. The works were to be carried out by CMC, a member of Lega delle Cooperative. CMC is the Cooperativa Muratori e Cementisti di Ravenna, the cooperative of bricklayers and cement workers, which is now a major international contractor and one of the biggest participants in Italian aid projects.

But Italy is hardly unique. Just five companies have received one-third of all Britain's aid and trade grants since 1979 – a total of £277 mn ($450 mn). These five firms contributed £1.5 mn ($2.5 mn) to the governing Conservative Party in that period. Indeed, the House of Commons Foreign Affairs Committee said that strong lobbying is more likely to gain funds than merit (Guardian 26 June 1987 and 18 October 1990).

Italy was, however, more blatant and complex. The system was quite informal, with companies and NGOs being told that contracts would be extended as necessary for cost overruns. Suddenly in 1989 this did not happen. After spending $28 mn (£17 mn) on a much-needed water supply system for Pemba, the project suddenly ground to a halt when the promised extra $2 mn (£1 mn) to complete the project was not released. Work on a hospital halted in a similar way. NGOs which had been told that more money would be paid, and had spent their own money in anticipation, were suddenly told that their promised grants would not be made; several closed or cut back their Mozambican offices.

Italian aid is also more tightly tied than that of almost any other big donor. Italian contractors even bring prefabricated housing from Italy rather than build housing locally. Italian architects must be used, even when type plans already exist, for example for health units.

The extreme example was Italian-funded emergency airlifts, which were only allowed to carry Italian goods. At one of the national emergency meetings, a provincial official noted that "in some zones displaced people need salt and clothing. We have salt and clothing to give them. But the Italians won't let us use their planes. We have trouble explaining to local people why we bring them extra Italian beans and rice they don't need, and why we can't bring them what they do need."

World Bank opposed

This is one of the few areas where the World Bank sides with Mozambique against the donors. The wide range of ties obviously goes against the Bank's free market principles, and such ties are manifestly inefficient to the recipient country. The Bank supported UCPI and every World Bank document on Mozambique calls on donors to "respond positively to the government appeal of untying a larger proportion of their aid" (WB 1989b). Under the special appeal for debt-distressed sub-Saharan countries, Mozambique is supposed to be a priority country for donors to untie their aid (WB 1988b). But obtaining a "return" on aid is just too important to the donors for this to happen.

Various World Bank studies also point out that Mozambique's entire "investment budget" comes from aid, but that too much is project-based. This forces Mozambique to turn everything into "projects"; even major maintenance sometimes becomes a development project, in order to satisfy donor demands. A Bank study warns that "while this tendency to 'projectize' recurrent expenditures in order to enable donors to supplement the current materials budget is not necessarily bad, there is a danger of creating a long-term dependence on foreign assistance for the running costs of essential services and excessive fragmentation of sources for recurrent expenditure" (WB 1988c).

This has also led to finance availability being the main criterion for development projects, rather than suitability or capacity to maintain and operate the new investments. The World Bank points to "the lack of donor support for rehabilitation projects; donors generally prefer new projects." This has prevented Mozambique from shifting its emphasis from new projects to rehabilitation. The Bank stresses the need for "quick-dispersing balance of payments or commodity support", rather than project aid (IMF 1987; WB 1987b, 1988b, 1989a, 1989d).

Finally, the Bank is pressing donors "to take account of the administrative burden being placed on the government by the aid programme [and] to minimize the complexities of the assistance" (WB 1988b). As the Mozambican government stressed, "delays in disbursements by donors and bureaucratic controls which differ from donor to donor continue to cause problems and are a significant factor retarding growth in various areas, particularly manufacturing. Those enterprises dependent on imported raw materials financed with grants and loans are often forced to suspend operations due to these problems." Donors should recognize and use the UCPI (RPM 1989).

The Begging Bowl

The need is so great that Mozambique and the donor agencies must try to find new funds while at the same time competing for a greater share of existing funds. Enlightened self-interest may be the main motivator of aid, but conscience, charity, and politics also play major roles. The funding process is quite complex, which leaves plenty of room for agency competition.

Nearly all aid money comes from government aid budgets. Governments have many different "budget lines". Some money is allocated to individual countries, some to UN agencies, and some to NGOs. Sometimes the money is for particular things; a country may give general funds to Unicef but also give it money specifically for the supply of drugs to Mozambique. Finally, there are aid budget lines for a host of special interests, including emergency, women, environment, education and scholarships, privatization, and trade-aid packages to promote exports. Thus agencies and countries are first trying to increase their formal allocation in a country's aid budget, and second are trying to dip their hands in the special money pots not allocated to named countries or agencies.

Similarly, NGOs engage in public fund raising. They, too, will have core funding coming from a parent church, Oxfam shops, etc. And they will raise extra money from famine appeals and government contracts. In part, then, NGOs compete with each other for money, and Third World countries compete with each other for NGO funds.

But NGOs and the UN also compete with the Third World governments they claim to be helping. Even when funds from the emergency budget are allocated for Mozambique, they can go directly to the Mozambican government, or to an NGO or UN agency for use in Mozambique. In the jargon, this is competition between aid "channels".

Pictures of starving black babies

To encourage the public, NGOs, and governments to give aid requires a highly developed publicity machine. The photographs of the ambassador handing over lorries to the DPCCN and of the UN official with the nurse helping pot-bellied children are firm parts of the aid iconography. Agencies hope that pictures of starving black babies may tug at heartstrings and wallets. Equally important are photographs of successful projects, to show that money has been well used.

Mozambique accepts and understands this; it is quite good at organizing tours for Harry Belafonte, Bob Geldof, Princess Anne, and their ilk. They raise the profile of Mozambique in competition with other disaster areas and other news in general. The TV crews and journalists that travel in their wake provide essential publicity, and the visiting celebrities become a focus for fund-raising when they return home.

But donor agencies are often forced to consider what is fundable and photogenic, rather than what is needed. Certain kinds of projects, such as crèches, raise money when general health and education projects do not. Donors prefer buildings or other objects that can be photographed; there are no pictures of salaries or petrol. Despite their rhetoric, donors are reluctant to fund training. The problem is most serious with repair. Few donors will repair or rehabilitate a building that already exists, especially if it was initially built by another donor. A new coat of paint simply isn't very impressive in the publicity photos.

Where local aid staff are cooperative, a bit of compromise and fudging can satisfy the needs of both the donor agency and Mozambique. For example, two donors can be given credit for building the same crèche, and the second lot of money can be diverted actually to run the crèche (which officially neither would pay for). Or an agency can build a training centre for the photos but some of the money can then be used for the training that Mozambican needs and wants.

Unicef success

One of the most successful agencies in the Mozambique emergency is Unicef, the UN Children's Fund. Its spending jumped from $2.6 mn (£1.6 mn) in 1984 to $10.7 mn

(£6.4 mn) in 1987 and $29.2 mn (£17.5 mn) in 1989 – a ten-fold increase (Unicef 1989b).

Unicef is unusual (but not unique) in the UN family in that it has little money of its own, and instead administers money given to it by UN member governments, NGOs, and national Unicef committees. In Mozambique, it received money from more than 40 sources including Sport Aid and the government of Trinidad and Tobago. Thus it must act like an NGO and fund-raise. Unicef is also unusual, however, in that it, in turn, channels some of its funds to NGOs.

Marta Mauras, who arrived in Maputo at the end of 1984 as Unicef head, was a highly effective publicist who played an important role in increasing Unicef's budget. She was rewarded with a promotion to be head of Unicef's Africa Section in 1989. Perhaps her biggest success was to promote the report *Children on the Front Line* (Unicef 1987, 1989a). This set out in graphic detail the impact of destabilization, and made an effort to quantify the human and material devastation (see also Chapter 3). This report caused an important change in public opinion, because it put the UN's name behind the estimates; this, in turn, made it much harder for right-wing forces to oppose aid to Mozambique.

Unicef always supported the government, and made important contributions to the Ministry of Health, for example for rural vaccination.

But some Unicef fund-raising and publicity actions raised eyebrows. In 1986 Unicef produced an expensive 48-page colour magazine full of pictures of pathetic Mozambican children, which seemed excessive in the face of such misery. Unicef was adept at linking its name to successful Mozambican projects such as vaccination in Maputo. By February 1986, the Ministry of Health had vaccinated 84% of all children in Maputo; it aimed to reach 90% by the end of the year, and surely would have. Unicef jumped in and gave cars, refrigerators, and funds (all sorely needed by the city health department, although not for that project) and then proudly took credit when the 90% target was reached.

Does Unicef's success benefit Mozambique? In the end, does Mozambique get more or less money because of Unicef? Unicef officials argue that many countries allocate funds which must be spent through multilateral agencies as part of their political support for the UN; the only way Mozambique can get those funds is if Unicef taps them. But Unicef also dips into money pots for emergency, health, and other areas where funds could go directly to the government. Thus Unicef is directly competing with the government of Mozambique and with NGOs for funds it will later give to them, having first taken a hefty cut for overheads and administrative costs.

As Unicef aid is largely tied to using Unipac (an important aspect of building up Unicef worldwide), Unicef is sometimes paying higher prices. It is effectively taking a commission on all donations. Unicef salaries and many other costs are also higher than the Mozambican government would pay. Because Unicef has substantially higher costs and overheads than the Mozambican government, Unicef must raise significantly more money than that which would have gone to Mozambique anyway if Unicef is to be profitable to Mozambique. I doubt whether Unicef really did raise that much *new* money.

Finally, Unicef's publicity for Mozambique, especially *Children on the Front Line*, undoubtedly raised the profile of Mozambique and this increased bilateral assistance. But Unicef also has independent appeals for Mozambique, and one was launched in 1988 just days before the main UN emergency appeal for Mozambique (*Guardian* 16 April 1988), which surely confused donors and may have reduced contributions.

On balance, then, Unicef's high-profile, high-expense operation probably has been a net cost rather than a net benefit to Mozambique.

Leverage and the 3 Cs

In the battle for funding, another well-tried route of international capital is "leverage" – putting up only a small amount of your own money and using that to gain control of much larger sums. Donors and especially the World Bank also use "leverage" to mean using their control of money to force policy changes. Conditionality, co-financing, and coordination are three ways to use leverage.

The IMF and World Bank have tried to muscle in and take a dominant role through "conditionality". For relatively small loans, they impose a package of conditions generally know as "structural adjustment". The Bank and Fund put their people into government ministries, and impose detailed budgetary and policy control. Their power comes because most of the large Western donors have agreed that they will not provide aid unless there is an ongoing and agreed programme with the IMF and World Bank, and those institutions are already making loans. Arguably, Nils Tcheyan, World Bank representative in Maputo, is one of the most powerful men in Mozambique. This is not because of the amount of money at his disposal, but because he has massive leverage: his approval is needed for most other aid projects.

The World Bank does use some of its own money. Its chief economist, Stanley Fisher, at a meeting in London in July 1990, set out two new ways to "maintain overall leverage" by linking the Bank's own funds more closely to conditionality. These are "slow disbursement loans" in which money is released only in response to agreed policy changes, and "hybrid loans" in which project loans are linked more directly to conditionality (*Southscan* 20 July 1990).

"Co-financing" is another trick developed by the World Bank. It asks existing donors to divert some of the money they had been giving directly to the government to fund jointly projects organized by the World Bank. This shifts the control of the project to the World Bank and away from the donor and recipient governments. After acquiescing, at least publicly, to World Bank demands, Mozambique has drawn the line at this; government officials openly requested donors not to co-finance. Unicef and NGOs also operate a form of co-financing. They will use some of their own funds as seed money to start a project, and then ask donor governments to come up with the additional money to complete or continue the project.

The third form of leverage is "coordination". Clearly with more than 200 donor agencies running around Mozambique, some coordination is needed. And if one agency can "coordinate" others, it gains at least partial control over those funds. Again, the World Bank heads the list, with its annual Consultative Group meeting in Paris. Another route is for donors to try to have their consultants in key positions in coordinating ministries and government agencies. Several different agencies – bilateral, multilateral, and NGO – have sent consultants to help the government reorganize the finance and cooperation ministries. Several different consultants assured me that "their" plan for reorganizing cooperation and the emergency was about to be adopted. Mozambique is forced to accept these consultants; either they simply arrive unannounced, or a donor says privately that it will be difficult to continue to fund Mozambique unless the government "asks" for consultants to tell it how to operate more efficiently. Mozambican officials have become quite skilled at dumping unwanted consultants in offices and ignoring them. But some of the problems in the Ministry of Cooperation must be due to the large number of consultants offering conflicting advice.

Consultants are often sent to "help" the Mozambican government, as a form of technical assistance. But one minister complained that some people were being sent who did not speak Portuguese and were totally useless. The funds would have been much better used if they had simply been given to the Mozambican government. At the closed Wilton Park seminar in Britain in 1988, donors actually urged the government to adopt a stronger policy to ensure an adequate standard of competence among foreign aid personnel posted to Mozambique. But that was hypocritical, since those same donors would be offended if the government of Mozambique rejected their consultants.

An alternative way of gaining leverage is for an agency to support a particular client within the state apparatus, and to try to ensure that its client becomes coordinator. Thus in the battle to dominate the emergency, the WFP supports the Ministry of Commerce, Unicef and Care (with US backing) work through the DPCCN, and other bilateral donors and UNDP back the Ministry of Cooperation and CENE. On the development front, UNDP appears to have gained ascendance in the Ministry of Cooperation, while the World Bank is ascendant in the Ministry of Finance. This latter division also leads the two agencies to fuel the battle over the relative roles of the emergency, where UNDP remains the paramount agency, and development, where the World Bank is dominant through the Consultative Group and its presence in the Ministry of Finance.

As the various agencies jockey for control of emergency and development funding, there is often quite bitter competition between them, as well as a great deal of backbiting. Thus World Bank officials argue that the Mozambican government bureaucracy is relatively efficient, all things considered, and complain bitterly that IMF spending limits mean that the Mozambique government is not allowed to hire enough people to service World Bank projects. There are similar disagreements on credit policy and the social impact of adjustment. Meanwhile, UNDP officials in Maputo are unhappy about being coordinated by World Bank staff who fly in from Washington, and so they try to ignore the Bank. The battle between Unicef, UNDP, and WFP for the dominant position in the emergency is quite fierce.

One of the most serious side-effects of these bureaucratic and financial battles is that the donors encourage their Mozambican clients to compete rather than cooperate. Attempts to deal with war-traumatized children developed into a similar struggle. One donor worked with the Ministry of Education while another worked with the Ministry of Health. Rather than encourage the two Ministries to work together, the donors followed their own bureaucratic imperatives and encouraged their respective ministries to fight for control of the traumatized children programme.

Aid Workers

Nurses, doctors, social workers, and many others spend their working lives helping others. Similarly, it is reasonable and honourable that people should want careers in aid. In the so-called caring professions, some people become careerists and put their own power, wealth, or life style ahead of those they are supposed to be helping. Hospitals, public health services, and so on exhibit the same bureaucratic struggles that occur in any large organization. We must assume the same conflicting motives and bureaucratic battles in the aid industry.

In the caring professions, a great deal of trust is placed in individuals; they have considerable personal control of their work, but they are expected to live up to a code of professional ethics. Checks are limited and a profession closes ranks to protect its members, so practitioners are only disciplined for misconduct so gross that it disgraces the profession as a whole. (With medical malpractice, this is perhaps less true in the US, but remains the case elsewhere.)

The aid profession shows some similar features of trust and closing ranks, but it is different in two critical ways which make it even harder to check misconduct. First, there is no agreed code of ethics. Second, the international nature of aid means that head offices are far away from the location of action; either the practitioners are in a recipient country and so far away from central control as to make checks impossible, or decisions are taken in a head office so far away from the results of the decisions that no one knows if they were correct or not.

First priorities

Aid workers face a number of instabilities. Frequent travel and postings in various countries make it difficult to have a settled life style. The vagaries of funding mean that many aid workers are on short contracts, for a few weeks, months, or at most two years. Thus aid professionals and those in the caring professions have very different lives.

For many, of course, this is an advantage. Foreign postings are exciting. Aid workers sent to foreign countries have much more power than they would in a comparable job at home. I should not deny my own interest in this. I find working in southern Africa exciting and enjoyable. And as a journalist, I can make sweeping generalizations about foreign countries that no British editor would ever allow me to make about Britain.

Despite the advantages, the instabilities mean that the first responsibility of all aid workers is to ensure their own jobs and salaries. You cannot help anyone else if you cannot feed your own family. Working abroad presents extra problems: you must maintain two homes, you need to arrange schooling for children and sometimes a job for your spouse, you must have home leave and holidays, and you need to ensure you have a pension and some financial cushion while you are between jobs. For full-time UN or bilateral agency staff, this is part of their contracts. Consultants, short-contract staff, and some NGO people must do this themselves out of their earnings. In practice, as with doctors, many aid workers do very well by doing good; the expatriate life style in Maputo is far more luxurious than many people could ever expect at home. Once your job is assured and you have a salary, a pension plan, regular holiday provision, and the basic accoutrements of a European life style, then you can begin to think of helping people in Mozambique.

Guaranteeing your own job also means ensuring that you are not dismissed for misconduct or a wrong decision. This leads to a form of collective protection. It is very difficult for any agency to monitor its field staff, or to have any way of measuring the effect of its head office staff and flying consultants. Because reporting is so spotty, despite attempts at evaluation, a single bad report can end a career. The UN system provides jobs for many Third World people (including three former Mozambican ministers). Some UN staff were parts of old governments thrown out in coups or elections and cannot easily return home, so they need these jobs. Thus the convention is that you may slang off your competitors at cocktail parties and in local gossip, but you never speak ill of other aid workers in a way that will affect their careers. You keep your job, and the other incompetents continue to be sent on ever more important assignments based purely on their length of experience and lack of complaints against them.

But the poor quality of some UN staff sent to Mozambique finally provoked Cooperation Minister Jacinto Veloso to make a very unusual attack on UNDP. He said that the "low level of implementation of programmes" was due in part to the "poor technical quality in formulation of projects." UNDP needed to "strengthen the capacity of the field offices" by "supplying them with competent personnel equipped with skills, experience, and technical capabilities." This clearly implied that some existing staff in Maputo were neither competent nor skilled (Veloso 1989).

Transients

Even the most committed aid workers rarely stay in Mozambique more than four years, and most stay only two. That inevitably creates a kind of short-termism which has several implications. First, it is hardly surprising that aid workers would like to see some results before they move on, especially if they have a direct interest in the work. But that militates against long-term solutions and slower but more effective development strategies.

Second, if you are only going to be somewhere for a relatively short time, then keeping records and files is a low priority. That means aid offices tend to be very disorganized. It also means that aid agencies rarely have an "institutional memory"; they don't know what has been done before, even by their own agency. This leads agencies totally to reverse policy without even knowing they are doing so, as seems to have happened with Care and DPCCN lorries carrying cargoes for agricultural marketing. It also leads to reinventing the wheel: I have seen examples of a series of aid workers reproducing the same plan or study, simply because no one knew it had been done before. This is also compounded by donor secrecy and a tendency not to circulate copies of reports inside Mozambique.

These factors combine to cause newly arrived aid workers to refuse to carry on existing projects and to start again. For many people, the desire to have a quick success means imposing your own ideas quickly; almost inevitably your predecessor was incompetent and got the whole thing backwards. In any case, the lack of institutional memory means that you have no idea what your predecessors tried or why they made the choices the did. Often, you make the same mistakes again.

The short memory also means that donors have forgotten the period of the late 1970s and early 1980s when Mozambique had a world-respected health service, economic growth, and so on. Aid workers arrive, see what seems to be a basket case, and assume an even greater lack of skills and experience than is the case.

Consultants

As the world has become more complex, businesses have increasingly employed consultants for specialist tasks. And it makes sense for the aid industry, too; there is no reason why a field worker or desk officer should know obscure details of areas ranging from agronomy to medicine to engineering. Consulting, however, has taken on a life of its own.

Even in donor countries where contracts for goods and projects are subject to tight, open-tender regulations, people are not. Consultants are chosen from limited lists or by very restricted tender. Friendship, the aid old boy network, and having produced acceptable reports in the past are the things that guarantee consulting jobs.

Consultants are expected to produce, promptly, reports which give the "right" answer for the funding agency. For example, a report for the World Bank will stress the importance of private sector involvement. If an agency wants to go ahead with a project, then the consultant will provide the support; if the agency wants to reject a project, the consultant will support that choice. Normally the consultant recommends more studies for himself (only very rarely herself) and his friends. Consultants being sent to do reports for the Mozambican government are naturally expected to recommend what the sponsor wants done.

Consulting is lucrative and is only difficult for those who are serious about doing a good job. The per diem or per week rate is so high that donors cannot afford to send people for more than a week or two to do a study. This means that most consultants rarely leave Maputo. Many do not even speak Portuguese, which further limits what they can do. Thus when they go to Mozambique, it is a "desk study" plus a few official interviews, and they rarely spend much time actually looking at the subject of the study. But sufficient data is normally there – in government reports, at the university, or in studies done by past consultants. So in a brief visit it is not hard to produce an acceptable report and still have time to sit beside the swimming pool.

The consulting sector is an important part of the aid industry. Consultants are often former staff members of aid agencies who receive contracts from their former colleagues, and who in turn provide the "right" answer. Consultants' reports have the veneer of independence and objectivity, but in fact help to build the empires of the people who commission them. Mutual self-interest rules. It is interesting that when donors actually want answers, for example to help in project design, they tend to hire Mozambican consultants who know the background and language. But when they want reinforcement, they hire consultants from their own country.

A few consultants are good and provide useful expert advice; sometimes a skilled outsider really can stand back and see things which are not obvious to the insider immersed in a mass of detail. For much of the time, however, consulting is a racket. "Consultants do reports that I would not accept from a first-year student", a Mozambican academic told me. Or they try to con the Mozambicans. "I saw one report where the consultant submitted the same report as he had done before, but in several places he had forgotten to replace Tanzania with Mozambique."

Researchers

A related group of people actually do carry out studies, often involving extensive field work. These people are either PhD students or researchers carrying out socio-economic or anthropological surveys as part of projects. Sometimes they produce genuinely new and interesting material. But the original data and documentation are taken back to the home country; sometimes a single copy of the thesis or report will be sent back to Mozambique and sometimes not even that. Just as in the colonial era, even knowledge is removed from Mozambique. This was successfully controlled before 1984 (as it still is in Zimbabwe) by requiring that all foreign research be done in partnership with the university, that it involve Mozambicans, and that it be on topics of Mozambican interest. Now researchers come and go at will as part of aid projects; often the university does not even know they are there. Increasingly academics from the North look to Third World countries as a subject for research and journal articles, which will generate them grants and contracts.

In one instance, an NGO was working in a district where the Centro de Estudos Africanos (CEA – Centre of African Studies) of Universidade Eduardo Mondlane had already done a survey. The NGO made contact with the CEA to draw on its original data, but then objected when the CEA suggested that the new research be linked to the old to allow comparisons. In the end, NGO staff did their own theses without contact with CEA. But the NGO had substantial EC money, so no one could object.

There seems to be a whole new science of "disasterology", and the emergency has drawn a flock of researchers. As Dr Ratilal commented, "some people have sought to profit from the tragedy by treating it as a research laboratory" (Ratilal 1990a: 123). A doctor commented: "With Lebanon, Mozambique, Uganda, El Salvador and so on there is a burgeoning traumatized children industry." Researchers get contracts to compare children in various countries, supposedly for the purpose of eventually helping them. One research group wrote to Mozambique with plans to administer long written questionnaires to several hundred children in three weeks. Mozambican officials wrote back and said it was impractical, but a researcher turned up in any case. The researcher, who did not speak Portuguese, went to schools and asked teachers to administer the questionnaire in local languages. The questions were complex and badly translated into Portuguese, so the teachers did not understand them. Several teachers were overheard telling the pupils just to make up the answers.

The doctor commented: "Surely it is unethical to ask children questions they will find traumatic and disturbing and which is of no use to anyone."

17 The New Missionaries

"It's identical to what happened 100 years ago. After the Berlin conference there were wars to establish colonial control of the continent. Then in came the missionaries, and they cleared the way for the capitalists. Again we have wars, this time followed by the NGOs. They are the new missionaries clearing the way for big foreign capital." That was the view from a provincial education director.

"All 'non-government agencies' are really government. They get money from their government and work toward their government's goals", a provincial governor told me. "They come and they do things 'for the people'. They build schools and dig wells, which do improve people's lives. But development takes time; it takes time to build up the local capability to dig wells and build schools. But they don't train us or build our capabilities. Why do they do this? They give us things but try to keep us dependent. They are trying to take the place of Frelimo and the government; they want to show that it is the agencies who improve the life of the people and not the government. They are trying to show that the old colonizers are really interested in the people after all; that they can bring you water today whereas Frelimo can only give you a well tomorrow."

In public, honey drips from the lips of Mozambican officials as they praise the NGOs and other donors. In private, the view is very different. Initially many Mozambicans were cautious with me, but if I was introduced by a mutual friend or when they became convinced that what they said would not get back to the donors, they became more outspoken. Standing chatting while waiting for a plane, over a cup of coffee after dinner, or after a long meeting, very different attitudes finally emerge. One of my strongest impressions in researching this book was that so many Mozambicans that I respect are angry and hostile about NGOs. And this anger is growing as NGOs become a major conduit for aid funding.

PVOs

Some NGOs are outgrowths of the old missionary societies. Some are linked to evangelical and right-wing religious sects. And some, like Oxfam and Care, were set up for famine relief after the Second World War. Some money, particularly in Britain, comes from fund-raising campaigns. But most comes from governments. Projects are initiated by either side; sometimes a government tries to find an NGO to do a specific job, and sometimes an NGO applies to a government, a UN agency, or the EC for funds for a project. In many ways, the US term "private voluntary organization" (PVO) is more appropriate than the now widely accepted term "non-government organization" (NGO).

This is because they are private bodies which receive most of their funding from governments, and so are not really "non-government".

This position was summarized by Diego Ungaro, second secretary in the Italian embassy in Maputo. He told me: "Italian NGOs receive all their money from the government. So from my point of view they are no different from a firm, except that they do not make a profit. They are just implementation agencies for us."

Some NGOs have become big businesses. Several have budgets of over $100 mn (£60 mn) per year, and some like Care and World Vision have become transnational with affiliated groups in several countries. (This has also led to some confusion: both Oxfam and Médecins Sans Frontières spawned groups elsewhere which now try to distance themselves from the original on political grounds.) As with any transnational business, the essential first requirement is to stay in business and to generate a surplus. The "business" of an NGO is to distribute money, food relief, and services; the surplus comes from the percentage of all grants which can be used for overheads. As the NGOs have grown, an increasing number of staff are accountants, managers, fund raisers, and others who have no contact with the actual recipients of the "help". Whatever humanitarian impulses may have caused the formation of NGOs many years ago, most are now driven by the same forces which drive any large corporation or large bureaucracy: to expand and increase turnover, while guaranteeing the jobs of those employed.

Why they flourished

NGOs grew rapidly with the aid boom of the 1970s and the famine and privatization of the 1980s. In the Thatcher-Reagan era, they were seen, in Ungaro's words, as private non-profit firms which would take over tasks done by the government. In this case, it is the implementation of foreign policy which is being privatized. Most NGOs have an anti-government bias, so donors were also able to use NGOs to undercut and bypass recipient governments as part of their Third World privatization strategy.

The US, for example, has a $7.5 mn (£4.5 mn) per year "PVO [NGO] Support Program", one of the purposes of which is "helping government reduce its direct involvement in the activities that can be performed by the private sector" (USAID budget submission FY 1991).

Funding has been organized in such a way that often NGOs must compete with each other to get projects approved, which ensures that they put forward projects most acceptable to donor governments. Even when NGOs don't support the donor government line, they cannot go strongly against it because they depend on their government for funding.

Small businesses and NGOs are supposed to be more flexible and responsive, as well as cheaper and more efficient, than traditional large and cumbersome state bureaucracies. NGOs are said to be staffed by younger and more enthusiastic people who work long hours for low salaries, and who are prepared to endure hardships to work at grassroots level. Thus NGOs should be able to respond more quickly and appropriately to the needs on the ground, and resolve bottlenecks more expertly. With these advantages, they would be more acceptable than official aid agencies to recipient governments and local people.

One purpose of this chapter is to argue that these assumptions are often false. NGO workers are all too often bumbling amateurs who go to Mozambique for a bit of adventure, to gain experience, and perhaps to further their careers. They frequently totally misunderstand local conditions, and are arrogant into the bargain. By contrast, bilateral and multilateral aid workers can be professionals who may respond more slowly, but make a more intelligent contribution which has more long-term benefit. The professionals sometimes show more respect for local knowledge and expertize.

Of course, neither generalization is always true. The professionals are often as bureaucratic, incompetent, and inefficient as they are alleged to be. And at their best, NGOs can be spectacularly good.

NGOs Can be Creative

In one province an NGO arrived and wanted to support health. It asked what was needed, and was told the most urgent need was for training – particularly upgrading and refresher courses for existing staff in the districts. So the NGO built a training centre, assigned two staff from the NGO, and provided all the material needs. The centre does two- or three-week courses as requested by the provincial health directorate. These involve normal Ministry programmes as well as special ones that often cater to the needs of refugees. In the first year, 200 primary and community health workers attended courses. The two NGO staff also go out to the districts to follow up and to support people who attended the courses.

The training centre is popular and successful, both with officials and with the health workers themselves. It satisfies a felt need in the province; the NGO provides the material conditions such as food and lodging, notebooks and manuals, and transport from rural areas; but the centre remains under government control and trains government staff in government-backed programmes. Thus the NGO is seen to be helping the government, not competing with it, and health workers feel that they are being trained by the Ministry and not by an NGO.

The centre and this NGO have been successful in part because the NGO is supportive and creative at the same time. The provincial health director was complaining that district health directors never filled in the disease notification forms and often failed to carry out national policy, but he admitted it was not surprising because they were all young and most had only been trained as nurses or medical technicians and not as administrators. The NGO suggested a course at the training centre. This was readily agreed; it was worked out jointly with the NGO and provincial government, and was largely taught by provincial health staff. Fourteen district directors were flown in for a three-week seminar, at which it was explained, probably for the first time, how to direct a district and how to carry out national policy and guidelines. A doctor in the province told me: "It was marvellous. The district directors loved it. They said that it was the first time some of them had been given any management skills."

The province was one that was badly hit by war, and it was only possible to reach some district headquarters towns by light plane. With IMF spending limits, the government could never afford to hire planes, so all transport was controlled by donors. Normally it was donors who flew out to the district, so local officials and people rarely saw the government; it seemed that only the NGOs cared about them. An NGO saw this problem, and assigned some of the seats on its hired plane to government; district directors could fly to the provincial capital and provincial staff could fly out to support their local staff on the ground. When I flew in an NGO plane to Mopeia, a man from education and a woman from agriculture flew with us. The man from education met with the teachers, who told him their problems – particularly their ragged clothes (they had been refugees too) which embarrassed them when they taught. The woman from agriculture improved the seed storage in the local warehouse. These were small things, but they were psychologically of huge importance; Frelimo had not abandoned them, and the government had sent people to help. They did not know or care who had provided the airplane.

To me, the health training centre and the places on the plane for government were simple examples of how NGOs could help government to do its job better. Even more important, they were doing what NGOs always say they can do best – responding creatively and imaginatively to local needs.

There are other examples. Two NGOs jointly set up a small $15,000 (£9000) foreign exchange fund for the Ministry of Health to use as it saw fit, so long as it accounted for the money. In one case, the ancient air conditioner in the intensive care unit of the Maputo Central Hospital finally stopped working at the peak of the hot season. Normally the hospital director would have had to petition the Ministry of Finance for foreign exchange (a delay of weeks at best) or make a formal request to an NGO (which would have taken months). Instead, he was able to use the fund and have a new air conditioner working in days – saving the lives of gravely ill patients who would have died in the sweltering heat.

A simple tale of two NGOs will show why it is impossible to make sweeping generalizations. An NGO was working in a coastal district. The Maputo representative visited the district and met with fishing people, who said they needed nets. "There are some problems. There is no local market, so how will they pay for the nets? And men are pushing women out because of the lack of other jobs, so we want to ensure that women take part", explained the representative. So a consultant came from Europe to study the problem. He suggested it needed another consultant. Another NGO working in the adjoining coastal district had already provided fishing nets. Their representative told me: "The Institute of Fisheries man in the provincial government knew exactly what was needed. He went and talked with the fishing people, organized an association, and set up a system for paying for the nets. We didn't need a consultant; the government could determine what was needed." It may not have been the best possible programme, but it was much cheaper and put people back to work more quickly.

Campaigning

Other examples of creative and successful NGO support could be mentioned, and many more disasters will be cited. But NGOs are most important not for what they do in Mozambique, but for what they do at home. It was NGOs, not bilateral donors or the UN, which alerted the world to the impending famine in late 1986. Solidarity groups and a few NGOs were also the first publicly to raise the idea of protecting food convoys and projects. NGO campaigns have played a crucial role in convincing larger donors and the general public that the basic problem is destabilization. Mozambican officials credit the more political, campaigning NGOs with an important role in reorienting and increasing the much larger bilateral aid that comes from governments.

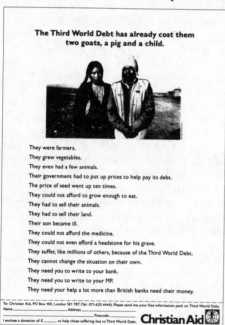

The Third World Debt has already cost them two goats, a pig and a child.

They were farmers.
They grew vegetables.
They even had a few animals.
Their government had to put up prices to help pay its debt.
The price of seed went up ten times.
They could not afford to grow enough to eat.
They had to sell their animals.
They had to sell their land.
Their son became ill.
They could not afford the medicine.
They could not even afford a headstone for his grave.
They suffer, like millions of others, because of the Third World Debt.
They cannot change the situation on their own.
They need you to write to your bank.
They need you to write to your MP.
They need your help a lot more than British banks need their money.

To: Christian Aid, PO Box 100, London SE1 7RT (Tel: 071-620 4444). Please send me your free information pack on Third World Debt.
Name_____Address_____
_____Postcode_____
I enclose a donation of £_____ to help those suffering due to Third World Debt.   **Christian Aid**

One of a series of advertisements on Third World debt run by Christian Aid in 1990.

For some Mozambican officials, this is the central importance of progressive NGOs. They are encouraged to do projects not because these projects are of any use to Mozambicans, but rather because they provide a platform for campaigning. Such projects often cost Mozambique more time and money than they are worth; their publicity value, however, may be much greater.

Finally, some of the NGOs working in Mozambique have played central roles in campaigns on the debt crisis, apartheid, and other issues which directly affect Mozambique. Their activism grew in part from their experiences in Mozambique.

Campaigning NGOs can come into conflict with their governments when they challenge policy. The British Charity Commission objected to Oxfam's call for sanctions against South

Africa in its 1990 Front Line States campaign. The Canadian solidarity organization TCLSAC warned of the danger of NGOs being less willing to speak out in order to ensure funds and contract work; of the government "buying the silence" of the NGOs. "With severe budget cuts, the hustle to get CIDA funds takes on more intensity. No one can live in the Ottawa milieu without becoming finely tuned to the limits of critical discourse about government policy. The structural relation of the development agencies to CIDA funding is such that, consciously or unconsciously, these agencies carry out a kind of self-censorship" (SAR February 1990: 28).

This must affect the way NGOs conduct their education campaigns at home. Collecting money and used clothes with pictures of starving babies helped by kindly white nurses reinforces stereotypes and charity consciousness, but it does not offend governments. Fund raising explicitly to help the victims of South African aggression makes a political point which may influence the policies of governments, and be of more use to Mozambique. To make the further point that people are hungry because of IMF structural adjustment policies supported by the NGO's own government would be most useful but is probably unacceptable. Dom Helder Câmara is often quoted in this context: "When I give food to the poor they call me a saint. When I ask why the poor have no food, they call me a communist."

Small is Not Beautiful

Nearly all the 180 NGOs working in Mozambique are quite small. No NGO has ever been among the 15 biggest donors (Table A.3b). Only two NGOs in Mozambique could be considered medium size; in 1989 Care had an emergency budget in Mozambique of $12.4 mn (£7.4) and WV $10.6 mn (£6.4). Little of this was their own money; most of it was contract funds from governments and other third parties (Table A.5a).

It is then a big step down to the next four foreign NGOs – Caritas, ICRC, MSF (France), and SCF (Norway) – which had emergency budgets of around $4 mn (£2.4) in 1989. Then there is another jump down to nine NGOs with emergency budgets around $2 mn (£1.2 mn). Of these 13, only four provided more than $500,000 (£300,000) of their own money (Table A.5a). These NGOs can have a major impact in an individual district, but they are tiny by the standards of the aid industry in Mozambique. Oxfam, the biggest British charity, launched an appeal in April 1990 to raise £1 mn ($1.7 mn) for the Front Lines states; Mozambique's share of this will be less than one-tenth of one percent of all its foreign aid in 1990.

Thus, nearly all the 180 NGOs working in Mozambique are tiny. Necessarily, NGOs argue that their small size is an advantage, making them more flexible, creative, and efficient. In Mozambique, however, the big agencies have shown that there are sometimes efficiencies of scale. The large organizations can be surprisingly flexible and move quickly. Being bigger, they usually have more money to spend, and they are often more professional and businesslike.

On the other hand, in Mozambique the things for which NGOs are normally praised have proved to be the root of major problems. Young staff are often inexperienced; enthusiasm to get on with solving the problem often means an unwillingness to listen; low overheads mean inefficiency and very long delays; small groups lack the resources to have much impact. NGOs are intrinsically amateurs who want to do their own thing; they have bigger egos (in inverse proportion to the amount of money they have to spend) and expect more personal satisfaction from their project.

At the core is attitude, and the very concept of a "non-government" organization. NGOs may not be able to avoid the constraints of the governments that pay them, but most work very hard to avoid, ignore, and bypass the recipient government. Instead, some try to create local NGOs or to work directly with loose groups of peasants. As former emergency head Prakash Ratilal commented, "some NGOs cherish their independence overmuch, to the detriment or even exclusion of a government's attempts to establish a coordinated strategy for their use" (Ratilal 1990a: 197). Some use this independence to pursue goals directly opposed to those of the government.

A paternalistic charity consciousness dominates the attitudes of many NGOs. Like the kind ladies and earnest missionaries running soup kitchens and doing good works in Victorian England, they want to help the "deserving poor". Their overriding assumption is that the poor are poor not because of lack of money or because of the actions of outsiders, but because of ignorance and superstition. The rich assume that their wealth gives them the right to pontificate, while the poverty of the poor means their views are also valueless – after all, if they knew what to do, they wouldn't be poor, whereas we wouldn't be rich if we weren't smarter.

NGOs seem to feel that they are the only ones who ever promote development. Sitting in a lovely flat overlooking Maputo Bay, with glasses of chilled white wine in our hands, an NGO worker told me: "No third world government ever wants to help its people. Why is it that in Manila slums and rural areas throughout the Third World, you see so many foreigners who are the only ones who want to help the people? Mozambique is no different."

Attitude towards foreign staff in Mozambique is perhaps symptomatic of the problem. Many NGOs are openly hostile to the old-style cooperantes who still work for the government; they are seen as supporters of the "wrong side" since governments are "never" interested in helping the poor.

Similarly, head offices are wary of appointing local staff who are too sympathetic to the government; the worst charge against a local representative is that they were "too cooperantish", the local equivalent of "going native". One NGO sent a consultant to Mozambique several times, and the consultant's manner succeeded in offending many of the Mozambican officials with whom he dealt. The local representative telexed the head office to say this man should not be sent back; the head office ensured that he was the next consultant they sent, on the grounds that if the locals didn't like him, he must be telling some useful home truths.

A few of the poorest

The struggle between NGOs and the government often revolves around who is to be helped. In the Third World the concept of "deserving poor" has been replaced by the phrase "poorest of the poor". The socialist goal of Frelimo was a broad development that would provide basic services and a minimum standard of living to all. The shared goal of NGOs, churches, and most aid agencies is to provide a better standard of living and better quality services to a few. They differ only in choosing which few: NGOs help a favoured group of peasants, churches help their members, and some of the bigger donors help the better off. It is all part of the trend toward privatization and reduced power of government. Furthermore, a key element in the new era of greed and private enterprise are charities and self-help organizations to pick up the pieces; NGOs play that role in the Third World, often as part of the "social dimensions of adjustment" (SDA) programmes.

In many countries selective help reaches the extreme of NGOs arranging for Western families to "adopt" a poor child or a granny, who is then given special privileges; so far Mozambique has successfully resisted attempts to pick out and privilege individuals and small groups. But NGOs keep pushing because this is an important way to raise money; one NGO advertised for sponsors for Mozambican children in refugee camps in Zimbabwe, since they were not allowed to "adopt" children inside Mozambique.

'My' peasant

It has proved much more difficult to stop NGOs from picking out a favoured group of peasants to help. The enthusiastic amateurs of the NGOs gain much more pleasure and self-satisfaction from helping specific peasants, just as concerned people in developed countries gain more vicarious satisfaction from "adopting" a Third World child. It is a clear case of the donor's personal self-interest taking precedence over any questions about what would be the most useful way to assist these people and their neighbours.

As well as the political issue raised by selecting one individual or a tiny group for special privileges, there are basic practical issues. It is doubtful how relevant the experience of a middle-class Westerner is to a Mozambican peasant; the aid worker will probably learn more than the peasant from the experience. All too often, working directly with the poorest creates expectations of levels of material and technical support that can never be maintained by the government. NGOs dismiss criticism of this sort by saying that they do "pilot" projects, and that when Mozambique sees the success of the project it will be implemented everywhere; NGOs never explain where Mozambique is to find the money and staff. Often the NGO worker leaves after the end of two-year contract – very proud of his or her success – and the project just collapses, leaving nothing behind.

Even if the project does succeed, it just creates a new highly privileged group to join the private sector (even if they call themselves a cooperative or peasant association). This supports the goals of those donors who promote privatization and want to widen rather than reduce divisions.

In any case, there are serious grounds for questioning the technical efficiency of this approach. The salary and overhead costs of an NGO worker helping an individual peasant or small group are astronomical; thousands of dollars or pounds or tens of thousands of kroner or francs, enough to make that poor peasant wealthy if it were given to her directly, and permanently rich if invested. NGOs want to target the poorest, whose biggest problem is simply lack of money. Thus the most useful thing would probably be to give each poor person a few 10 Rand notes. After generations of living close to the margin, most peasants would use the money wisely to buy clothing, agricultural inputs, education, or whatever else they needed. Some might even form associations and hire their own agricultural advisers.

If groups of poor peasants were convinced of the merit of NGO-style projects, and if they were in control of those projects, it seems likely that given the choice they would prefer advisers from other developing countries. They would understand peasant problems better, and have more relevant experience. Furthermore, other Third World people would be much cheaper, allowing the available money to go further.

Working directly with the poorest can never be cost-effective for a foreign NGO, and it is not often very productive. The really useful thing to do is to train and support Mozambicans who will work with the poorest. In Mozambique, that means supporting those agencies in the government (and related to the government) which provide long-term appropriate help to the poorest peasants and workers – the DPCCN, health, education, agricultural extension, green zones directorates, and cooperative unions. This is treating NGO work as political rather than charitable. Instead of helping handfuls of peasants, it is more productive to help government to develop the capacity to provide permanent support which will operate even after the NGO has moved on to helping the poorest somewhere else.

A former country representative of a major NGO in Mozambique told me: "We have the money and skills and the Mozambicans don't. So we should give them the money and the skills to use it. We shouldn't be telling them how to use it. The only thing useful that an NGO can do is to train people. I told this to my head office, but it was totally unacceptable to them, so I quit."

"It shows an extremely high level of arrogance to believe that you know how to communicate with peasants. Instead we really just impose our cultural values", commented one long-term aid worker. The only choice is to train Mozambicans to work with peasants.

Unfortunately, many people join development NGOs because they want to help the poorest personally while having an adventure in a foreign country; it is less personally satisfying to train other people to help the poorest. And there are few jobs for NGO people in simply handing out money, or in promoting South–South cooperation. Here the bureaucratic and institutional issues become paramount: NGO workers need to find a role that ensures their jobs. And their self-justification often requires them to believe that governments do not want to help their own poorest.

To be sure, there are other countries which are now so dominated by self-serving elites that only outsiders will work with the poorest. As I argue in the next chapter, donors are trying to create that situation in Mozambique. But everywhere in Mozambique that I went in researching this book, I found people in government who are still struggling to help the poorest.

Lady Bountiful

The small size and low overheads on which NGOs pride themselves mean that they are stretched very thinly. They keep their official overheads down by not training staff and by not developing elaborate accounting systems. Untrained staff and sloppy books mean they waste a lot of money, but that counts as project spending rather than overheads.

Lack of staff means NGO heads fly into Mozambique for a few days, where they are whisked off to look at projects and be received by grateful and hungry natives, and then make pledges and dole out charity like latter-day Lady Bountifuls. But they have no time to assess the suitability of their bounty.

A Maputo NGO representative told me how she got her job. "The director of the NGO came here for four days. He doesn't speak Portuguese and didn't have an interpreter, so he only talked to a few people who speak English. In the four days, he wrote a programme and looked around for a local rep. My husband is working here; we only arrived recently and I was free, so he hired me. I have no experience of this, and I wouldn't have hired me. I suggested he hire a Mozambican, but he said no." But the NGO takes full account of her inexperience. "I cannot take any decisions. I need approval from head office to spend more than the equivalent of $300 (£180), and for anything over $3000 (£1800) they call in outside advisers – who normally have no experience of Mozambique. Then everything must be approved by the director, but he is travelling most of the time. I was asked to provide some equipment which was obviously necessary for a health unit, but I can't promise anything and I can't get an answer in less than three months. Mozambican tenders are normally good for only two months, and I can't get a reply within that time."

More importantly, she feels strongly that she is not serving a useful function. She and her Maputo office cost more than $30,000 (£18,000) per year. The head office has a Mozambique/Zimbabwe desk officer, an Africa desk officer, an emergency desk officer, and various accountants and secretaries – probably the equivalent of two more full-time staff dealing with Mozambique. The NGO deals primarily with the Ministry of Health. "We should just give the money to the Ministry. Some things will go wrong. But people seem to care and to use money effectively, so they would lose less than my NGO pays me." She also suggested they work through an NGO already active in Maputo with established links with the Ministry of Health, but the director stressed they had to have a separate identity in Mozambique.

Is it worth the cost?

The plethora of small NGOs take up a disproportionate amount of government time, housing and office space, and people. For Mozambique, the local administrative cost, in both time and money, is very high for aid projects. Reams of paperwork are different for each donor, and donors resist any attempt at standardization. At the same time, donors are notoriously unwilling to provide word processors, paper, printer ribbons and various other items which are essential to produce the reports they demand. Every donor expects to meet ministers and to have top provincial officials at their beck and call; they expect cars and hotels to be arranged, of course.

What is striking is that administrative demands seem inversely proportional to the amount of money on offer. The big bilateral agencies are accustomed to spending large amounts of money and have developed simplified systems to monitor it. NGOs, on the other hand, want a personal involvement in each project. They agonize over tiny projects, bring in consultants, and organize seminars. This is, of course, precisely the merit of NGOs, but it is also the core problem. I once saw a woman spend a week in Maputo organizing to spend $10,000 (£6000). She needed a car and a hotel, and talked with at least a dozen officials. Surely the value of their time was worth more than the $10,000 she was going to spend.

In one case, a donor visited Mozambique and gave $16,000 (£10,000) to rebuild two classrooms. The donor wanted before and after pictures and regular progress reports. And the donor was to fly out again for an opening ceremony. The expenses will surely be more than the original donation.

Similarly, evaluations sometimes seem to cost the NGO more than the project. Mozambique is also expected to participate in these evaluations, which can take several weeks. Some projects are evaluated more than once. All too often, the seminars and evaluations are needed to try to fit the Mozambican square peg into the round hole of experience and theory based on India or Ethiopia.

Integrating Mozambicans into the evaluations is laudable, but is it worth the time and opportunity cost? In many provinces, there are dozens of NGO projects, which means that at least one is being evaluated at any time. The Mozambican directors who have to support the NGOs and help in the evaluation are taken away from their normal work, which doesn't get done. It becomes a no-win game. If the Mozambican director declines to participate in the evaluation, it is taken as further evidence that he doesn't care about the poor. If he does participate and is therefore out of his office, then the other NGOs that come pounding on his door with their demands say: "Look, Mozambican directors are never there. They don't care about the poor."

NGOs are increasingly hiring Mozambican staff and even local field directors, as part of an apparently praiseworthy localization policy. But Mozambique's biggest shortage is of skilled people. NGOs rarely train people at the level they recruit, because they say their job is to help the poorest and not to train administrators. But every accountant, secretary or manager hired by an NGO is one lost to the economy or, more often, to the state. NGOs strip people out of the state apparatus, which weakens the state, which further justifies NGO claims that the state cannot help its own people and that NGOs must be there to help the poor. With the best of intentions, NGOs that localize without training an equal number of people are supporting the big donors that are trying to weaken the state.

Unguided Missiles

The independence, self-importance, charity consciousness, do-goodism, and amateurism of the NGOs have created innumerable problems for Mozambique. Perhaps the most blatant combination of arrogance, disdain, and incompetence is NGOs promising things they do not deliver. Mozambicans are supposed to be grateful for whatever they receive, and NGOs become quite angry if Mozambique complains of unfulfilled promises. (By contrast, big donors don't want gratitude; they want policy changes.)

One of the oldest and most famous NGOs arrived in a coastal province, and asked what was needed. Provincial officials pointed to the shortage of coastal transport, and suggested a small boat that could carry 50 tonnes of cargo. The NGO sent a consultant to evaluate the request and the consultant suggested a larger 200-tonne-capacity boat. This was agreed. The NGO and province signed a detailed contract setting out that the boat could not leave provincial waters without written permission of the NGO, that the NGO could send its cargo free of charge, and that the boat was to be named Quionga. The contract was announced in *Noticias*. Plans were made to use the boat. But it never arrived. The NGO decided the boat was a bad idea, and without further discussion with the province, reneged on the contract.

A European NGO arrived in Mozambique, and was sent to a district. It did a small and successful development project, and then asked to expand. It made extravagant promises of development projects in several adjoining districts, which were accepted because of the success of the first. But then nothing was heard. The first small project ended, and the NGO quietly withdrew. Finally it returned to admit that it had never had the money for its multi-district project; the "promises" were merely plans and the EC had turned down its project proposal. A provincial government official said to me: "Not only is it bad for the districts, it also makes the government look bad. We appeared side by side with these people when they made their promises, and it looks like our fault that they did not deliver." But the embarrassed NGO said it did have a little bit of money and would like to return to its first district. This was approved, and the NGO agreed to rehabilitate the hospital. A local contractor was appointed, and was eventually told that materials were on the way and he should start work. He removed the roof from the hospital and waited. Eventually the rainy season started. Drugs were damaged and patients were moved from the roofless hospital to adjoining houses. When I visited the province, no one knew where the new roofing sheets were, and the NGO representative could not be found.

The head of an NGO visited Mozambique and toured one of the provinces. He was asked to rebuild a war-damaged health post and readily agreed. I was in the province 18 months later, and was told no more had been heard from the NGO. On my return to Maputo I asked the local representative, who explained that the promise had been made in August. The budget cycle of the organization is 1 September to 31 August, so the promise was made too late to get into that budget. Therefore no money could be spent until September of the following year. The NGO is one of those which does not buy in Mozambique, so the building materials had to be ordered from Swaziland. But the Maputo office person told me proudly that the materials were finally on their way. Unfortunately, after a year with no contact, provincial officials had assumed the project had been forgotten; they had found another NGO to do temporary repairs and the health post was back in use. No doubt if the first NGO discovered this, it would have been very offended and complained bitterly about the "ungrateful Mozambicans". I hope the province took the alternative route and quietly diverted the building materials to a different health post, telling both NGOs they fixed the same one, and hoping they never compared detailed notes.

Part of the problem is that far from being flexible as claimed, small NGOs are often highly bureaucratic and do not permit local representatives to take decisions. An NGO representative told how they agreed to provide seeds and food to a group of refugees. At Mozambique's request, they agreed to supply both at the same time, so that the refugees would not be forced to eat the seed. The Maputo office ordered maize for food in Zimbabwe, because it could be shipped on time; head office overruled this, saying it was "irresponsible" to pay a higher price in Zimbabwe, and ordered the maize in Kenya. With no regular shipping link, the maize did not arrive until well after planting time. In fact, however, the refugees did not eat the seed. The NGO head office was so slow in approving the seed order that it did not arrive in time either.

We know better

The arrogance of NGOs is also shown by their automatic assumption that they know better than the recipient country – and better than other donors. As one Mozambican said to me, NGO workers are "the lesson givers".

NGOs often see themselves as "fixers" flying in from outside to fix what is wrong in the Third World. In particular, NGOs assume that their broad worldwide experience is directly applicable to Mozambique. Thus some NGOs feel they can simply replicate the projects they ran in India or Costa Rica. And the "emergency experts" who have flown to floods in Bangladesh and droughts in Chad arrive in Mozambique convinced they know exactly what to do; time spent talking to Mozambican officials only delays their help to the poor and hungry.

One NGO has actually set up "a programme to demonstrate that the bicycle is still a useful means of transport", and it is importing bicycles from Taiwan (*Noticias* 13 June 1990). No one needs to tell Mozambican peasants about the utility of bicycles, which are among their most prized possessions; their problem is the lack of money to buy the bicycles. And there is already a privately owned bicycle factory in Maputo, so there should be no need to import bicycles.

Mozambique's health service has won justifiable international praise for its stress on primary and rural health care, and for its emphasis on extending health services to the mass of the population. One major NGO sent in an evaluation team, which after three weeks concluded that Mozambique's health policy did not help the poorest, and thus should not be supported. Several other evaluation teams from this NGO, which has cultivated a progressive image at home, criticized the local office for working too closely with the government and not spending enough time with the peasants.

Another NGO sent a technician to work with urban producer cooperatives, such as carpenters and salt producers. One of his successful ventures was to send two shoemakers and two potmakers to work with companies in Maputo; when they returned, their production quality was much higher and sales increased. Another success was arranging for the state salt producer to send someone to help the salt co-ops. But the NGO technician made all the links himself. He flew regularly to Maputo to find or import raw materials for his co-ops, to arrange training places, and to find advisers. He was so busy that he asked his NGO for two more foreign staff. There was a suggestion that the two should work within the government, to build up government capability to support co-ops. The government was anxious to do this. The provincial planning director, who is a strong advocate of small enterprises, including co-ops, wanted the support. The director stressed the need to build up local capacity so that some of the raw materials could be supplied to co-ops locally, rather than be brought by the NGO from Maputo. But the NGO rejected the proposal. "It is our policy not to work with government", the NGO technician told me as we sat in a beach-side restaurant drinking South African beer. "In any case, don't believe what those officials tell you. This government does not want to help co-ops." It was just an exception that the state timber company and state salt company were anxious to work with the co-ops, and that government officials had encouraged those links.

'It worked in Asia...'

It is worth giving one example (from many candidates) which encapsulates the problems of NGOs. In this case, the NGO seemed to start out well. As usual, it had been assigned to a district; it accepted the Mozambican bias toward integrated development and was to work in both health and agriculture. The health segment was a rapid success. An enthusiastic doctor used the district health centre as a basis for training and upgrading local health workers. A Ministry of Health survey found that his district had shown the best improvement rate in the area, and concluded that the project showed that an NGO-based spurt of training could be highly effective. Vaccination rates doubled. For diarrhoea treatment, oral rehydration was commonly used and understood; misuse of antibiotics was unusually low. The Minister of Health visited the project and praised it as a model, the best NGO project he had seen.

Unfortunately, however, the other parts of the project were soon in deep trouble.

Whenever the project leader was questioned about decisions, the reply was simply: "Our development philosophy worked in the country I was in before, so it must work here." Officials both in the province and in Maputo were unhappy with the agriculturalists, seeing them as unskilled volunteers so committed to a "small is beautiful" philosophy that they only helped a handful of peasants and had little to contribute to the district as a whole.

The project had three cars – by far the largest transport pool in the district – but they were used only for project staff; cars could not even be used by rural vaccination teams. Cars are always a source of conflict, but this was extreme; a high Maputo official openly accused the project manager of being racist and not wanting black people to use his cars. The project leader responded by refusing to deal with local government staff.

Meanwhile, the project head came into increasing conflict with the doctor. The head said that they were there to help the poorest of the poor. In the previous country that had meant spending time in rural areas on preventive health, and the head accused the doctor of spending too much time in the health centre and too much time on curative medicine. This was the only health centre in a district affected by war, and many people came to the centre for treatment; the doctor also used the centre as a basis for training. Nevertheless, the doctor did spend half his time out in the countryside. But that was not enough.

The Minister of Health's praise of the doctor only underlined what the project head saw as a misguided government policy of trying to balance curative and preventive work. When the Ministry of Health planned to send one of its staff to do a nutrition survey in the district, the project head banned her, saying in an open meeting that if she came to "his district" he would close the project. The provincial director of health objected, but eventually agreed because he wanted a model project to continue.

Finally the project head sacked the doctor. In an almost unprecedented action, the Minister of Health personally sent a telex to the NGO headquarters saying that the "decision to suddenly remove the doctor ... creates a difficult situation for us because of the very negative effects on the community. I therefore request the continuation of the present health team."

The NGO head office backed up its project head, and refused to rescind the dismissal. But it did try to pacify Mozambique with extra aid: 5000 tonnes of grain for the province and, in a reversal of previous policy, a car for the district administrator and a pledge to rehabilitate the health centre.

This presented a problem for the Mozambican government. The NGO had substantial financial backing from a medium-sized country which had just changed its policy to channelling more of its aid through NGOs. Furthermore, this country was giving strong political backing to the Front Line States, and could not be offended. Deciding that discretion was the better part of valor, the Minister of Health backed off and allowed the project to continue without the doctor. But he appointed the sacked doctor as a government "cooperante" doctor in the adjoining district.

Growing Power

NGOs are becoming increasingly wealthy and powerful within Mozambique, especially through the emergency. In part, this is because a number of donors, including the US, UK, and Norway, have taken a policy decision to channel aid through NGOs and not the Mozambican government. In other cases it is less overt, and systems are developed which make it difficult or impossible for a government like Mozambique's to tap funds directly, but easy for NGOs in the donor country.

US policy is quite open: "USAID will channel rehabiliation assistance through PVO [NGO] grants." On health, the US has opted to work through NGOs to "minimise dependence on national public health infrastructure." Food will be consigned less to the

DPCCN and more to WV and ADRA (USAID 1990b: 48ff). WV is being encouraged "to convert the emergency program to regular program feeding activities targetted at specific vulnerable groups and rehabiliation activities" (USAID budget submission FY 1990).

A high UN official in Maputo told me in 1990: "Some of the bigger NGOs here are so flush with resources that they cannot maintain an adequate rate of dispersal if they have a well planned programme, so they are just throwing money around. One of the big donors says the government is corrupt and inefficient, but its NGOs are much worse."

But the question is neither saving lives nor efficiency. Donors are trying to bypass and undermine the Mozambican government. They want foreign private organizations rather than the Mozambican government to be offering food aid as well as health, education, water, and agricultural extension services. And they want it to be clear to all Mozambicans that it is not the government but foreign NGOs that keep them alive and help them to develop. It is a direct attack on the power and credibility of the Mozambican government, and of Frelimo.

Some NGOs "use the donations channelled through them to spread a religious message or their own policy on development", complained Dr Ratilal, the former emergency head. "Aid is ultimately tied to a particular doctrine and interest" (Ratilal 1990a: 196, 200). Some of the large religious NGOs give priority treatment to members; a major charity, for example, would only support a small irrigation project if church members were given preferential access. Some use their aid to proselytize; they bring in missionaries under the guise of aid staff, distribute bibles, build churches, and give out food and clothing at the end of church services.

Local NGOs

As part of their anti-government bias, donor NGOs try to work with local NGOs. This is a particular problem in Mozambique, where there have been only a handful of local NGOs. Mozambique may be an extreme case, but it is an issue elsewhere in Africa as well. The NGO answer is simply to set up NGOs in Mozambique. US policy is to "encourage PVOs [NGOs] to help strengthen or initiate counterpart indigenous NGOs" (USAID 1990b: 58).

The argument is justified in terms of popular participation and accountability, which is good in principle. Yet it seems strange coming from NGOs which are accountable to no one except the donor government which provides the contracts, and which rarely have any democratic structure of their own. Moreover, the NGOs they create in Mozambique will clearly have to accept what their parent donor NGO says, or they will lose their foreign funding. Thus these "Mozambican" NGOs will be subsidiaries of foreign NGOs, just as some Mozambican businesses are subsidiaries of foreign firms.

Nevertheless, some Mozambicans have noticed that the foreign NGOs working in Mozambique are not normally grassroots organizations. Rather, they are autonomous groups created by a few prominent people, which are usually close enough to their governments to obtain substantial funding from that source. Mozambique had already begun to follow this route and create local NGOs on the Western model, from the top down and headed by the local equivalent of "the great and the good". Thus they have a great deal of autonomy, but still reflect Frelimo priorities.

By the mid-1980s, a few such NGOs were active. Undoubtedly the most successful is the General Union of Cooperatives, which grew out of the Maputo green zones project. Initially subordinate to the city council, it grew to be an independent, national, grassroots body which both promotes the welfare of its members and promotes the government's policies on cooperatives. It serves as a pressure group for cooperatives, as well as a service body. The Christian Council, a grouping of Protestant churches sympathetic to Frelimo, also grew in importance and took on a significant emergency role.

Because of the demand by foreign NGOs for local partners, Mozambique is setting up further NGOs on the Western model. Janet Mondlane, the widow of Frelimo's first president, took over as head of the Mozambican Red Cross in 1987; she effectively and publicly established it as a pro-government alternative to the local representation of the International Committee for the Red Cross (ICRC). Marcelina Chissano, the wife of the President, has set up an Office of the First Lady. Graça Machel, the widow of Frelimo's second president, is Executive Director of the Community Development Association, which was set up in 1990. Several special interest NGOs have emerged, including associations of diabetics and of the handicapped.

Finally, Frelimo has made clear that the "mass organizations" of women, youth, workers, and so on will have to become independent. The party will no longer be able to provide funds; members will need to replace the party hacks that dominate the leadership. Some of these will simply wither and die without party backing, but others, such as the workers' organization, could find a role as an NGO representing their members' interests.

Although many foreign NGOs would like to see their Mozambican counterparts become implementing and development agencies, as alternatives to the government, local NGOs seem unlikely to be able to build up the capacity to do that in the near future. It seems more likely that their role will be to put pressure on the government to carry out official policy towards cooperatives, rural development, the handicapped, and so on, and to push government to provide the resources, extensions workers, and the like.

Flaunting power

Mozambicans are slowly setting up NGOs, but foreign NGOs are moving much faster. They are flaunting their new wealth and power, and in a very public way displacing the Mozambican government. One NGO was using money from a global allocation from its parent government. Mozambique objected to the NGO not following government guidelines, so the NGO simply withdrew on short notice, abandoning its project, and took the money to another country.

The issue is perhaps clearest within the health sector. Renamo has shattered the rural health network which Mozambique is trying to rebuild, but IMF funding limitations prevent Mozambique from rebuilding health posts and hiring doctors unless they are funded by donors. Mozambique's health service still has the commitment and administrative capacity to operate good rural facilities, if funds were made available. Instead, donors give the money to NGOs.

In the emergency appeal in April 1989, the government asked for $4.2 mn ($£2.5$ mn) to rehabilitate health posts, provide vital medicines and transport, and help children. Donors provided only three-quarters of this, leading to severe drug shortages in many areas. But $16 mn ($£9.6$ mn) was allocated to NGO projects that Mozambique did not ask for; the EC was the biggest donor of unrequested health projects, while not providing any funds for emergency health projects proposed by the government (*Priority Requirements*, 30 April 1990).

As a result, at least six different teams of flying doctors were working with displaced people. Mozambique has three objections to this. First is use of resources. Airplanes and foreign doctors are very expensive, and for a similar amount of money Mozambican health workers could be put in more places providing health care to more displaced people. Even if security is a problem and medical staff must fly in, the government would prefer it to be Mozambican doctors and nurses. But NGOs will only use their planes for their own staff.

Second is that these NGOs are providing a short-term emergency health service rather than building up a Mozambican one; when they think the emergency is over they will go away, leaving no health provision behind. Several of the NGOs providing this service bring in young and often inexperienced doctors for only six months at a time. Thus they never learn Portuguese and do not follow government guidelines; there is no continuity of care.

Third, some of the flying doctors refuse to even liaise with the government. They fly to towns without advance notice, bring in medicines not on the national restricted drugs list, and do nutrition surveys without giving the government the results. Mozambique has cajoled some of the flying doctors into better cooperation, but it has no real power over them.

In areas where they are working, this new breed of NGO doctors are displacing the government health service, and setting up an independent one. In effect they are creating a new form of the old mission hospitals.

Who brings the food?

Increasingly, donors are giving food aid and transport to NGOs rather than the government. A US embassy official told me that since early 1989 "we have been very eager to get PVOs [NGOs] into the distribution of food". Mozambican agencies and the UN are becoming more open in their objections to this. The government news agency AIM noted in mid-1990 that "certain other donors, most notably the United States, have been trying to marginalize the DPCCN, and are insisting on the distribution of food aid by their own non-governmental organizations, a procedure which some of the United Nations staff in Maputo consider extremely inefficient." This was a reference to the World Food Programme, which had just pointedly and very publicly given a large food donation to the DPCCN. Mark Latham, WFP head in Maputo, said that the donation is a "recognition of the ability of the Mozambican government to use this assistance effectively" (MIO 15 June 1990).

In one instance in 1990, an NGO was given food which was assigned to only one district. According to government officials there were only 1450 displaced people in the district, who would normally receive 10.5 kg each per month – a total of just over 15 tonnes. Over a three-month period, the NGO brought in 420 tonnes of maize and gave it out free to nearly everyone in the district, most of whom were producing their own food. The government was appalled: it destroyed incentives to produce and totally destroyed the agricultural marketing campaign in the district. If people were getting free food, why should they produce extra to sell?

In 1989, an NGO had money for an airlift to one district, and had its own plane. Funds had run out for airlifts to adjoining districts, and people were starving. But the NGO refused to divert its plane to serve other districts, even though the people in "its" district already had enough food. If the donor had given the money to Mozambique instead of to an NGO, it would have been much more wisely used, and saved more lives.

In a third case, the DPCCN had food for a district but no transport. An NGO known to be hostile to Frelimo had lorries provided by its parent government. The NGO said it would transport the food only if it could have exclusive rights to the district. It would transport *and distribute* the food. And it would also take over agricultural support. An NGO more sympathetic to Frelimo had been distributing seeds and tools through the government, but it would have to withdraw; the other NGO would instead distribute seeds and tools itself. The provincial government was unhappy and angry, but the NGO stressed that it had the lorries and the government didn't. Furthermore, the NGO was prepared to let people starve if its conditions were not met.

In some cases, church groups are giving assistance only to the members. As one aid official commented, "if DPCCN was selective in that way, it would cause an international scandal." In other cases NGOs were acting without informing the government. In March 1990 at a meeting of the CENE Emergency Operations Committee, DPCCN directors from five provinces appealed for help. They reported that NGOs were ignoring agreements signed with government, and were totally out of control. NGOs were putting people into the districts without notice, staking a claim to that terrain, and effectively displacing the government. NGOs were distributing food and medicines without even informing the DPCCN, in some cases duplicating DPCCN deliveries. It made any kind of rational planning impossible, and meant some hungry people went without food while others received too much.

NGOs are also using their power to control the flow of information. A journalist told me that an NGO which controlled the only flights to a district town in Zambézia said it would fly him there only if he agreed to do a puff piece about the NGO. "They were quite open about it", he said. "And I refused."

What role for the new missionaries?

Northern NGOs are "even more prone – with a few exceptions – to bypass their Mozambican NGO and civil society counterparts than government agencies are to bypass the Mozambican government", notes Professor Reginald Green, of the Institute of Development Studies and an adviser to the Mozambican government. "NGOs may well be part of the answer, but only if it is recognized that they are today a not insignificant part of the problem." (Green 1990b)

At their best, NGOs are flexible, imaginative, useful, and boost government efforts. More often, they are arrogant, corrupt, incompetent, and undercut government. Of course Mozambique has gained from some NGO projects. But an equal number have done permanent damage. And most have been useless.

One of six windmills installed by an NGO in the Pemba green zone. None still work and they have been abandoned. (J. Hanlon)

What would NGOs leave behind if they packed their bags now? A food aid distribution system that Mozambicans cannot administer. Hand pumps that break and cannot be fixed. Windmills that don't work. Handfuls of peasants who expect one-to-one agricultural extension from foreigners. In other words, hundreds of collapsed small projects. On balance, NGOs have probably done more harm than good in Mozambique.

Most NGOs are depressing mixes of good and bad. In my studies, I did not find one NGO with an unblemished record. And even the worst one had a few good projects. But Mozambique has little choice. Donors increasingly insist on NGOs. In part it is a political problem. NGOs have created such a good reputation for themselves at home that to keep them out would look exactly like not wanting to help the poor. Furthermore, keeping out right-wing church groups would bring an outcry – "godless Marxists" – and the hostile publicity might reduce bilateral aid.

Donors are increasingly channelling funds through NGOs. Such NGOs are simply contractors, and are no different from private companies, cooperatives, consulting companies, and individuals who execute contracts in Mozambique. In part they are doing jobs because of the arrogance and racism of bilateral donors who do not trust Mozambicans to carry out the projects.

More than anything else, however, the NGO bias is part of the anti-government privatization ethic of the large donors. Whether they agree or not, NGOs are being used to weaken and bypass the Mozambican government. As Mozambique becomes poorer, even progressive NGOs and solidarity groups increasingly need funds if they are to be of any use. But the need to raise money from governments means that progressive NGOs must be careful what they say and do. It is a restricted and unsympathetic milieu in which to work.

This chapter starts with a quote about NGOs being the "new missionaries", and this may be the best way to see their role. Some of the biggest of the NGOs are religious groups and are, in fact, the old missionaries. But even the non-religious NGOs are much like the missionaries of a century ago. They are individuals and small groups with a genuine dedication and commitment to help the people. They represent a wide range of interests and do health and development work as a way of promoting those interests. They are "opening up" Mozambique and they are being followed by agents of the new colonialism. As before, there is competition between the missionaries.

The old missionaries did important and often progressive work. In both Mozambique and Zimbabwe, for example, some missionaries supported the liberation struggles. In Latin America, missionaries played a role in the development of liberation theology.

The NGO new missionaries can also play a progressive role in Mozambique. But they will only do so if they understand that they are, indeed, missionaries who have been sent to Mozambique as part of the recolonizing mission.

Missionaries from Mozambique?

Perhaps the most useful role that progressive NGOs could play would be as missionaries *from* Mozambique rather than *to* Mozambique. In that form, their role would be to bring to Europe and North America the message that destabilization continues and that structural adjustment is wreaking havoc. Instead of reinforcing a false picture of "civil war", "black-on-black violence", and white people helping the benighted natives, the new missionaries could present a more accurate picture of Africans suffering at the hands of white recolonizers.

NGOs have not proved very successful as development agencies in Mozambique. But a few have proved very effective in campaigning at home for support for Mozambique. For example, NGO campaigns alerted the world to hunger in Mozambique and undoubtedly triggered more government and EC aid than the NGOs themselves could ever have hoped to provide. Similarly, NGO campaigns which stressed that destabilization continues, and which have publicized Renamo atrocities, have surely done Mozambique much more good than the tiny development projects those NGOs were carrying out in Mozambique.

NGOs have shown that they can change the views of their own governments, and in so doing generate much more help for Mozambique than they could ever provide themselves. Surely that is the vocation of the progressive new missionaries.

18 OK for Some

War, emergency, structural adjustment, and the aid invasion have widened class divisions and accelerated class formation. In Chapters 1 and 2, I pointed to the growth of two groups of what Frelimo called "aspirants to the bourgeoisie." The *state group,* sometimes also called the "nomenclatura", is composed of directors and higher level state officials whose power comes through control of state resources. The *commercial group* of farmers and traders gained in the early 1980s from the black market and from the privatization of shops and farms. To these must be added a new *comprador group* which depends on foreign interests for its wealth and power. These groups are not well defined, are shifting over time, and often overlap.

As the economy was squeezed in the early 1980s, the state group was increasingly defined by its access to goods and other privileges. As the bulk of the population found life ever harder, this group was cushioned and often improved its living standards. Directors with state-supplied Ladas did not have to worry about the city bus that never came because there were no bus tyres. Officials could send their children to party schools and had access to military hospitals or special wards. A string of special shops opened to supply goods that ordinary people could only find on the black market; increasing numbers of officials were given foreign currency and access to the Loja Franca – the hard currency shop.

There had been a traditional view that "chiefs should eat first". President Samora Machel used this as part of his nation-building project. He argued that people expected their leaders to be well dressed, and to live properly. He insisted that the new national leaders were to have the traditional status and respect. Thus the highest official always entered the room last, and everyone stood when the official entered. This was true at all levels; students stood when the teacher entered the room, and journalists stood when a minister entered a press conference.

Similarly, it was only sensible that high state officials could not be expected to work 12-hour days if they also had to queue for bread and buses. Initially, no one objected, because Frelimo maintained an attitude of common sacrifice; privilege was paired with puritanism. Ministers and high officials lived modestly and were manifestly honest. They did not abuse their positions; they were not getting rich and building grand houses.

But this began to change, at first imperceptibly and then, by the mid-1980s, quite blatantly. Privilege and class division grew from what was at first seen as nation building and a necessity for the functioning of the state. A class division that had been hidden was now clear.

Privatization of small state and intervened businesses had started in 1980, and it accelerated after the Fourth Congress. As declared policy, former state farms and other parcels of land were to be given to larger farmers who already had tractors, or at least oxen, on the grounds that they could get more rapid results. This, too, accelerated class divisions.

An important change in the mid-1980s was the realization by some in the state group that the state itself was no longer the most sensible means of accumulation. Some ministers, directors, and civil servants began to acquire farms for themselves, or to use their families to establish businesses, so that they had a foot in both commercial and state camps. There were fierce battles over land in the Limpopo valley and in the green zone around the capital, with private farmers, high officials, and cooperatives all fighting for prime farmland.

Frelimo encouraged party or state officials and army officers to move into farming and private business; Frelimo's statutes, which as a Marxist-Leninist party had banned members from employing wage labour, were liberalized to allow this. Three reasons were given. First, with the growing shortage of food, it was argued that everyone had a responsibility to produce. "Bearing in mind the need to make use of the organizational capacity that party members possess for increasing food production, all restrictions concerning the number of workers they may employ should be lifted" (Frelimo 1989a). Second, Samora Machel had begun a programme to retire former guerrillas who were now ineffective as army officers; they were given land, funds to set up businesses, and other preferences. Third, it was argued that with donors promoting the private sector, it was better that Frelimo supporters had a firm foothold there and that the private sector not be left to its enemies.

With the justification afforded by all these quite valid reasons, the nomenclatura was using its access to state power as a way to expand into the commercial sector.

The role of aid

Class differentiation was already well under way by the mid-1980s, but the arrival of the aid industry significantly accelerated the process. There are three different aspects. First, the imposition of structural adjustment and privatization widens class divisions and supports the emerging bourgeoisie. Second, the aid industry, and to a lesser extent foreign companies, have become a major source of wealth and highly paid employment. Third, and not to be underestimated, is a social factor. The thousands of foreigners in the aid industry have set new standards of consumption for the Mozambican elite.

Structural adjustment in Mozambique has made the poor poorer and ensured that the new elite is much better off. The new free market, with the general removal of price controls, means that some traders and business people are wealthy by Mozambican standards. Top government salaries have risen faster than inflation, while those of the worst off have not. There are goods in the shops on which to spend the money, and the loosening of import controls means that luxury goods are available for those with more money. A full page advertisement in the daily *Noticias* (8 June 1990) offered colour television sets for sale for 1.5 mn meticais ($1600 or £960 at the official exchange rate) – roughly 100 times the minimum monthly wage.

IMF restrictions on government spending on health and education, together with the Fifth Congress's lifting of restrictions on private health and education, point the way to a class-based two-tier system of social services. The new Unicef–World Bank emphasis on "social dimensions of adjustment" stresses a charity approach. Selected groups of poor people are targeted for help. Food subsidies will only be allowed on less desirable foods. Free medicines are no longer a right, but are paid for from a fund for the deserving poor. All of this points to the creation of an underclass which is the recipient of charity.

As so often in Mozambique, the US is the most upfront about its intervention. Its import support programme is only to help the private sector, and its main programme has been importing tractors to sell to larger private farmers. US support for privatization means higher salaries for people who switch from being managers in the state sector to working in the private sector.

The whole structural adjustment process particularly benefited a small group which had been able to accumulate during the hard times of the early 1980s, mainly traders and private farmers and fishermen who had been able to take full advantage of the black market. They were able to use their ill-gotten gains to take over land, buy USAID tractors, acquire boats, and in other ways consolidate their position for the new period of legal free market trade. To a lesser extent, those peasants who were already better off were also able to take advantage of the changes.

Donor dollars

The aid community pumped dollars into the economy. They illegally sublet houses and flats and paid in dollars, sometimes into Portuguese bank accounts. They bought fish and other items on the black market, and paid dollars. And, of course, they changed money on the black market.

But the biggest and most divisive impact was the way in which they bought up scarce trained people and pushed wages up dramatically. Everyone who had regular dealings with the aid community was given dollars. Part of the pay of drivers, gardeners, and servants was in dollars. Many Mozambican staff of aid agencies received a "food basket" – either a direct cash payment, or the right to buy a certain amount (usually not including liquor and cigarettes) from the Loja Franca. Higher officials were given top-ups in dollars, or were given consultancy contracts paid in dollars. If they travelled abroad, they were always given a hefty per diem in dollars; sometimes they were even given hard currency per diems for attending meetings in Mozambique. Most of this was legal, or at least acceptable. But it was totally unregulated; officials even did consultancies related to their normal work where there was a clear conflict of interest.

"The winners are the aid agencies", comments Professor Reginald Green, because they are giving consultancies to buy civil servants' time for their own, and not the governments', priorities. In so doing, the aid agencies "are rapidly decapacitating the Mozambican government and public service" (Green 1990b).

Wage differentials reached absurd levels. A UN official told me his driver received $250 (£150) per month ($150 plus $20 per child up to five children) in dollars, plus 30,000 MT (then equivalent to about $30 or £18); a government minister at that time earned the equivalent of only $180 (£110) per month.

Although some officials just took consultancies, many shifted over to the aid sector. Highly trained Bank of Mozambique officials became UN secretaries, a DPCCN logistics coordinator was hired by an NGO, an absolutely essential ministry budget official joined an NGO as an accountant for five times his former salary, and so on. One NGO ran a half-page recruitment advertisement in *Noticias* offering "good salaries and job security" but demanding the ability to speak English plus various other qualifications; only higher-level government staff would have qualified. Some donors, including the World Bank, paid skilled local staff more than $3000 (£1800) per month – low by international standards but a fortune in Mozambique – to attract national directors to their projects. At the craziest level, the World Bank would hire a director who had a skill which could not be replaced easily, and then send him back to his old job, always reminding him he now worked for the World Bank and not the government. The growing private sector is also attracting people from government service by paying very high salaries.

A government minister told me: "The state is losing its capacity. The best directors are leaving to be paid in dollars, while the worst – the bureaucratic and inefficient – stay. This is very dangerous, but the World Bank and IMF are happy." The Mozambican response has been to introduce its own top-up programme, in which high officials and technicians receive $100-200 per month plus a car to stay in their present jobs. It is paid for with aid funds from a sympathetic donor. With consultancies and other perks, highly skilled people can earn significant amounts and still stay in government. It is still much less than they could earn working for the donors, but it is enough to keep people in government; before the top-up began, even militants began to feel they were stupid to stay in government and have to take a second job in order to feed their families.

"The serious tendency for cadres to leave the state apparatus to seek jobs in companies and in international organizations has merited special attention", the Central Committee told the Frelimo Fifth Congress. Therefore "a conscious choice" has been made to "provide benefits for cadres and leading figures. By giving them privileges in relation to the workers as a whole, these measures seek to preserve the quality and motivation of these people who are key for the proper functioning of the entire apparatus" (Frelimo 1989a). The 1990 state plan revealed this would include higher salaries and access to the Loja Franca.

This creates serious heart searching on the part of old Frelimo militants and their supporters, and it is one of many unresolvable contradictions in Mozambique today. The new high state salaries clearly accelerate differentiation, but what else can be done once there is a free labour market and foreigners have what seems like unlimited funds to buy staff?

Different standards

As well as bringing money, the aid industry brought very different life styles. In the first years after independence, Frelimo leaders had a standard of living that was almost spartan compared to those in other African countries, while few people in the private sector were conspicuously rich. Initially cooperantes had Mozambican salaries and lived only a bit better than the Mozambican middle class; indeed, many consciously tried to avoid displays of wealth that would set them apart from Mozambicans. Diplomats and UN experts lived the luxury expatriate lifestyle, but there were few enough of them and they spent most of their time in Maputo; they did not really create a model for the Mozambican elite. For many outside Maputo, television and video recorders were the height of luxury, and the illegal import of videos by a network of private traders made front page news.

The economic crisis of the early 1980s made the first changes. Even cooperantes were forced to go to the foreign currency shop to buy essentials. I can remember when I first arrived in Mozambique, I could be invited to a Mozambican house for dinner and invite Mozambicans to my house in return. By 1982 Mozambicans were embarrassed to invite foreigners home, because food was short, there was no beer, etc. Middle-class lifestyles had been hit hard by destabilization and the growing economic crisis, and the differentials between foreigners and their Mozambican counterparts were much more noticeable.

The gap widened dramatically with the aid invasion. These were professional expatriates who expected a high standard of living wherever they worked; this was their job and they were not making sacrifices to help the poor and hungry. A tiny group of 3000 foreign technicians earns an incredible $180 mn (£109 mn) per year, according to Finance Minister Magid Osman (MIO 21 February 1991). Salaries are as high as $25,000 per month, he said, and this all comes out of Mozambique's foreign aid and technical assistance grants. The wage bill of this tiny group is three times the wage bill of the entire Mozambican civil service of 100,000 people, including teachers and health workers. It is also equivalent to 15% of Mozambique's entire gross domestic product.

There is a definable expatriate lifestyle set by people who are no longer committed to Mozambique in particular, but might be living and working anywhere in the Third World. Nightclubs and good restaurants charging dollars have opened; the yacht club has come back to life.

To make regular visits to Mozambique as I did was to watch a physical transformation, not just in Maputo but in provincial capitals as well. There were more cars on the streets. Mozambican friends began to acquire stereos and, in Maputo, TVs. Where the odd beer had been the middle-class norm, now there was wine and whiskey. Clothing and food improved for the middle classes. But how did this happen? A surprising amount was linked to aid. Most of the cars were donor or diplomatic cars, although often supplied to government officials. The stereos and whisky were often gifts of donors, or bought on foreign trips paid by donors.

The donors brought with them European and US lifestyles, with salaries to match, at a time when most Mozambicans are either subsistence farmers or refugees partly dependent on handouts. The gap is huge and, in the short term, unbridgeable. Donors transformed expectations, and government bureaucrats increasingly aim for the same standard of living as aid workers. The Mozambican elite depends on donors for both its values and its resources.

Many Mozambicans (as well as the early cooperantes) had been prepared to make significant sacrifices to build the new Mozambique. Now, like the new aid workers, they have realized that development takes a long time and they feel they deserve an advance on the good life now.

A Mozambican official commented to me: "We Mozambicans are sometimes a bit slow. And it has taken us a long time to learn. But we have finally learned from you the first rule of development: that you must have a house and a car, whisky and a stereo, before you can start to help the peasants."

When self-interest and policy coincide

Some Mozambicans are now openly in support of widening class divisions. They argue that a bourgeoisie is essential for development. "When we started PRE we also started the market economy, and with the market economy comes inequality between people. Standard of living varies according to the location people have in the market," said Finance Minister Magid Osman (*Domingo* 3 June 1990).

He stressed that "Mozambique needs an elite of entrepreneurs who feel that society values their importance." And he backs high salaries, luxury cars, and other perks to keep highly skilled technicians in government because there is intense competition for trained people. But he warns that "the current tendency is towards the creation of a class based on dubious business deals, and which requests various kinds of 'bonuses' and protectionism from the state, to the detriment of the consumer. In my opinion, the creation of a large, dynamic, and enterprising Mozambican entrepreneurial class is essential" (Osman 1990).

Structural adjustment is in the personal interest of officials at the middle and higher levels, and of ministers. If they do what the IMF says is good for Mozambique, they help themselves, so why should they question those orientations? It is hardly surprising that debate is sometimes suppressed, or that officials fail to look for alternatives. The IMF tells them that greed is good, and that by looking after number one they are actually helping the people. As Graham Hancock comments, for government officials "structural adjustment is like a dream come true. No sacrifices are demanded of them personally. All they have to do – amazing but true – is *screw the poor*, and they've already had plenty of practice at that" (Hancock 1989: 60).

Structural adjustment and aid give some groups substantial power to implement policies in their own class interests: rents, salaries, land distribution, and even specific aid projects. It had long been apparent that rents did not even cover the maintenance costs on the blocks of flats which had been nationalized at independence. With the post-1984 economic crisis and the need to cut subsidies, an obvious target was that very small percentage of the population who by luck lived in nationalized rented property.

The question was how to implement rent increases. The system introduced was similar to the one used in colonial times and in capitalist countries. Rent was to be based purely on the flat or house itself, considering size, age, location, and condition. Flats with sea views or in preferred neighbourhoods would be more expensive. Previously rents had been based on a fixed portion of salary; now this was no longer an issue. Even the UK has a system of rent reductions for the low-paid, but this was not to be in socialist Mozambique. The reasoning was obvious: housing was tight in Maputo and the new high rents would force out poor workers, leaving sea-view flats for the nomenclatura.

In fact, other interests moved faster. A World Bank rehabilitation programme was predicated on the assumption that if people had to leave buildings because they could not pay the rent, then those buildings could be rehabilitated to a higher standard and rented out to foreigners paying in forex. When the new rent levels were finally set, however, they were not as high as people had expected, probably because middle-level flat-dwelling civil servants had succeeded in defending their own interests.

In setting salary scales, the state group again looked after itself. Higher salaries were closely tied to academic qualifications, which clearly benefits top civil servants over others. The Frelimo Fifth Congress was forced to note that "within wages policy, in addition to academic qualifications, professional experience should be taken into consideration. Frequently this has not been given its due value" (Frelimo 1989b). In other words, the upper classes received much higher wage increases than skilled workers.

The trade unions complained that the biggest wage rises were going to the bosses and "to the minority not linked to the production of material goods". And it warned that those who had received big rises might slip into "thinking that the economy is growing when in fact it is declining" (OTM 1989). The UN confirmed that statistics showing growth in per capita consumption should be treated with caution because they "are excessively influenced by the relative weight of higher income urban consumers, neglecting the stagnating or even declining consumption patterns of large groups of Mozambican population" (UNDP 1989a: 16).

There is growing evidence that the Frelimo leadership is losing touch with its base, and may now be so cushioned that it does not realize how badly the poor are squeezed. One hint of this came at the opening of an electricity generating station, where a government minister told a mass meeting of local people: "Now you can have cold beer in your refrigerators." Only a handful of people in the audience could afford beer; even fewer had fridges.

Aid funds are sometimes used for luxury consumption. A loan and technical assistance from China was used to set up The Sheik, an exclusive Chinese restaurant and nightclub in Maputo. A joint World Bank and French loan for $8 mn (£5 mn) was used to buy 243 Peugeot taxis and 270 minibuses (*Noticias* 8 June 1990). Both will transport relatively few people at a high standard; a larger number of cheaper and simpler vehicles would have provided better public transport, but the Peugeots will be more comfortable for the officials who took the decisions.

Cars are a special status symbol and an obsession. The Council of Ministers has had extended secret debates about what model cars should be given to different levels of directors. Scarce foreign exchange has been allocated to import them. And high officials have given themselves the right to buy these cars at a low price.

The new compradors

Within the growing upper strata, the new comprador group is gaining a special role. Because foreigners control virtually all hard currency resources, and large slabs of meticais as well, advancement for a Mozambican demands an alliance with a foreigner.

Even progressive, committed Frelimo officials must build good relations with donors if they are to undertake any kind of development. The government has no money of its own; every tractor, lorry, car, seed or hoe comes from a donor. Inevitably, Mozambican officials must think in terms of donors and projects, and of satisfying donor demands.

What bureaucrat would turn down a project which would provide him with the resources to do rural development and thus benefit the peasants, and at the same time give him foreign travel, a car and a higher standard of living? Increasingly, the quality or suitability of the project and whether or not it satisfies national goals and norms become immaterial in comparison to the resources on offer.

As we have already seen, many in the growing Mozambican elite have left the government to work directly for the aid donors. If there is a growth in foreign investment, then it will be TNCs and smaller South African and Portuguese firms that will provide the better paid jobs and perks.

The aid industry, structural adjustment, and privatization have forced a level of class and wealth difference unprecedented in post-independence Mozambique. And there is a new comprador group whose social and economic standing is entirely dependent on foreigners. If the donors leave, then this group loses the resources that give it political power, as well as the means to maintain its living standard. Thus this new comprador group has a vested interest in the donors staying and in the continuation of IMF involvement, privatization, and structural adjustment.

Who benefits?

"Frelimo and the people of Mozambique shared a dream", a friend told me. "That dream had a lot of power. People sacrificed and suffered together. When there wasn't much food, we all ate the same thing. Now the dream has collapsed. The chiefs eat better, and have something to lose. We no longer share the same goals and the same experience."

Class divisions are widening, and class struggles are intensifying. Mozambicans are increasingly looking at just who is benefiting. The Fourth Congress pointed to "citizens originating from social strata that were already privileged in the colonial period", and they have gained ground since; it is another aspect of the recolonization process. In rural areas, those who had bigger farms before independence have been able to obtain land and hire landless refugees. Sérgio Vieira, director of the Centre of African Studies, notes that it is largely former settlers who have benefited from USAID tractors.

In its report to the Fifth Congress, Frelimo's Central Committee had to admit that many of those who now had high state posts had been privileged before independence. Those with the highest academic qualifications (who by "conscious choice" had received wage increases vastly above those of ordinary workers) "come from regions where colonialism ensured a greater implantation of its political and administrative domination" and thus some Mozambicans in those areas had access to better schooling. "A further section of those in leading positions was constituted by cadres of European or Indian origin, or by people of mixed race" who had greater access to training during colonial times, the Central Committee admitted (Frelimo 1989a).

In 1989 and 1990 this led to an upsurge of black nationalism and northern regionalism. This was fuelled particularly by black Mozambicans from Zambézia and Nampula provinces who felt they were being kept out of high-salaried jobs by white and Indian Mozambicans, as well as by black Mozambicans from the Gaza and Maputo provinces. In 1990 there was even an unsuccessful attempt to define Mozambican nationality in such a way as to exclude non-blacks, and at the same time to try to block non-Mozambicans from owning property – a quite transparent attempt by one part of the emerging bourgeoisie to marginalize another part.

Initially there was little opposition to the growth and consolidation of elite groups. But that has ended. The strikes and riots of 1990 showed that working people were no longer prepared to be squeezed to satisfy the new comprador-donor alliance. Workers in the ports, sugar plantations, and elsewhere showed they have reached their limit.

The late 1980s also saw the petty bourgeoisie become an identifiable and different group. This includes the vast majority of civil servants who are not directors and not part of the nomenclatura. In the first years of independence, they gained in prestige and status; leaders like Samora Machel (a former nurse) came from this group, and they identified closely with Frelimo. But they have been badly hit both by the war and by PRE. These are the teachers, nurses and clerks whose living standards have been badly squeezed. Students have also become a leading force in this group.

Teachers and nurses, in particular, were the vanguard of the social services that made Frelimo popular, and striking teachers gained wide popular support. If teachers and nurses blame Frelimo for their falling wages (and Frelimo has, after all, told Mozambicans that PRE is its programme) and turn against Frelimo in the elections, they could be a potent force.

Will this petty bourgeoisie side with the state group in an attempt to retain relative privilege, or will it ally with the workers?

So far, this group seems to taking the first choice. For example, striking nurses turned their anger not on government officials, but on the patients; in the January 1990 strike nurses actually blockaded Maputo Central Hospital. Another indication is the intermittent demand of the petty bourgeoisie that they not be taken to work in the same buses as manual workers, but have separate transport. The new Peugeot minibuses, the relatively small rent increases, and a September 1990 supplementary budget with extra money for civil service salaries can be read as attempts by the state group to placate the petty bourgeoisie.

There are also sharpening rural class divisions, with a growing number of landless labourers and peasants marginalized by PRE. When the war ends and refugees return home there will be bitter battles over land. There are also likely to be battles with foreign investors. It is notable that in the debate over the new constitution overwhelming popular pressure forced Frelimo to withdraw proposals allowing the sale of land, and to maintain the national ownership of land. Ordinary people felt that their access to land was better protected by state ownership, while the elite supported privatization.

Another question is what will happen when thousands of demobbed soldiers and returned Renamo fighters join the unemployed in the city and the landless in rural areas.

There have been some very rapid shifts in class formation, alliances, and divisions; the position remains volatile and it is too early to predict an outcome. But three important changes in the upper stratum can be underlined. One is the emergence of a comprador group which needs the continuation of aid and investment and thus supports recolonization. Also important is the move of the state group into commercial activity, often using its base in the state as a springboard. Third is the growth in conflict within the elite, initially expressed in terms of race, but likely to lead to the emergence of contending parties.

19 Lead Us Not into Temptation

Soon after Nigel Lawson retired as Chancellor of the Exchequer (finance minister) of Britain, he took a £100,000 per year part-time job with Barclays Bank. As Chancellor, Lawson had been responsible for bank regulation. Margaret Thatcher, former Prime Minister of Britain, is married to a wealthy businessman with business interests in countries affected by foreign policy once determined by his wife; for their retirement he bought them a house in the London suburb of Dulwich. In Mozambique, a man who spent 10 years in the bush fighting for independence and 15 years as a government minister, and who now has no property and no pension, has been given a farm by the government. He has also received materials to build a house for his retirement.

All of these ministers are trying to ensure that their final years are comfortable after they retire from arduous public service. Are any of them guilty of corruption?

More than half of all new cars in the UK are company cars. That is, they are bought by companies for their staff to use on company business. It is widely accepted that these cars are taken home at night and on weekends, where they are used for shopping and other family purposes. In Mozambique, many aid workers are provided with cars in order to carry out their jobs; most use those cars for shopping and weekend travel. In the evening, a provincial hospital director takes her children to the beach in a car provided to the hospital by a UN agency.

Are any of these people corrupt?

When I was on the staff of a magazine, I used the magazine's telephone and its paper and typewriter to do freelance articles. Everyone on the staff did so. Professionals and office workers normally make personal telephone calls from work, use the office photocopier for party invitations, put a few personal letters in the office post, etc. I watched a man in a ragged shirt unloading sacks of aid flour in Quelimane. Each time he returned to the lorry he scooped up a handful of spilled flour and put it in a small basket at his feet. At night, he took the basket home to help feed his family.

Are any of us corrupt?

Developed and underdeveloped corruption

The US government is being forced to pay an incredible $325 billion (£195 bn) to bail out the savings and loan institutions (building societies) after deregulation led to widespread and massive corruption. Fraud and corruption are "pervasive" in the US Savings & Loan industry, according to FBI Director William Sessions (*Guardian* 13 April 1990, *Financial Times* 7 April 1990).

Workers unload sacks of flour from a lorry on the quay in Quelimane (Left). Each time he returns from carrying a sack, one man scoops up a handful of spilled flour and puts it in a basket behind the wheel of an adjacent lorry (Right). Is this corruption? (J. Hanlon)

A university study estimated that over a decade Italian public officials and their business allies misappropriated 400 trillion Lira ($28 bn, £17 bn). Trillions of Lira for earthquake reconstruction have gone astray, some of it to build luxury seaside villas (*Observer*, 15 January 1989). The London and New York stock exchanges have been hit by scandals involving hundreds of millions of dollars. The US CIA has been deeply involved in international drug trading.

In the Third World, local corruption is as underdeveloped as the economies, while big corruption is necessarily linked to the industrialized world. The biggest form of Third World corruption must be transfer pricing, in which transnational corporations cook the books of their subsidiaries in theThird World; they overcharge for goods they sell to their own subsidiary and underpay for what they buy, and then they tell the government that they lost money for the year and need pay no taxes and cannot afford to raise wages. We have all read numerous tales of bribes, kickbacks, and Swiss bank accounts; but this requires the agreement of the company making the payment, and of the Swiss bank that allows the account to be established. The late President Marcos of the Philippines and the present President Mabuto of Zaire have been able to salt away hundreds of millions of dollars only because the US continued to provide economic and political support in exchange for military bases.

Corruption is very much part of our culture and history. We learn about it in our history books, read about it in novels, and see it on television programmes like Dallas. Many of our well-known corporations initially grew on theft, dishonesty and illegality. How many American family fortunes were founded on bootlegging during prohibition? A German UN official commented to me: "When you look at my country after the war, we were all black market dealers. Now we are all honourable businessmen." One of the most famous British writers, the seventeenth-century diarist Samuel Pepys, used his journals not only to note observations of his times, but also to record his sexual conquests and the large bribes he received as a navy purchasing officer (Latham 1970: cxxiv).

Corruption is deeply embedded in the fabric of the industrialized world. Not all corruption is large, however. In many places, if the dustman does not receive his annual Christmas present, then your dustbin is always left lying in the middle of the road. I lived in one city where planning applications were always submitted with $10 bills between the pages; officials would never violate the rules and allow an unacceptable building, but without the money to keep them reading they would never even consider the application. In many countries, buyers for large companies are given holidays, parties, and Christmas presents by suppliers. Glasnost has revealed widespread petty corruption in the USSR.

Corruption or perk?

Whether it is emolument, a perk, turning a blind eye, or full-blown corruption probably depends how high up in the hierarchy you are. For the managing director the house and car are included in the contract. For lower-level managers, the company car and executive lunches are recognized "perks". This is an abbreviation of "perquisite", which the *Concise Oxford Dictionary* defines as "casual profit additional to normal revenue or emolument; customary gratuity". Perks are so common that the word has entered normal English usage. For me and many like me, using the company telephone for personal calls is not a recognized perk; but our managers clearly turn a blind eye to reasonable use, and there would be outrage if this privilege was withdrawn. At a lower level still, building workers often take materials home; normally the blind eye applies, but sometimes there are outraged cries of "corruption and theft". The very use of the word "corruption" implies something different and, perhaps, more civilized than certain other crimes. We do not view corruption as seriously as mugging, street theft, or breaking into a building to steal the same things.

In drawing the line some offences are balanced against more serious ones. The magazine where I was able to do freelance work in the office had a clear rule: we could not write for competing magazines but only for those in other fields. Writing for a competing magazine was a sin which could get you dismissed; using the company telephone for freelance work was a perk institutionalized by years of the blind eye.

Corruption, perks, and the blind eye are endlessly fascinating precisely because our views are so confused and contradictory. How many church newsletters have been sent out through company post? Similarly, any discussion of corruption in Mozambique must be put into context.

End of Puritanism

After more than a decade of fighting colonial exploitation, Frelimo came to independence with very strict views on corruption. People were to be paid the right wage for the job. Tipping, even in restaurants, was ended. Cars were strictly for official use.

An army uprising in Maputo in 1975 was caused in part by demands of former guerrillas for special treatment in payment for their years in the bush. Some of the early defectors to Renamo were Frelimo officers who could not accept the new code of ethics. But for the most part the new morality held. Ministers and high government officials accepted that the new rules banning private renting of houses applied to them as well; they gave up their former homes and moved to government houses – in effect tied housing – without considering what would happen if they were dismissed or retired. When cooking oil or other essentials went short, ministers' households went short too.

To me, several examples typified the new morality. When I first arrived in Mozambique in 1979, the war with Rhodesia was still on and there were many military checkpoints on the roads. Soldiers carefully checked your documents and said you could pass. Only then did they ask for cigarettes. They made it clear that cigarettes were not a condition of passage. Indeed, as a non-smoker I did not carry cigarettes and always went on without a hassle. Similarly, soldiers often waited at checkpoints for lifts, but they never came up to you while you were having your documents checked – they always ran up as you were pulling off. The new morality meant that not only was there no corruption, but that people wanted to be seen to be squeaky clean.

An acquaintance bought electronic equipment for the army. Worldwide, this is an area of massive corruption and kickbacks, because the competition between international electronics companies is so fierce. Yet he lived in a normal army house. He had a stereo and tape deck, but they were old and partly hand made, and clearly not gifts from military suppliers. His modest living standard was both an end in itself and a reason, because if he suddenly produced a giant new stereo, all his friends would know he had not bought it on an army salary. That would have been totally unacceptable.

This was demonstrated by the suicide of Francisco Langa in 1980. Langa was one of Frelimo's earliest militants. He was a Central Committee member and was in charge of support for Zimbabwean refugees. He was, however, caught taking money from the refugee programme. In a remarkable communiqué, Frelimo praised him for his courage and for his contribution as chief of logistics in Tete during the liberation war. But it went on to tell of the embezzlement, and said that he when he was caught he was overcome with shame and committed suicide rather than face his comrades.

There were few other places where someone like Langa would have committed suicide, and where the ruling party would publicly say why. Langa's suicide and public anger at corruption showed that many people expected that at least the leadership should maintain the new morality. But Langa's suicide was really the end of an era. At the time Langa died a wide-ranging investigation into government corruption was already under way; more than 100 people had been arrested. There were other scandals, too, including one in the state housing agency that involved over-invoicing and forging documents. But even in the early 1980s, corruption was still relatively uncommon.

Perks and shortages

Shortages often create the first corruption. Frelimo tried to maintain fixed prices and ensure a reasonably wide distribution of scarce goods. But some people were prepared to pay extra, which created the black market; some people felt they deserved privileged access, which created perks. Special shops for party and government officials were opened in the cities. In rural areas the private wholesalers ensured that the district administrator and other officials had adequate supplies of oil, sugar, and other essentials; this was often in exchange for the district administrator turning a blind eye to the growing black market. I once hitched a lift with a trader who had a permit to carry a few sacks of maize across a provincial border to feed his workers in the next province. But the permit was undated, and I have no doubt that the district administrator knew it would be used over and over again.

The nature of perks changed, too. Many factory workers had a right to buy part of the output at wholesale prices, which had been a relatively minor perk. When goods became short, however, cloth or biscuits commanded high prices on the black market; workers could earn more than their official salary by selling their small allocation of goods.

Some forms of corruption involve patronage or family links. Flats are allocated to relatives rather than people on the waiting list. Scarce cement goes to a cousin who is building a house. The driver of a beer lorry who can no longer buy beer on the open market will inevitably keep a few bottles for himself and his friends; perhaps he can trade some beer for a chicken.

It is at this point that the free marketeers step in and argue that this corruption only exists because there is an allocation system. If things were sold on the open market there would be no black market and no informal allocation systems. This is true, but only up to a point. What happened in Mozambique was that allocation-based corruption was replaced by outright theft. For example, staff stole batteries out of lorries in company garages because they could be sold for so much.

In any case, it was deregulation and the lack of control that led to the savings and loan scandal in the US. Deregulation is a licence for corruption.

Finding enough money to live

From 1986 the economic crisis caused by the war and structural adjustment introduced a form of corruption increasingly evident in Africa and the Third World. Goods are no longer scarce, but no one has money. Few salaries are large enough to support a family. Nearly everyone needs additional income, and people find it in any way they can.

Those with access to resources use them; for example, state and company vehicles are used quite openly to carry paying passengers and goods, and as a result are often not available for their proper purpose. Anyone with access to tools or a workshop does private repairs and building work. Officials do freelance work and consultancies. Others, who cannot use work facilities to generate a second income, take time off to buy and sell, or to raise chickens. The problem is that some people spend more time arranging their second income than they do earning their first.

Those who can, steal. Sacks of aid food, crates of beer, cloth, and anything else which can be used or sold "falls off the back of the lorry". It is hard to criticize a DPCCN porter who steals a bit of food to feed his children.

Meanwhile, those who deal with the public begin to demand bribes; it is the only way they can earn enough.

Now big time

But corruption is not just handfuls of flour. Theft from the state and from the emergency programme has grown; the days of Langa's suicide and the Frelimo morality are gone.

People see corruption spreading around them in ways inconceivable a decade ago. A friend commented: "In my ministry we sell bread to the staff. Four small loaves a day cost one quarter of the minimum wage. People on that wage buy the bread. Where do they get the money? They must be corrupt or steal." Another index of corruption is alcohol consumption. A few middle-level government officials seem permanently drunk and spend their days in bars; others do their jobs, but every night spend more that a week's official salary swilling down expensive cans of South African beer. Where do they get the money? Some provincial directors show how far corruption has gone when they brazenly take things from government warehouses to sell.

At the armed forces' Frelimo party conference in June 1989, before the Fifth Congress, many soldiers and officers denounced corruption. "There is degradation and material corruption in the armed forces. There is abandonment of leadership of the troops [because] many high-level officers are busy with private business deals", complained Lt Patricio Gimo of the Frontier Guards. "How can an officer who wastes his time inspecting the fish in the market have any time for leading his troops?" And Lt Gimo went on to accuse some officers of having foreign bank accounts (*Mozambiquefile* June 1989). Corruption and diversion of supplies have become serious enough to affect the fighting capacity of some army units.

For many people, theft or diversion of emergency relief supplies was the most shocking form of corruption. In Zambézia it was reported that people starved because food aid was sold to traders (*Noticias* 10 June 1989). This was very unusual and extreme. What seems to occur is not large-scale thefts, but consistent skimming by various people in the distribution chain. Losses of food grain have clearly risen above the 10% to 15% that many donors consider normal and acceptable. Systematic looting of trains and major thefts from the ports have occurred; the army and militias are implicated.

UN officials dealing with the emergency cite two moderating factors. First, theft from ports is not unique to Mozambique, and widespread theft in their own ports was one of the factors that pushed European and US shippers into containerization. In general, aid is not containerized and it is unreasonable to expect Mozambique to be better able to police its ports than the US was in the pre-container days. Second, in a country as hungry as Mozambique, diverted food is not going to waste – it is being eaten. Nevertheless, food and other emergency aid is being diverted from its intended recipients in a systematic and not just a random or casual way.

It is particularly depressing that high Frelimo officials have been implicated in the thefts. One high official regularly took emergency goods while his wife had been sorting through donated clothes and taking out the best to sell. A high DPCCN official had been diverting food to a restaurant he owned. In one province, the governor and two-thirds of the district administrators were systematically diverting emergency supplies.

President Chissano condemned the theft of relief supplies, declaring that "we must end this evil." He stressed that "officials must enjoy the confidence of the people" (*Mozambiquefile* May 1989). But little has been done to encourage that confidence. The report of two commissions of enquiry was never published inside Mozambique, although it was distributed to donors ("Executive Summary", 1990). Many middle- and lower-level DPCCN officials have been tried or publicly dismissed for corruption, but so far no district administrators, governors, or high-level officials. The lack of prosecutions leads to rumours that corruption reaches to very high levels and that corrupt officials are being protected.

Although most of the discussion is over theft and diversion of emergency goods, two other forms of corruption are also growing. Although demands for bribes are not yet widespread, they are becoming much more common. Especially notable are demands for small bribes from low-paid civil servants, such as teachers.

The other area is use of influence to obtain contracts and property. Generals and high government officials have used their rank to demand farmland; in some instances peasants have been pushed off land so that officials can have it. There are also rumours of contracts going to businesses owned by family members of high government officials.

Need or Greed?

As I noted at the beginning of the chapter, corruption is a worldwide issue. One difficulty is defining what is acceptable. What is a perk and what is theft?

One way to consider the issues is to look at the reasons for corruption. In Mozambique there seems to be a spectrum ranging from greed to need. At one end of the spectrum, large-scale thefts from the army or the emergency to obtain luxury cars or set up businesses are clearly a major crime. At the other end of the scale, structural adjustment and PRE have made it impossible for the poorest to survive on their wage. They must have an extra source of food or income. Few would complain about the man taking handfuls of flour to feed his family.

In some cases perks have been institutionalized. Workers and military guards on food convoys are often given food, in part simply to prevent them stealing it. One government department which has an electronics workshop for its own repairs now allows technicians to bring in outside private work and use the tools and test equipment. They did it anyway, and the officials felt that this was a good way to keep technicians working for the government. What previously was corruption is now an official perk.

Pension?

It is in the wide gap between greed and need that the issue is most complex. It is here that international standards vary most, and also here that Mozambican norms have shifted most in the past decade. For Mozambicans, there is a shift in both needs and expectations.

In the early years of independence, high officials could legitimately expect to have a house, perhaps a car, an adequate standard of health care, a reasonable education for their children, and to be taken care of in their old age. The struggle to build socialism was precisely to ensure that basic needs were satisfied for all. This is no longer true. And with the coming of the multi-party system, if Frelimo loses an election government ministers could find themselves homeless.

Mozambican officials have no pension plan and no assurance of somewhere to retire to. For most aid workers, part of their salary (and thus part of what is officially "aid" to Mozambique) goes into savings at home and into a pension fund. Mozambicans do not have this. For them, their house and a small family farm or business is their pension. Just as we put aside something for our retirement, so should they. But for them it may be building materials and a pump. Sometimes these are diverted from aid projects or from the government. But just because these are solid objects, are they, in principle, any different from the portion of project funds that goes into aid workers' pension funds?

Similarly, aid workers receive a reasonable salary, while structural adjustment and IMF restrictions on government expenditure mean that many Mozambicans cannot earn a living wage and must top up their salaries. They have no choice but to use official cars for a few paid trips, to take small bribes, and to allow a few sacks of maize to fall off the back of the lorry.

Although the label is different, it seems hard to argue that these are not legitimate parts of the overheads of aid projects.

Class and expectations

But the other half of the shift is in expectations, and that is much more difficult. As the previous chapter showed, the expectations and consumption patterns of the Mozambican elite have risen much more rapidly than average incomes.

This is one of the starkest contradictions of trying to do structural adjustment in time of war. On the donor side, there is much moralizing and muddle. Adjustment says that greed is good and top people should live well. But charity attitudes say that people are starving and those Mozambicans working with the poor should live modestly themselves; there is an "us and them" sense as well, with many foreigner aid workers holding the view that they are making a sacrifice by being in Mozambique and thus have a "right" to a much better living standard than Mozambicans. Which model officials should follow depends on which set of foreigners they are dealing with.

So how corrupt is corrupt? What is acceptable? Where do we draw the line? Should foreigners expect more of Mozambicans than of themselves, or should we draw the line in the same place for Mozambicans as for ourselves – using a bit of lateral thinking to take into account issues like how one provides pensions? To do otherwise is to be puritanical and hypocritical.

I have a friend who is a high official in a state organization. He lives in a suburb and his wife runs a small market garden. When I first met him ten years ago, he had no electricity and drove his own car – an old banger that constantly broke down. Today he has electricity and drives a company car. The organization he works for has a well-drilling rig, which was sent to his home to drill a well for his wife's garden. Although he paid full price for the pump, he used his connections in order to be allocated one sooner than might otherwise have been possible. Electricians from his organization installed the pump. When I first went to his house for dinner, there were one or two bottles of beer; now he has an entire shelf of whisky given to him by foreign consultants and aid workers. He has been abroad on courses and has a stereo and TV. He and his family live comfortably, although not luxuriously. He and his wife still work long, hard days. He remains an active Frelimo party member who is well respected both at home and at work. Is he corrupt? I think not.

Big bucks

But there is real corruption in Mozambique. When Mozambique arrested a UN staff member who had transferred large amounts of money abroad from a Mozambican state company, the UN intervened and said it would cut off all UN assistance unless he was released; UN aid was worth much more than he had embezzled, so he was freed. Tens of millions of dollars go in corrupt payments on aid projects: suppliers charge much more than the going international price for goods, contractors make kickbacks to politicians and officials in the home countries in exchange for the contracts, the contract calls for new goods and second-hand ones are sent instead, false evaluations are written to justify projects, and so on. Mozambicans cannot really complain, because they know some use comes from these projects, and if they object the aid will go elsewhere.

There is also widespread corruption in emergency aid that is supposed to save starving people. Rotten food and tainted powdered milk has been sent because kickbacks were paid somewhere. Containers of medical supplies arrive with the donor NGO citing a value ten times the real worth; someone back home pocketed the difference. "Consultants" who fly to Maputo turn out to be someone's wife or cousin on holiday. That "emergency" trip to buy spares in Harare just happens to correspond with a trip to a game park.

Mozambicans take their share. In at least two cases, millions of dollars have been embezzled from the Bank of Mozambique. Private traders must be moving hundreds of thousands of dollars into foreign bank accounts.

On the whole, however, Mozambicans cannot approach the scale of foreign corruption, simply because they do not have access to the resources.

Dreams and practical morality

When Frelimo militants had a dream of socialist development, they were able to make immense sacrifices. One goal of destabilization has been to destroy that dream. And destabilization works.

The death of the dream also meant the death of a corresponding puritanism and self-abnegation. The enthusiasm of independence and of the revolution was wearing off. Mozambicans were worried about their children and families, concerned about their own living standards, and wondering about their own old age. The time for jam tomorrow was over; they wanted a bit of jam today. Structural adjustment has changed the rules. A government minister told me sadly: "There was a moral constraint that was lifted with PRE. Now to be honest means to be stupid."

The war has created two problems relating to corruption and ethics. In an environment of generalized mayhem, destabilization has numbed the senses. Corruption seems less serious to some people. This is reinforced by the amnesty, under which Renamo guerrillas who have massacred people and committed unspeakable atrocities can go free, and are even given land and helped to start anew. Secondly, a decade of destabilization has made the military an extremely powerful force in the country. The lack of prosecutions of corrupt army officers supports the widespread belief that the government is afraid to probe too deeply into military corruption for fear of provoking a coup.

That deepens the moral ambiguity. If the two biggest sources of corruption – foreign donors and the army – are untouchable for justified fears of retaliation, why should smaller-scale corruption be singled out for contempt.

In this context, the case of the high official and his wife who were involved in taking emergency goods has caused substantial private discussion. They have been supported by some Frelimo officials on the grounds that they did not take much, worked hard, and still lived modestly. And their actions were minor compared to Renamo atrocities, theft by army officers, or the millions of dollars diverted by some donors – none of which will be punished.

It is genuinely difficult to create an island of honesty in a sea of corruption. When the poorest state workers have to steal to eat and those at the top seem to get away with anything, what should those in the middle do? One of the central problems in Mozambique is that there is no agreed definition of corruption. Conditions and expectations are simply changing too rapidly. A first step was taken in late 1990, when parliament passed a law governing the conduct of high ranking state officials. They must make annual declarations of their bank accounts and property, cannot be administrators or managers in a private company, and must put any shareholdings in trust. They cannot intervene administratively in any matter in which they or their immediate family have a direct interest (*Mozambiquefile* October 1990). Loopholes remain, but it is a first effort to define a code of conduct which begins to resolve the moral ambiguities.

Donors Fuel Corruption

I remember a newly arrived FAO expert back in the early 1980s telling me how it only cost him a few dollars – much less than in other African countries, he said – to "successfully" bribe a customs official. This was when corruption was most unusual, so I asked him to tell me in detail what happened. He outlined the various papers passing back and forth, then how he gave the customs man a few dollars, and then how his bags were cleared. Mozambique has always been very bureaucratic (inherited from the Portuguese), and it was clear to me that the procedure had been totally normal: he was, in fact, about to be cleared when he gave the man the money, quite unnecessarily. And the surprised customs official simply pocketed it.

The *offering* of bribes by aid workers is becoming more common. An acquaintance was standing in a queue at a customs office, and noticed that the NGO worker in front of her handed in an envelope of money along with the paperwork. A different acquaintance was in a queue at Maputo airport. A prior plane to Tete had been cancelled so there were two sets of people trying to squeeze on to only one plane. Too far back in the queue to get a seat was an NGO official. Quite openly, where all could see, he waved a handful of dollar bills. He got a seat.

This creates a sort of optional corruption, which I saw later when I arrived at Maputo airport. I handed my passport to the immigration officer, and when he was ready to return it, he asked me for "a dollar for some beer". I said no, and he shrugged and handed me my passport. He knew that some of the UN people and high-paid consultants would give him money, if others would not.

It is also clear that aid agencies, and especially NGOs, create a very different relationship with the Mozambican officials they deal with regularly. They often provide whisky, calculators, video recorders, and even holidays. I remember one Mozambican government official who was sent on a course in Europe by an NGO which seemed genuinely surprised that he wanted to attend the course; they saw it as an excuse for a paid holiday.

When do these gifts become bribes? In some cases donors are literally buying Mozambican officials, and shop around to find who will be most bribable. In other cases, the NGO may not expect permission to do anything illegal, but it surely expects that in exchange for the holiday its proposals get straight to the top of the pile on his desk. Perhaps it expects preferment over a competing NGO.

What is striking is that donors often do not see it in this light. They accuse the Mozambicans of obstruction, laziness, and cupidity, and say they are using their gifts to encourage officials to do what they should be doing anyway. But what foreigners see as obstruction may actually be officials defending Mozambican policy – for example on using local contractors, following the official drugs list, installing recognized handpumps that can be maintained, only distributing approved seeds, and not setting up parallel structures. I have seen any number of cases where NGOs and other donors bribe officials to waive these rules, and justify it to themselves on the grounds that the donors know best and are just speeding up the process of helping the poor benighted black people of Africa. Paternalism breeds corruption.

Lack of control

Donors are actually making it more difficult for Mozambique to control corruption. In direct opposition to the appeal in the Lord's Prayer, donors are leading Mozambicans into temptation.

For example, the IMF demands ever fewer regulations on foreign trade, allowing the creation of private import-export firms which use false invoices to transfer money abroad. This is particularly easy for families where some members left at independence and went to Portugal, South Africa, or Macau, while a few stayed behind in Mozambique. The Mozambican branch of the family imports goods from family members abroad who are operating under a company with an innocent-sounding name that seems to have no link to them. They pay inflated prices for the goods, thus transferring money out of Mozambique.

Another problem relates to food aid. The US forced Mozambique to accept the services of Care to organize the DPCCN Logistic Support Unit. Several reports, including that of the commission of enquiry into corruption in food relief, have criticized Care by name (highly unusual in the aid business) for its failure to organize an effective monitoring system for food aid ("Executive Summary" 1990). This left the warehouse door open, and provided an invitation to corruption.

US grain was sent to Mozambique in bags labelled "not for sale" even when, in fact, the grain was legally and officially designated for sale in urban areas. On one hand, it looked like free grain was being diverted to the market when it was not, creating a false image of corruption. On the other hand, there was no visual control of grain which was diverted.

At the very least, the US has made it more difficult for Mozambique to control corruption. And then the US has exaggerated the resulting corruption for propaganda purposes.

Indeed, donors have not proved very enthusiastic about helping Mozambique to combat corruption. In 1990, following bitter donor complaints and a subsequent government investigation of thefts of emergency supplies from the ports and railways, the government asked for $150,000 (£90,000) for a study to identify measures to improve port and railway security. No donor was interested (GM 1990).

Changing money

Donor venality breeds corruption too. One of the most widespread forms of petty corruption is changing money on the black market. Undoubtedly this was encouraged in the period around 1984 when the exchange rate was significantly out of line, and goods were expensive in international terms if money was changed at the official rate. But with the first devaluation goods and services became cheap by international standards, and subsequent devaluations have made them cheaper still. A currency black market will always exist, because private traders want to smuggle money out to put in foreign bank accounts, and because the genuine shortage of foreign currency due to falling exports means there will always be a shortage of imported goods.

But who provides the foreign currency in the first place? The main supply of dollars comes from diplomats and aid workers, who see it as perfectly normal to change money on the black market. After all, when a dinner of nice prawns in a good restaurant costs $10 (£6) at the official exchange rate (less than half of what it would cost in Europe), they think it silly not to change on the black market so it only costs $5 (£3).

The IMF-imposed regulations ensure that this black market continues. The IMF demanded as part of the relaxation in exchange controls that anyone be able to bring in up to $500 in goods with no questions asked. Traders in Maputo buy dollars from aid workers, go to Swaziland to bank some of the dollars and legally bring back $500 in goods to sell. Totally inessential items like South African grapes in Maputo Central Market and South African beer in the bars of Quelimane are imported legally in this way. This ensures that the black market rate will always be at least double the official rate, because that is the difference needed to allow some money for foreign accounts and still make the trade profitable.

Who benefits?

It is important to ask who benefits from corruption. Of course, those who actually take the land, food, or money benefit directly. Fundamentally, they are the ones who are corrupt and guilty. But the aid industry sets irresistible temptations, and creates fertile conditions for the growth of corruption. The aid workers who offer bribes and gifts without being asked are creating a culture of corruption. The donor agencies that weaken state structures, steal government staff, create complex parallel systems, and block the creation of monitoring systems make it impossible for Mozambique to stop corruption. Deregulation promotes corruption. By demanding that people not be paid a living wage, the IMF creates conditions in which corruption is essential for survival. But why?

Corruption is in donor interests, first, because it further demolishes Mozambique's uniqueness and destroys Frelimo's moral superiority. Mozambique becomes just like other African countries.

Corruption in Mozambique makes it easier for donors to be corrupt.

Corruption provides an excuse further to bypass and weaken the government.

Corruption is fundamental in the creation of a new comprador group. It creates patron-client relationships in which the Mozambican client becomes dependent on the foreign patron. And when the link is corrupt or illicit, it gives the patron additional power. It makes it easier for donors to demand policy changes.

Publicly, donor agencies make a big song and dance about corruption. Privately they promote corruption, because it is in the interests of the new colonizers.

V Who Calls the Shots?

20 Greed is Good

There is no "'third way' between central planning and a market economy", according to IMF Managing Director Michel Camdessus. And if countries are changing their system, it is "a mistake to take a piecemeal approach" (*Financial Times*, 20 April 1990).

The IMF's message for eastern Europe as well as for Africa is that there is nothing between Stalinism with a sclerotic central planning system, on one hand, and the untrammelled free market with the glorification of greed, on the other. And yet this is manifestly false. There are many varieties of capitalism and various brands of socialism. Sweden, West Germany, and Italy have all mixed capitalism with a high degree of state involvement in a form of social democracy. Following their "third way", they have been markedly more successful than those nations like the US and UK which followed the chimera of the free market. Japan and newly-industrialized Asian countries like South Korea have succeeded by mixing capitalism with extensive state involvement and tight controls.

The IMF and World Bank are promoting the view of the Thatcher-Reagan new right that greed is the main motivating force in the world. Everyone wants more, they say, and the way to encourage prosperity and development is to remove impediments to grasping more. Welfare and minimum wages must be cut back, to encourage the feckless poor to go out and work. As people get rich, they create jobs. The old discredited trickle-down theory (crumbs from the rich man's table) is alive and well. Greed is good and we should be proud of it.

In Africa, those states which have received the strongest backing from the West for their version of free market capitalism, such as Kenya, Malawi, Zaire, and Ivory Coast, are hardly advertisements for the success of the policy. Central planning may not have been a panacea for Third World countries, but the unregulated free market has proved an even greater failure.

Greed is great for those at the top who benefit from it. In the Third World the balance of the evidence shows greed and the gap between rich and poor to be self-perpetuating, with an increasing share of resources providing goods and services for the better-off. In Britain, a decade of Thatcherism has shown clearly that the free market widens the gap between rich and poor, and creates immense suffering. I sit writing this book a short distance from a part of London where many homeless live on the pavement; walking through what is known as "cardboard city" feels very much like walking through parts of Bombay. These are the victims of free market Thatcherism. I remain convinced that there must be a "third way", for both Britain and Mozambique, and that Camdessus is cruelly wrong.

The experience of the European social democracies points to this third way, not as a single path (there is no unique "third way", any more than there is one socialism or a single capitalism) but as variants of social democracy or market socialism.

'Counter-productive and unsustainable'

It is increasingly recognized that structural adjustment programmes have been "counter-productive, unsustainable, and short-lived", according to Adebayo Adedeji, executive secretary of the Economic Commission for Africa (ECA) (Adedeji 1990).

Adedeji is an under-secretary-general of the UN, and the ECA is as much a UN agency as are the World Bank and IMF. So when he says that "orthodox structural adjustment programmes have only succeeded in rending the fabric of the African society without bringing sustainable development", surely Adedeji's views deserve equal weight with those of Camdessus?

Kenneth Dadzie, secretary-general of the UN Conference on Trade and Development (Unctad), also deserves an equal hearing. He notes that those developing countries in the 1980s "which recorded the fastest rates of growth of exports, followed policies of selective intervention rather than neutrality of incentives", as demanded by structural adjustment (Dadzie 1990). The state must intervene in the economy to ensure growth.

"What Africa needs are fundamental change and transformation, not just adjustment", Adedeji argues. "The change and transformation required are not just narrow, economistic and mechanical ones of book-keeping and financial balancing, but broader and more fundamental changes. ... We should avoid the unforgivable mistake of trying to fit development into the adjustment process. This has led in the past decade to putting on hold the long-term development of Africa."

Even the detailed policies of the IMF and World Bank have been proved wrong. "From the empirical evidence in many of our countries, it has become apparent, for instance, that generalized devaluation of the exchange rate, with its associated severe inflationary pressures, capacity under-utilization, and higher level of unemployment and speculative investment, has been particularly damaging and not the way forward", the ECA executive secretary continued. High interest rates "make matters worse. Nor will the removal of production subsidies, especially input subsidies and price support for agricultural production, help in the attainment of the goal of increased food production."

Dadzie stresses that devaluation and trade policy reform has not stimulated African exports: "not only did the resulting acceleration of inflation erode the initial competitiveness, making further devaluation necessary, but the increase in exports due to the relative price changes was limited since most African primary commodities have low responsiveness to price changes."

Both Adedeji and Dadzie argue that African countries must increasingly process their primary products and add more value before export, and must develop new exports, because the outlook for the next two decades shows a continuing fall in commodity prices. But Dadzie notes that donors have been extremely reluctant to fund projects to diversify the economies of Third World countries.

What way for Mozambique?

Twenty years ago, Frelimo drew widespread support in part because it understood the fallacy of the trickle-down theory. The record of many other countries was that only a tiny elite – typically 10% or 20% of the people – joined the modern sector and benefited from "development". The rest became ever poorer. Frelimo put forward a development policy which tried to build on the experiences of both socialist and newly independent African countries. There was to be development which benefited the broad mass of people, and not just a tiny stratum at the top. The goal was clothes for everyone rather than air conditioners for a handful.

More recently many in Mozambique appreciated the fallacy of structural adjustment, but Frelimo failed to gain widespread support for this view.

Although its failures in the 1980s owe more to destabilization than to Marxism, Frelimo undoubtedly followed an over-centralized model and made many errors. It did not give enough scope to democracy, private initiative, and the market. The collapse of the eastern European form of Marxism underlines the fact that Mozambique can never go back to the policies of the late 1970s – nor would it want to.

Divisions have now appeared in the Mozambican leadership. Some have replaced misunderstood Marxism with ill-digested free-market capitalism, and now believe that greed is good. Others, however, adhere to the original goals, but are rethinking the means and the possibilities. Much of the struggle in the second half of the 1980s has been about attempts to find a "third way".

This was shown in the writing of Mozambique's new constitution. The drafters had included a number of sops to the US and IMF. The word "People's", which had caused unaccountable offence in the US, was dropped wherever it had been used – for example from "People's Republic of Mozambique" and "People's Assembly". Similarly, the draft constitution approved by the Frelimo Central Committee defined Mozambique as a "market economy".

Parliament, however, threw out the reference to "market economy". The move was led by Eneas Comiche, governor of the Bank of Mozambique and one of the negotiators with the IMF and World Bank. Part of a new generation of Mozambican professionals trying to find that "third way", Comiche dismissed the idea that the market economy is "the remedy of all evils".

After much debate, Comiche and his allies won. The constitution now says that the Mozambican economy "rests on the value of labour, on market forces, on the initiative of economic agents, on the participation of all types of property, and on the action of the state to regulate and promote economic and social growth and development, seeking to satisfy the basic needs of the population" (MIO 5 November 1990).

The key phrases are "regulate and promote" and "satisfy the basic needs" – the social democratic mid-way between market and planned economy. Chapter 14 looked in much more detail at the role of the state. The Central Committee report to the Fifth Congress argued that "an irreplaceable task falls to the state – namely preventing social differences from being established or perpetuated on the basis of privileges of birth or other privileges. The state must constantly promote equality, by guaranteeing access, in identical circumstances, to the enjoyment of basic rights such as education and health care" (Frelimo 1989a).

"The system of directing the economy that we wish to implant envisages the state acting increasingly through instruments of economic policy, permitting greater administrative and financial autonomy to economic agents" (Frelimo 1989b). Thus the state should still "direct the economy", but no longer through rigid central planning.

Finance Minister Magid Osman told me: "In the case of Mozambique, you cannot say that the free market will make the miracle and stimulate production. Market forces cannot succeed on their own; development cannot be oriented by the market. We still believe the public sector has a very important role to play."

In the early 1980s, Mozambique "ignored economic laws", admitted Prime Minister Mario Machungo. "We thought we could solve everything through administrative decisions, and that a simple desire for rapid development had to result in practical and concrete achievements.... We learnt and we changed." Machungo denied that Mozambique had to choose between planning and a market economy, and said there was a place for both. He argued that the state must define priorities, direct public investment, and set norms and policies in fiscal matters, allocation of credit, and the fixing of wages and prices. "Certain guidelines must prevail, and there must be a certain presence of the public sector in the economy" (MIO 2 August 1990).

Various documents see a continued place for state farms and industries. The state must also intervene in commerce to ensure that private monopolies do not develop. Based in part on the success of the Maputo green zones, the Fifth Congress called for increased support for producer and consumer cooperatives, as a form of socialist enterprise. "Experience teaches us that where appropriate support is provided to cooperatives, that have been voluntarily set up by those interested in them, then noteworthy successes have been achieved" (Frelimo 1989b).

No one now would argue that there is a place for hugely inefficient, loss-making state farms or for state shops with empty shelves. But in rural areas the market is relatively small, and the free market leads not to competition but to monopoly; indeed, this is already happening. Agricom as an alternative wholesaler and marketing agent, and consumer cooperatives as alternatives to private shops, ensure competition. The free market in fruit and vegetables led only to a cartel; it was state participation in the market, through Hortofrutícola, that brought down prices (see Chapter 10). Hortofrutícola occupies a small portion of the market and is profitable as a company, yet it provides essential competition. Similarly, to encourage state-owned farms and producer cooperatives is simply to encourage plurality in a truly mixed economy. The state and cooperative sectors can also provide alternative forms of employment and of labour relations.

The point about trying to find a "third way" or middle road is to ensure that any switch to the market includes some degree of equity, and that structural adjustment is linked with growth. "Of equal value to controlling the budget deficit is assuring that the vast majority of the population has access to the growing internal market", commented Sérgio Vieira, director of the Centre of Africa Studies at Eduardo Mondlane University in Maputo (Vieira 1990).

Finance Minister Osman admits that structural adjustment "does not guarantee harmonious economic and social development, much less social justice" (*Mozambiquefile* September 1990). Therefore, at the Fifth Congress Frelimo stressed that "the basic concerns are to preserve the workers' living standards and purchasing power, to preserve our social gains, to prevent the illicit accumulation of wealth, and to defend the socialist patrimony" (Frelimo 1989a).

Another issue is the weakness of productive forces in Mozambique. Mozambican capitalists respond quite sensibly to the free market by stressing commercial and speculative activities with rapid turnover and quick profits. Only the state (or foreign capital) has the ability to make longer-term productive investments in industry and agriculture.

Finally, it is clear that development all over the world has required a high level of state involvement. This has been true even in alleged bastions of the free market ranging from the American West in the last century to South Korea and other east Asian newly industrialized countries in the 1960s and 1970s. Training, subsidy, regulation, planning, social reform, and protection have all played vital roles. Whether there ever was a genuine free market development in the mythical past, it is clear that no nation has successfully developed in the second half of the twentieth century without extensive state involvement.

The IMF and the big Western donors are committed to preventing this, and to forcing Mozambique to implement a completely free market. They want to prevent the emergence of a *regulated* market economy, and block any state *intervention* in the economy which would ensure plurality and competition.

Behind the fundamentalism

Many of the World Bank and IMF officials that I have met and many of the aid executives who visit Maputo seem quite genuine in their belief in a particular free market approach to development. And the strength of their faith is remarkable, considering the total lack of evidence that it will work. But this is an era of fundamentalism, and some people choose free market fundamentalism just as others choose Christian or Islamic fundamentalism. For the industrialized world, Greed has become the fashionable creed.

When the missionaries set out a century ago to bring God to the heathen natives of Africa, they did so with the best of motives and with a genuine faith. But they and their converts also had other motives. And the people who paid for and sent the missionaries to Africa had a very different agenda; the missionaries were the advance guard of colonialism.

Much the same thing is happening today. The faith and good motives of most aid workers in Mozambique cannot be questioned. But it is essential to look beyond the aid foot soldiers, both to those who pay the bills and to the new converts, and to ask why they insist on a system which will prevent an independent and equitable development in Mozambique. Their goal is to bury as deeply as possible the dreams of the 1970s, when independence led to attempts to change North-South relations and there could be talk of a "new international economic order".

The 1980s have seen world market prices of Africa's commodities decline steadily. On top of this, the net flow of resources *from* Africa *to* the industrialized world reached $6 bn in 1989. Of that, $1.5 bn went to the IMF and World Bank – precisely the agencies which are supposed to be "helping" African countries (Adedeji 1990). In the 1980s in the US and UK, the rich got richer and the poor, poorer; similarly, the rich countries of the North became richer and the poor countries of the South became poorer still. This is not accidental; it is the goal of policies established by the industrialized countries and increasingly enforced by agencies which they control.

"The goal of the IMF is to make Mozambique just like any other country in Africa", a frustrated government minister told me. Professor Bade Onimode of the University of Ibadan and the Economic Commission for Africa talks of the "economic recolonization of Africa by the Fund and the Bank" (Onimode 1987).

Recolonization

IMF boss Camdessus stresses the need for all countries to "open their economy to foreign competition" and of the need for "participation in the world trading system". As the world trading system is presently organized, Mozambique can only participate in a subservient position as a producer of agricultural commodities and raw materials, and as a supplier of services such as transport and tourism. The US and IMF are pushing for nothing less than the recolonization of Mozambique, albeit with a newer and more acceptable face called the "world market". Many bilateral donors and NGOs are witting or unwitting agents of the recolonizing mission.

The intention is that South Africa should return to its former status as the dominant regional power, and as the local agent of the industrialized world. The West expects South Africa to join and dominate SADCC, and thus the region. Any international aid package for the region after the end of apartheid would probably be channelled through South Africa. Western leaders have repeatedly stressed that a post-apartheid South Africa will be, in the words of UK Foreign Secretary Douglas Hurd, "a powerful engine of growth and prosperity in the region" (Hurd 1990).

In Mozambique, Pretoria's renewed role can already be seen. The South African citrus exchange (Outspan) has taken over the marketing of oranges that formerly went to East Germany. South African companies are investing in and taking over the running of large farms and plantations in excess of 100,000 ha (400 sq miles). The Ministry of Agriculture now has a group dealing specifically with requests from South Africa (*Noticias* 6 June 1990; AIM May 1990).

South African business people have taken back the management of hotels and firms they ran before independence. Some are originally of Portuguese origin, and left in 1975. Gencor of South Africa along with Lonrho are taking a major role in the Moatize coal mine, which was nationalized after two serious accidents raised questions about the safety consciousness of the former South African management.

Portugal will also play a role. In 1988 I met one of the World Bank's industry team. He accepted that there were no local entrepreneurs and said that the Portuguese should come back and that the old Portuguese holding groups like Entreposto should play a bigger role. "After all, Mozambican industry was foreign-controlled in colonial times, so why not now?" he asked. The US embassy, too, was quite open in encouraging Portuguese businessmen to come back to Mozambique.

Part of the debt renegotiation with Portugal involved a debt-equity swap, in which Portuguese entrepreneurs can use a quarter of the debt (about $42 mn, £25 mn) to buy an interest in Mozambican state companies (*Noticias* 8 February 1988). Several have already done so. This is not new foreign investment; rather it is giving away assets to pay off an otherwise unpayable debt, rather like a mortgage foreclosure.

Portuguese involvement seems closely linked to continued support for Renamo. The Serviços de Informaçao Militar, a branch of Portuguese military intelligence, is openly backing Renamo. The early support of the MNR/Renamo by Portuguese businessmen was connected to their demands for the return of property they had abandoned. Manuel Bulhosa, who is widely suspected of helping to finance Renamo, visited Maputo in 1990 to demand the return of his oil refinery, which had been nationalized by Frelimo (AIM September 1990)

There has been some non-Portuguese and non-South African investment, most notably from Lonrho. Its name is based on LONdon-RHOdesia, and in the colonial era it built the oil pipeline from Beira to Rhodesia (which it still owns and operates). Lonrho head Tiny Rowland built a good personal relationship with President Samora Machel (as he has with many African heads of state). Lonrho was the first major foreign company to take over state farms and to create a private army to protect them from Renamo. Lonrho has set up plantations in at least five provinces, taken over the Hotel Cardoso in Maputo, and is involved in gold and coal mining.

Lonrho received $2.5 mn (£1.5 mn) from the World Bank's International Finance Corporation (IFC) and DMark 10 mn ($5 mn, £3 mn) from the (then West) German Agricultural Investment Bank (DEG) for its agricultural activities in Mozambique (IMF 1988, *Noticias* 14 October 1988). Although the money goes to Lonrho, on the books it counts as aid to Mozambique.

Lonrho's activities seem modelled on a mix of Frelimo state farms and the old colonial plantation and chartered companies in Mozambique. In Cabo Delgado Lonrho is to take over a project developed by Romania, which pulled out due to security problems. Lonrho will run it in much the same way as before, with "large-scale mechanized farming" and aerial spraying of pesticides. (So much for the argument that mechanized state farms were inherently impractical.) But at least half the cotton will come from peasants, and Lonrho is being given exclusive rights to the commercialization of peasant produce in its 200,000 ha "concession area" (Lonrho 1990, C&D August 1990).

In a similar way, two Portuguese-Mozambican companies, Entreposto and João Ferreira dos Santos, are to manage peasant cotton production in parts of Nampula province, just as they did before independence (*Noticias* 31 May 1990). Entreposto is owned by Companhia de Moçambique, set up in 1888 as one of the chartered companies to exploit the Portuguese colony (*Financial Times* 15 August 1988).

The form of foreign involvement also recalls the colonial era. A World Bank official admitted that nearly all investment has been in quick return areas, notably real estate, tourism, and mining, and only to a lesser extent in agriculture. It is just like the shopkeeper colonialism of the 1960s.

Thus what is happening in Mozambique is not neo-colonialism, but an actual recolonization – sometimes by the same people or companies. Clearly, the revolution of 1975 is being rolled back.

Local agents

Some of those who previously were faithful adherents of Marxism and non-alignment are now equally faithful to the new cult of the free market, and a regional doctrine that supports the dominant role of South Africa. Politburo member Jacinto Veloso talked of "the integration into SADCC of South Africa as the country which could become the motor of regional development." These are almost identical words to those used by the British Foreign Secretary.

For many, the new faith is genuine. But, just as the Portuguese did in the 1960s, so the recolonizers are winning allies with money, ideology, and brute force. As in the colonial era, there are those who judge their personal interests to be best served by acting as agents for the recolonizers.

In a parliamentary debate on PRE in September 1990, there were complaints that foreign business interests were benefiting more than Mozambican. Interior Minister Manuel Antonio said that "we should prioritize the Mozambican entrepreneur more than the foreign one, who ends up transferring his foreign exchange out of the country." (MIO 5 October 1990). But the reality is that unlike Zimbabwe, Mozambique has not developed a prominent national capitalist class. The Mozambican business class is largely interested in commerce or quick returns from restaurants or tourism. This group is rarely interested in long-term investments in manufacturing or farming, and has no reason to keep the South Africans and Portuguese out. Indeed, the private commercial sector, which stands to make quick trading profits from free trade, is exactly the group that benefited in the old days of shopkeeper colonialism. The exceptions are those who took over tiny businesses abandoned by the Portuguese at independence, and who don't want to be pushed out by returnees. This may be happening and could cause increasing tensions.

Many people, however, are anxious to be compradors – agents for the recolonizers. They want to be managers or front men for foreign companies, or officials for NGOs or other donor agencies. Indeed, the whole process of structural adjustment is designed to replicate on a domestic level the widening gap between rich and poor that is occurring internationally. It is only the wealthiest Mozambicans that can benefit from the new free market and new support for the private sector; only they have the capital to expand and take advantage of people who are being forced, as part of public policy, to work for less than the minimum wage. This reserve army of labour cannot effectively participate in the domestic "free" market, just as Mozambique cannot effectively participate in the international "free" market. But that small group of Mozambicans who receive personal benefits clearly supports the change, even if the overall effect is to make Mozambique poorer.

This can be seen most clearly with privatization. Sérgio Vieira points out that "the main beneficiaries of privatization are the transnationals and those local speculators who frequently accumulated … through black market deals" (Vieira 1990). Smaller properties such as shops and pieces of state farms have been taken over by traders who accumulated vast sums during the black market period of the early 1980s. They, in turn, are helped by USAID which provides them with tractors and inputs.

But on a bigger scale, because there are no large Mozambican capitalists, it is only foreigners who can take over bigger state and intervened firms – sometimes on the cheap through debt-equity swaps. In some cases, Mozambicans are simply fronting for foreigners who have the money. The danger is that South Africa, Portugal, and Britain will again come to dominate the modern sector of the economy.

Kenneth Hermele comments that "private capital is emerging as the dominant internal force. But even the private sector remains utterly dependent upon the resources which are made available by external forces: the World Bank, multinational enterprises, regional development banks, etc." It is, he says, "a subservient capitalism.… A weak, dependent form of capitalism, which basically is serving the South African economy with labour, transport routes, markets, and raw materials" (Hermele 1990: 41).

Finally, as well as direct business interests, there are social and consumption reasons to want to return to colonial patterns. There is a stratum of people in both government and private sectors who have, or would like to, become accustomed to a higher level of consumption. They reject locally made products and want clothing and consumer durables from Europe, or at least from South Africa, which they have always seen as the local metropole and a surrogate for Europe. This group will encourage free trade. It will be particularly anxious to lower barriers with South Africa, and will argue that the ending of apartheid removes the need for SADCC and makes it sensible to allow South African dominance.

South Africa also provides important services, and it is already using them for propaganda purposes. In 1989 South Africa sent a letter to the UN arguing that its improving relations with Mozambique gave the lie to continued claims of South African incursions and support for Renamo. It gives as an example its claim that "a patient programme for Mozambique has been approved and the first Mozambican citizen to benefit [from treatment] by the arrangements was the former Minister of Health, Dr Fernanco [sic] Vaz" (Shearar 1989).

First weaken the state

Mozambique is a much more divided country than it was a decade ago when Frelimo pursued its aims of socialism and non-alignment. Nevertheless, the state remains important, because it still provides social services, at least partially directs the economy, and still battles with the IMF and TNCs in an effort to maintain a measure of sovereignty. This seems likely to be true whoever wins the 1991 election.

Thus the fundamental struggle is over state power. Destabilization, structural adjustment, and the actions of many donors all have the same goal: to reduce the power and influence of the Mozambican state and of Frelimo within that state. This is an absolutely essential requirement for recolonization. Only then can foreign interests have free rein. There is also a related political issue: the state must be weakened sufficiently to prevent Mozambique from aspiring to an independent, non-aligned stance. Indeed, this was one of the main goals of destabilization.

A central goal of destabilization is to destroy the structures of civil society in rural areas – to eliminate all vestiges of the state, including health, education, and political administration – and to undercut the position of the state by demonstrating that it cannot protect its citizens from bandit attack. The IMF's structural adjustment programme with its cuts in state expenditure has the same effect. The state cannot afford an adequate defence or provide sufficient health and education services. Low salaries drive the best people out of state service.

The issue of health and education is particularly critical, precisely because Frelimo's popularity rested in large part on its rapid and successful expansion of health and education. Both destabilization and the IMF have targeted health and education. And it is here that the political content of the World Bank line is clearest – to develop a two-tier structure with higher-quality private services for the better-off, and lower-quality state services for the poor. One World Bank study of Mozambique argues that "given the acute shortage of skilled personnel within the Ministry of Health, and the destruction of health facilities in many rural areas, a common thread throughout the recommendations is the need to use alternative organisations and channels outside the Ministry", rather than rebuild the government health service (WB 1989g: xiv).

The World Bank's *World Development Report 1990* is explicit. In health, "the case for the state's being sole provider of curative care is weak." In education, "where demand exceeds supply and budget constraints are tight, greater reliance on the private sector will allow the government to direct more of its scarce resources toward education for the poor" (WB 1990e: 84).

For health care, the report takes Chile in 1974–75 as its main success story. This was just after General Augusto Pinochet overthrew the elected government of Salvador Allende in a US-backed coup, and launched a brutal dictatorship. For education, the

Bank again cites Chile under Pinochet, as well as Pakistan in 1979, the year in which General Zia ul-Haq executed the former Prime Minister Zulfikar Ali Bhutto, whom he had overthrown in a coup (WB 1990e: 84,85).

It is worth noting that the World Bank thinks its health and education policies are best introduced under repressive military dictatorships. World Bank free marketeers may argue for a minimal state that does not interfere in the economy, but they seem happy to support heavy state involvement in repression of trade unions, the press, and popular organizations. This seems a hidden admission that structural adjustment really is incompatible with democracy. Are the military dictatorships of Chile and Pakistan the World Bank model for Mozambique?

21 Aid is Political

I was walking out from an interview with World Bank officials, when one of them asked me the title of my book. I replied: "Who calls the shots?" The Bank official laughed and said: "In any country receiving $1 bn from outside, it's those who pay the piper that call the tune."

Donors hold the power of life and death over millions of Mozambicans. Many perished in Inhambane in 1983 because donors withheld food; others suffered from the 1986 donor strike. But many survived in Inhambane in 1984 and Zambézia in 1987 because of effective donor response following political capitulations by Frelimo.

Aid is explicitly political. At a global level there is IMF conditionality, as well as demands for further "turns to the West" and correct votes in the UN. At a local level there are NGO demands to be allowed to distribute food, and donor demands to push economic and social policies to help preferred groups, ranging from children to private farmers.

Despite the shift of the World Bank on issues like education and poverty, it is clear that North and South are still at loggerheads on the role of the state in the economy, and on structural adjustment. ECA evidence of the failures of structural adjustment (Chapters 13 and 20) is simply rejected.

The British Foreign Secretary Douglas Hurd laid down the line in June 1990: "Aid donors ... should consider potential recipients' of aid in the light of certain criteria.... Governments who persist with repressive policies, with corrupt management, or with wasteful and discredited economic systems should not expect us to support their folly.... Prudent macro-economic programmes, well-judged public expenditure, a lesser role for the state in production and distribution and prices and exchange rates based on the market are increasingly seen as essential. With the support of aid donors, many countries have worked out adjustment programmes which reflect these principles" (Hurd 1990).

The changing international climate can only make matters worse, as was made clear at a conference in Maputo in May 1990 on Rethinking Strategies for Mozambique. The East-West confrontation has cost Mozambique particularly dear. Politburo member Jacinto Veloso spoke for many Mozambicans when he told the meeting that "the East-West confrontation ... is the fundamental explanation for the existence of the main armed conflicts that today continue in southern Africa", because South Africa "has been integrated on the Western side in the East-West conflict."

"Nevertheless, the [East-West] bipolarity offered alternatives, within certain limits ... that increased the influence of the South and its capacity to negotiate with the decision-of hand-out programmes like food-for-work, it wants to give people salaries to buy the food. In parallel, it wants to sell food and clothing if at all possible, only giving them to those who have absolutely no money. Donors, as their name implies, want to "donate" food to people, or at least give it to them personally in exchange for work. Eneas Comiche, Governor of the Bank of Mozambique, warned that although food aid can prevent starvation, it does not necessarily reduce poverty, and often leads to dependence. "In some parts of the country, foreign aid has prejudiced agricultural production", he warned, because people were becoming accustomed to living on free food aid (*Mozambiquefile* September 1990). It is ironic that those who claim to support capitalism actually promote charity, while Frelimo and the socialists push for cash payments and the market. This again gives the lie to the claims of the self-proclaimed advocates of the market; it shows they are in fact promoting a two-class system, a charity consciousness, and permanent dependence.

Donors also consistently refuse to provide adequate back-up to the emergency, or to link emergency with rehabilitation. They give food for the starving, but decline to provide transport, local costs, and protection – despite IMF restrictions which make it difficult for Mozambique to do this. And donors seem unwilling to look to rehabilitation and to Mozambican society after the war and the emergency end. They are even willing to pay much more to fly in food rather than repair bridges. Some refuse to support local industry, and instead compete with it by importing things made in Mozambique.

In part, this is because some donors have different development and emergency budgets (although surely the onus must be on donors to sort out this problem). But the overriding problem is the charity attitude; donors consistently refuse Mozambique's requests for assistance for development and for repairing war damage, and instead give additional emergency and relief contributions.

Women of the Laulane cooperative in the Maputo green zone (AIM: Joel Chiziane).

A more political issue is foreign support for economic sectors. President Joaquim Chissano, in a speech in Matola on 18 April 1989, noted that foreign support was largely going to the private sector. The state, he said, should not follow this path, but should prioritize its own companies, the agricultural cooperatives, and subsistence farming, assisting them in organization, technical support, management, and marketing (*Mozambiquefile* May 1989).

The World Bank, the US, and various other donors are giving preferential treatment to larger private businesses, and in practice are discouraging competition and plurality. Thus if progressive donors simply want to be even-handed, they should be supporting the state and cooperative sectors. But President Chissano is saying more than that. If state companies and cooperatives are to succeed, they will need substantial and long-term support in the form of training, technicians, managers, and so on. Transnational corporations will provide this for a few subsidiaries; the US and World Bank will help some bigger local capitalists. This will give them a competitive advantage against the state and cooperative sectors, and progressive donors can help to redress this balance.

The choices that donors make now will set a development pattern for decades to come. If there is any hope of finding a "third way" and of laying the groundwork for alternative forms of ownership, then it is essential to support the cooperative and state sectors to ensure that they remain as efficient and productive as the more heavily promoted private sector.

Parallel structures

"The strategy should always be to strengthen national structures", according to former emergency head Dr Prakash Ratilal (1990a: 193). One of the conclusions of the 1988 Wilton Park conference on aid to Mozambique was that "donors should work through local government in an attempt to strengthen it, rather than operating in parallel", even though "in the short run this may slow down aid work" (*Times* 6 February 1988). Yet another conference, this one at the Institute of Development Studies, called on donors in Mozambique to "support the existing institutional structures rather than create parallel structures" (Clay 1987: 33). The sixth national emergency conference in June 1989 stressed "the principle of not creating parallel structures". The 1989 mid-term emergency evaluation stressed that "a priority objective for NGO activity should be to strengthen Mozambican institutions through training and material support" (CENE 1989b).

Despite this message being so clear and repeated so often, this has proved to be the most difficult area. This is precisely because so many donors are creating parallel structures as a way of weakening the state, or are at least following Sir William Ryrie's injunction not to strengthen the state accidentally.

This can be seen in food distribution where donors said it was not acceptable to have Agricom distributing food aid, and that the DPCCN must set up a parallel distribution system. Inevitably these two were weaker separately than they would be together, and donors used this as evidence of the inability of the state to carry out its functions. Thus they argue for another parallel structure to distribute food, through NGOs and the private sector.

At all levels, donors are creating parallel systems either within or in competition with the state, for example with business people in Maputo, in care of traumatized children, in support for local small-scale industry, and in the supply of seeds and agricultural extension. In health, donors are rejecting requests to support the Ministry of Health, while providing substantial funds for independent NGO health projects.

With refugees, donors often create special charity systems rather than providing social support through normal channels. In refugee camps people tend to establish the organizations they had before, with a health worker, teacher, Frelimo party secretary, women's organization head, and so on. Food and other relief can go through these normal structures. Similarly, some donor agencies do vaccination campaigns with the normal

Mozambican Ministry of Health teams, while others run independent programmes.

Mozambique tries to avoid special feeding programmes, put orphaned children into new families instead of institutions, and cares for traumatized children through the schools. The need for donor support is obvious: teachers and health workers need help, including training, transport, materials, and sometimes even clothing. But by being involved in helping their own people, they will gain in confidence and experience and be more effective when the donors leave. Too often, however, donors demand their "own" individual programme rather than a Mozambican one, and do not trust Mozambicans to care for their own children.

A related problem which has been repeatedly underlined by the government is the unwillingness of donors, and particularly NGOs, to coordinate their activity, because they allege that it limits their freedom. The result is duplication, both of Mozambican government actions and of activities by other NGOs (UNDSPQ 1990: 43).

Another problem is the hundreds of tiny NGO projects which are not related to each other or to anything the government is doing, and which will simply collapse when the NGO moves on. "A multiplication of projects does not necessarily represent a multiplication of development", commented a study done for the Canadian NGO Cuso-Suco. "Projects must be inserted in global programmes and cannot be realized in isolation." And they must be coordinated by the state (Castel-Branco 1989).

Where does the money go?

Mozambique's biggest problem is lack of money. But just as donors try to create parallel structures for implementation, so they try to ensure that finance goes to these structures instead of the government.

The World Bank is increasing the pressure to divert donor funds into channels that it controls, notably through co-financing, control over some emergency funding, and the system of non-administrative allocation of foreign exchange (SNAAD). In their strongest stand against the Bank, Mozambican ministers have repeatedly requested donors not to co-finance but instead to leave the funds as part of the normal bilateral aid frame.

Donors are increasingly giving funds to NGOs and UN agencies, particularly Unicef, which have a good public image. But there is little evidence to suggest that they use the funds any better than the government, and they are often simply other intermediaries that take commissions to support their own overheads. Furthermore, they tend to be the main advocates and creators of parallel structures in Mozambique.

The World Bank is also trying to push donors to fund health and education rather than development and rehabilitation, which contradicts Mozambique's own goals. In fact, in some circumstances donors can do both. If they provide assistance to economic sectors, this generates counterpart funds, which can then be used for health and education; the money works twice, whereas it works only once if it is given directly for health and education local costs.

Worldwide, two-thirds of all bilateral aid is tied (WB 1990e: 128). But if money must return home, at least it should do the maximum amount of work while it passes through Mozambique. That means finding ways to use tied aid to support the projects that the government wants, rather than doubling the tie by creating independent projects. It also means supporting Mozambican institutions and industry. For example, it may be possible to use tied aid to provide raw materials or intermediate goods for industry, rather than finished products. Similarly, tied aid and direct material aid can be used to stimulate commerce and generate counterpart funds, and thus do double duty. This can be done, for example, by allowing the sale or swap of donations for the emergency.

People

Mozambique is so short of skilled people that over the next five years it will continue to need at least 1000 outside accountants, engineers, and other middle-level staff, according to estimates by Reginald Green (1990a). These are not simply for training, but also for filling essential gaps. Donors often want to feel that they are training Mozambican staff, which is not a bad thing, and demand that any technicians they send should have Mozambican counterparts. But the skills gap is simply too large, and donors must help to plug these gaps over the next few years until more Mozambicans graduate from technical schools and university.

Green calls for donors to "place cooperantes in Mozambican-run institutions regularly reporting to Mozambicans (at managerial and professional, not just ministerial levels) in fact as well as form." He urges concentration on training of Mozambicans inside Mozambique, as being more efficient and allowing people to remain on the job. But he also calls for donors to give "more accountability to Mozambicans" and to "accept that Mozambicans do know a great deal about Mozambique which outsiders do not" (Green 1990b).

Donors are still providing some of the large numbers of skilled people that Mozambique needs. Some have set up "personnel funds", which allow Mozambique to hire its own skilled technicians, usually from other developing countries at a fraction of the cost of those from the big donors. Others send traditional cooperantes, who work directly for the government rather than for the donor; donors are also providing the salary and other support such as transport and word processors these cooperantes need to be effective.

Increasingly, however, donors do what Green calls "decapacitating the state". For example, they send skilled people only as part of projects, and these people work for the donor and not the government. Or they set up projects without providing adequate servicing and back-up, so that Mozambican mechanics and accountants are diverted from other programmes. These are examples of weakening the government and creating parallel structures. Donors also steal Mozambican staff from the government – often by paying substantially more than the government is allowed to pay. They are widening the skills gap. Partly it is intentional; some donors have said openly that they want to weaken the Mozambican state.

Well-intentioned NGOs try to localize their programmes by hiring Mozambicans. This further depletes the tiny pool of bookkeepers, administrators, and other technicians. It would seem sensible and supportive to train as many Mozambicans as they hire, but NGOs normally refuse. They say their priority is to help the poorest of the poor rather than to train middle-class city dwellers.

Green argues that donors have a responsibility to increase Mozambican capacity to initiate programmes. Instead donors tend to demand that Mozambique use its limited pool of skilled people to assist donors to put their own proposals into action.

The Frelimo Fifth Congress recognized the problem being created by aid. It stressed that "technical cooperation should, wherever possible, function as one more mechanism for training and developing national cadres and technicians, as well as for performing the specific tasks attributed to each technician."

Even the World Bank, which has done so much to weaken the state, has become more and more worried about this. Each draft of its "Poverty Framework Paper" (WB 1990b, 1990f, 1990j). contained a stronger statement, and the final version said: "Every effort should be made by the donor community to build up implementation capacity [of local and national government], while at the same time avoiding overloading the system through new and diffuse initiatives. In particular, resources – including personnel – should normally be channelled through the appropriate Mozambican institutions in ways enhancing their capacity, not via expatriate-run, isolated, parallel projects which can disable and reduce Mozambican capacity" (WB 1990j: 5).

Donors seem happy to hire consultants to run an installation in Mozambique, or send someone for a few weeks for a consultancy, or even provide a grant for a course in the donor country. The real problem is to find donors who will provide a package of long-term technical support with cooperantes to fill the gaps and appropriate training when people become available, without taking over the running of the project or enterprise themselves.

The Mozambican Role

Mozambique is the mendicant and the donors are trying to call the tune. Nevertheless, Mozambique has retained a surprising amount of power to set policy and direct donors. Indeed, much of this book has been about Mozambique's struggles, and there have been some successes. From a position of apparent weakness Mozambique has pushed and even forced donors to follow its policy and guidelines. The government has retained an economic role in the face of near total donor opposition. It has finally convinced even the World Bank of the need to link growth with adjustment. And Mozambique has retained a surprising ability to direct development funding.

Mozambique has persuaded donors to consider the nature of the structural emergency, convincing most that destabilization is the root of the problem. This is a signal victory – Mozambique and not the donors defined the terms of the emergency. It has drawn the donors into planning emergency relief and prevented them from setting up their own independent coordination mechanism.

The emergency commission has directed NGOs into specific geographical areas, largely preventing them from shooting about like unguided missiles. By pushing donors into districts, it has promoted integrated rather than vertical development. It has probably pushed donors into doing more rehabilitation and repair of war damage than they originally intended. In health and nutrition, water and sanitation, and some aspects of agriculture such as seed provision, it has coerced donors into following government policy and guidelines.

But none of these victories are permanent. Nearly every battle must be fought again and again as donors try to recoup lost ground. Often they are rearguard victories, simply slowing the retreat. When I wrote the first draft of this book, I said that Mozambique had kept effective control over the distribution of food and other relief supplies. But in my visit to Mozambique in mid-1990 it was clear that the government was finally losing that battle, too; NGOs with powerful bilateral donor backing were doing their own distribution.

In early 1988 a Mozambican delegation visited Ethiopia and Somalia; they found it difficult to believe that every agency had its own distribution programme, warehouses, trucks, and personnel, creating duplication on a grand scale. The Mozambicans asked officials in the Ethiopian government's Relief and Rehabilitation Commission why the government did not impose on the operation one unified structure like Mozambique's DPCCN. Now the Mozambicans know why.

Are they victories?

For the million dead Mozambicans, and for their friends and relatives, ten years of destabilization have meant despair and defeat. The turn to the West, accepting the IMF and structural adjustment, spells defeat for the dream of socialism. Thus, at the most basic level, Washington calls the shots in Mozambique.

Suppose that ten years ago someone had said to the Frelimo leadership: "If you do not join the West and accept capitalism, we will kill one million of your people and flatten your country." What would have been the reply? But no one asked that question. Frelimo was never given the choice. Who in Mozambique could have predicted the cost of non-alignment and socialism?

One problem, then, is to figure out the right question. Do we look at the magnitude of the defeat, or should we be pleased that something has been saved? Under fire, Mozambicans continue to win small victories which, taken together, could guide the country on a more humane and equitable path. Are these pyrrhic victories, which only extend the course of destabilization? Donors have made it clear that they are prepared to allow thousands to starve to death in order to obtain political concessions. Will the dying only end with abject surrender?

In 1980 I did not forecast the holocaust that hit Mozambique, and my judgement may be no better now. Nevertheless, I feel that some kind of settlement is in sight, and that Mozambique retains some limited room to manoeuvre. In other words, I think the victories are real, even in the face of much larger defeats; it is a victory to be able to call even a few of the shots.

Setting out the line cautiously

Inevitably Mozambicans tread very cautiously for fear of needlessly offending notoriously thin-skinned donors. Sometimes, Mozambican discretion pays dividends. The decision not to publicize the expulsion of aid workers has meant that there has been no bad publicity, but that the donor community knows the limits. The acceptance of a certain amount of donor corruption has also been useful, because Mozambique has been able to win favours in exchange.

In the early 1980s when I was working as a journalist in Mozambique, Frelimo spoke with a relatively consistent voice. What was said in public was not dissimilar to what was said in private. That is no longer true. For example, while some ministers publicly proclaimed that PRE was entirely Mozambique's idea, others privately admitted that it was structural adjustment as imposed by the World Bank and IMF, and that they were not happy with it. But even in private conversations some high officials stuck to the line that Mozambique had initiated PRE.

There are two reasons for this. Most important is the need to satisfy the US and end the war – at all costs. As they have shown by their paranoia about Mozambican press criticism, US officials want to be loved, or at least respected. Part of this is the demand that Mozambique not simply acquiesce to US demands, but that it *believe*. It is not good enough to say greed is good; it must be said with conviction. Mozambican officials and ministers understand this, and it partly explains their reluctance to contradict the IMF and the privatization bias of US policy. This is especially true because the US controls not just the IMF and money, but also Renamo and thus the duration of the war.

The second reason is that recolonization has gained allies, even at ministerial level. Some Mozambicans like the new lifestyle and have abandoned Frelimo's socialist goals, even though they maintain the rhetoric. They have their own reasons for blocking debate and backing structural adjustment and privatization. Greed is indeed good for them. Thus there are many examples like that of the NGO which said it wanted to follow Frelimo guidelines and help cooperative farms, and was told by the provincial agriculture official that the real priority was to help private farmers – including him!

In researching this book, several donor representatives complained to me that they received "mixed signals" from Mozambican officials, and were not always sure what Mozambique wanted. And I do think Mozambique has not pushed donors hard enough, particularly its traditional friends. Frelimo often overestimates the perceptiveness and intelligence of its friends, and gives too much credence to their ability to read between the lines.

Nevertheless, this is undoubtedly the most difficult area; splits within even the progressive donor camp mean that closed meetings can be reported back to the US or World Bank, and a decade of destabilization must make any Mozambican minister think twice about the impact of any hint that Washington is not the fount of all truth and wisdom.

Sometimes, what allegedly sympathetic donors treat as "mixed signals" is their unwillingness to hear, or their failure to ask the right question. If Mozambique is asked: "Do you want NGO doctors?" the answer is naturally yes. But if the question is: "Would you prefer cooperante doctors in the Ministry of Health, or independent NGO doctors?" Then the answer is very different; that Mozambique doesn't really want the NGO doctors.

But it isn't a mixed signal at all – NGO doctors are better than none, and Mozambique will take them if they are the only ones available. There is no point in offending a donor, or the US, by asking for something that is not available.

But for those who want to listen, the policy is frequently clear. For example, on the issue of private versus state and cooperative, no statement could be clearer than President Chissano's complaint about donors only helping the private sector, and stressing the need to assist cooperatives and state farms.

Clear guidelines

Mozambique has had its best success precisely in those areas, like water and health, where it has a clearly defined policy, and was prepared to defend it. At a practical level, it became increasingly hard for donors to argue for alternative handpumps when they manifestly did not work and could not be maintained. At a political level, the clear understanding about Mozambique's socialist health policy that permeates all levels of the health service means that those who undercut and bypass it are patently out to sabotage the state health service.

Industry is instructive here. First, the Ministry did make maximum use of general socialist guidelines to direct assistance from progressive donors to support the state sector. But it did not start out with a fully defined policy. Instead it used alternative sources of expertise, especially Unido and former cooperantes, to help it formulate a clear policy with which to battle successfully with the World Bank and other donors.

On the other hand, one of Mozambique's greatest weaknesses is that sometimes officials are unable to articulate a clear policy, and are too embarrassed to ask for help. At the worst, as with agricultural extension, there was no policy at all, which gave donors a free hand.

Sometimes a policy existed but was never spelled out in a clear and simple way. For example, the chaos about the new health charges, with wide variations as to who was charged and who was not, occurred because the Ministry of Health failed to distribute a simple list of charges and exceptions. Similarly, the Ministry of Health had an excellent policy against creating new orphanages. But a donor who had not been able to give an orphanage to the Ministry was able to give it to a provincial governor, who did not know it was against national policy because it was not written down in readily accessible form.

Often this is a function of inexperience and the lack of skilled people, which leads to bureaucratization – people are afraid to write clear policy statements, or afraid to approve those written by subordinates, for fear that they may contain errors or oversimplifications. This is compounded by an unwillingness to correct mistakes, for fear of losing face.

"Local policies and strategies, if poorly articulated and transmitted, carry no weight", one sympathetic donor official complained. "By reacting to donor initiatives, the Mozambicans are systematically on the defensive. By more aggressively pursuing their own goals, and advising this to the donors, they would at the same time strengthen the bargaining position of the Maputo offices of friendly donors vis-à-vis their headquarters."

The position is improving, however. The weekly emergency meetings proved to be important forums both for donors to demand policy guidelines and for the government to present them. For example, the government used these meetings to distribute very detailed regulations on what kinds of seeds were to be distributed to peasants, to ensure that they were suitable for the soil and were open pollinating types that the peasants could use to produce their own seed.

Not in Mozambique

The resolution of Mozambique's problems does not rest with guidelines on seeds and pumps, or even with correct donor decisions on projects. Rather, the need is for fundamental changes in the policy of the industrialized world toward Mozambique.

The first need is for an end to the war. By late 1990, Renamo still had active support in South Africa, Kenya, and Portugal. None of these countries could back Renamo without at least the acquiescence of the US. Thus there must be a political commitment by the US and the West to stop the war.

Mozambique's children will be paying the cost of destabilization for the rest of their lives. Traumatized by the war and deprived of an education, they will still be expected to spend their adulthood repaying more than $4 bn in international debts. These debts are not the result of their parents' profligacy, but of a war cruelly imposed on Mozambique to ensure Western hegemony. Now that the West has won its war, surely Mozambique deserves at least the cancellation of that debt? No development is possible while the debt burden remains.

Nor will it be enough just to write off debts. Mozambique needs more than $1 bn (£600 mn) each year for the rest of the century. Whatever one thinks of aid and the aid industry, the industrialized world must continue to pour money into Mozambique to rebuild the infrastructure and living standards to 1980 levels. Professor Green estimates that it will cost $5.6 bn (£3.4 bn) just to resettle the refugees, the dislocated, and the demobbed. And he warns that "it is brutally pragmatic. To demobilize men with guns into pauperism is to ensure either an instant coup or an instant tidal wave of 'self help' banditry" (Green 1990b). With the end of apartheid, with starvation in Mozambique reduced simply to acute malnutrition, and with Western attention turned to eastern Europe, it will be too easy for donors to forget Mozambique.

Reagan has gone and his version of the free market has proved to be "voodoo economics" with massive deficits and widespread corruption and profiteering. Thatcher is gone and her version of market forces is on the wane in its home country, where it has done huge economic damage. Only the IMF retains the fanaticism of the true believer, trying to impose on Mozambique a version of the fundamentalist free market faith that was never acceptable in the US. Even if structural adjustment made any sense in the countries for which it was originally designed, it makes no sense in war-ravaged Mozambique. It must be lifted if there is to be reconstruction at the end of destabilization.

No one doubts that Mozambique must increase its exports to survive, and that it must be part of the world economy. But the US, EC, and Japan only want to impose the free market on others and not accept it for themselves. Thus, they force down the price of raw materials and block any attempts at cartels or other methods to boost prices. But when developing countries try to do at least some processing of these raw materials, the developed states impose trade barriers against manufactured goods. Furthermore, as Unctad head Dadzie notes, "oligopolistic industry and market structures" dominate the food and beverage exports such as tea and sugar that many African countries, including Mozambique, are dependent on. There can be no growth for Mozambique and for the rest of Africa without a more equitable trade relationship.

And what relationships is the West going to impose on southern Africa as a whole? Will it permit the growth of SADCC and PTA as development cooperation bodies and preferential trading blocs which encourage joint development and industrialization? Or will it insist on a totally free market to ensure fragmentation and perpetually small local markets? And will the West insist that South Africa becomes the regional power, or will it allow a balance between South Africa and the states to the north?

Although Mozambique can lobby, negotiate, and campaign on these issues, their resolution lies in Washington, Brussels, New York, and Tokyo. And it is here that solidarity organizations, progressive NGOs, and enlightened donors of all sorts can play their most important role. Their actions at home, to change the policies of their own governments and of the major Western powers, are worth more than thousands of tiny development and relief projects in Mozambique. Ending the war, halting structural adjustment, or cancelling the debt will benefit millions of Mozambican peasants in a way that no aid project can.

22 Forced to Beg

"Aid is not bad, however, because it is sometimes misused, corrupt, or crass; rather, it is *inherently* bad, bad to the bone, and utterly beyond reform. As a welfare dole to buy the repulsive loyalty of whining, idle and malevolent governments, or as a hidden, inefficient, and inadequately regulated subsidy for Western business, it is possibly the most formidable obstacle to the productive endeavours of the poor", writes Graham Hancock in his book *Lords of Poverty* (Hancock 1989: 183)

A decade ago, Frelimo would have agreed. But Mozambique has been forced to bend its knee and beg. Destabilization, carried out by South Africa with the active connivance of the major Western powers, has killed one million Mozambicans and impoverished most of the others. For Mozambique, it is not a question of whether aid is good or bad. Mozambique has been battered until it was forced to accept Western aid and all of the conditionality that goes with it.

A decade ago Mozambique refused to join the IMF and World Bank, and did not ask for big programmes with the major Western aid donors. A long-serving government minister who watched this process told me privately: "I have no doubt that destabilization was intended to force us to reach this point, to force us to negotiate with the IMF."

What is even more striking is the way in which the IMF and destabilization work to the same end. Renamo destroys schools and health posts. Then IMF rules make it impossible to rebuild those schools and health posts and pay salaries sufficient for nurses and teachers to return to the rural areas. Finally, NGOs and churches rebuild the schools and pay more for their health workers and teachers to take the place of the state ones, creating an alternative private or mission system.

Destabilization, aid, and recolonization are intimately linked. Without destabilization, Mozambique would never have accepted an IMF structural adjustment programme nor allowed the US to dictate so freely. Thus, at the very least, it has not been in the interests of the IMF and the US to end destabilization. Indeed, despite their protestations, until the end of the decade continued war was in the interests of the IMF and World Bank.

It is like what in the US is called "urban renewal" and in Britain is called "comprehensive redevelopment". In both cases an entire neighbourhood is flattened and something completely different built in its place. This is what is happening in Mozambique. Destabilization is to demolish the old, and the aid agencies are now moving in to rebuild Mozambique in a new capitalist image.

Thus the destruction wrought by destabilization is an end in itself. There is no need to replace Frelimo as the government if instead the power of the government is destroyed.

The shared goal of destabilization, structural adjustment, and aid is to do just that.

Sowing division

Destabilization works. Low-intensity warfare is effective. Mozambique's economy is shattered. Mozambicans are demoralized and exhausted. The dreams of independence have been turned to ash. There is no time or place to dream of a just society. Now the priorities are feeding and clothing one's own family, educating one's own children, and worrying about one's own old age.

Frelimo came to power with dreams of unity and equity. Destabilization was intended to destroy that dream. Now the donors are building division, inequality, and self-interest in its place. Whether they say they are helping the poorest of the poor or the richer private farmers, they are promoting privilege and division, and working against unity and equity.

Corruption is at the heart of this process The continued war and destabilization leads to a breakdown in social values and to corruption. And aid is corrupting. Officials are bribed to turn a blind eye to donor corruption. Government staff are bribed to take decisions that donors want. Mozambican counterparts are encouraged to have a living standard like that of foreign staff. Lower-level workers are paid so little that they must find extra sources of income.

At the same time, donors try to weaken, erode, and bypass the state. They create parallel structures and entice Mozambicans away from government. They weaken the state, then stress its incapacity and lack of authority. Instead of increasing Mozambique's capacity, donors reduce its capacity and make it permanently dependent.

Destabilization, the IMF, and aid work together to divide, corrupt, and undermine Mozambican society.

Belfast and babies

Part of the process is to justify recolonization by convincing both Mozambicans and the outside world that what is happening is the fault of the Mozambicans themselves, and thus the problem should be solved by the industrialized North. The former colonizers, who caused such appalling suffering and underdevelopment the last time they were in charge, should be put in control again. Those who have made such a mess of their own economies with their fundamentalist faith in the free market should now be put in charge of Mozambique's economy.

Thus Mozambique is told that its economy is in crisis not because of destabilization and the colonial heritage, but because of policy mistakes by doctrinaire Marxists; Mozambique's growth of the late 1970s and the failures of doctrinaire IMFism are ignored. So the solution is not a Keynesian war-time formula of a strongly managed economy, but an IMF free-market structural adjustment package.

The war is accepted as a cause of suffering, but it is a "civil war" or "black-on-black violence". It reinforces the deepest white prejudices that black people are fundamentally barbarous and need the civilizing white influence. It is still further evidence that black people cannot rule themselves and need their old white masters back. This is underlined by the aid icon of white nurses helping black babies – which is itself part of a vicious circle, because aid agencies say that donors will not give unless their prejudices are confirmed. Indeed, one purpose of destabilization has become the creation of just such pictures. For South Africa, they reinforce the arguments against majority rule; majority rule only brings chaos and blacks will always be dependent on whites. For the industrialized world, such photos underline the continued dependence of South on North. And for the donors, such images underline their continued role in succouring the heathen.

Even our media images of the war are distorted to present an image of all of Mozambique having descended into chaos. To be sure, many have died, millions have been made refugees, and a majority of Mozambicans are indirectly affected by the war. But this does not mean continued warfare everywhere. Rather it means just the opposite, that most areas are at peace and most people are trying to rebuild and improve their lives. A journalist from "war-torn Mozambique" visited Britain in early 1990, and was taken to Belfast. He was shocked by the heavily armed soldiers on the streets, the armoured personnel carriers zooming around the city, and the repeated searches. "This is real war, nothing like

Despite the war, people try to live relatively normal lives. This is a militiaman in a village outside Pemba
(J. Hanlon).

Maputo", he said. Indeed, visitors from New York and Washington to Maputo worry about the dangers, when in reality they are safer than they would be at home.

The IRA has run a bombing campaign against the railway between Belfast and Dublin. The line was cut more than 70 times in the first ten months of 1989 (*Guardian* 30 October 1989). This is significantly more often than the railway between Beira and Zimbabwe is disrupted (Johnson 1989: 56). Yet it is the Beira corridor and not the Belfast-Dublin link which is portrayed as war-disrupted and dangerous.

Real hunger

Whatever the question of false images, the cost to Mozambicans of the campaign to drive Mozambique into the arms of the donors has been massive. One million are dead. The economic costs exceed $18 bn (£11 bn). Hunger and deprivation are real and widespread.

Now there are hopeful signs that destabilization is ending. If the war stops, and babies are no longer starving, will the charities lose interest? Emergency aid will be needed for several years just to resettle refugees and help them to begin producing. Hundreds of thousands of tonnes of food aid will be required to prevent starvation.

If Frelimo wins the coming election, will destabilization continue?

And if Frelimo loses, will the West celebrate its victory and lose interest? When Mozambique has finally done all that the IMF wants, will the big donors lose interest because they no longer need to put pressure on Mozambique? Will eastern Europe be more interesting than southern Africa?

And what about the progressive forces? Judith Marshall, a long-time cooperante and supporter of Frelimo, was citing Frelimo's slogan "the struggle continues" when she noted wearily that with the continued impact of war and structural adjustment, "it becomes increasingly difficult to identify whether and where the struggle actually does continue" (Marshall 1989). As Mozambique makes more and more concessions to the IMF, are the progressive forces to abandon Frelimo?

Are the charities moving on to the next famine, and the progressives moving on to the next revolution?

The new struggle begins

For Mozambique the first priority is peace. Perhaps by the time this book has been published, a peace agreement will have been reached, although such hopes have been raised and dashed several times in the past six years. But an agreement will not end the fighting. South African and US backers of Renamo have provided it with arms to last for years to come; some Renamo fighters will return home, but others will find that banditry is a soft option and will remain in the bush. The fighting may slacken, but it will not end for several more years.

Whether or not an agreement is reached, Mozambique must begin now to rebuild and return to its campaign against underdevelopment. What route will it take now? Have structural adjustment and destabilization firmly closed the door on socialism or on a "third way", and must development benefit only a handful? Or can Frelimo still lay the ground-work for a form of development that highlights equity and unity?

"For some, peace is merely the absence of war. It is the possibility for unbridled capitalist development, which marginalizes the majority of people from the use and benefit of the product of the labour of all. For us, peace is indeed the absence of war, as the first condition. But it is much more than this. It is a society of democracy and social justice. It is respect for the sovereignty of each people. It is the use of our resources for our own well-being. It is relationships of equality and mutual respect with other countries and nations", declared Graça Machel (Machel 1990).

This is the new struggle, which begins now. Donors and other outside forces will play a determining role. Progressive donors can help to lay the foundations for development based on justice instead of greed. Or they can turn away.

"We have no choice"

It will be difficult to end the "exploitation of the Mozambicans by our 'partners'", admitted President Joaquim Chissano in a TV interview in early 1990 ("Compass", Channel 4, UK, 24 April 1990). "But we will try to keep the maximum we can keep from what they are going to bring to us. We have no choice."

Surely the role of progressive donors is to help Mozambique make the best of a very difficult situation, and to help Frelimo and the Mozambican people maintain some vestiges of the goals of equality and development that inspired the first years of independence, and which seemed so threatening to the big Western powers.

"Our main struggle is independence and survival. We don't want to be the object of the hunt any more", a Politburo member told me. "Wanting to be free brought us war. Now the developed world wants us to remain dependent, to always be recipients. But even slaves rebel. The colonized rebelled."

"How do we react to people who talk under torture? We say they were victims, and we give them a new chance. Otherwise we destroy them", another minister counselled me. "One day, we will be able to raise our heads again. We must continue with our project, so that we can fight again, even if only in ten or twenty years. Do not abandon us now."

Appendices

Appendix 1:
Further Economic Tables

Tables A.1 Basic Economic Data

Table A.1a Rates of exchange

	1974	1975	1976	1977	1978	1979	1980	1981	1982	1983	1984	1985	1986	1987	1988	1989	1990
MT/$	25	27	31	33	33	32	32	35	38	40	42	43	40	282	528	747	950
MT/£	58	60	56	57	63	68	76	70	66	61	56	56	59	460	940	1225	1660
£/$		2.33	2.22	1.81	1.74	1.92	2.12	2.36	2.03	1.75	1.52	1.33	1.30	1.47	1.63	1.78	1.64	1.75

Average rate for year, except 1990 which is mid-year rate
Where rates have been given for comparison in the text, the following have been used:
  £ = $2 $ = 0.5 £ through 1981
  £ = $1.65 $ = 0.6 £ from 1982

Table A.1b Terms of trade (1980 = 100)

Year	1975	1976	1977	1978	1979	1980	1981	1982	1983	1984	1985	1986	1987	1988	1989
Terms of trade	113	105	103	92	94	100	103	89	88	101	94	90	83	75	66

Source: 1975–87: Unctad 1988
        1988,89: WB 1990c 1988,89 rates of change applied to Unctad 1988 value for 1987.

Note that Unctad 1988 and WB 1990c do not agree on terms of trade calculations for Mozambique, with the WB basing its calculation entirely on values in US$ and claiming that terms of trade actually improved up to 1986. Unctad estimates seem more realistic, and so have been used when they are available. The 1988–89 deterioration in terms of trade is based on changes as calculated by the WB, but applied to 1987 Unctad data to keep the series consistent.

Table A.1c Basic information

Area	799,380 sq km
Gross domestic product	$1.2 bn (1990 estimate)
	$78 per capita
Population	12.1 million (1980 census)
	16 million (1991, author's estimate, including
	refugees temporarily outside Mozambique)

Population by province, 1980 census:

Niassa	514,000
Cabo Delgado	940,000
Nampula	2,402,000
Zambézia	2,500,000
Tete	831,000
Manica	641,000
Sofala	1,065,000
Inhambane	997,000
Gaza	990,000
Maputo	491,000
Maputo City	755,000

Source: DNE 1985

Note: Maputo City counts as the 11th province

Table A.1d Foreign trade, by country

Imports by origin	Value ($ mn)			Share (%)		
	1981	1985	1988	1981	1985	1988
Main trading partners						
South Africa	101	50	98	12%	12%	14%
USSR	15	83	73	2%	20%	10%
Italy	35	23	68	4%	5%	10%
USA	20	49	56	2%	12%	8%
Portugal	37	16	41	5%	4%	6%
UK	28	13	40	3%	3%	6%
West Germany	52	13	32	3%	3%	4%
Zimbabwe	5	4	31	1%	1%	4%
France	86	24	29	11%	6%	4%
Netherlands	20	19	29	3%	5%	4%
Sweden	36	11	29	2%	1%	4%
Japan	25	11	24	3%	3%	3%
Canada	3	8	24	...	2%	3%
East Germany	52	11	15	6%	3%	2%
TOTAL IMPORTS	809	424	715			
Imports by region						
OECD	353	215	419	44%	51%	59%
Africa	166	61	166	21%	14%	23%
Socialist	114	108	95	14%	25%	13%
Other	173	39	34	21%	9%	5%
Exports by destination						
Main trading partners						
Spain	23	18	22	8%	23%	21%
Japan	21	13	17	8%	16%	17%
USA	49	14	16	17%	19%	16%
Portugal	15	4	8	5%	6%	8%
South Africa	na	3	7	na	4%	6%
East Germany	39	10	6	14%	12%	6%
USSR	9	2	6	3%	2%	5%
Netherlands	21	1	2	7%	1%	2%
West Germany	na	1	2	na	2%	2%
TOTAL EXPORTS	283	77	103			
Exports by region						
OECD	148	54	72	52%	70%	70%
Africa	na	9	18	na	12%	17%
Socialist	57	14	13	20%	18%	13%

Sources: CNP 1984b; DNE 1985, 1987, 1989; WB 1990c

Note: na = data not available

... = less than 0.5%

Table A.1e Foreign trade, by commodity

Imports by commodity	Value ($ mn)		
	1981	1985	1988
Food	114	121	172
Non-food consumer goods	64	45	94
Chemical products	72	25	30
Metal products	52	19	18
Petroleum and products	167	69	51
Electricity	5	6	10
Other intermediate goods	70	44	100
Parts	104	47	101
Capital goods	151	49	138
TOTAL imports	801	424	715

Exports by commodity	Value ($ mn)			Volume (000t)		
	1981	1985	1988	1981	1985	1988
Prawns & lobster	52	33	47	8	5	5
Cashew nuts & oil	55	12	27	17	4	8
Sugar & molasses	29	7	5	112	33	12
Cotton	25	5	5	15	5	4
Copra	5	5	4	12	13	14
Petroleum products	52	4	4	na	na	na
Citrus	5	3	2	16	10	6
Wood	7	1	1	na	na	na
Tea	14	2	0	16	2	0
Coal	10	0	0	236	9	15
TOTAL exports	281	77	103			

Other exports include cement, tyres, tantalite, and sisal.

Sources: CNP 1984b; DNE 1985, 1987, 1989; WB 1990c

Note: na = data not available

Table A.1f Balance of payments (US$ mn)

	1980	1981	1982	1983	1984	1985	1986	1987	1988	1989
Trade & Services										
Receipts										
Exports	281	281	229	132	96	77	79	97	103	93
Transport	93	82	83	66	34	39	45	35	42	42
Migrant labour	53	64	64	75	57	41	50	58	72	70
Other	25	32	24	24	27	27	24	44	102	109
Payments										
Imports	800	801	836	634	540	424	543	625	715	766
Other	69	87	80	78	70	83	123	136	123	141
TOTAL Trade & Ser.	-417	-429	-516	-415	-396	-323	-468	-527	-519	-593
Aid & Capital										
Receipts										
Donations	56	57	79	90	168	139	213	302	364	380
Loans	503	718	725	339	265	227	284	301	232	275
Payments										
Interest	6	36	60	88	81	117	155	148	117	159
Loan repayments	139	309	329	296	338	278	336	384	378	292
TOTAL Aid & Capital	414	430	415	45	14	-29	6	71	101	204
Errors & omissions	-30	-67	-41	9	26	-3	-27	29	46	-15
GLOBAL BALANCE	-33	-66	-142	-361	-356	-355	-489	-427	-372	-404
Run down reserves★	32	69	148	47	-23	20	-23	-73	-49	-5
Further unpaid debt★	0	0	0	285	206	153	482	-884	0	0
Debt relief	0	0	0	0	213	193	0	1359	397	398

Source: DNE 1987, WB 1990c

Note: In "run down reserves", negative (–) entries indicate increase in reserves. "Further unpaid debt" shows new or additional arrears for that year; a negative entry indicates payment or relief of back debt.

Comment: Sources differ even on something as fundamental as balance of payments, so this table shows some discrepancies with others in this book.

Table A.1g Government budget, 1988 ($ mn)

Government Income		Government Expenditure	
Company profits tax	46	Defence	110
Income tax	9	Health & education salaries	33
Circulation (sales) tax	57	Other civil service salaries	14
Beer & tobacco taxes	26	Goods and services	49
Import duties	35	Interest	29
Other taxes	35	Price subsidies	14
Rents from houses	6	Subsidies to state industries	21
Fishing licences	7	Other current	11
Other government revenue	25	Investment	265
Foreign aid for projects	92		
Counterpart funds & other aid	82		
TOTAL INCOME	421	TOTAL EXPENDITURE	546
Budget deficit	125		

Source: DNE 1989

Tables A.2 Official Development Assistance as Defined by OECD

Table A.2a Aid to Mozambique ($ mn)

	1980	1981	1982	1983	1984	1985	1986	1987
Net ODA								
From DAC donors	115	110	161	161	190	217	319	532
From non-DAC bilateral	26	16	29	22	63	65	63	61
From multilateral agencies	34	33	41	49	66	77	95	115
TOTAL net ODA from all donors	175	159	231	232	320	359	477	708

Source: UNDP 1989b

Table A.2b Estimate of ODA from socialist bloc ($ mn)

	1980	1981	1982	1983	1984	1985	1986
Non-DAC ODA (from UNDP 1989b)	26	16	29	22	63	65	63
OPEC ODA (from UNCTAD)	10	1	2	2	3	6	7
Difference = socialist ODA	16	15	27	20	61	59	56

Table A.2c Financial flows to Mozambique ($ mn)

	1979	1980	1981	1982	1983	1984	1985	1986	1987	1988
Net ODA	162	184	171	228	231	320	359	477	710	875
Net non-concessional	2	174	277	139	24	-57	31	-63	-98	-84
TOTAL financial inflows	164	358	448	367	255	263	390	414	612	791

Source: Hansma (1990) as modified (see Comment 3)

Notes to Tables A.2

Definitions:
ODA is "official development assistance", and includes grants and concessional loans with a grant element of at least 25%. Certain kinds of assistance, such as debt relief, are not included.
DAC is the "Development Assistance Committee" of the Organization for Economic Cooperation and Development (OECD). The DAC donors are the 18 industrialized countries.
OPEC is the "Organization of Petroleum Exporting Countries.
Non-concessional finance includes export credits, non-concessional loans, and investment.
Net means that all figures are net after subtracting repayments from new inflows, including repayments of concessional loans. Figures are also for aid actually received by Mozambique and not aid pledged.
Comments:
1. No two sources agree on aid flows. OECD, Unctad, WB, and UNDP all give different figures, although there is vague agreement, especially on general trends.
2. Table A.2b surely underestimates the volume of concessional loans made by the socialist bloc. Compare this to Table A.3b.
3. Hansma (1990) is based on OECD data, which includes OPEC but not socialist bloc assistance. Although it is not precisely correct to do so, in Table A.2c I have added the socialist bloc aid from Table A.2b to Hansma's figures, and I have made estimates of socialist aid for the missing years.

Tables A.3. Development Assistance as Reported by Donors to the UN

Table A.3a Types of assistance ($ mn)

	1982	1983	1984	1985	1986	1987	1988
Technical	80	65	54	73	109	159	167
Capital	163	154	154	364	452	394	479
Emergency	17	30	72	104	130	349	312
TOTAL	261	249	281	542	693	903	960

Source: UNDP 1989a: 32 as amended (see note 2 below)

Table A.3b Donors to Mozambique ($ mn)

Donor	1985	1986	1987	1988
Italy	95	110	135	160
Sweden	46	78	95	103
USSR	130	112	48	96
UK	11	32	45	64
EC	nd	nd	73	64
Netherlands	37	37	50	57
US	61	53	76	52
Norway	14	25	34	44
West Germany	14	15	22	35
Canada	12	22	26	29
France	20	32	37	20
Denmark	3	14	27	19
East Germany	nd	22	29	19
Switzerland	9	4	17	13
Australia	4	5	5	10
Finland	3	5	10	3
Japan	5	22	15	nd
3rd world	4	6	8	7
Other Europe	3	5	5	0
World Food Programme	26	16	14	20
UNDP	8	9	8	10
UNICEF	2	10	19	8
Other UN	8	8	10	9
World Bank	5	0	25	44
IMF	0	24	15	25
Other banks	13	12	18	nd
NGOs	10	15	39	35
TOTAL	542	692	902	960

Comment: This is data as reported by donors to the UN in Maputo. This means that it will differ from other aid tables in three ways:

1. Western aid as reported here is more than $200 mn per year more than is shown in table A.2a, which means that in their reports to the UN, donors are claiming as aid substantial amounts that would not qualify as ODA under the DAC definition.
2. Coverage of socialist bloc aid is probably more accurate here than the OECD estimate in tables A.2.
3. Most NGOs do not reply to the UN questionnaire. Of those which do, most claim some funds already claimed by bilateral donors, leading to double counting. There may be similar double counting with some UN agency funds as well. For emergency funds, this is clarified in tables A.5.

Source: UNDP 1987a, 1987b, 1988b, 1989a

Notes:
1. Columns do not add correctly because of omissions in the UNDP reports.
2. UNDP 1989a, covering aid delivered in 1988, contains two omissions and one questionable inclusion, which have been corrected. Two major USSR donations of material aid are listed in Table 6 of UNDP 1989a but omitted from the totals. They are $28.4 mn in petroleum derivatives, given as balance of payments support, and $25 mn in consumer goods given as relief assistance, (UNDP 1989a: 206, 212) and have been included in table A.3b. West Germany has claimed $103.6 mn in debt cancellation (UNDP 1989a: 168). Such debt pardons are never included as aid, and no other country has claimed its debt cancellations as aid, so this item has been ignored in calculating table A.3b.
3. nd = no data reported

Table A.4 Grain Imports

Table A.4a Grain imports (000t, actual arrivals)
Calendar year, except 1987–89, agricultural year (May– April)

Year	73	76	77	78	79	80	81	82	83	84	85	86	87	88	89
Aid	0	114	75	114	168	139	137	194	221	332	249	253	560	527	393
Commercial imports	118	36	112	190	192	196	187	112	72	24	71	0	0	0	0
TOTAL imports	118	150	187	304	360	335	324	306	293	356	320	253	560	527	393

Table A.4b Grain donations: 1976–86 (000t)
(Donated grain arrivals in calendar year)

Donor	76	77	78	79	80	81	82	83	84	85	86	TOTAL	SHARE
European Community	22	15	63	26	12	30	44	57	55	59	55	438	22%
USA	21	7	8	59	55	2	10	33	52	52	57	356	18%
Canada	16	11	0	11	4	11	16	17	49	7	21	163	8%
Sweden	15	15	11	22	20	33	21	8	6	0	0	151	8%
World Food Programme	0	0	0	0	0	11	14	8	41	19	31	124	6%
Denmark	20	15	0	27	8	0	15	0	22	0	0	107	5%
UK	0	5	27	8	15	12	0	3	8	9	14	101	5%
Netherlands	0	0	0	0	12	8	6	0	45	23	5	99	5%
Japan	0	3	0	2	10	0	20	18	5	9	26	93	5%
Italy	0	0	0	4	0	8	5	17	12	10	6	62	3%
France	0	0	4	0	1	10	4	2	9	7	7	44	2%
Australia	4	0	0	4	0	0	0	4	5	7	14	38	2%
USSR	0	0	0	0	0	0	17	10	0	3	0	30	2%
West Germany	0	0	0	0	0	8	2	4	3	5	7	29	1%
Zimbabwe	0	0	0	0	0	0	0	25	0	0	0	25	1%
Others	16	4	1	5	2	4	20	15	20	39	10	136	7%
TOTAL	114	75	114	168	139	137	194	221	332	249	253	1996	
"Like-Minded Group"	67	41	11	63	44	52	66	25	122	30	26	547	27%

Table A.4c Grain donations: 1987–89 pledges (000t)
Grain promises made by donors during year
Agricultural year (May–April)

Donor	87	88	89	TOTAL	SHARE
USA	131	179	171	481	30%
European Community	161	102	73	336	21%
Canada	56	52	36	144	9%
World Food Programme	8	31	71	110	7%
Australia	27	34	43	104	6%
Italy	47	27	9	83	5%
UK	37	19	19	75	5%
Japan	34	13	19	66	4%
Netherlands	19	13	18	50	3%
West Germany	14	21	14	49	3%
Denmark	12	16	0	28	2%
France	5	7	9	21	1%
Others	42	17	9	68	4%
TOTAL	593	531	491	1615	
"Like-Minded Group"	89	81	54	224	14%

Source: author's estimate based on Ministry of Commerce data

Notes to Tables A.4:

1. There is wide disagreement as to actual quantities of grain imported. Different ministries and donor groups keep their own records and disagree. Furthermore, even within the same file folder within one ministry, there can be wide disparities between documents. The figures here are the author's selection from various sets of data from the Food Security Department of the Ministério do Comércio (previously Ministério do Comércio Interno).

2. With the big increase in food aid in 1987, reporting formats changed. From 1987 there was a switch from the calendar year to the agricultural year, so "1987" means 1 May 1987–30 April 1988. That means there is a three month gap in table A.4a.

3. Tables A.4a and A.4b attempt to show grain which actually arrived in Mozambique in the year in question. The time between a pledge of grain and its actual arrival is between 6 and 24 months. Because of changed reporting formats, Table A.4c refers to pledges of aid rather than actual arrivals, but comparison with the totals of actual aid arrivals in Table A.4a shows that in that period the quantities were relatively similar for those 3 years.

4. The "Like-Minded Group" is a very loose association of the Nordic states (Denmark, Finland, Norway, and Sweden) plus Canada and the Netherlands. The group has tended to support Mozambique quite strongly, so its combined grain donations are also shown in Tables A.4b and A.4c. (These countries are already included individually so the amount for the "Like-Minded Group" should not be added again to the total.)

5. "Other" grain donors include Algeria, Argentina, Austria, Belgium, China, Finland, India, Kenya, North Korea, Norway, Pakistan, Spain, Swaziland, and Switzerland, as well as several NGOs, notably the Mennonite Church and the World Lutheran Federation.

Table A.5 Response to emergency appeals

Table A.5a Pledges by donor and by channel ($ mn)

AGENCY	SOURCE OF FUNDS 1988 appeal			SOURCE OF FUNDS 1989 appeal			CHANNEL 1988 appeal			CHANNEL 1989 appeal			PORTION OF FUNDS DISBURSED BY FUNDER 1988 appeal			PORTION OF FUNDS DISBURSED BY FUNDER 1989 appeal		
	against appeal	other	TOTAL	against appeal	other	TOTAL	against appeal	other	TOTAL	against appeal	other	TOTAL	against appeal	other	TOTAL	against appeal	other	TOTAL
COUNTRIES																		
Australia	2.9		2.9	7.2		7.2	1.8		1.8	2.5		2.5	62%		62%	35%		35%
Austria	1.4		1.4	0.6		0.6							0%		0%	0%		0%
Canada	24.0	0.6	24.6	16.2		16.2	13.2		13.2	9.4		9.4	55%	0%	54%	58%		58%
Denmark	4.9		4.9	3.3		3.3				0.3		0.3	0%		9%			9%
EC	22.2	4.4	26.6	46.5	13.4	59.9	17.2	2.9	20.1	39.0	3.0	42.0	77%	66%	76%	84%	22%	70%
Finland	1.4	0.4	1.8	1.2	0.3	1.5							0%		0%	0%	0%	0%
France	4.1		4.1	2.2		2.2	4.1		4.1	1.7		1.7	100%		100%	77%		77%
Germany - West	12.1	0.3	12.4	5.8	1.0	6.8	0.6		0.6	0.4		0.4	5%	0%	5%	7%	0%	6%
Italy	43.9	5.7	49.6	2.2		2.2	41.2	4.2	45.4	1.7		1.7	94%	74%	92%	77%		77%
Japan	6.1		6.1	4.1		4.1	5.3		5.3	4.1		4.1	87%		87%	100%		100%
Netherlands	10.4	0.1	10.5	4.0		4.0	3.4	0.1	3.5				33%	100%	33%	0%		0%
Norway	5.8	0.4	6.2	2.8		2.8	2.2		2.2	1.4		1.4	38%	0%	35%	50%		50%
Sweden	26.8	8.7	35.5	26.9	7.5	34.4	20.5	5.7	26.2	15.4	2.8	18.2	76%	66%	74%	57%	37%	53%
Switzerland	0.9	1.1	2.0	3.6	1.0	4.6	0.2		0.2	0.6		0.6	22%	0%	10%	17%	0%	13%
UK	12.2	2.9	15.1	10.3	0.2	10.5	2.1		2.1	3.2		3.2	17%	0%	14%	31%	0%	30%
US	56.9	4.0	60.9	60.8	3.5	64.3	40.6		40.6	48.2	3.3	51.5	71%	0%	67%	79%	94%	80%
USSR	1.2	5.7	6.9	5.2		5.2	1.2	5.7	6.9	5.2		5.2	100%	100%	100%	81%	100%	100%
Other	5.9	0.2	6.1	2.5	0.3	2.8	4.4		4.4	1.8		1.8	75%	0%	72%		0%	77
TOTAL GOVT	243.1	34.5	277.6	200.2	32.4	232.6	158.0	18.6	176.6	129.7	14.3	144.0	65%	54%	64%	65%	44%	62%

AGENCY	SOURCE OF FUNDS						CHANNEL						PORTION OF FUNDS FROM OTHER SOURCES					
	1988 appeal			1989 appeal			1988 appeal			1989 appeal			1988 appeal			1989 appeal		
	against appeal	other	TOTAL	against appeal	other	TOTAL	against appeal	other	TOTAL	against appeal	other	TOTAL	against appeal	other	TOTAL	against appeal	other	TOTAL
UN SYSTEM																		
UNDP	0.6		0.6	0.2		0.2	2.1	0.1	2.2	1.8		1.8	71%	100%	73%	89%		89%
UNDRO				0.4		0.4	1.1	0.2	1.3	2.9	0.4	3.3	100%	100%	100%	86%	100%	88%
UNHCR	0.5		0.5				5.8		5.8	3.2	1.7	4.9	91%		91%	100%	100%	100%
UNICEF	1.5	0.4	1.9	1.2		1.2	8.3	1.1	9.4	5.0		5.0	82%	64%	80%	76%		76%
WFP	13.1		13.1	13.4	7.8	21.2	32.4		32.4	20.7	7.8	28.5	60%		60%	35%	0%	26%
Other UN	0.2		0.2				0.5	0.1	0.6	0.2		0.2	60%	100%	67%	100%		100%
TOTAL UN	15.9	0.4	16.3	15.2	7.8	23.0	50.2	1.5	51.7	33.8	9.9	43.7	68%	73%	68%	55%	21%	47%
NGOs																		
Action Aid	0.6	0.2	0.8				2.6	0.2	2.8	0.6		0.6	77%	0%	71%	100%		100%
ADRA							1.2	0.3	1.5	1.7		1.7	100%	100%	100%	100%		100%
ARO							1.6		1.6		1.6	1.6	100%		100%		100%	100%
Care							4.5	2.0	6.5	12.4		12.4	100%	100%	100%	100%		100%
Caritas	0.1		0.1	0.4		0.4	9.7	1.7	11.4	3.5	0.8	4.3	99%	100%	99%	89%	100%	91%
CCM	4.4		4.4	3.8	0.5	4.3	5.7	0.3	6.0	7.0	0.6	7.6	23%	100%	27%	46%	17%	43%
E. Mondlane Fdn.							0.4		0.4	1.3		1.3	100%		100%	100%		100%
Emmaus											2.3	2.3					100%	100%
FHI	1.0		1.0	0.2	0.2	0.4	1.0		1.0	0.4	1.4	1.8	0%	0%	0%	50%	86%	78%
FOS (Belg)		2.2	2.2					2.2	2.2					0%	0%			
German Agro Ac.							2.2	0.3	2.5	1.3		1.3	100%	100%	100%	92%		92%
ICRC				0.1		0.1	0.2	3.8	4.0	3.6	0.5	4.1	100%	100%	100%	100%	100%	100%

AGENCY	SOURCE OF FUNDS 1988 appeal			SOURCE OF FUNDS 1989 appeal			CHANNEL 1988 appeal			CHANNEL 1989 appeal			PORTION OF FUNDS FROM OTHER SOURCES 1988 appeal			PORTION OF FUNDS FROM OTHER SOURCES 1989 appeal		
	against appeal	other	TOTAL	against appeal	other	TOTAL	against appeal	other	TOTAL	against appeal	other	TOTAL	against appeal	other	TOTAL	against appeal	other	TOTAL
LWF	1.4		1.4	0.8	0.4	1.2	2.0	0.1	2.1	1.2	0.9	2.1	30%	100%	33%	33%	56%	43%
MSF (Belg)							0.5		0.5		2.5	2.5	100%	100%	100%		100%	100%
MSF (France)					1.2	1.2	0.4		0.4		3.8	3.8	100%	100%	100%		68%	68%
MSF (Neth)							1.0		1.0		2.3	2.3	100%	100%	100%		100%	100%
Oxfam (Belg)							0.0			1.8		1.8				100%		100%
Oxfam (UK)	0.5	0.4	0.9	0.9		0.9	4.7	0.4	5.1	2.1		2.1	89%	0%	82%	57%	57%	57%
SCF (Nor)							0.9	2.5	3.4	4.2		4.2	100%	100%	100%	100%	100%	100%
SCF (UK)	0.3	0.7	1.0	0.6		0.6	2.7	1.5	4.2	2.4		2.4	89%	53%	76%	75%	68%	75%
SCF (US)							0.2	0.8	1.0	0.9		0.9	100%	100%	100%	100%	100%	100%
World Vision I.	1.1	0.4	1.5	0.1	1.3	1.4	15.0	0.9	15.9	10.4	0.2	10.6	100%	100%	100%	100%	100%	100%
Other NGO							3.7	1.8	5.5	3.6	2.6	6.2	70%	78%	73%	97%	50%	77%
TOTAL NGO	9.4	3.9	13.3	6.9	3.6	10.5	60.2	18.8	79.0	58.4	19.5	77.9	84%	79%	83%	88%	82%	87%
(non-Moz NGO)	5.0	3.9	8.9	3.1	3.1	6.2	54.5	18.5	73.0	51.4	18.9	70.3						
TOTAL	268.4	38.8	307.2	222.3	43.8	266.4	268.4	38.9	307.2	221.9	43.7	265.6						

Source: Ratilal 1990a (deleting category "non-related"), *Priority Requirements* 4 April 1990 (deleting unconfirmed Italian pledges)

Notes:
Against appeal = funds pledged to cover a specific request
Other = funds for items not requested by the government of Mozambique
Source of funds = actual donor of money
Channel = agency which administers and disburses the funds

Includes all agencies which pledged or were to administer more than $1 mn in 1988 or 1989.

Appendix 2:
Periodization

Events have moved very quickly since independence, and it is useful to divide the past fifteen years into phases. Each author sets their own periodization, and I see the following points as marking sharp breaks:

- *25 June 1975:* Independence.
- *February 1977:* Third Congress.
- *Late 1980 and early 1981:* First SADCC conference, rapid international changes, and the start of destabilization.
- *Late 1983 and early 1984:* Fourth Congress, Nkomati, defaulting on the debt, and start of the aid invasion.
- *Late 1986:* Escalation of destabilization, death of Samora Machel, and agreement to structural adjustment.

That leads naturally to five periods. The first three are discussed in detail in *Mozambique: The Revolution Under Fire* (Hanlon 1984a), while the last two are the subject of this book.

1975–76: Consolidating independence

This was a period of rapid transformation, when Frelimo took control of state power and the economy and introduced major social changes. Health, education, law, and rented property were nationalized. Other economic sectors were not nationalized, but most Portuguese fled and abandoned their property, leaving Frelimo to try to keep the country running – which it did. Politically this was the period of revolutionary voluntarism and mass mobilization; Frelimo was still a broad front, while neighbourhood and workplace committees (groupos dinamizadores, GDs, dynamising groups) became both administrative and local political bodies. Internationally, Mozambique imposed mandatory UN sanctions on Rhodesia, while South Africa began imposing economic sanctions on Mozambique.

1977–80: Building socialism

Having created some degree of order and stopped the post-independence economic decline, Frelimo moved into its Third Congress with confidence. Economically it set out to socialize and modernize the country, with an emphasis on state farms and new industry. Internationally, Rhodesia attacked central Mozambique heavily during 1977-79, delaying economic development projects, but Zimbabwe became independent in 1980 and

SADCC was founded. Several countries (East and West) promised substantial credits for major industrial and agricultural development projects, and financial inflows increased. The army was converted from a guerrilla to a modern army, and won notable victories against Rhodesia.

Socially, Frelimo hardened its stand against traditionalism; the position of women improved substantially. Politically, Frelimo was converted from a broad front to a Marxist-Leninist Vanguard Party and GDs formed the basis for party cells. Frelimo still talked of "people's power", but increasingly power rested with the Frelimo party and the state apparatus.

1981–83: drought and destabilization

There was a sharp change in the world political environment, with the US, UK, and West Germany hostile to Mozambique and SADCC. Other European states backed Mozambique and SADCC, but it was not enough because the US licensed South African destabilization which brought economic chaos.

Destabilization came on top of the worst drought of the century and the worsening world economic climate, which meant deteriorating terms of trade and an end to credits, causing a sharp drop in financial inflows. Rapid modernization was already running into problems, due to over-ambition, excessive centralization, a lack of skilled people, and delays caused by Rhodesian attacks. Lacking foreign exchange, Mozambique stopped importing raw materials and consumer goods, which alienated the peasants and hit industrial production. Shortages led to an explosive growth in the black market with massive profits for traders. The rapid spread of the MNR was largely due to the high level of South African support, but it also reflected peasant alienation and the inability of the newly modernized and mechanized army to fight a guerrilla war.

The Fourth Party Congress in 1983 marked an effort by Frelimo to return to its populist roots and encourage debate, but this was not maintained and did not lead to formal democratization. Authoritarianism increased. The Congress also took steps to liberalize the economy, and give more freedom to private traders and farmers.

1984–86: searching for a way out

Frelimo looked for a middle way to end destabilization, trying to avoid aligning itself with either East or West. It signed the Nkomati Accord with South Africa and joined the IMF. There was some economic liberalization, but Frelimo did not abandon socialism and did not introduce the full IMF structural adjustment package. East bloc aid increased to support the new approach, but eastern and Nordic partners pressed Frelimo to make a deal with the US and its allies. Western donors poured in, but western aid increased only slowly as the West tried to force policy changes. US policy became more confused, but the US and its friends largely shifted from trying to destroy Frelimo to attempting to co-opt it. Destabilization increased and the economic situation worsened.

In 1986 aid jumped, which meant goods in urban shops. But destabilization peaked in 1986, which meant that half the population needed food aid. The death of Samora Machel in 1986 ended the post-revolutionary era. Forced to choose between the great powers, Mozambique finally turned to the West. Agreement to an IMF structural adjustment marked the failure to find an alternative way out, and concession to western pressure.

1987–90: adjustment

Destabilization was slowly rolled back from 1987, reflecting South Africa's weaker position due to sanctions and internal uprisings, as well as increased support for Mozambique from its other neighbours. Structural adjustment accelerated privatization and social differentiation. Poverty and hunger became more widespread, while conspicuous wealth and consumption increased. Health and education, the two pillars of Frelimo's popularity, were hit hard by destabilization and structural adjustment.

Aid flows rose rapidly, and donor agencies dominated the country. The entry and return of foreign companies accelerated. A comprador group began to emerge, as the massive inflow of aid provided opportunities for Mozambicans to earn high salaries working for the foreigners. Corruption became more obvious in the state apparatus and the army.

Politics became more contradictory. The Frelimo Fifth Congress in 1989 was much less democratic than the Fourth; dissent was curtailed. But the national People's Assembly (parliament) became more than a rubber stamp, and debated and criticized on a wide range of issues. There were a series of strikes and protests in 1990. A new constitution was approved which was much more democratic and which introduced a multiparty system.

After 15 years of remarkable unity, the Frelimo leadership began openly to show divisions. The Fifth Congress jettisoned Marxism-Leninism, and part of the leadership backed capitalism with the same passion with which they had backed socialism two decades earlier. Other parts of the leadership, however, pushed for a more social democratic line. 1990 saw the first direct talks between the government and Renamo.

References

Articles and Books

Adam, Yussuf *et al* (1987), "Programa de Ábastecimento de Água Potável na Província de Cabo Delgado em Moçambique, Avaliação 1987", Maputo.

Adam, Yussuf *et al* (1989), "Preparatory Study on Markets and Prices in the Rural Areas", Centre for African Studies, Maputo.

Adam, Yussuf (1990), *Foreign Aid to Mozambique: Needs and Effects*, Centre for African Studies, Maputo, and Chr Michelsen Institute, Bergen, Norway, February 1990.

Adedeji, Adebayo (1990), statement at a conference "The Prospects for Africa in the 1990s", sponsored by the Overseas Development Institute, London, 6 June 1990.

Association of West European Parliamentarians for Action Against Apartheid (AWEPAA 1989) and African-European Institute, *Mozambique's Unnatural Disaster Persists,* report of a working visit to Mozambique 18–26 November 1988, AWEPAA, Prins Hendrikkade 48, 1012 AC Amsterdam.

Azam, J P and Faucher, J J (1988), *The Supply of Manufactured Goods and Agricultural Development: The Case of Mozambique,* OECD Development Centre, Paris.

Berger, Lewis, Inc. (1988), "Evaluation of OFDA and FFP Grants to Care International in Mozambique", Washington, 11 June 1988.

Butler, M B, Sanera, M, and Weinrod, W B (eds) (1984), *Mandate for Leadership II,* Heritage Foundation, Washington.

Brennan, Tom and Lockwood, Richard (1985), "Evaluation of OFDA Grant ASB-0000-G-SS-4108 to Care/Mozambique to establish an emergency assistance logistical unit", US Office of Foreign Disaster Assistance (OFDA), September 1985.

Brochmann, Grete and Ofstad, Arve (1990), *Mozambique: Norwegian Assistance in a Context of Crisis,* Chr Michelsen Institute, Fantoft, Norway.

Carrilho, João (1990), untitled paper on the Programa dos Distritos Prioritários (PDP), 12 March 1990.

Castel-Branco, Carlos Nuno (1989) "Reflexão sobre a Cuso-Suco na economia Moçambicana", Cuso-Suco, Maputo.

Clay, Edward and York, Susan (1987), *Information and Emergencies: a Report of the 5th IDS Food Aid Seminar 21–24 April 1987*, Institute of Development Studies Discussion Paper 236, Brighton, UK.

Cliff, Julie *et al* (1986), "Mozambique Health Holding the Line", *Review of African Political Economy*, Sheffield, UK, September 1986.

Crocker, Chester (1987), "US Policy Toward Mozambique"; statement to the Africa Subcommittee of the Senate Foreign Relations Committee, 24 June 1987, and published by the US State Department as "Current Policy No. 983".

Dadzie, Kenneth (1990), statement at a conference "The Prospects for Africa in the 1990s" sponsored by the Overseas Development Institute, London, 6 June 1990.

Disch, Arne (1989), "Social Dimensions of Adjustment in Mozambique", Norad, Maputo, 7 July 1989.

Eduards, Krister *et al* (1990), *Market Intervention and Price Policies for Agricultural Marketing in Mozambique*, Stockholm Group for Development Studies.

Egero, Bertil (1987), *Mozambique: A Dream Undone*, Scandinavian Institute of African Studies (Nordiska afrikainstitutet), Uppsala, Sweden.

Francisco, António (1987a), *A Produção e a Comercialização de Hortofrutícolas da Zona Suburbana para a Cidade de Maputo no Contexto da Liberalização dos Preços*, Maputo, March 1987; Tese de licenciatura.

Francisco, António *et al* (1987b), *Estudo do Sistema de Marcado de Hortícolas e Frutas e Impacto da Liberalização dos Preços*, Maputo, November 1987; study for the World Bank.

Geldenhuys, Deon (1982), "Destabilisation Controversy in Southern Africa", Southern African Forum Position Paper vol 5 no 18, Johannesburg.

George, Susan (1988), *A Fate Worse than Debt*, Penguin, London.

Gersony, Robert (1988), "Summary of Mozambican Refugee Accounts", US State Dept. Bureau of Refugee Programs, April 1988; this has been reprinted in various publications, notably in *Mozambique – a Tale of Terror*, African-European Institute, 1989, available from AWEPAA, Prins Hendrikkade 48, 1012 AC Amsterdam.

Green, Reginald H (1989), "Poverty in Mozambique", February 1989; paper prepared for Unicef and the Ministry of Finance, also known as "Estudo SDA" and "the Green report".

Green, Reginald H (1990a), "Mozambique into the 1990s", paper presented at the AWEPAA Child Survival conference, Harare 24 April 1990.

Green, Reginald H (1990b), "Poverty, Rehabilitation and Economic Transformation: The Case of Mozambique", paper presented at the Institute of Social Studies, The Hague, 1 November 1990.

Green, Reginald H (1990c), "Toward Rural Transformation in Mozambique", paper presented to the Association of Agricultural Economists of Namibia, Swakopmund.

Grosh, Barbara (1990), "Public, quasi-public, and private manufacturing firms in Kenya: the surprising case of a cliché gone astray", *Development Policy Review*, Sage, London, Vol 8.

Gumende, Antonio (1989), "Emergency/NGOs" article sent out by AIM, Maputo, 19 October 1989.

Hackett, James (ed.) (1986), "The Resistance Can Win in Mozambique", *National Security Record*, June 1986, Heritage Foundation, Washington DC.

Hancock, Graham (1989), *Lords of Poverty*, Macmillan, London.

Hanlon, Joseph (1981), "Mozambique's 'new realities' confront Comecon", *Guardian*, London 28 July 1981.

Hanlon, Joseph (1984a), *Mozambique: The Revolution Under Fire*, Zed, London.

Hanlon, Joseph (1984b), "Too little, too late", *New Statesman*, London 3 February 1984.

Hanlon, Joseph (1984c), "National plan promises radical changes", *Africa Economic Digest*, London 11 May 1984; written under pseudonym "Antonio Johala".

Hanlon, Joseph (1986a), *Beggar Your Neighbours: Apartheid Power in Southern Africa*, James Currey, London.

Hanlon, Joseph (1986b), *Apartheid's Second Front*, Penguin, London.

Hanlon, Joseph (1989), *SADCC in the 1990s*, Economist Intelligence Unit, London.

Hansma, Tamme (1990), *Basic Data on SADCC and International Cooperation*, AWEPAA, Amsterdam.

Heatherly, Charles (ed.), (1981), *Mandate for Leadership*, Heritage Foundation, Washington.

Heatherly, Charles and Pines, Burton (1989), *Mandate for Leadership III*, Heritage Foundation, Washington.

Hedges, David (1989), "Notes on Malawi-Mozambique Relations, 1961–1987", *Journal of Southern African Studies*, October 1989.

Hermans, Arnoldus *et al.*, (1990), "Mozambique's Priority District Programme", letter from the Like-Minded Group in Maputo to Cooperation Minister Jacinto Veloso, 1 June 1990.

Hermele, Kenneth (1988), *Land Struggles and Social Differentiation in Southern Mozambique*, Scandinavian Institute of International Affairs, Uppsala; Research Report No 82.

Hermele, Kenneth (1990), *Mozambican Crossroads*, Chr Michelsen Institute, Bergen, May 1990.

Hurd, Douglas (1990), statement at a conference "The Prospects for Africa in the 1990s" sponsored by the Overseas Development Institute, London, 6 June 1990.

Irwin, Michael (1990), "Inside the World Bank", lecture at the Institute for African Alternatives, London, 17 July 1990.

Jansson, Kurt *et al.* (1987), *The Ethiopian Famine*, Zed, London.

Jeggle, Terry (1987), testimony before the Senate Africa Subcommittee, 24 June 1987, Care, Washington.

Johnson, Phyllis and Martin, David (1989), *Apartheid Terrorism*, Commonwealth Secretariat and James Currey, London.

Kanji, Najmi (1988), "Drug Policy and Financing in Mozambique", M.Sc thesis, London School of Hygiene and Tropical Medicine.

Latham, R C and Matthews, W, (eds) (1970), *The Diary of Samuel Pepys – Vol 1: 1660*, Bell, London.

Lewis, T W L (1990), "Proposal for the Rehabilitation and Development of the Family Sector in the Montepuez District", January 1990.

Lonrho (1990), "Montepuez Agro Industrial Complex Project", March 1990.

Macaringue, Joao *et al.* (1989), "An Evaluation of the Airlift Operation in Sofala Province, 26 September – 1 October 1989".

Machel, Graça (1989), "Fundamental forces that have dominated events in southern Africa", paper given at the AWEPAA Child Survival conference, Harare 24 April 1990.

Machungo, Mário (1988), statement at the Consultative Group for Mozambique, Paris 3 November 1988.

Mandate. See Heatherly 1981 and 1989 and Butler 1984.

Marshall, Judith (1989), "On the Ropes: Socialism & Frelimo's Fifth Congress", *Southern African Report*, Toronto, November 1989.

Marshall, Judith (1990), "Structural Adjustment and Social Policy in Mozambique", *Review of African Political Economy*, Sheffield, UK, Spring 1990.

Mauras, Marta (1987), "Unicef Mozambique Emergency Programme", paper presented at ESARO Regional Management Team Meeting, 8–12 November 1987.

Morrison, J Stephen (1987), "The Battle for Mozambique", *Africa Report*, September–October 1987.

Mistry, Percy (1989), "The Present Role of the World Bank in Africa", talk delivered at the Institute for African Alternatives, London, 16 October 1989.

Mutemba, Abel (1981), *Operação 6 Aniversário*, *Notícias*, Maputo.

Noormahomed, Abdul and Cliff, Julie (1988 & 1990), "The Impact on Health in

Mozambique of South African Destabilisation", Ministry of Health, Maputo; second and third editions.

Norrbin, Clay *et al* (1988), "Knowledge development within the sister industry concept", SIDA, Stockholm.

O'Brien, Peter *et al*. *(*1990), "Evaluation of Norway's Non-Project Financial Assistance to Mozambique", Chr Michelsen Institute, Derap, Norway.

Onimode, Bade (1987), opening address at a conference on the Impact of IMF and World Bank Policies on the people of Africa, Institute for African Alternatives, London, 7 September 1987.

Osman, Magid (1990), "Economic and Social Recovery", talk given at a meeting of the European Campaign on South African Agression Against Mozambique and Angola (ECASAAMA), Paris, 23 November 1990.

Pécoul, Bernard *et al*. (1990), "Mozambique: Mortality among displaced persons", *Lancet*, 17 March 1990.

Pililão, Fernando (1989), *Moçambique: Evolução da Toponimia e da Divisão Territorial 1974–1987*, Universidade Eduardo Mondlane, Maputo.

Ratilal, Prakash (1988), speech at the Conference on Emergency Assistance to Mozambique, Maputo 26-27 April 1988.

Ratilal, Prakash (1990a), *Mozambique: Using Aid to End Emergency*, UNDP, New York.

Ratilal, Prakash (1990b), *Enfrentar o Desafio*, Editoria Globo, Maputo.

Riddell, Roger (1987), *Foreign Aid Reconsidered*, James Currey and ODI, London.

Rutherford, George and Mahanjane, Amós (1985), "Morbidity and Mortality in the Mozambican Famine of 1983", *Journal of Tropical Pediatrics*, June 1985.

Ryrie, William (1990), statement at a conference "The Prospects for Africa in the 1990s" sponsored by the Overseas Development Institute, London, 6 June 1990.

Shearar, Jeremy (1989), letter published as UN General Assembly document A/44/226 of 13 April 1989.

Smart, Teresa (1984), "Starving Mozambicans cross border to Zimbabwe", *Guardian*, London, 17 February 1984.

Stacey, Roy (1987), Statement to the House Select Committee on Hunger, 7 October 1987.

Thompson, Carol (1990), "Beyond the Nation-state? Democracy in a Regional Economic Context", University of Southern California, Los Angeles.

Torp, Jens Erik *et al*. (1989), *Mozambique, São Tomé & Príncipe*, Pinter, London.

Urdang, Stephanie (1989), *And Still They Dance*, Earthscan, London.

Veloso, Jacinto (1989), statement to the UNDP governing council, New York, 14 June 1989.

Vieira, Sérgio (1990), "Prospectivas nas Relações Norte Sul", talk delivered at a seminar May 1990.

Vines, Alex (1990), "Several Years Behind the Leash", *Southern African Review of Books*, London, June/July 1990.

Vines, Alex (1991), *Renamo: A Study in Terrorism*, James Currey, London.

Official Documents

Care (1983), "Care probe to Mozambique", September 1983.

Comissão Executiva Nacional de Emergência (CENE 1987a), various documents relating to the Reunião Nacional de Emergência in Tete, 12–18 August 1987.

CENE (1987b), "Preliminary Evaluation of the Emergency Programme", Maputo, 22 December 1987.

CENE (1988a), *Rising to the Challenge*, Maputo, April 1988.

CENE (1988b), "Resumo do Relatorio Sobre a Execução do Programa de Emergência", Maputo 24 September 1988.

CENE (1989a), "VI Reunião Nacional de Emergência Documento Final", Maputo, 1 June 1989.

CENE (1989b), "Mid-Term Evaluation of the 1989-1990 Emergency Appeal", November 1989.

Comissão Nacional do Plano (CNP 1984a) *Economic Report*, Maputo January 1984.

CNP (1984b), *Complemento à Informação Económica*, Maputo May 1984; document distributed to OECD creditor governments in response to questionnaire following the publication of the *Economic Report*.

CNP (1990), "Estudo sobre as Condições Actuais de Produção e Consumo de Alimentos em Cinco Provincias", Maputo, April 1990.

Departamento de Prevenção e Combate às Calamidades Naturais (DPCCN 1983a), *Food Emergency in Mozambique in 1983*, Maputo 18 January 1983.

Direcção Nacional de Estatística (DNE 1985), *Informação Estatística 1975–1984*, Maputo.

DNE (1986), *Informação Estatística 1985*, Maputo.

DNE (1987), *Informação Estatística 1986*, Maputo.

DNE (1988), *Informação Estatística 1987*, Maputo.

DNE (1989), *Informação Estatística 1988*, Maputo.

Economic Commission for Africa (ECA 1989a), *African Alternative to Structural Adjustment Programmes: A Framework for Transformation and Recovery*, April 1989; E/ECA/CM.15/6/Rev.2

ECA (1989b), "Statistics and Policies: ECA Preliminary Observations of the World Bank Report 'Africa's Adjustment and Growth in the 1980s'", 24 April 1989.

ECA (1989c) and UN Inter-Agency Task Force, Africa Recovery Programme, *South African Destabilisation: The Economic Cost of Frontline Resistance to Apartheid*, PO Box 3001, Addis Ababa and Room S-805, UN, New York.

"Executive Summary of the Report of the Commission of Enquiry Appointed by the Council of Ministers to Investigate Misappropriation and Theft in the Management and Distribution of Emergency Programme Goods", Maputo, 14 April 1990; drawn up by a joint donor-government working group.

Frelimo (1989a), "For the Normalisation of Life – Report of the Central Committee", English translation, MIO London.

Frelimo (1989b), "Economic and Social Directives", English translation, MIO London.

Government of Mozambique (GM 1990), "Update of the Emergency Situation in Mozambique and Provisional Assessment of 1991 Relief Needs", December 1990.

House Select Committee on Hunger (HSCH 1987), "Mozambique: Origins of a Famine", Washington, nd but probably 1987.

International Committee of the Red Cross (ICRC 1983) "Missão de Avaliação à Província de Inhambane", Maputo, 5 July 1983.

International Monetary Fund (IMF 1987), "People's Republic of Mozambique – Staff Report for the 1987 Article IV Consultation", 20 October 1987.

IMF (1988a), "People's Republic of Mozambique – Request for Second Annual Arrangement Under the Structural Adjustment Facility", 24 February 1988.

IMF (1988b), "Statement by the staff representative of the IMF at the Mozambique Consultative Meeting, Paris, November 3-4, 1988".

Ministério da Agricultura (MA 1983), "Monap Annual Report 1982", Maputo.

Ministério da Agricultura (MA 1984), "Monap Annual Report 1983", Maputo.

Ministério do Comércio (MC 1988), Departamento de Seguranca Alimentar, "Cidade de Maputo 1988 – I Inquerito Nutricional e do Orcamento Familiar".

Ministério do Comércio (MC 1990), "Proposta para a futura intervenção do estado na comercialização agricola e areas relacionadas", Maputo, May 1990.

Ministério do Comércio Interno (MCI 1983a), Food Security Office, "Perspective of Food Aid 1983", 24 June 1983.

MCI (1983b), "Information on the Drought Situation in Mozambique", Maputo, December 1983.

MCI (1984), Direcção de Economia, "Informação Sobre a Situação Alimentar", 30 May 1984.

Ministério da Educação, Nùcleo de Emergência (Mined 1987), untitled maps dated 14 November 1987.

Ministério da Informação (Minfo 1985), *Documentos da Gorongosa (extractos)*, photocopies and translations of parts of a diary maintained by a Renamo official named Vaz and captured at the Renamo base "Casa Banana" at Gorongosa on 28 August 1985.

Ministério da Saùde (Misau 1986a), "Medicamentos: Necessidades e Financiamento: Mesa Redonda", Maputo, 29 August 1986.

Misau (1987b), "The Essential Drugs Programme", Pharmaceutical Department, Maputo, 31 December 1986.

Misau (1987), "Comissão de Emergências do Misau: Procedimentos e Recomendações", Maputo, 6 October 1987.

Misau (1989), "Manual de Atenção a Saùde em Situação de Emergência", Maputo.

National Planning Commission, see Comissão Nacional do Plano (CNP)

Office of Foreign Disaster Assistance (OFDA 1987), *Mozambique: a Country Profile*, USAID, Washington, April 1987.

Organização dos Trabalhadores de Moçambique (OTM 1989) "Analise do Impacto do Programa de Reabilitação Económica na Vida do Trabalhador", Maputo, October 1989.

Organization for Economic Co-operation and Development (OECD), *Development Co-operation*, Paris, annual.

Parliament of the Commonwealth of Australia (PCA 1989) *Report of the Australian Parliamentary Delegation to Ethiopia, Tanzania, Mozambique, and Zimbabwe: June–July 1988*, Canberra.

Província da Zambézia Comissão Províncial de Emergência (PZCPE 1988), "Relatório", Quelimane, September 1988.

República Popular de Moçambique (RPM 1984), "Address to the creditors of the People's Republic of Mozambique", Maputo 30 January 1984.

RPM (1985), *Report*, Maputo, January 1985. (No ministry identified)

RPM (1987), "Strategy and Program for Economic Rehabilitation 1987–90, Report prepared by the Government of Mozambique for the meeting of the Consultative Group for Mozambique, Paris, July 1987", Maputo June 1987.

RPM (1988), "Strategy and Program for Economic Rehabilitation 1988–91, Report prepared by the Government of Mozambique for the meeting of the Consultative Group for Mozambique, Paris, November 3–4, 1988", Maputo 7 October 1988.

RPM (1989) "Strategy and Program for Economic Rehabilitation 1989–92, Report prepared by the Government of Mozambique for the meeting of the Consultative Group for Mozambique, Paris, November 16, 1989", Maputo 3 October 1989.

Southern African Development Coordination Conference (SADCC 1980), *Southern Africa: Toward Economic Liberation*, a declaration by the governments of independent states of southern Africa made at Lusaka 1 April 1980.

SADCC (1990), *SADCC: the productive sectors – engine of growth and development*, document for annual conference, Luanda, February 1990.

UN Children's Fund (Unicef 1986), "Mozambique", Maputo, September 1986.

Unicef (1987), *Children on the Front Line*, New York.

Unicef (1989a), *Children on the Front Line – 1989 Update*, New York.

Unicef (1989b), *Unicef Annual Report – Mozambique, Swaziland 1989*, Maputo.

Unicef (1990), "Supply Division Annual Report 1989".

UN Conference on Trade and Development (Unctad), *Handbook of International Trade and Development Statistics*, New York, annual.

UN Department of Special Political Questions, Regional Cooperation, Decolonization and Trusteeship (UNDSPQ 1990), *The Emergency Situation in Mozambique. Priority*

Requirements for the period 1990–1991, UN, New York; document ST/SPSRCDT/1. (Appeal document for the 1990 New York conference.)

UN Development Programme (UNDP 1987a), *Development Co-operation Report – 1985*, Maputo, September 1987.

UNDP (1987b), *Development Co-operation Report - 1986*, Maputo, September 1987.

UNDP (1987c), "Programme Planning – Country and Intercountry Programmes and Projects – Third Country Programme for Mozambique", New York 9 March 1987; document DP/CP/Moz/3

UNDP (1988a), "UNDP Administrator to Visit Mozambique", Maputo 7 March 1988; press release.

UNDP (1988b), *Development Co-operation Report – 1987*, Maputo, December 1988.

UNDP (1989a), *Development Co-operation Report – 1988*, Maputo, December 1989.

UNDP (1989b) and the World Bank, *African Economic and Financial Data*, New York & Washington.

UN Industrial Development Organisation (Unido 1987), *Study of the Industrial Sector in Mozambique/ Situação da Indústria em Moçambique*, Vienna; 2 vol, DP/ID/Ser.B/586.

UN Industrial Development Organization (Unido 1989), *Industry and Development: Global Report 1989/90*, Vienna.

Unipac (nd), "A World of Goods", booklet published by Unipac (Unicef Procurement and Assembly Centre), Copenhagen, nd but perhaps 1985.

UN Office for Emergencies in Africa (UNOEA 1989), *The Emergency Situation in Mozambique, Priority requirements for the period 1989–90*, New York 8 March 1989. (Appeal document for the 1989 New York conference.)

UN Special Coordinator for Emergency Relief Operations in Mozambique (UNSCERO 1987), and the Government of Mozambique, *Priority Emergency Assistance Requirements of the People's Republic of Mozambique for the Year 1987*, Geneva, 14 March 1987. (Appeal document for the 1987 Geneva conference.)

UN Special Coordinator for Emergency Relief Operations in Mozambique (UNSCERO 1988), and the Government of Mozambique, *The Emergency Situation in Mozambique: Priorities for Emergency Assistance for 1988–1989*, Maputo, 17 March 1988. (Appeal document for the 1988 Maputo conference.)

US Agency For International Development (USAID), various years, *Annual Budget Submission*, Washington. Budget for fiscal year is submitted in calendar year two years before, eg FY 1990 budget submission is dated May 1988.

USAID (1986a, 1986b, 1987a), Evaluations of the Mozambique Private Sector Rehabilitation Programs I, II, and III, Maputo.

USAID (1987b), "Action Plan" for Mozambique for FY 1989, Maputo.

USAID (1988a), draft agreement between USAID and MSF-France for Zambézia Child Survival Project, 12 August 1988.

USAID (1989a), *Mozambique Private Sector Support Programme*, Washington, August 1989.

USAID (1989b), *Mozambique Pilot Child Survival Project 656-0207 Project Paper*, Maputo, 30 June 1989.

USAID (1990a), "A Discussion of Commercial Food Aid", Maputo; nd but probably May 1990.

USAID (1990b) "Mozambique Country Strategic Programme FY 1990-1992", Washington, March 1990.

US Commerce Department (USCD 1980), *Foreign Economic Trends and Their Implications for the United States – 80-026 – Mozambique*, prepared by the US Embassy, Maputo April 1980.

US State Department (USSD 1987), "Mozambique: Charting a New Course", Current Policy No. 990, Washington, June 1987.

World Bank (WB 1985a), "Mozambique: Discussion Paper on Economic Policy", 31 October 1985.

WB (1985b), "Discussions of Economic Policy with the government of the People's Republic of Mozambique, Aide-Mémoire", 18 November 1985.

WB (1986), "World Bank Mission to Assist in the Preparation of an Economic Rehabilitation Program, Aide-Mémoire", 11 December 1986.

WB and IMF (1987a), "People's Republic of Mozambique Economic Policy Framework, 1987–89", 5 May 1987.

WB (1987b), "Report to the Consultative Group for Mozambique on the Government's Economic Rehabilitation Programme", 16 June 1987.

WB (1987c), "The World Bank's Role in Promoting the Private Sector", 27 October 1987.

WB (1987d) "Aide-Mémoire of the World Bank Mission to Review Progress of the Second Rehabilitation Credit", 28 November 1987.

WB (1988a) and IMF, "People's Republic of Mozambique Economic Policy Framework, 1988–90", 2 March 1988.

WB (1988b), "Report to the Consultative Group for Mozambique on the Government's Economic Rehabilitation Programme", 3 October 1988.

WB (1988c), "Mozambique Public Expenditure Review", 28 October 1988, draft.

WB (1988d), "Special Program of Assistance Status Report for Mozambique", 4 August 1988.

WB (1988e), "Current Economic Situation"; statement by the WB at the Mozambique Consultative Group Meeting, Paris, 3–4 November 1988.

WB (1988f), "Statement on External Financing Requirements by World Bank", Mozambique Consultative Group Meeting, Paris, 3–4 November 1988.

WB (1988g), "Social Dimensions of Adjustment (SDA) Project Identification Mission", Aide-mémoire, 16 April 1988.

WB and IMF (1989a), "People's Republic of Mozambique Economic Policy Framework, 1989–91", 21 February 1989.

WB (1989b), "Report to the Consultative Group for Mozambique on the Government's Economic Rehabilitation Programme", 4 October 1989.

WB (1989c), "Staff Appraisal Report, Mozambique, Health & Nutrition Project", 7423-Moz, 1 February 1989.

WB (1989d) "Public Expenditure Review", 7615-Moz, 6 April 1989.

WB (1989e), "Business Environment Study", 7705-Moz, 20 June 1989.

WB (1989f), "Food Security Study", draft.

WB (1989g), "Food Security Study", 7693-Moz, 12 October 1989.

WB (1989h), *Sub-Saharan Africa: From Crisis to Sustainable Growth*, November 1989.

WB (1990a), "Population, Health and Nutrition Sector Report", 7244-Moz, 9 January 1990.

WB (1990b), "Poverty Alleviation Framework Paper", 31 January 1990.

WB (1990c), "Country Economic Memorandum", 8370-Moz, 14 March 1990.

WB (1990d) ,"Staff Appraisal Report, Mozambique, Agricultural Rehabilitation and Development Project", 8467-Moz, 10 April 1990.

WB (1990e), *World Development Report 1990* Oxford University Press, Oxford, June 1990.

WB (1990f), "Poverty Policy Framework Paper", 14 September 1990; update of WB 1990b.

WB and FAO/WB Cooperative Programme (1990g, 1990h), "Mozambique Rural Rehabilitation Project Approach Paper", versions of March and May 1990.

WB and FAO/WB Cooperative Programme, (1990i), "Mozambique Rural Rehabilitation Project Preparation Mission Aide-Mémoire", draft, 9 June 1990.

WB (1990j), "Poverty Reduction Framework Paper", 31 October 1990; update of WB 1990b, 1990f.

WB (1990k), and IMF "Mozambique Economic Policy Framework, 1990–92", May 1990.

Mozambique-Related Periodicals

AIM Information Bulletin (AIM), published monthly by the Agência de Informação de Moçambique. Name changed in November 1988 to *Mozambiquefile*.

BCG Bulletin, Beira Corridor Group, PO Box 1697, Harare.

Boletim Informativo do DPCCN. See DPCCN Newsletter.

Boletim Trimestral, Seção de Nutrição, Ministerio da Saùde, Maputo.

Cooperação & Desenvolvimento (C&D), published monthly from February 1989 by Ministério da Cooperação, CP 1101, Maputo.

Diario de Moçambique (DM), daily, Beira.

Domingo, weekly (Sunday), Maputo.

DPCCN Newsletter, published monthly from 1985 by the Departamento de Prevenção e Combate às Calamidades Naturais, Maputo. (Also called *Boletim Informativo do DPCCN*.)

Emergency Mozambique, published irregularly by the National Executive Committee for the Emergency, Rua da Resistência 1746, Maputo.

Encontro, Maputo; first issue April 1990.

Extra, 3 times a year, Centro de Formacação Agrária, Maputo.

Mozambique Briefing, Information Department, Frelimo Party Central Committee, Maputo.

Mozambiquefile, published monthly by the Agência de Informação de Moçambique, CP 896, Maputo. US$20/yr. Was called *AIM Information Bulletin* until November 1988.

Mozambique Information Office News Review (MIO), fortnightly, 7a Caledonian Rd, London N1 9DX. £14–28/yr.

News Bulletin, 10 issues published in 1984 by UNDP Maputo.

Noticias, daily, Maputo.

Priority Requirements, computer print-out updated fortnightly, office of the UN Special Coordinator for the Emergency, Maputo; list of pledges in response to most recent appeal.

Revista Fiscal, 4 times a year, Direcção Nacional de Impostos e Auditoria, Maputo.

Tempo, weekly, Maputo.

Other Periodicals

Africa Analysis, monthly, London.

Africa Confidential, fortnightly, London.

Africa Recovery, quarterly, UN, New York.

Afrique-Asie, Paris.

Financial Mail, weekly, Johannesburg.

Financial Times, daily, London.

Guardian, daily, London.

Independent, daily and Sunday, London.

Market South East, monthly, London.

New Statesman, weekly, London.

Observer, weekly, Sunday, London.

Southscan, weekly, London.

Southern African Report (SAR), quarterly, 427 Bloor St W, Toronto, Canada.

The Times, daily, London.

Weekly Mail, Johannesburg.

Index